Readings on Religion as News

Readings
on Religion
as News

edited by Judith M. Buddenbaum and Debra L. Mason

Iowa State University Press /Ames

#42397808

Judith M. Buddenbaum is a professor in the Department of Journalism and Technical Communication at Colorado State University. Besides teaching journalism, Buddenbaum has been a newspaper religion reporter, a free-lance magazine reporter specializing in religion, and a communication researcher for Lutheran World Federation. Widely published, she is the author of *Reporting News about Religion* (1998).

Debra L. Mason is an associate professor in the Department of Communication at Otterbein College, Ohio, and the executive director of the Religion Newswriters Association. Mason is a former award-winning religion reporter and has researched religion in the media for nearly a decade.

© 2000 Iowa State University Press
All rights reserved

Iowa State University Press
2121 South State Avenue, Ames, Iowa 50014

Orders: 1-800-862-6657
Office: 1-515-292-0140
Fax: 1-515-292-3348
Web site: www.isupress.edu

Authorization to photocopy items for internal or personal use, or the internal or personal use of specific clients, is granted by Iowa State University Press, provided that the base fee of $.10 per copy is paid directly to the Copyright Clearance Center, 222 Rosewood Drive, Danvers, MA 01923. For those organizations that have been granted a photocopy license by CCC, a separate system of payments has been arranged. The fee code for users of the Transactional Reporting Service is 0-8138-2926-7/2000 $.10.

♾ Printed on acid-free paper in the United States of America

First edition, 2000

Library of Congress Cataloging-in-Publication Data

Readings on religion as news/edited by Judith M. Buddenbaum and Debra L. Mason—1st ed.
      p.   cm.
   Includes bibliographical references.
   ISBN 0-8138-2926-7 (alk. paper)
   1. Mass media in religion—United States—Influence. 2. Mass media in religion—United States. 3. Christianity and culture—United States.
   I. Buddenbaum, Judith M. II. Mason, Debra L.
   BV652.97.U6 R43 1999
   070.4′49200973—dc21   99-047158

The last digit is the print number: 9 8 7 6 5 4 3 2 1

Contents

12 Revivalism   161

13 The Spirit of Reform   177

14 Faith, Science and Scripture   197

15 Pulling Together   211

Preface

This book is a labor of love. It is also one born of frustration.

As former religion reporters, we share a long-standing fascination with religion and with its influence on individuals and society as well as deep respect for those journalists who have covered and who now cover news about religion. But as academics, we have found it difficult to help our students see the connections between religion and the media that we believe are important for understanding our culture and reporting on it.

Religious histories of America are plentiful, but few even mention the role of the press in spreading religious ideas through society. Standard journalism histories give short shrift to religion both as a cultural force and as a subject for press coverage. While there are, to be sure, occasional articles in scholarly journals, trade and general circulation publications that address some aspects of the subject, material showing the interplay between religion and news is scattered and hard to find. Therefore, we set out to produce an anthology of news stories that illustrates both the role of religion in shaping public opinion and the role of the media in spreading religious beliefs and opinions through society and in shaping people's opinions about religion.

At first we thought the task would be relatively simple: identify a few episodes and issues when religion and/or religion news coverage clearly made a difference, then find a few stories that would show how newspapers and newsmagazines covered the story. But quickly we found ourselves inundated with examples of times when religion made a difference. Similarly, we found so many interesting and varied examples of news coverage that helped shape public opinion that we very quickly found ourselves facing hard choices about what could be included in this anthology and what would have to be excluded.

To keep the book to a manageable length, we chose to focus on religion in the United States. We also chose to eliminate most examples of religion news that those interested in the subject can obtain rather easily without resorting to anthologies. That means there are no stories primarily about religion abroad: the Middle East, Northern Ireland, or Bosnia, the Pope or the Dalai Lama, for example. Neither are there examples of routine stories from modern religion pages or those that have won Pulitzer Prizes. Citations for prizewinning stories can be found by checking the list of stories at *www.pulitzer.org/archive/;* routine ones can easily be found simply by going to a library and looking through recent issues of newspapers or magazines.

Some other stories were eliminated simply because they were so long that including them would have precluded using several other interesting and useful stories. Initially we had intended to include an appendix of other useful stories, but there were so many that the idea proved unworkable. Instead, we have included references for a few particularly noteworthy ones in the introduction to each chapter.

The resulting collection is, admittedly, somewhat eclectic. We tried for variety in subject matter and writing style. We also sought stories from different regions of the country, from a variety of publications and authors— both those that are well known and those that are not. At the same time, we tried to be mindful of our original purpose.

Taken as a whole, the collection illustrates both continuity and change in religion and in reporting. As such, the collection is designed to meet the need for supplementary material in journalism history and media and society courses, as well as allied courses in American history, American studies and religious studies.

In most cases, we used stories from the publication where they originally appeared, but we have sometimes used a version published in another paper as a way of showing how stories from one region spread through the nation in an era when travel was difficult and journalists had neither the news services nor the communication technologies they now use to cover news from around the nation. To the extent possible, we have also preserved the original typographic features, spelling, grammar and punctuation, adding a "[sic]" or an omitted word only where necessary to make it clear the problem is in the original, not in the reproduction. While the stories from earlier years have historical importance, the chapters devoted to the modern era were designed to show the breadth and range of current concerns. Unlike the stories from earlier years, the more recent ones were selected for their value as examples of good religion reporting and writing. Therefore, these stories lend themselves to use in reporting courses.

Chapters in Part 1 treat the period from the first American newspaper through the early years of the nation, when ideological, even religious, journalism was the norm. Part 2 covers the period from the Penny Press through the end of World War II, when newspapers were privately owned and reflected the views of those owners. Part 3 treats the era when individual ownership began to give way to chain ownership. It covers the years between the end of World War II and the constellation of events in the mid-1970s that mark the birth of renewed concern for religion as news. That era of renewed concern is the subject of chapters in Part 4.

Within each section, chapters are arranged as chronologically as possible, given the overlapping and intertwining nature of the subjects that are their focus. For the most part, stories within chapters are also arranged chronologically, but imposed on that arrangement is some grouping by theme.

Many people helped us select the episodes and issues that form the basis for each chapter; many others helped us find the stories. We thank the religion reporters who shared their work with us and other reporters and colleagues in academia who pointed us to important stories. We also thank the librarians at Colorado State University, the Graham Archives at Wheaton College, Indiana University, Ohio University, Ohio State University, Otterbein College, the University of Colorado and the Westerville Public Library for their help tracking down stories as well as those at other schools who provided materials through interlibrary loan. We also thank the librarians at the *Detroit Free Press* and the *Toledo Blade* for their help.

We gratefully acknowledge the newspapers and magazines that gave us permission to use their stories, an Otterbein College National Endowment for the Humanities faculty development grant to cover copyright costs and additional support from Religion Newswriters Association.

Special thanks go to our assistants Hilary Kimes, Carrie Troup, Brian Batch, Elizabeth Honeycutt, Diane Wootton and William Hayes for countless hours of research work and for typing stories or scanning them into computer-readable files. Most of all, we thank our husbands, Warren Buddenbaum and Jack McManus, for being there for us and for helping us in so many ways.

Introduction

According to the conventional wisdom, Americans were once a highly religious people living together in a nation that was truly "under God." But over time both the people and the country lost their religious moorings as they adopted a secular outlook that is inimical to the well-being of both individuals and the nation. The blame for that change rests partly, if not entirely, with the press, which once supported religion but now treats it as irrelevant at best, a joke at worst.

But the reality is not quite that simple. Certainly over time there have been changes in religion and in the religious climate. There have also been changes in the practice of journalism. But from the Puritans to the Promise Keepers, religious people have left their mark on American culture and they continue to do so. And the press has been there, at every step along the way, spreading religiously inspired beliefs and behaviors throughout the country and policing the boundary between "acceptable" and "unacceptable" forms of religiosity.

During the colonial period, almost all Americans who were religious were Christian. But not all Americans were religious. According to recent research published by Roger Finke and Rodney Stark in their 1992 book, *The Churching of America 1776–1990,* a young woman living in the colonies was more likely to have been sexually active before marriage than to have been a member of a church. Even those who were religious and who tried to live their lives according to the tenets of their faith were not religious in the same way. Although the religious diversity existed primarily within a rather narrow range of Protestantism, disputes were bitter.

Puritan Congregationalists vied for power with the Anglicans with whom they shared an uneasy arrangement of multiple established churches in Massachusetts. They were even more suspicious of the generally less pious Anglicans in the southern colonies. By the eve of the Revolution, southern Anglicans had reason to fear both the Massachusetts Congregationalists and the Baptists who, having been driven from Massachusetts into Rhode Island, were now making such inroads in the south that they were beginning to outnumber members of the established Anglican Church. In Maryland, the only officially Roman Catholic colony, Catholics made up only about 10 percent of the population. As in the other Middle Colonies, the overwhelming majority of residents who belonged to any church belonged to a Protestant one but no denomination had a majority or even a strong plurality. Even in Pennsylvania, the Quaker State, Quakers made up less than 10 percent of the population. There were nearly twice as many Baptists, Episcopalians and Presbyterians.

With so many churches to choose from, diversity was becoming the norm. Although some states continued to have an established religion until well into the 19th century, with so many denominations present, establishments of religion were breaking down even in the religiously most homogeneous regions. With each church fearful lest the others gain too much power, any attempt to establish a religion for the nation as a whole would have thwarted attempts to create one nation from disparate colonies.

Although the First Amendment, with its guarantee that there would be no established church and that everyone would have religious freedom, was adopted for both ideological and practical reasons, whether a nation could exist without a unifying religion to undergird it was, and is, the subject for much debate. But, where many feared, and still fear, that the absence of a unifying religion inevitably leads to a decline in religiosity, the opposite has been true.

Every survey confirms that the United States is the most religious of all western developed nations. Nine out of 10 Americans believe in God; more than half are affiliated with a church and 90 percent of those with a Christian church. Even more consider themselves Christian.

But if religiosity flourishes under the conditions of religious freedom that exist in the United States, religious options have also proliferated. Jews and Muslims each make up at least 3 percent of the population; there are almost as many Hindus and Buddhists. An accurate count for other smaller religions is almost impossible, but their combined membership probably does not exceed 10 percent of the total population. Christians remain the majority.

Today there are at least 100 varieties of Christian religions and well over 1,000 other options. Each religion promotes its own beliefs and its own vision of how people should behave and how society should be ordered. With so many diverse beliefs, no single religion can put its stamp on society the way Puritans were initially able to do in colonial New England. As a result, it is easy for members of every religion to assume the result is evidence that religion has lost its influence.

But religion still leaves its mark. As Alexis de Tocqueville noted when he visited the United States in 1831, the freedom the First Amendment grants to all religions has turned them into voluntary associations that must compete with each other for members and for money. This competition has produced a kind of religious vitality and sense of purpose unknown elsewhere. Freed from government control—and support—religion shapes the manners and mores of society. But to do so, religion, like other kinds of voluntary associations, needs the press. As de Tocqueville also noted, only the press has the ability to plant the same idea simultaneously in thousands of minds.

Needing press coverage and getting it can be a two-edged sword. The news about religion that the media choose to cover spreads those ideas throughout society; the choices teach people which religions and which religiously inspired ideas are important and unimportant, which ones are acceptable and unacceptable. That was as true in colonial times as it is today.

Until well into the 20th century, most newspapers were individually owned and operated to give voice to the particular world views of their printers/editors/owners or backers. Writers often used religious arguments, couched in religious language, to promote proper religion as they understood it and to support other causes that they favored. They also used their papers to attack religions and religiously inspired opinions and behaviors with which they disagreed. People expected each newspaper to have a distinctive viewpoint and to be true to it. Neutrality and objectivity were foreign concepts. Anyone who attempted fair and balanced coverage would have been seen as lacking in conviction and, therefore, as morally suspect.

The resulting coverage often exacerbated culture wars even as it fueled revivals and reforms promoted by those religious options fortunate enough to find a newspaper to promote their causes. The result was generally acceptable to most people so long as the marketplace of ideas was understood as consisting of multiple newspapers and magazines each championing their own views and so long as there were many such competing media circulating within the same city or town.

But with the decline in multiple newspaper towns and the rise of corporate ownership, such views became untenable. In order to attract an audience large enough for it to survive, each publication had to become all things to all people. Religious rhetoric dropped out of popular discourse, partly because religious diversity meant the language was no longer as widely shared as it once was and partly because the language of one tradition would be offensive to another. The result was, first, a fairly neutral kind of stenographic journalism and then the kind of objectivity attempted today.

But in spite of the changes, the result has been remarkably the same regardless of whether each religion or religious viewpoint is covered in a separate publication, each one is covered in the same publication by a separate story relatively free from outside interpretation, or whether multiple perspectives are combined into a single story.

The news media pick up on some religions and their attendant behaviors and viewpoints, spreading them throughout society while virtually ignoring other religions and their concerns. The coverage inevitably has an agenda-setting and socialization effect.

Sometimes the coverage has been, and is, hostile to religion or to a particular religion. However, in general it has, and does, support certain themes that, as Mark Silk points out in his 1995 book, *Unsecular Media: Making News of Religion in America,* support widely shared values that are deeply imbedded in a culture that is, at core, religious.

The more things change, the more they stay the same.

The chapters and stories in this book illustrate continuities in issues, arguments and styles of coverage. The stories show religious influence on American culture. They also provide examples of news coverage that helped shaped the religious climate and opinions about religion.

The beliefs and behaviors that concerned and sometimes divided our colonial forebears fuel public debates today. The religiously inspired arguments used then resurface in current debates over very similar issues. The events of the past have their impact on the present.

The kinds of news colonial printers published in their papers are staples today. If the religious essay is no longer the norm, it has not disappeared. Its traces linger on editorial pages, in magazines and as the inspiration for stories that break free of the inverted pyramid. Individual viewpoints are now more often compressed into single stories, but the viewpoints, and the issues themselves, remain a constant feature of religion news. Voices from the past serve as a cautionary tale, a challenge and an inspiration for students of history and for the journalists who write its first draft.

PART 1

Ideological Journalism in a New Jerusalem

When they landed at Plymouth Rock in 1620, the Pilgrims signed the Mayflower Compact in which they "covenanted together," binding themselves to each other and to God. But their Plymouth Colony was absorbed into the Massachusetts Bay Colony founded by the Puritans. Like the Pilgrims, the Puritans came to the New World primarily for religious freedom. But that was a freedom they were unwilling to share with others. Where the Pilgrims had separated church and state, the Puritans combined them.

For the Puritans, America was to be the "New Jerusalem," a "shining city on the hill." To make it just that, both church and state were to be governed by church members—the "elect"—as God's agents in this world. Making that religio-political system work required an educated clergy and a literate church membership, so the Puritans established schools, including Harvard University. They also established printing presses and founded newspapers.

Harvard's press printed books and tracts; clergy, faculty and students contributed to Boston's newspapers. Printed material from Boston spread Puritan ideas through the colonies. But in spite of their best efforts, the Puritans were unable to convince those living in other colonies to adopt their religious beliefs and powerless to prevent other churches from making inroads into their territory. Still, Puritanism left its mark.

If others could not accept the Puritan form of government or agree to their strict moral code, they did agree that people needed instruction in correct beliefs and protection from influences that might lead them astray. They also readily accepted the Puritan vision of America as a special place. Like William Penn, who described his Pennsylvania colony as a "holy experiment," Americans came to see themselves as creating a society that would be "an example to the nations."

That basic idea was reinforced through sermons, tracts, books and

1

finally through newspapers. Until well into the 19th century those newspapers could more properly be described as "viewspapers." In the early years of the Republic, a few printer/editors opened their pages to people on all sides of a controversy. But that model was generally suspect. From the establishment of the first newspaper in 1690 through the era of the Party Press, the prevailing view was that people should have the courage of their own convictions. Those who published, without comment or contradiction, views with which they disagreed were generally seen as morally suspect.

During that period, most papers represented a distinctive viewpoint—first that of the paper's proprietor or his financial backers and then that of a political faction or party. On matters of religion, ideological journalism produced a kind of religious news designed to promote and protect correct beliefs and behaviors according to the standards of the newspaper printer/editor and his supporters.

The stories reproduced in the chapters in this section show continuity and change in journalistic practices during the years from 1690 through the early 1800s. They also illustrate changing and competing views of what the New Jerusalem should look like.

Chapter 1 includes the press philosophies of early newspapers and some very early examples of news about religion. Chapter 2 covers the attempt by Anglicans to capitalize on controversy over a vaccine for smallpox to break Puritan hegemony in Massachusetts. Although that attempt failed, chapter 3 provides accounts of the first period of religious revival, the Great Awakening, which undermined Puritan power by splitting churches and even families. Turning from primarily religious controversies to political ones, chapter 4 includes stories illustrating religious arguments for and against the Revolutionary War. Chapter 5 treats religiously inspired arguments that accompanied attempts to define a course for the new nation.

1

Early Press Philosophy and Practice

In Puritan New England, the first newspaper publishers saw their newspapers as fulfilling both informational and religious functions. Those twin functions can be seen in the statements published in the first issue of the first newspaper, Benjamin Harris's *Publick Occurrences Both Forreign and Domestick,* and later ones, including Samuel Kneeland's *New-England Weekly Journal.*

After just one issue, government authorities shut down *Publick Occurrences* because Harris apparently published it without first obtaining the required license. By the time the next newspapers appeared, the requirement for a license had been lifted. Although the subsequent custom of publishing "by authority" also died out after 1721, most early printers were careful not to print anything that would offend the community.

The first newspapers downplayed politics. Active newsgathering was minimal. News consisted primarily of short items reprinted or summarized from other papers that arrived in a city via boat from Europe or stagecoach from other colonies. Those items, as well as simple observations about life in the community, blended together. Headlines and typographic features other than italics were rare. As with Harris's philosophy and the news piece that follows, the beginning of a new item was marked only by indenting for a new paragraph.

The philosophy expressed in Kneeland's paper is unusual because it promises contributions from correspondents who would provide news from surrounding communities. An example of that news is an account of the ordination examination of a new minister. However, in Kneeland's paper, as in most other early papers, news of religion consisted primarily of personal experiences that also served as cautionary tales or of first-person accounts that attributed "remarkable events" to divine pleasure or divine displeasure. Those forms are illustrated by Jeremiah Collier's account of a shipwreck and by the "Confession of a Woman Accused of Murder," to which are appended related items and an example of the record of baptisms Kneeland promised in his first issue.

The prospectus for the Georgia Colony is an unusually long example of the kind of documents that newspapers of the era often reprinted in full. It also provides evidence of existing assumptions about the beneficial effects of life in the New Jerusalem.

Although printer/editors outside Massachusetts were less inclined to express a religious purpose in their paper's prospectus or first issue, they, too, generally avoided publishing material that would be offensive to their community. Believing their papers should provide material that would be uplifting and instructive for moral improvement, they often reprinted tracts or sermons. But not everyone found their efforts laudatory.

At age 25, Ben Franklin wrote his "Apology for Printers" after many in the community complained about an offensive reference to Anglican clergy in an advertisement he had printed. The Apology ends with a fable that Thomas Whitmarsh repeated in his *South-Carolina Gazette* of October 14, 1732, in response to his critics.

In opening his paper to all views, Franklin was more successful than most other colonial printers who tried that approach. But his Apology glosses over occasions when he may well have given offense to the religious community: the satires of religion he published under the name of Silence Dogood (see chapter 2), and a fictional story of a witch trial at Mount Holly, which he may or may not have written, but did publish in the *Pennsylvania Gazette* on October 22, 1730. However, the Apology is remarkable for Franklin's view of publishing, which is more in tune with journalistic practices of today than those of his own era, and for his description of problems that continue to plague journalists who cover religion.

Benjamin Harris: Philosophy and First News

Publick Occurrences Both Forreign and Domestick, September 25, 1690

It is designed, that the Countrey shall be furnished once a month (or if any Glut of Occurrences *happen* oftener) *with an Account of such considerable things as have arrived unto our Notice.*

In order here unto, the Publisher will take what pains he can to obtain a Faithful Relation *of all such things; and will particularly make himself beholden to such Persons in* Boston *whom he knows to have been for their own use the diligent Observers of such matters.*

That which is herein proposed is, First, *That* Memorable Occurrents *of* Divine Providence *may not be neglected or forgotten, as they too often are.* Secondly, *That people everywhere may better understand the Circumstances of Publique Affairs, both abroad and at home: which may not only direct their* Thoughts *at all times, but at some times also to assist their* Business *and* Negotiations.

Thirdly, *That some thing may be done towards the* Curing, *or at least the* Charming *of that* Spirit *of* Lying, *which prevails among us, wherefore nothing shall be entered, but what we have reason to believe is true, repairing to the best fountains for our information. And when there appears any* material mistake *in any thing that is collected, it shall be* corrected *in the next.*

Moreover, *the* Publisher *of these* Occurences is willing to engage, *that whereas, there are many* False Reports, *maliciously made, and spread among us, if any well minded person will be at the pains to trace any such* false Report, *so far as to find out and Convict the* First Raiser *of it, he will in this Paper (unless just Advice be given to the contrary) expose the Name of such person as* A malicious Raiser of a False Report. *It is supposed that none will dislike this Proposal, but such as intend to be guilty of so villanous a Crime.*

THE Christianized *Indians* in some parts of *Plimouth,* have newly appointed a day of Thanksgiving to God for his mercy in supplying their extream and pinching Necessities under their late want of Corn, and for His giving them now a prospect of a very *Comfortable Harvest.* Their Example may be worth Mentioning.

Samuel Kneeland's Philosophy of News

The New-England Weekly Journal, March 20, 1727

It would be needless to mention here the particular Reasons *for Publishing this Paper; and will be sufficient to say, That the* Design *of it is with Fidelity and Method to Entertain the Public every* Monday *with a Collection of the most Remarkable Occurrences of* Europe, *with a particular Regard from time to time to the present Circumstances of the Publick Affairs, whether of Church or State. And to render this Paper more Acceptable to its* Readers, *immediate care will be taken (and a considerable progress is herein already made) to settle a Correspondence with the most knowing and ingenious Gentlemen in the several noted Towns in this and the Neighbour-Provinces, who may take particular Care seasonably to Collect and send what may be Remarkable in their Town or Towns adjacent worthy of the Public View; whether of Remarkable Judgments, or Singular Mercies, more private or public, Preservations & Deliverances by Sea or Land: together with some other Pieces of History of our own, &c. that may be profitable & entertaining both to the Christian and Historian. It is likewise intended to insert in this Paper a Weekly Account of the Number of Persons* Buried, & Baptiz'd, *in the Town of* Boston; *With several other Things that at present can only be thought of, that may be of Service to the Publick; And special care will be taken that nothing contrary thereto shall be inserted.*

Jeremiah Collier's Reflections on a Storm and Shipwreck

The Boston News-Letter, June 5 to 12, 1704

Mr. Jeremiah Collier, writing a Letter to a Person of Equality upon occasion of the late Tempest concludes thus,

We have lately felt a sad Instance of God's Judgments in the terrible Tempest: Terrible beyond any thing in that Kind in Memory, or Record. For not to enlarge on the lamentable Wrecks, and Ruins, were we not almost swept into a Chaos? Did not Nature seem to be in her last Agony, and the World ready to expire? And if we go on still in such Sins of Defyance, may we not be afraid of the Punishment of *Sodom,* and that God should destroy us with *Fire* and *Brimstone.*

What impression this late Calamity has made upon the *Play-house,* we may guess by their Acting *Macbeth* with all its Thunder and Tempest, the same Day: Where at the mention of the *chimnies being blown down (Macbeth, p. 20)* the *Audience* were pleas'd to *Clap,* at an unusual Length of Pleasure and Approbation. And is not the meaning of all this too intelligible? Does it not look as if they had a Mind to out-brave the Judgment? And make us believe the Storm was nothing but an Eruption of *Epicurus's* Atoms, a Spring-Tide of Matter and Motion, and a bland Salley of Chance? This throwing Providence out of the Scheme, is an admirable *Opiate* for the Conscience! And when Recollection is laid asleep, the *Stage* will recover of Course, and go on with their Business effectually.

Thus, Sir, I have laid before you what I have to offer upon this Occasion, and am,

Your most Humble Servant,

December 10.
1703   J.C.

Confession of a Woman Accused of Murder

The New-England Weekly Journal, June 19, 1727

(In our Numb. 10, we mention'd the Execution of a Molatto Woman at *Plymouth* for the Murder of her Child, since which we have receiv'd a Paper which was found in the Prison after her Execution, supposed to have been taken from her own mouth by one who was in Goal with her some time of her Imprisonment, and is here inserted, without the Addition of One Word.)

A Short Account of the Life of *Elizabeth Colson,*
a Molatto Woman, who now must Dye
for the Monstrous Sin of Murdering her Child.

I was born at Weymouth *and my Mother put me out to* Ebenezer Prat, *who was to learn me to read, but I fear they never took that pains they should have done to instruct me, my Mother being School-Mistress was loth I should come to School with other Children, and so I had not that Instruction I wish I had in my Youth. I was carry'd very hardly too by my Mistress, and suffer'd hunger and blows, and at last was tempted to Steal, for which I have reason to lament, for although I stole at first for necessity as I tho't, yet the* Devel *took that Advantage against me, and led me further into Sin, for one Lord's Day the People being gone to Meeting, I broke into a Neighbour's House, and stole some Victuals, and looking for more I saw a piece of Money, which I took, and afterwards telling a Lye, & saying I found it, so was led by one sin to another.*
After-wards I was Sold to Lieut. Reed, *where I had some good Examples set me, but having got a habit of Sin, I still grow worse & worse, and was left to fall into the Sin of Fornication, and after my Time was out with Master* Reed, *I was in great distress what to do with my Child, but carried it from place to place, till I left it at Dighton and ran away from it, and soon fell again to that shameful & Soul destrowing Sin of*

Fornication the Second time; and not having the Fear of God before my Eyes, I was justly left of God to this horrid Sin the Third time, that led me together with the Instigation of the Devil, and the wretchedness of my own Heart, to that monstrous Sin for which I must now Dye: And so I have not only brought my Body to dye a shameful Death, but my Soul in danger of Death & Damnation.

O that all People would be Warned to flee from the Sins I have been Guilty of, least they run themselves into more terrible Distresses than they can easily imagine, amongst their ungodly Companions, who will not be able to help them out of their Distresses, when they have left God and God hath left them. I would therefore earnestly intreat all Young People to watch against the beginnings of Sin in themselves, for you know not where you will stop this side Hell if once you allow your selves in Sin, tho' you may think you can: For I remember that when I was Young, I heard of a Woman that Murdered her Child, and I said, I never would do so. *I may say to you as my Mistress did to me,* you do not know what you may be left to. *Therefore, I would intreat all Young People to beware of Stealing, Lying, and especially that shameful Sin of Uncleanness, which hath been the leading Sin to that horrid Sin for which I must Dye. O then take this Advice from a poor Dying Malefactor, who must suffer a Shameful Death as the just demerits of a sinful Life.*

O that all People would take Warning by me, of grieving the Holy spirit of God by sinning against the light of their own Conscience, and of Prophaning the Sabbath Day, and not regarding the Warnings of Christ's faithful Embassadours, but be now advised to take fast hold of Instruction, and let it not go, keep it for it is thy Life: And let them then, that think they stand, take heed lest they fall.

We hear from *Hinghan,* that on Tuesday morning the 9th of this Instant June, was found Dead, the Child of Capt. *Stephen Cushing,* 'tho going to Bed well. As also on the same Day was Scalded in a very remarkable manner the Child of *Daniel Cushing* of *Hingham* aforesaid, which dyed the Night following.

Burials in the Town of BOSTON, *since our last,*
Seven Whites ; One Black
Baptiz'd in the several Churches,
Six.

Extract from the Designs for the Georgia Colony

The South-Carolina Gazette, December 2 to 9, 1732

Christianity will be extended by the Execution of this Design; since the good Discipline established by the Society will reform the Manners of those miserable Objects, who shall be by them subsisted; and the Example of a whole Colony, who shall behave in a just, moral, and religious Manner, will contribute greatly towards the Conversion of the *Indians,* and taking off the Prejudices received from the profligate Lives of such who have scarce any Thing of Christian but the Name.

The Trustees in their general Meetings will consider of the most prudent Methods for effectually establishing a regular Colony; and that it may be done is demonstrable. Under what Difficulties was *Virginia* planted; The Coast and Climate then unknown, the *Indians* numerous, at Enmity with the first Planters,who were forced to fetch all Provisions from *England*; yet it is grown a mighty Province and the Revenue receives 100,000 for Duties with the Goods that they send yearly Home. Within this 50 Years *Pennsylvania* was as much a Forest as *Georgia* is now; and in these few Years, by the wise Occonomy of *William Penn,* and those who assisted him, it now gives Food to 80,000 Inhabitants, and can boast of as fine a City as most in *Europe.*

This new Colony is more likely to succeed than either of the former were, since *Carolina* abounds with Provisions, the Climate is known, and there are Men to instruct in the Seasons Nature of cultivating the Soil. There are but few *Indian* Families within 400 miles, & those in perfect Amity with the *English; Port-Royal,* the station of his Majesty's Ships, is within 30 and *Charlestown,* a great Mart, is within 120 miles. If the Colony is attacked, it may be relieved by Sea from *Port-Royal,* or the *Bahamas*; and the Militia of *South-Carolina* is ready to support it by Land.

For the continuing the Relief which is now given, there will be Lands reserved in the Colony; and the Benefits arising from them is to go to the carrying on of the Trust. So that at the same Time the Money by being laid out preserves the Lives of the poor, and makes a comfortable Provision for those whose Expences are by it defrayed; their Labour in improving their own Lands will make the adjoining reserved Lands valuable, and the Rents of those reserved Lands will be a perpetual Fund for the relieving more poor People. So that instead of laying out the Money upon Lands with the Income to support the People, this is laying out Money upon the Poor, and by relieving those who are now unfortunate, raises a Fund for the perpetual Relief of those who shall be so hereafter.

There is an Occasion now offered for every one to help forward this Design, the smallest Benefaction will be received and applied with the utmost Care; every little will do something, and a great Number of small Benefactions will amount to a sum capable of doing a great deal of Good.

If any Person, moved with the Calamities of the Unfortunate, shall be inclined to contribute towards their Relief, by encouraging this Design, they are desired to pay their Benefactions into the Bank of *England,* on Account of the Trustees for establishing the Colony of *Georgia* in *America,* or else to any of the Trustees, who are as follows, *viz.* The Rt. Hon. the Lord Visc. *Percival,* the Rt. Hon. the Lord *Carpenter,* the Hon. *Edw. Digby,* Esq; *James Oglethorp, George Heathcote, Robert Moor, Robert Hacks, John Larvebe, James Vernon, Thomas Tower, Francis Eyles, William Sloper, William Belitha, Rogers Holland,* Esqrs. The Rev. *Mr. Stephen Hales,* B.D. the Rev. *Mr. John Burton, Richard Bundy, Arthur Bedford, Samuel Smith, Adam Anderson,* and *Thomas Corant,* Gents.

Benjamin Franklin's Apology for Printers

The Pennsylvania Gazette, June 10, 1731

Being frequently censur'd and condemn'd by different Persons for printing Things which they say ought not to be printed, I have sometimes thought it might be necessary to make a standing Apology for my self, and publish it once a Year, to be read upon all Occasions of that Nature. Much Business has hitherto hindered the execution of this Design; but having very lately given extra-ordinary Offence by printing an Advertisement with a certain *N.B.* at the End of it, I find an Apology more particularly requisite at this Juncture, tho' it happens when I have not yet Leisure to write such a thing in the proper Form, and can only in a loose manner throw some Considerations together which should have been the Substance of it.

I request all who are angry with me on the Account of printing things they don't like, calmly to consider these following Particulars

1. That the Opinions of Men are almost as various as their Faces; an Observation general enough to become a common Proverb, *So many Men so many Minds.*

2. That the Business of Printing has chiefly to do with Mens Opinions; most things that are printed tending to promote some, or oppose others.

3. That hence arises the peculiar Unhappiness of that Business, which other Callings are no way liable to; they who follow Printing being scarce able to do any thing in their way of getting a Living, which shall not probably give Offence to some, and perhaps to many; whereas the Smith, the Shoemaker, the Carpenter, or the Man of any other Trade, may work indifferently for People of all Persuasions, without offending any of them: and the Merchant may buy and sell with Jews, Turks, Hereticks, and Infidels of all sorts, and get Money by every one of them, without giving Offence to the most orthodox, of any sort; or suffering the least Censure or Ill-will on the Account from any Man whatever.

4. That it is as unreasonable in any one Man or Set of Men to expect to be pleas'd with every thing that is printed, as to think that nobody ought to be pleas'd but themselves.

5. Printers are educated in the Belief, that when Men differ in Opinion, both Sides ought equally to have the Advantage of being heard by the Publick; and that when Truth and Error have fair Play, the former is always an overmatch for the latter: Hence they chearfully serve all contending Writers that pay them well, without regarding on which side they are of the Question in Dispute.

6. Being thus continually employ'd in serving all Parties, Printers naturally acquire a vast Unconcernedness as to the right or wrong Opinions contain'd in what they print; regarding it only as the Matter of their daily labour: They print things full of Spleen and Animosity, with the utmost Calmness and Indifference, and without the least Ill-will to the Persons reflected on; who nevertheless unjustly think the Printer as much their Enemy as the Author, and join both together in their Resentment.

7. That it is unreasonable to imagine Printers approve of every thing they print, and to censure them on any particular thing accordingly; since in the way of their Business they print such great variety of things opposite and contradictory. It is likewise as unreasonable what some assert, *That Printers ought not to print any Thing but what they approve;* since if all of that Business should make such a Resolution, and abide by it, an End would thereby be put to Free Writing, and the World would afterwards have nothing to read but what happen'd to be the Opinions of Printers.

8. That if all Printers were determin'd not to print any thing till they were sure it would offend no body, there would be very little printed.

9. That if they sometimes print vicious or silly things not worth reading, it may not be because they approve such things themselves, but because the People are so viciously and corruptly educated that good things are not encouraged. I have known a very numerous Impression of *Robin Hood's Songs* go off in this Province at 2*s.* per Book, in less than a Twelvemonth; when a small Quantity of *David's Psalms* (an excellent Version) have lain upon my Hands above twice the Time.

10. That notwithstanding what might be urg'd in behalf of a Man's being allow'd to do in the Way of his Business whatever he is paid for, yet Printers do continually discourage the Printing of great Numbers of bad things, and stifle them in the Birth. I my self have constantly refused to print any thing that might countenance Vice, or promote Immorality; tho' by complying in such Cases with the corrupt Taste of the Majority, I might have got much Money. I have also always refus'd to print such things as might do real Injury to any Person, how much soever I have been solicited, and tempted with Offers of great Pay; and how much soever I have by refusing got the Ill-will of those who would have employ'd me. I have heretofore fallen under the Resentment of large Bodies of Men, for refusing absolutely to print any of their Party or Personal Reflections. In this Manner I have made my self many Enemies, and the constant Fatigue of denying is almost insupportable. But the Publick being unacquainted with all this, whenever the poor Printer happens either through Ignorance or much Persuasion, to do any thing that is generally thought worthy of Blame, he meets with no more Friendship or Favour on the above Account, than if there were no Merit in't at all. Thus, as Waller says,

> *Poets loose half the Praise they would have got*
> *Were it but known what they discreetly blot;*

Yet are censur'd for every bad Line found in their Works with the utmost Severity.

I come now to the particular Case of the *N.B.* above-mention'd, about which there has been more Clamour against me, than ever before on any other Account. In the Hurry of other Business an Advertisement was brought to me to be printed; it signified that such a Ship lying at such a Wharff, would sail for Barbadoes in such a Time, and that Freighters and Passengers might agree with the Captain at such a Place; so far is what's common: But at the Bottom this odd Thing was added, N.B. *No Sea*

Hens nor Black Gowns will be admitted on any Terms. I printed it, and receiv'd my Money; and the Advertisement was stuck up round the Town as usual. I had not so much Curiosity at that time as to enquire the Meaning of it, nor did I in the least imagine it would give so much Offence. Several good Men are very angry with me on this Occasion; they are pleas'd to say I have too much Sense to do such things ignorantly; that if they were Printers they would not have done such a thing on any Consideration; that it could proceed from nothing but my abundant Malice against Religion and the Clergy: They therefore declare they will not take any more of my Papers, nor have any farther Dealings with me; but will hinder me of all the Custom they can. All this is very hard!

I believe it had been better if I had refused to print the said Advertisement. However, 'tis done and cannot be revok'd. I have only the following few Particulars to offer, some of them in my Behalf, by way of Mitigation, and some not much to the Purpose; but I desire none of them may be read when the Reader is not in a very good Humour.

1. That I really did it without the least Malice, and imagin'd the *N.B.* was plac'd there only to make the Advertisement star'd at, and more generally read.

2. That I never saw the Word *Sea-Hens* before in my Life; nor have I yet ask'd the meaning of it; and tho' I had certainly known that *Black Gowns* in that Place signified the Clergy of the Church of England, yet I have that confidence in the generous good Temper of such of them as I know, as to be well satisfied such a trifling mention of their Habit gives them no Disturbance.

3. That most of the Clergy in this and the neighbouring Provinces, are my Customers, and some of them my very good Friends; and I must be very malicious indeed, or very stupid, to print this thing for a small Profit, if I had thought it would have given them just Cause of Offence.

4. That if I have much Malice against the Clergy, and withal much Sense; 'tis strange I never write or talk against the Clergy my self. Some have observed that 'tis a fruitful Topic, and the easiest to be witty upon of all others. I can print any thing I write at less Charge than others; yet I appeal to the Publick that I am never guilty this way, and to all my Acquaintance as to my Conversation.

5. That if a Man of Sense had Malice enough to desire to injure the Clergy, this is the foolishest Thing he could possibly contrive for that Purpose.

6. That I got Five Shillings by it.

7. That none who are angry with me would have given me so much to let it alone.

8. That if all the People of different Opinions in this Province would engage to give me as much for not printing things they don't like, as I can get by printing them, I should probably live a very easy Life; and if all Printers were every where so dealt by, there would be very little printed.

9. That I am oblig'd to all who take my Paper, and am willing to think they do it out of meer Friendship. I only desire they would think the same when I deal with them. I thank those who leave off, that they have taken it so long. But I beg they would not endeavour to dissuade others, for that will look like Malice.

10. That 'tis impossible any Man should know what he would do if he was a Printer.

11. That notwithstanding the Rashness and Inexperience of Youth, which is most likely to be prevail'd with to do things that ought not to be done; yet I have avoided printing such Things as usually give Offence either to Church or State, more than any Printer that has followed the Business in this Province before.

12. And lastly, That I have printed above a Thousand Advertisements which have not the least mention of *Sea-Hens* or *Black Gowns;* and this being the first Offence, I have the more Reason to expect Forgiveness.

I take leave to conclude with an old Fable, which some of my Readers have heard before, and some have not.

"A certain well-meaning Man and his Son, were travelling towards a Market Town, with an Ass which they had to sell. The Road was bad; and the old Man therefore rid, but the Son went a-foot. The first Passenger they met, asked the Father if he was not ashamed to ride by himself, and suffer the poor Lad to wade along thro' the Mire; this induced him to take up his Son behind him: He had not travelled far, when he met others, who said, they were two unmerciful Lubbers to get both on the Back of that poor Ass, in such a deep Road. Upon this the old Man gets off, and lets his Son ride alone. The next they met called the Lad a graceless, rascally young Jackanapes, to ride in that Manner thro' the Dirt, while his aged Father trudged along on Foot; and they said the old Man was a Fool, for suffering it. He then bid his Son come down, and walk with him, and they travell'd on leading the Ass by the Halter; 'till they met another Company, who called them a Couple of sensless Block-heads, for going both on Foot in such a dirty Way, when they had an empty Ass with them, which they might ride upon. The old Man could bear no longer; My Son, said he, it grieves me much that we cannot please all these People: Let us throw the Ass over the next Bridge, and be no farther troubled with him."

Had the old Man been seen acting this last Resolution, he would probably have been call'd a Fool for troubling himself about the different Opinions of all that were pleas'd to find Fault with him: Therefore, tho' I have a Temper almost as complying as his, I intend not to imitate him in this last Particular. I consider the Variety of Humours among Men, and despair of pleasing every Body; yet I shall not therefore leave off Print-ing. I shall continue my business. I shall not burn my Press and melt my Letters.

2

Playing God and Playing for Power

For those living in colonial America, disease was a constant threat. In September 1690 *Publick Occurrences Both Forreign and Domestick* reported that already that year, 320 people in the Boston area had died from smallpox, but the epidemic was not as bad as the one 12 years earlier. In the epidemic of 1677–78, 700 residents—12 percent of Boston's population—died. When smallpox threatened again in 1721, hundreds of Boston residents left the town; of those families who remained, almost all had at least one member who contracted the disease.

On May 26, 1721, the Puritan clergyman Cotton Mather wrote in his diary that he planned to "procure a Consult of our Physicians" on the matter of inoculation against the disease although inoculation had "never been used in America, nor indeed in [England]." In spite of Mather's support for the procedure, only one of Boston's 10 physicians, Dr. Zabdiel Boylston, agreed to try it. However, his efforts caused as much consternation as the disease itself.

The *Boston News-Letter* printed a letter highly critical of the untried procedure in its July 17–24, 1721, issue. In response, Cotton Mather, joined by other Puritan clergy, published an open letter to the writers and to the community. The version included in this chapter is from the *Boston Gazette* of July 27–31. In that letter, Mather argued that inoculation would work and that the method should be viewed as a gift from God that should not interfere with people's faith in God or their submission to Him. But others were not convinced. To them, the new procedure appeared to be an example of people "playing God" on matters of life and death.

It is in this context that James Franklin began printing the *New-England Courant.* James, the older brother of Benjamin Franklin, has been portrayed as a champion of journalistic and religious freedom because he ignored the custom of publishing "by authority" and his *New-England Courant* carried many articles attacking the Puritan religious establishment. However, prominent members of the only Anglican church in Boston set Franklin up in the newspaper business because they saw the inoculation controversy as an opportunity to attack the Puritan clergy, undermine their authority and, with luck, make the Church of England the established church in the colony.

In contrast to other Boston newspapers, the first issue of the *New-England Courant* promised a witty and irreverent newspaper. However, the publisher's statement in the August 21, 1721, edition concluded with words signaling that the smallpox issue would be its main theme: "Pray hard against Sickness, yet preach up the POX!"

And "preach up the POX" the paper did. Both the *Boston Gazette* and the *Boston News-Letter* printed items relating to the controversy during the summer and early fall of 1721, but the *New-England Courant* had them in virtually every issue. It also kept the controversy alive even after the epidemic of 1721 ended.

The item attributed to Frank Scammony is an example of the issue-oriented letters printed in early newspapers. The "Dialogue between a Clergyman and a Layman," the second installment of which ran in the next issue of the *New-England Courant,* is a very early example of that form for presenting arguments. The objections to inoculation presented in the *Courant* are much like those used by religious people today who oppose procedures ranging from blood transfusions to abortions and cloning.

The final item is one of Benjamin Franklin's "Silence Dogood" letters. Like the other letters, it shows the influence of English essayists on the opinions and writing style of the young Benjamin Franklin. Because the letter in this chapter was published at the height of the smallpox epidemic, it very likely contributed to the inoculation controversy. Although other Silence Dogood letters were quite critical of the Church of England, in context this one was probably understood as an attack on the Puritan establishment. The "ingenious Political Writer" to whom Franklin refers is Thomas Gordon, one of the authors of the series known as "Cato's Letters." The letter containing the quote was published in the *London Journal* on May 27, 1721.

An Open Letter Defending Inoculation

The Boston Gazette, July 27 to 31, 1721

To the Author of the Boston News Letter

Sir:

It was a grief to us the *Subscribers,* among Others, of your Friends in the *Town,* to see Dr. *Boylston* treated so unhandsomely in the *Letter* directed to you last Week, and published in your Paper. He is a *Son* of the *Town* whom Heaven (we all know) has adorn'd with some very peculiar *Gifts* for the Service of his Country, and hath signally own'd in the Successes which he has had.

If Dr. *Boylston* was too suddenly giving into a new Practice and (as many apprehend) dangerous Experiment, being too confident of the Innocence and Safety of the Method, and of the Benefit which the Publick might reap thereby; Altho' in that Case we are highly obliged to any Learned and Judicious Person who kindly informs us of the hazard and warns against the practice, yet what need there of injurious Reflections and any mean detracting from the known worth of the Doctor?

Especially how unworthy and unjust (not to say worse) is it to attempt to turn *that* to his reproach, which has been and is a singular honour to him, and felicity to his Country? We mean those words in the Letter,—*a certain Cutter for the Stone*—Yes, Thanks be to GOD we have such a One among us, and that so many poor *Miserables* have already found the benefit of his great tenderness, courage and skill in that hazardous Operation cannot enough value the *Man* and give praise to GOD. And we could easily speak of *other Cases* of equal hazard wherein the Dr. has serv'd with such Successes, as must render him inestimable to them that have been snatch'd from the Jaw of Death by his happy hand.

The Town knows and so does the Country how *long* and with what *Success* Dr. *Boylston* has practic'd both in *Physick* and *Surgery*; and tho' he has not had the honour and advantage of an *Academical* Education, and consequently not the *Letters* of some *Physicians* in the Town, yet he ought by no means to be call'd *Illiterate, ignorant, &c.* Would the Town hear that Dr. Cutler or Dr. Davis should be so treated? no more can it endure to see *Boylston* thus spit at.

Nor has it been without considerable *Study expense in travel, a good*

Genius, diligent Application and much Observation, that he has attain'd unto that knowledge and successful practice, which he has to give thanks to GOD for, and wherein we pray GOD that he may improve and grow with all humility.

The mean while we heartily wish that Men would treat one another with decency and charity, meekness and humility, as becomes fallible creatures, and good Friends to one another and to their Country.

As to the *Case of Conscience referred to in the Divines,* we shall only say—What *Heathens* must they be, to whom this can be a question.

"Whether the suffering more the entire grounds of Machinations of Men, than to our Preserver in the ordinary course of Nature, may be consistent with that Devotion and subjection we owe to the All-wise Providence of GOD Almighty?"

Who knows not the profanity and impiety of trusting in *Men* or *Means* more than in GOD? be it the most learn'd Men or the most proper Means? But we will suppose what in fact is true among us at this Day, true Men of Piety and Learning after much *serious tho't* have come into an Opinion of the Safety of the faulted method of *Inoculation for Smallpox;* and being perswaded it may be a means of preserving a Multitude of lives, they accept it with all thankfulness and joy at the gracious Discovery of a *Kind Providence* to Mankind for that end:—And then we ask, Cannot they give into the method or practice without having their *devotion and subjection to the All-wise Providence of* GOD *Almighty* call'd in question? Must they needs *trust more in Men than in their great Preserver* in the use of *this means than of any other?* What wild kind of Supposition is this? and the *Argument* falls with the *Hypothesis* in our *Schools.*

In a word, Do we not in the use of all means depend on GOD's *blessing?* and *live* by that alone? And can't a devout heart depend on GOD in the use of this means with much Gratitude, being in the full esteem of it? For what hand or art of *Man* is there in this Operation more than in *bleeding, blistering* and a score more things in *Medical use?* Which are all consistent with a *humble Trust in our Great Preserver, and a true Subjection to His All-wise Providence.*

Increase Mather
Cotton Mather
Benjamin Colman
Thomas Prince
John Webb
William Cooper

Boston, July 27
1721

Frank Scammony Questions Inoculation

The New-England Courant, August 21 to 28, 1721

To the Author of the New-England Courant

Sir,

The story of *Inoculation* I see finds Employment for several Hands, some labouring to maintain, while others strive to destroy a base *Hypothesis.* And being of a public Nature, as most Disputes are, has given Birth to several Printed Speculations, which seem on one side not so much to defend the Practice, which was expected, and that justly, as on the other to condemn it as Mal- Administration, because disagreeing with the Modes of Physick, besides a little low Treatment on both sides. Verberations and Reverberations as if in Time they would look on one another, to be neither Christians nor Gentlemen, because they cannot agree in their Opinion.

A Distemper so awful as the *Small Pox,* could not but spread Fear and Amazement in and around a Place, which had escap'd a Visitation of so terrible a Nature so long. But the Concern, I observ'd, in some measure began to abate with some, upon the News of a much safer way of taking it by *Inoculation.* The Lawfulness and Safety of such a Practice was the next thing to be considered. *Two Select Men* of your Town, prudently conven'd, desiring the *Practitioners of Physick* to join them and give their Opinion on the Case before them; which they did, and after some Deliberation, it was unanimously agreed, saith my author (for I was not there) to be *rash and dubious, &c.* And in another Place he tells us, B_____n is desired by the Select Men to desist, and so 'tis thought were his Followers (or Directors which you please) *in an ordinary way.* I quietly submitted to the Decision of those whom I thought to be the properest judges; and thought no more of it for a time.

But some being inclin'd to countenance and receive the Practice, (which I imagin'd a culpable Transgression of the Charge given by the *Eybort,* and disputing the Opinion of the Judges) this I say, indue'd me to throw a few Reflections together, and see what I could find for or against it. Whether *Inoculation* might be admitted or not, in the Places under my Oeconomical Jurisdiction: And tho' they may be thought trivial, yet as they proceed from an honest Principle for the Publick Good, I hope they will prevail upon a disinterested Reader (and such I hope you are) to pardon their Intrusion.

I was puzzled a little at first to know how to state the Case, whether according to my own or the *Inoculating Plan,* but concluded to draw up both, and then both might be satisfied, they as well as my self.

The Case stated in my own manner was, *Whether Self-Infection was lawful.* I soon past it in the Negative: and my reason was, because I thought in the end it might prove a Species of Self-Murder, if the Infection carried me off; and I had no Assurance to the contrary, but it might.

The Case as it was stated by the Opponent Side is, *Whether it is unlawful to produce on one's Self a lesser Sickness to prevent a greater?* This, as it consisted of more Parts, requires more time for it's Resolution, at least a satisfactory & sufficient one, because several interrogatories are to be made, as Whether you are sure of having this greater *Illness* and whether mortal or not, and whether the lesser *Sickness,* as it is term'd, might terminate so, of which in these Places.

I look upon it very strange, believe me Sir, that there should be so many, who, blest with a sound and vigorous Constitution, should be desirous to bring upon themselves a *Distemper,* of which themselves are afraid, and from which so many flee, that they should be so discontented when God brings it upon them, yet can be very well satisfied to bring it upon themselves, after the new Fashion! We have been fore-acquainted with the fearful Effects and dangerous Consequences that have attended some who have undergone the *Operation,* of which we have had sufficient Testimonies, and which we are oblig'd to believe unless disapproved, and that after a better manner than affirming them to be *Industrious Reports, meer ungrounded Rumours,* and *uncertain Guesses.* You may as well persuade the Attestant he has no Eyes. It is a very weak way of disapproving Testimonies. If, I say, they have impos'd Falshoods upon the World, and you know it to be Imposition, then in Justice to the Operation, and its Followers you should have detailed it, otherwise it was not fair to force People to believe the contrary. If, after all the terrible Apparatus's presented to our view, or Evils which may reasonably be apprehended as Consequences of *Self-Infection,* we go on in an uncertain, insecure and dangerous manner, to hazard and endanger, what ought to be most dear to us, our own and our Neighbor's Life and escape: Let us *bless* God that he suffered us not to perish in the presumptuous way of our own Inventions, and own *it was of the Lords Mercies we are not consumed.*

But if we perish, what a Confluence of Evils are there, and at whose hands shall it be required? If *Infection* is communicated to another by means of *Self-Infection,* and this *Contagion* spreads it self among others, and any of those thus infected perish, at whose Hands shall their Blood be required? Since it was probable they might have escaped the *Natural Pock,* and thereby came to an untimely End.

Self-Love or Self-Preservation (the great Duty of the Sixth Commandment) is a universal Maxim or Principle, which the Great Creator has planted in the whole *Animal Creation;* it puts a Man upon seeking and securing that which is good, and avoiding that which is evil; it teaches him to seek *Health* and Safety, and to avoid Pain and Insecurity; for Pain and Insecurity must threaten our Preservation. It labours to find by what means *Health* may be made defensible, where the Approaches and Avenues to Danger lie open, and make suitable Preparations to let and hinder them, and all this in Subordination to the Divine Will and Rule.

The *Indispositions* and Ailments of *Human Bodies,* as they arise from several Causes, so have they several Ways and Means, as second Causes, for the Removal, and restoring to the *Body* a State of *Health,* to such a Degree as the Constitution of the Body is capable of receiving, or the Medicaments subordinately administered, are capable of conveying unto it, referring all to Him who is the Disposer of all things, and in whose Hands are the Issues of Life and Death. And he who neglects to use means when there is a Call for it, contributes so far to the destroying himself, as the neglected Remedies (if procurable) might have done him good. But *Epidemical distempers, as they more immediately proceed from a Divine stretched out Anon, and are sent as Judgments from an angry and displeased God, so they require a different Physick, a different* Way *of Prevention, Being the greatest Marks of the greatest displeasure, so they call for the greatest Humiliation, the greatest Observation of the Duties of Repentance.*

Thus our LEGISLATORS recommended in the *Proclamation for observing a Fast upon this Occasion,* which abounds with a true Christian Spirit and Concern, the very reading of which must needs affect a Soul (if capable of being mov'd) with a most awful Contemplation of the Divine Judgements, and excite a thorow Resolution, (with the Divine Assistence) to repent of and forsake those Iniquities, which have stirred up against us, the Wrath of an offended God. This, and this alone is the Prescription, even of God himself, to prevent his Judgments from falling upon us. This being observ'd, the Prophet then tells us, *Who knoweth but he may return and repent, and leave—Blessing behind behind [sic] him.* How far *Inoculation* suits with this *Directory,* and how far it helps us to *meet the Lord in the day of his Judgments,* is beyond my Ability to determine.

As *Boils* and *Blasms* are reckoned amongst the Judgments of the most High, what must the invading his Province be by bringing them upon our selves? If the Undertakers of *Inoculation* proceed after the Methods of those poor People mention'd, I adminish 'em to repent and forbear to *DIRECT AND MANAGE Small Pox* to any in such a Manner, than in an *ORDINARY WAY they shall be SURE OF NONE but a GENTLE VISITATION,* this with all Submission God Almighty never instructed poor People either to say or do, and therefore ought to have been rejected as an *Hypocrosie,* exceeding Christian Decency. I recommend to their Perusal the Judgment denounced *Deut. 28.17. The Lord thy God will smite thee with the Botch of Egypt, with the Emerods, with the Scab & with the Itch, whereof thou canst not be healed.* How far this may countenance an easy way of introducing what all good Men esteem a Judgment, I leave to be determin'd.

Men of Piety and Learning, Men whom I sincerely believe to be highly valuable and great for both, and whom I honour, may be perswaded that the *Inoculated Small Pox may be a Means for preserving a multitude of Lives,* but then are they perswaded that it may not be a means of taking away some? This wanted a *serious thought* as well as the other, but I had nothing of it. And unless I am perswaded that no such thing is to be fear'd, I shall be so far from *giving into* this Method and *Practice,* that I should think it ought rather to be call'd in Question.

It may be replied the *Artificial Pock* is not of that spreading *Infectuous* Nature. It may be; but I fear some may have experience'd the Contrary. This Gentlemen you should have consider'd before you proceeded to the *Practice.*

In short, I affirm it unlawful for a Person in *Health* upon any Account to receive a less *Infection* to avoid a greater, because Our blessed Saviour, the Great, the Skillful Physician says, *He that is whole needs not a Physician, but he that is Sick.* He allows of Application to Physicians in Cases of *Illness;* but *Health* has no need of Recourse to them.

As God blesses us with *Health,* by the sixth Commandment we are oblig'd to maintain it, and use it to the End bestow'd *to glorifie Him that we may enjoy Him forever.*

You say it is to prevent a greater *Illness,* how know you that you shall have any, much more a great One, or what you term a lesser Sickness may not result in the greatest, even that of the Death of the Soul for your presumptuous running into it. If you think you might escape it, why bring you it upon yourselves? If you thought you could not, why wait you not God's appointed Time, but must present to themselves the time *NOW* and the measure of but Invite a *GENTLE VISITATION AND THAT AVAILS Such.*

I am asham'd that these things of so pernicious Consequence, so destructive to *human Security* cannot be seen without pointing to 'em, and am sorry for so mean a hand. All I have more to say at present of the *Practice of Inoculation,* into which we are running, is serviceable and Lawful, and tends to *Preservation of a Multitude of Lives,* and endangers none, I question not not [sic] but 'twill have the Blessing of God and the Protection of the Government. But if it is unlawful and destructive of the Lives of the Liege subjects of his Majesty King GEORGE, His Excellency our Governor and the Senate of this Land, to whose Care and Government this great People is committed, and whose welfare they have so much at Heart, will, I hope, in their Great Wisdom and singular Prudence Judge and Determine the Affair.

Little-Compton   *I am, Sir*
Aug. 17, 1721   *Your very Humble Servant,*
            Frank Scammony.

A Dialogue between a Clergyman and a Layman, Concerning Inoculation

By an unknown Hand, *The New-England Courant,* January 1 to 8, 1722

Clergyman. The last Time I discours'd with you, you seem'd to discover a bitter Aversion to the new and safe Way of *Inoculation*; are you yet reconcil'd to that successful Practice?

Layman. I have but little reason to entertain a more favourable Opinion of that Practice than formerly, unless the Death of several Persons under the Operation of late, should induce me so to do. I confess, I am not yet convinc'd, that it is either a *lawful or successful* Practice.

Cl. The Ministers of the Gospel who are our Spiritual Guides approve and recommend this Practice; and they are great and good Men, who would not impose on the World, and surely, you ought to fall in with their Opinion.

Laym. I think the Ministers who have drove on Inoculation so fiercely have not only impos'd on others, but themselves also, so that we have reason to say in the Words of the Prophet (Hos. 9:7) *The Days of Visitation are come; —the Prophet is a Fool, and our Spiritual Men is mad.* I have abundant Reason to think, that they and I are equally ignorant of Inoculation, especially as to the *Success* of it; and if the Blind lead the Blind, both shall fall into the Ditch.

Cl. But why won't you believe the *Ministers*? They can explain the dark Passages of Scripture, and answer Cases of Conscience, better than *illiterate Men.*

Laym. I will believe no Man (tho' he be a Minister) because he is great and good; for such *may err,* and have sometimes deceived themselves and others: Nor have any of our Casuists as yet given satisfactory Answers to the Objections and Scruples which are rais'd against this upstart Way: But all the Books they have written for it (as *Moses* began his) they have fill'd with a *Chaos.*

Cl. Well, but you will acknowledge they are good Men, I hope.

Laym. They *are* or *should* be good; but I remember a great Divine says, "When we are about our Enquiry into Truth, let it be remembered; that neither the Great, nor the Learned, nor the *Good* are absolutely to be confided in."

Cl. But I find, *all the Rakes in Town* are against Inoculation, and that induces me to believe it is a right Way.

Laym. Most of the *Ministers* are for it, and that induces me to think it is from the D_____l, for he often makes use of good Men as Instruments to obtrude his Delusions on the World.

Cl. You must not say it is from the D____l because of the *Success* of it, for the D____l was never the Author of any thing for the Good of Mankind.

Laym. As to the Success of this Practice, the learned Dr. *Edwards* shall speak for me, and the rather, because Dr. *C. Mather (Bonif. p. 130)* says *More* Edwards *would be past Blessings.* "Some fool themselves into the grossest Errors by looking at that *Success* and *Prosperity,* and (as they are pleased to call it) the *Providence* which attends their Opinions and Ways. It is a Maxim among the *Turks* generally, that whatever prospers hath God for its Author: And so from their Success in their Wars, they have been wont to conclude that their Religion is from God, and owned by him. But I think the Scripture forbids us to learn the Customs of the Heathen.

Cl. Inoculation is not the worse because the Heathens first practiced it. They make use of Food and Clothing, and shall we reject those Gifts of Heaven, because they receive them? God forbid!

Laym. The Gift of Food and Clothing, which you bring for an Instance, is noways purtinent, for the Sixth Commandment requires us to use those things for the support of our Lives. Are you willing to indicate the Heathen in other Things besides *Inoculation?* The King of *Calesus* in the *East-Indies* lies not with his Queen in the night, but one of the Priests doth, who have a Gratuity bestow'd on him for that Service. I suppose it is not a worse Sin to break the Seventh Commandment than the Sixth.

Cl. I should be loth to conform to that outlandish Practice, because it is a mortal Evil, which I think Inoculation is not.

Laym. You do not think it is not a *mortal Evil,* for you cannot prove that it is not; none of you have done it as yet, and I presume you are all asham'd of your Craft, and will write no more in favour of the Practice.

Cl. I see you are obstinate, and will not be convinc'd. I will adjourn the Discourse to our next Meeting.

Silence Dogood on Hypocrisy

The New-England Courant, July 18 to 23, 1722

To the Author of the New-England Courant

It has been for some Time a Question with me, Whether a Commonwealth suffers more by hypocritical Pretenders to Religion, or by the openly Profane? But some late Thoughts of this Nature have inclined me to think, that the Hypocrite is the most dangerous Person of the Two, especially if he sustains a Post in the Government, and we consider his

Conduct as it regards the Publick. The first Artifice of a *State Hypocrite* is, by a few savoury Expressions which cost him Nothing, to betray the best Men in his Country into an Opinion of his Goodness; and if the Country wherein he lives is noted for the Purity of Religion, he the more easily gains his End, and consequently may more justly be expos'd and detested. A notoriously profane Person in a private Capacity, ruins himself, and perhaps forwards the Destruction of a few of his Equals; but a publick Hypocrite every day deceives his betters, and makes them the Ignorant Trumpeters of his supposed Godliness: They take him for a Saint, and pass him for one, without considering that they are (as it were) the Instruments of publick Mischief out of Conscience, and ruin their Country for God's sake.

This Political Description of a Hypocrite, may (for ought I know) be taken for a new Doctrine by some of your Readers; but let them consider, that *a little Religion, and a little Honesty, goes a great way in Courts.* 'Tis not inconsistent with Charity to distrust a Religious Man in Power, tho' he may be a good Man; he has many Temptations "to propagate *public Destruction* for *Personal Advantages* and Security": And if his Natural Temper be covetous, and his Actions often contradict his pious Discourse, we may with great Reason conclude, that he has some other Design in his Religion besides barely getting to Heaven. But the most dangerous Hypocrite in a Common-Wealth, is one who *leaves the Gospel for the sake of the Law:* A man compounded of Law and Gospel, is able to cheat a whole Country with his Religion, and then destroy them under *Colour of Law:* And here the Clergy are in great Danger of being deceiv'd, and the People of being deceiv'd by the Clergy, until the Monster arrives to such Power and Wealth, that he is out of the reach of both, and can oppress the People without their own blind Assistance. And it is a sad Observation, that when the People too late see their Error, yet the Clergy still persist in their Encomiums on the Hypocrite; and when he happens to die *for the Good of his Country,* without leaving behind him the Memory of *one good Action,* he shall be sure to have his Funeral Sermon stuff'd with *Pious Expressions* which he dropt at such a Time, and at such a Place, and on such an Occasion; than which nothing can be more prejudicial to the Interest of Religion, nor indeed to the Memory of the Person deceas'd. The Reason of this Blindness in the Clergy is, because they are honourably supported (as they ought to be) by their People, and see nor feel nothing of the Oppression which is obvious and burdensome to every one else.

But this Subject raises in me an Indignation not to be born; and if we have had, or are like to have any Instances of this Nature in New England, we cannot better manifest our Love to Religion and the Country, than by setting the Deceivers in a true Light, and undeceiving the Deceived, however such Discoveries may be represented by the ignorant or designing Enemies of our Peace and Safety.

I shall conclude with a Paragraph or two from an ingenious Political Writer in the *London Journal,* the better to convince your Readers, that Publick Destruction may be easily carry'd on by *hypocritical Pretenders to Religion.*

"A raging Passion for immoderate Gain had made Men universally and intensely hard-hearted: They were every where devouring one another. And yet the Directors and their Accomplices, who were the acting Instruments of all this outrageous Madness and Mischief, set up for wonderful pious Persons, while they were defying Almighty God, and plundering Men; and they set apart a Fund of Subscriptions for charitable Uses; that is, they mercilessly made a whole People Beggars, and charitably supported a few *necessitous* and *worthless* FAVOURITES. I doubt not, but if the Villany had gone on with Success, they would have had their Names handed down to Posterity with Encomiums; as the Names of other *publick Robbers* have been! We have *Historians* and ODE MAKERS now living, very proper for such a Task. It is certain, that most People did, at one Time, believe the *Directors* to be *great and worthy Persons.* And an honest Country Clergyman told me last Summer, upon the Road, that Sir John was an excellent publick-spirited Person, for that he had beautified his Chancel.

"Upon the whole we must not judge of one another by their best Actions; since the worst Men do some Good, and all Men make fine Professions: But we must judge of Men by the whole of their Conduct, and the Effects of it. Thorough Honesty requires great and long Proof, since many a Man, long thought honest, has at length proved a Knave. And it is from judging without Proof, or false Proof, that Mankind continue Unhappy."

I am, SIR, Your humble Servant,
SILENCE DOGOOD

3

The Great Awakening

A hundred years after the Pilgrims landed at Plymouth Rock, America was no longer as dangerous a place as it once was, but neither was it the New Jerusalem so many had envisioned. Immigration brought new churches to what initially had been religiously homogeneous communities. With prosperity came spiritual complacency.

Something of the encroaching spirit of irreverence and indifference can be seen in the "Dialogue between a Clergyman and a Layman" included in chapter 2. But by the time the Anglicans in Boston tried to wrest power from the dominant Puritan Congregational Church by setting James Franklin up in the newspaper business, the major threat to the established churches in New England was already well underway. That threat came not from free spirits such as James and Benjamin Franklin but from clergy who took their faith quite seriously.

During the 1720s and 1730s the teachings of ministers such as Jonathan Edwards, William Stoddard and William Tennent split churches into "Old Light" ones and "New Light" ones. Some of the points of contention between the two groups were the subjects for public debates of the kind noted in an item appearing in the *New-England Weekly Journal* on June 27, 1727. Those debates also set the scene for the first of many recurring periods of religious revivalism in America.

The Great Awakening, as this period of revivalism came to be known, was set in motion through the efforts of itinerant preachers such as James Davenport, Gilbert Tennent, the son of William Tennent, and, most notably, George Whitefield. For decades preachers had been lamenting both false doctrine and the indifference to all things spiritual they saw around them. Therefore, initially many of them welcomed these preachers into their communities. But others saw them as a threat.

The "Old Light" churches eschewed enthusiasm—the 18th-century term for the belief that emotions, impulses and intense feelings are to be accepted as revelations from God. Calvinist churches taught that some people are predestined to salvation and others are not. But the preachers of the Great Awakening encouraged a personal, enthusiastic and experiential religion. They taught that all people can be saved if only they will accept Jesus as their Savior and then lead a life in accord with biblical precepts.

This new message resulted in many converts. But it also divided communities, churches and even families into those who accepted the new teachings and those who did not. With the Great Awakening, the older denominations saw their power wane as Methodist and Baptist influence increased.

The stories in this chapter document the work of the Rev. George Whitefield, the most important revivalist of the Great Awakening. Oxford educated and a member of the Church of England, Whitefield was greatly influenced by Charles and John Wesley, founders of Methodism. At their urging, Whitefield first visited America in 1738 and 1739. Over the years Whitefield preached in most of the colonies, but his impact initially was greatest in New England.

The "Report on George Whitefield in New York" documents Whitefield's reception, his preaching style and its effect on his audience. As that report and the subsequent "Letter from a Writer in New England" indicate, Whitefield was a persuasive and very popular preacher. However, the letter taken from the *South-Carolina Gazette* also show the controversy surrounding his ministry because of the religious enthusiasm he promoted.

Those 1741 letters also illustrate how news from one region spread throughout colonial America. They were undoubtedly of great interest to Charleston residents because Whitefield had preached there in January 1740. The first page of the *South-Carolina Gazette* for December 19–January 5, 1740, had a handwritten note announcing Whitefield's arrival; subsequent issues carried reports of his work in South Carolina, which gave rise to lengthy theological debates that were published in the paper during February and March 1740.

During 1741 Whitefield's criticism of the faculty and students at Harvard and Yale provoked additional complaints from New Englanders. The commentary on that criticism outlines both Whitefield's charges against Harvard and the underlying doctrinal differences the Great Awakening brought to light. Whitefield, who had already left Massachusetts for England at the time critical letters began to appear in Massachusetts newspapers, responded with a letter that was published in the *Boston Gazette & Weekly Journal* on March 16, 1742. In it, he tried to mollify his critics, but with only partial success.

While Whitefield was in England, both support for revivalism and criticisms of it appeared regularly in newspapers from Massachusetts to South Carolina. On February 2, 1742, the *Boston Gazette and Weekly Journal* carried a testimony in which clergy thanked the Revs. Gilbert Tennent and George Whitefield for the revival of religion in their community; however, one year later, on March 28, 1743, the *Boston Weekly Post-Boy* carried an account of "religious excess" at New London, attributable to the Rev. Mr. Davenport and the "New Lights"; three months after that, on July 1, the *Boston Weekly News-Letter* reported Davenport had been expelled from Connecticut.

When Whitefield made his last trip to America in 1770, the personal, enthusiastic and experiential religiosity he taught met with new challenges from the rationalism of Enlightenment era thought that fueled the American revolution. A month after the *Massachusetts Spy* published the letter from Thomas Young, a Deist, and an August 25, 1770, reply to it, Whitefield died suddenly in Newburyport, Massachusetts. Newspapers throughout the colonies carried obituaries. Most of those obituaries, like the one from the generally critical *Massachusetts Spy* of September 29–October 2, 1770, praised his work.

A Report on George Whitefield in New York

The New-England Weekly Journal, December 4, 1739

The Rev. Mr. *Whitefield* arrived at the City of N. York on Wednesday the 14th Inst. a little before Night. The next Morning he waited on the Rev. Mr. *Vesey,* and desired leave to preach in the English Church, but was refus'd: The Reason assigned for such Refusal was, because Mr. *Whitefield* had no Licence to Preach in any Parish but that for which he was ordained; and an old Canon was read. To this Mr. *Whitefield* reply'd, That that Canon was Obsolete, and had not been in Use for above 100 Years, That the whole Body of the Clergy, frequently preach out of the Bounds of their Parishes, without such Licence. These Arguments not prevailing, some Application was made to the Rev. Mr. *Boel,* for the Use of the *New Dutch Church,* but this also was refus'd. Then Mr. *Whitefield* had the offer of the *Presbyterian Church,* but did not care at first to accept it, not being willing to give any Offence to his Brethren of the Church of *England*; but said, *He chose rather to go without the Camp, bearing his Reproach, and Preach in the Fields.* At length being informed, that in some Parts of this Country, the Meeting Houses had been alternately us'd by the Ministers of the several Communions, and very often borrowed by the Church of the Dissenters, he consented to accept the Offer for the Evening. However, in the Afternoon he preached in the Fields to many Hundreds of People.

Among the Hearers, the Person who gives this Account, was one. I fear Curiosity was the Motive that led me and many others into that Assembly. I had read two or three of Mr. *Whitefield's* Sermons and part of his Journal, and from thence had obtained a settled Opinion, that he was a Good Man. Thus far was I prejudiced in his Favour. But then having heard of much Opposition, and many Clamours against him, I tho't it possible that he might have carried Matters too far—That some *Enthusiasm* might have mix'd itself with his Piety, and that his Zeal might have exceeded his Knowledge. With these Prepossessions I went into the Fields; when I came there, I saw a great Number of People consisting of *Christians* of all Denominations, some *Jews,* and a few, I believe, that had no Religion at all. When Mr. *Whitefield* came to the Place before designed, which was a little Eminence on the side of a Hill, he stood still, and beckned with his Hand, and dispos'd the Multitude upon the Descent, before, and on each side of him. He then prayed most excellently, in the same manner (I guess) that the first Ministers of the *Christian Church* prayed, before they were shackled with Forms. The Assembly soon appeared to be divided into two Companies, the one of which I considered under the Name of GOD'S *Church,* and the other the *Devil's Chappel.* The first were collected round the Minister, and were very serious and attentive. The last had placed themselves in the skirts of the Assembly, and spent most of their Time in Gigling, Scoffing, Talking and Laughing. I believe the Minister saw them, for in his Sermon, observing the Cowardice and Shamefacedness of *Christians* in Christ's Cause, he pointed towards this Assembly, and reproached the former with the boldness and Zeal with which the Devil's Vassals serve him. Towards the last Prayer, the whole Assembly appeared more united, and all became hush'd and still; a solemn Awe and Reverence appeared in the Faces of most, a mighty Energy attended the Word. I heard and felt something astonishing and surprizing, but, I confess; I was not at that Time fully rid of my Scruples. But as I tho't I saw a visible Presence of GOD with Mr. *Whitefield,* I kept my Doubts to my self.

Under this Frame of Mind, I went to hear him in the Evening at the *Presbyterian Church,* where he Expounded to above 2000 People within and without Doors. I never in my Life saw so attentive an Audience: Mr *Whitefield* spake as one having Authority: All he said was *Demonstration, Life* and *Power*! The Peoples Eyes and Ears hung on his Lips. They greedily devour'd every Word. I came Home astonished! Every Scruple vanished. I never saw nor heard the like, and I said within my self, *Surely God is with this Man of a Truth.* He preach'd and expounded in this manner twice every Day for four Days, and this Evening Assemblies were continually increasing. On Sunday Morning at 8 o'Clock, his Congregation consisted of about 1500 People: But at Night several Thousands came together to hear him, and the Place being too strait for them, many were forced to go away, and some (tis said) with Tears lamented their Disappointment.

Letter from a Writer in New England to Friends in South Carolina

The South-Carolina Gazette, June 18, 1741

We have passed thro' a Winter the most tedious and severe in the Memory of Man: But neither that nor the Desolation of, are half so bad as sectarian enthusiastick Madness. *Whitefield's* Place has been occupied by his prime Friend *Gilbert Tennent.*—Their Prayers are generally censured as imperfect, immethodical, &c. But their Sermons and Expositions—! There from the latter you might hear yourself *cursed, damned, double-damned,* the Generality stiled *unregenerate, proud, Hypocrites, rotten-hearted, old Sinners, and Devils, and worse than Devils;* and these repeated and deliver'd in a long String, which would take many Minutes to bring out of his Mouth. This Creature has stirr'd the World, occupied almost all our Pulpits in Town, drawn off People from their necessary Labours every Day in the Week 2, 3, or 4 Times in the Day, at the Meetings, or more private Conventicles; neither Cold nor Rain, nor Snow, cou'd keep the red-riding-Hoods at Home by Night or by Day; groaning, crying, fainting took Place of regular Attention. Notes have been put up in great Variety and Number, even to 50 at a Time; for some 6 and upwards, some 12, some 30, 50, 60 Years old; some under Hardness of Heart, some wicked Children, some converted themselves for their unconverted Relations, some under Conviction, some half convicted. People are dissuaded and discouraged from the Sacrament, terrified, bewilder'd, distracted: And some after Agonies and Torments, like those of Hell, are happily recover'd and new born, *forsooth,* and with as much heavenly Joy as any *Bedlam* People. Boys and Girls from 6 Years and upwards take upon them to meet together for religious Exercises, and to go the Rounds, praying, conferring and exhorting. Several of the neighbouring Towns tally with us; *Cambridge* particularly, where great Numbers of the Students are taken off from all learned Improvements, and under the practical Whims of *Tennent,* whose Tutors find it impossible, to oblige them to their Exercises in these Times of prevailing Distraction; and I expect that impregnated with *John Bunyan, Stoddard, Sheppard &c.* they will soon get into the Pulpits, and fill the Country with *Antinomian* Reveries.

Commentary on George Whitefield's Criticism of Harvard

The Boston Gazette and Weekly Journal, April 20, 1741

To the Reader,

The Author of the following Remarks is a true and hearty Lover of the Rev. Mr. Whitefield, thinks that he has been Instrumental in awakening and stirring up People to a serious Concern for the Salvation of their precious Souls; and it is the Author's daily Prayer that the Convictions and Awak'nings among us, may terminate in a sound Conversion, evidenced by newness of Life and new Obedience; but still he is not so blinded as to think that worthy Gentleman is infallible; and whoever reads his last Journal must be of the same Mind; there being many Things therein contained, and particularly with Relation to the College *in* Cambridge, *and the Ministers of* New England, *without Foundation: And least this partial Account of the former, and his uncharitable Thoughts of the latter, should do as much Hurt to Religion as his Preaching did Good, the following Remarks are made.*

Mr. Whitefield observes, that on the 24th of *September,* he preached at the *College:* that it has one President, and four Tutors—Here his Account is partial, for he ought to have said that there are two Professors; one of Divinity, the other of the Mathematicks; as also an Hebrew Instructor; and he had added that these three Gentlemen were as well qualified for their respective Trusts, as any he ever conversed with, he would have spoke the Truth, and done the College but Justice.

He observes, that Discipline is at a low Ebb there; in which he is intirely mistaken. I lived at the College in two Presidents Time, both very excellent Men; the first particularly remarked for being a Man of Authority; and I am perfectly acquainted with the Government of the College at this Time, and so am as capable of knowing the Truth of that Matter as Mr. *Whitefield,* who never was at College but once in his Life, and then not a quarter of an Hour (except whilst a Preaching) and I do solemnly declare that I never saw the Authority of Government more maintained than at this Time, and I believe no one ever thought the contrary, saving this Reverend Stranger.

Again, he observes that the Tutors neglect to pray with and examine the Hearts of their Pupils; by which Account any one must necessarily suppose that they are in a worse State at College than the Heathens; for they have their publick Prayers: but here is a Society that call themselves Christians, consisting of above an Hundred Persons, and yet there are no public Prayers offered up to Almighty GOD for them, by those unto whose Care they are committed. But now is this the Case at College; no, the President prays twenty-eight Times a Week in the College-Hall, and the Professor of Divinity four Times; so that there are thirty-two Prayers offered up to God by the President and Professors every Week with and for the Students, who by Law are obliged to attend the same. *David,* a Man after God's own Heart, prayed Evening and Morning, and at Noon; which makes twenty-one Times in a Week: these Gentlemen pray two and thirty Times in a Week with the Students; and yet, there are no Prayers at College. Again, are not the Holy Scriptures read by the President twice every Day in publick, and often expounded by him? Hath not the Professor of Divinity three Lectures every Week upon the best and most important Subjects? Again, I do not see how it can be called a *Neglect* in the Tutors should they not pray with their Pupils; it was what was never done in good Mr. *Shepard's* Day, nor since the College had an Existence; they are not obliged by the Laws of the College to do it, which if it was tho't necessary, undoubtedly it would have been injoined them by the Corporation and Overseers; b[ut] if it is necessary, and yet not injoined them, the Legislative Power in the College are more to blame than the Tutors. Again, the Tutors praying with the Pupils is what I believe was never known in any University, especially where there are so many Prayers every Day as at the College in *Cambridge.*

But then how does Mr. *Whitefield* know that the Tutors do not privately talk with their Pupils, with respect to their Souls. I know the Tutors never told him they did not, I know he never had it from the Pupils, how then came he by his Knowledge; I conclude he argues it from this, he finds no Journal printed giving an Account of these Things, and therefore these Things cannot be. Private and personal Instructions, Examinations, Advice, and the like in their own Nature ought to be kept secret; and because I do not know that a Man does this or the other Thing, shall I therefore infer he doth not do it. I never heard any Man pray in secret, must I therefore conclude and report abroad that no Man makes Conscience of that Duty, because he doth not publish it. But in Truth I believe the Tutors do talk with the Pupils about their Souls as Occasion requires: I was when at College under Mr. *Flynt,* who to my certain Knowledge was very faithful as to that Particular, as well as all other.

Again, Mr. *Whitefield* is pleased to observe that bad Books are read, *Tillotson* and *Clark,* instead of *Shepard* and *Stoddard.* If he means by the Undergraduates, it is a Mistake, they do not read them; if he means the Graduates, I believe they do read *Tillotson,* and I hope they will, but not in the room and stead of Bishop *Hopkins,* Bishop *Peirson,* Dr. *Bates,* Mr. *How,* Dr. *Owen,* Mr. *Baxter,* and Dr. *Wates,* who were as Great and as Good Men as Mr. *Shepard* and Mr. *Stoddard;* these they could not read till lately, because out of print; and therefore if they read other Books as good, I hope they will be forgiven: and if they should read Dr. *Tillotson* also, I do not know that it would be a Crime. Those that censure him undoubtedly have read him; pray then allow others the same Liberty you take yourselves. There are a great many excellent good Things in Dr. *Tillotson,* that the Enemies to Dr. *Tillotson,* as I have heard some of them acknowledge, have got a great deal of Good by, and so many others. It certainly would have been better for Mr. *Whitefield* to have treated Dr. *Tillotson,* unto whom the Protestant Religion, and the Dissenters are so vastly indebted, as he has done the great Mr. *Stoddard:* He speaks very honourable and justly of him, and his Works, and recommends them; but then he thinking differently from Mr. *Whitefield* in some Things, about unconverted Ministers (where by the way Mr. *Stoddard* was perfectly right in my Opinion, as also in his Thoughts about unconverted Persons going to the Sacrament) is pleased to say of him thus—'That he honours the Memory of that great and good Man, yet he thinks he is much to be blamed for endeavouring to prove that unconverted Men may be admitted into the Ministry.' So I think Mr. *Whitefield* might have spoke of Dr.

Tillotson; might have recommended his Works in General, and cautioned the Scholars against his Errors, none of which were more destructive to Christianity (allowing Mr. *Whitefield's* Thoughts to be just about unconverted Ministers) then are Mr. *Stoddard's* Tho'ts and Writings upon that Subject. But again, there are in Dr. *Tillotson's* Writings Things fundamentally wrong (in Mr. *Whitefield's* Opinion) or there are not, if there are not, then no such Crime to read them; if there are, still they ought to be read by those capable of making a Judgment: Because Mr. *Whitefield* may be mistaken in these Things as well as Mr. *Stoddard* in other Fundamentals. And upon Supposition Mr. *Whitefield* should be mistaken, and Dr. *Tillotson* in the right, what will become of those that have neglected reading him, upon Mr. *Whitefield's* Prohibition; will that plead their Excuse in the Great Day? And as to the Students reading Dr. *Clark* and other Arian Writers, I believe they never did. True it is, that about the Year 1735, Dr. *Clark* and many Books much worse than his were read, and some were then given up to strong Delusions, and began to deny the God that bought them; immediately upon which the Divinity Professor laboured more abundantly in asserting and proving the important Truths then denied; and by the Blessing of God upon his learned and faithful Endeavours, a Stop was soon put thereto.

In short, Mr. *Whitefield* had no Advantages of knowing the true State of the College; never had any Account about the College from any Persons of Truth, and that were acquainted with it; provided he had no other Account, that what he has given in his Journal; and therefore what Regard can be had to it.

But before I leave the College, I beg leave to observe that by Mr. *Whitefield's* and *Tennent's* Preaching, there, the Scholars in general, have been wonderfully wrought upon, and their Enquiry now is, *What shall we do to be saved?* Some I believe have lately been savingly brought home to God: These Gentlemen have planted, Mr. *Appleton* hath watered; and a blessed watering it hath been: but after all, it was GOD who gave the Increase.

A Letter to George Whitefield from Thomas Young

The Massachusetts Spy, August 28 to 30, 1770

To the Reverend GEORGE WHITEFIELD

Sir,

A PUBLICK reproach will doubtless at least excuse a public complaint. In your lecture delivered at the Old North meeting-house on Wednesday evening, you were pleased to inform us, That Cain was the founder of the Deists, and gave this argument for proof, that because no blood attended his offering it was not accepted. If these be very material points in divinity, I should like to see them much better elucidated, than by a bare quotation of the opinion of a Reverend Doctor who, you informed us, put the matter out of dispute, that Abel also brought the fruits of the ground in offering. Should this Reverend Doctor have any collateral history of superior authority to that ascribed to Moses, he may perhaps from thence deduce irrefragable evidence to the point in question: but in the fourth of Genesis the story runs thus: *And Abel was a keeper of sheep, but Cain was a tiller of the ground. And in process of time it came to pass, that Cain brought of the fruit of the ground in offering unto the Lord. And Abel brought of the firstlings of the flock and of the fat thereof. And the Lord had respect unto Abel and his offering. But unto Cain and his offering he had not respect.* One would imagine that, from the previous account of the respective occupations of the brothers, their offerings were naturally supposable the fruits of their respective industry; and your large acquaintance with the sentiments of divines on this head, renders it needless for me to inform you, that the non-acceptance of Cain's offering has been very frequently ascribed to another cause. However, not to labor this matter, I presume if the hands of Cain had remained free from blood and violence *"not for the want of goats and bullocks slain,"* would God or man have been so much offended with him. There is [but] another difficulty, which the mist of antiquity hides from vulgar eyes, i.e. to come at any shadow of proof, besides the bare word of the Priest, that Cain was a person of any tolerable figure in religion at all, much less the founder of a set whose principles are the acknowledged foundation of every religion that has yet appeared in the world. The learned Dr. Samuel Clark, speaking of the Deists, acknowledges some classes of them to have right apprehensions of the natural attributes of God and his all-governing providence, in the direction of the affairs of men, as also, the obligations of natural religion, *justice, mercy and fidelity,* but so far only as these things are discoverable by the light of nature, without believing any divine revelation, and concludes, that the priinciples of those men are so immaterially different from those of christianity, that he questions whether such Deists exist. The compilers of the Universal History, however warmly they espouse the cause of Christianity, are diffuse in their encomiums on the excellent system of true religion, among the ancient Persians, which they acknowledge was refined Deism, or the pure unallayed religion of nature, flourishing in, and blessing that vast empire for many centuries. That these refined Deists are wrong in any tenet they profess is not pretended, even by their avowed opponents; the whole accusation against them is therefore reduced to a complaint, that there are some necessary truths they do not believe; the remedy in such case is only force; the several kinds of force, are brutal, perswasive, and rational: the first, thank heaven, is wearing a little out of fashion, the second loses ground, and unless we are forced by unquestionable evidence, and rational argument, to believe the Deity is inexorable by other means than cutting the throats and spilling the blood of innocent animals, we must remain with good King David and the ancient Persians, at least doubters of the absolute necessity of embracing our hands in blood in order to please our Maker.

I am, Sir, your humble servant,
THOMAS YOUNG.

4

Religion and Revolution

By the time of the Rev. George Whitefield's last visit to America in 1770, the colonies were moving inexorably toward a break with England. Instead of deferring to authority, newspapers began to assert their independence of it. Where once printer/editors described the purpose of their paper in religious terms, now they more often presented their papers as fulfilling political functions. Although they still published news items, letters and essays intended to promote true religiosity, their frequency decreased as the number of items using religion to justify or oppose a break with England increased. Justifications for the break came both from traditional Christianity and from Deism.

Most American papers took up the patriot cause. Cato's Letter, "Arbitrary Government proved Incompatible with true Religion, whether Natural or Revealed," first published in the *London Journal* on February 21, 1721, was widely reprinted in colonial newspapers. A supplement to the *Boston-Gazette* of March 22, 1773, promoted John Locke's essay on civil government.

Themes from those works appeared and reappeared in letters and essays by patriot writers, but often with a twist. Instead of tightly reasoned, scholarly arguments, patriot writings such as the "Commentary on the Stamp Act" reproduced from the *New-York Gazette* but also appearing in other newspapers including the *South-Carolina Gazette and Country Journal* of December 31, 1765, took on an impassioned, somewhat frantic tone.

Other essays gave vent to colonial dissatisfaction with England through the use of religious forms to make political points. "The First Book of the Marks" is an example of writings that borrow their structure and language from the Bible."The Geneology [sic] of a Jacobite," from the *Pennsylvania Evening Post* of February 9, 1775, and "The American Chronicles of the Times," published in the *Virginia Gazette* during January 1775, also use biblical style; "An English Patriot's Creed," published in the *Massachusetts Spy* on January 19, 1776, mimics the style of the Apostles' Creed.

Patriot newspapers also routinely published prayers, proclamations for days of prayer and sermons favorable to their cause. An example of a proclamation for a day of prayer, signed by John Hancock, can be found in the *Boston-Gazette and Country Journal* for July 3, 1775; a sermon delivered by the Rev. Gilbert Tennent appears in the *Massachusetts Spy* for December 4, 1776.

Although their writings suggest the patriots were convinced that God would be on their side as long as they remained faithful to his commands, they sometimes adjusted their religious practices to make them compatible with their political beliefs. The item from the *Virginia Gazette* announcing changes in the Anglican form of worship was picked up by the *Pennsylvania Evening Post* of August 3, 1776, and then by other papers around the country.

While the patriots used religion to justify their cause, those who sympathized with England argued that true religion and revolution were incompatible. In Tory newspapers, those arguments became more frequent as British fortunes waned. The essay reproduced in this chapter from Jeremy Rivington's *Royal Gazette* traces revolutionary zeal to the same misguided beliefs and hypocrisy that led religious dissenters to break with the Church of England. Those arguments show up again in the *Gazette* on November 25, 1778; a year later, on December 16, 1778, the paper reprinted an essay from a collection first published in London, in which the author also complains that "the pulpit has been shamelessly prostituted" by clergy who do not attend to "That part of scripture which inculcates loyalty." On October 16, 1788, the *Newport Herald,* edited by Peter Edes, reprinted an essay from the *Pennsylvania Packet* that linked revolution and the Anti-Christ. A Quaker testimony in opposition to revolution, based on that religion's pacifist beliefs, can be found in the *New York Gazetteer* for December 8, 1774.

Commentary on the Stamp Act

New-York Gazette, November 14, 1765

OH! inhabitants of New-York, and the British dominions in North-America: Hear my voice! Attend to the dictates of your patron,—your instructor—your companion—your friend;—The Genius of Liberty addresses you, oh! hear her voice.—

—My origin is divine—I am co-existent with the Deity—My residence was in his mind, before his divine benevolence had formed the design of creation;—and I assisted in planning the glorious fabrick of the universe: When God created rational intelligences, *and made* man *in his own image;—the resemblance could not subsist without me; I gave* them *scope for the exercise of* their *natural powers of action, and was the test of* their *true characters: Without me vice could not be known, nor virtue subsist:—Benevolence, generosity, gratitude, religion, love—could have no place;—Nor without me could God or man ascribe either praise or blame to any design or action;—A mere machine cannot be the object of any resentment. Without freedom the whole universe must be a solitary desert, filled with unmeaning machines, blindly performing, without design, the will of their Director; and he that gave them all their motions, by irresistable impulses upon their minds, could never esteem and accept their actions otherwise than as his own,—not the Creature's,—which being entirely passive, could neither receive his approbation or displeasure, nor be capable of reward or punishment:—God alone would be the only actor in the universe;—and could he receive any pleasure in such a forced obedience to his will? Could he esteem the creature who paid it as an object of his love? As one that obeyed and adored him from gratitude and knowledge of the perfections of his nature? If these things could not be, it follows that God has made freedom essential, and united it to the very nature of man.* And what God has joined, let no man attempt to separate.

As all men sprung from the same common parent, they were all originally equal, and all equally free—Every man had a right to do what he pleased, provided he did not injure others who had the same rights as himself. This regard to the rights of others was the only boundary to the right of each particular. Whatever any one acquired, without injury to others, was his own property; which none had a right to take from him. When strength or cunning were employed to violate or encroach upon the rights of others, it became necessary for many *to unite in* defence *of their properties against their invaders, Hence government arose. By common consent some were chosen to act for the service of the rest, and by each individual invested with his power, to render that service effectual.* The sole end of government was the publick good: *By the security of private property, and the increase of the means of happiness—For the more convenient collection of the power of a whole society or people, to guard against or repeal the attempts of fraud and violence—To establish*

*prudent rules for the determination of property. To decide in difficult
cases, and accommodate justice to particular circumstances, so that
each one might enjoy his right; and to do whatever other matter should
be necessary to the publick good. It became also necessary to fix rules to
regulate the order and offices of government itself—These are various in
different places, but the design of all is the same, that is,* The publick
good. *So long as the end is pursued, the government is the peoples
friend—and it is their interest to support its offices and officers: But if it
happens, as it often does, that those who are invested with power and
authority to be employed for the publick good, make use of it to injure
and opppress their brethren, in direct opposition to the design of their
appointment—Then, if they cannot be removed, nor redress be obtained
by the ordinary methods of proceeding—the next consideration is,
whether the evils imposed upon them by those they have entrusted with
the administration of publick affairs, is greater than they would suffer
from the dissolution or suspension of government in its usual form. If the
latter is the least evil, then there always resides a power in the united
body of the people, sufficient to suspend or dissolve the powers they have
given, or oblige those who hold them to the performance of their duty.*

*This can only happen in cases that are very plain, and important to
the public, so that the whole body of the people concur in sentiment,
unite and determine as one man—Then they may naturally resume the
powers they gave—Powers that subsisted only in their consent to support
them—and take them again into their own hands, till their grievances
are redressed: for* the public good, *the sole end of government, is not to
be sacrificed to the form established, for attaining it.*

*It is needless to give cautions against this recurrence to the first prin-
ciples of government, but in cases important enough to justify it—for it
cannot happen at all but in such cases—without a discontent general
enough to occasion it, it cannot take place.*

*But as the Stamp-Act has given such an occasion for it, as never was
before known to Englishmen, which has excited more popular tumults
than ever till now happen'd in America, and, unless the fatal act, which
would utterly destroy liberty, is repealed, may yet occasion many more,
the effects of which may be terrible, unless properly regulated—*Some
advice upon that head, in case of any more such popular meetings may
be useful.

*All that compose such an assembly, especially those that act as lead-
ers and directors of the rest are advised, always to keep in mind, that the*

design of their meeting is to obtain a redress of grievances—not to occasion new ones,—therefore that no innocent person, nor any upon bare suspicion, without sufficient evidence, should receive the least injury.

They are advised to consider that while they are thus collected, they act as a supreme uncontroulable power, from which there is no appeal, where trial, sentence and execution succeed each other almost instantaneoulsly—and therefore they are in honour bound to take care that they do no injustice, nor suffer it to be done by others, lest they disgrace their power, and the cause which occasioned its collection. Wherever there is power, there is an implied obligation upon it, to do justice and redress grievances; so that when the collective body of the people, for a time, take the power out of the hand of magistrates, into their own; the obligation upon them to do justice is no less than it was upon the magistrates, while the power was in their hands.

They are advised to consider that such extraordinary measures are only taken upon very extraordinary and important occasions; and ought to be confined to such weighty matters of general concernment and complaint, as could not be redressed by the ordinary forms of proceeding, nor admitted of any other remedy: That therefore the mixing any other matters of less general concernment or consequences, injures the grand cause of their meeting, and helps to frustrate the design of it.

They are advised to consider, that many men of bad principles will take the opportunity of publick commotions to perpetrate their base or villainous designs, to indulge revenge, or prey upon publick property, by leading heated tho' generally well-meaning multitudes, into actions that disgrace their proceeding, and weaken that power that is often of the greatest use, and the most terrible to arrogant, overgrown offenders, who have contrived to screen themselves from being brought to the punishments they have deserved, by the ordinary methods of proceeding; the greatest care therefore is necessary to keep an undisciplined irregular multitude from running into mischievous extravagencies: and if any enormities are committed, it damps the spirits of all concern'd, and perhaps may not leave them courage enought for the necessary defence of their liberties.

Lastly they are advised, as soon as the grand design of their meeting is fully answer'd, and security given that the Stamp-act, shall not be executed, immediately to dissolve—and let government go on in its usual form.

The First Book of the MARKS: A Commentary on the Stamp Act

South-Carolina Gazette and Country Journal, July 22, 1766

In our Gazette *of the eighth Instant, we gave our Readers the second, third, and fourth Chapters of the Book of the* Marks: *since which we have obtained the first Chapter, which we now publish, as thinking it may prove diverting to our Readers, although it does not come in proper Order.*

The First Book of the M A R K S

Chap. I

1. The Murmurs of the People, and the Division amonst them. 9. Speech of a great Man in their Behalf in the Sanhedrin. 17. The Rejoicings in the great City on Account thereof. 23. A further Destruction of the S***p-p***r.

NOW it came to pass that after the People had waited in Expectation of Relief from the mighty Men of the great House, even in the House of a great Assembly.

2. That they grew exceedingly weary, and were very wroth, insomuch that they returned their Ships, and their Goods, and would not let them pass this Way nor that Way, but sent them afar off, from whence they came.

3. And they worked each Man for himself, and each Woman for herself, and each Child for itself also.

4. And they made themselves Cloathing and Raiment to put on, even from the Produce of their own Land in great Abundance.

5. Now it came to pass when the great Merchants, and the Traders upon the mighty Waters, heard all that was done, they murmured amongst themselves, saying,

6. What now can we do? Our Ships and our Trade are at a Stand, and the Things that we have sent, behold them returned upon our Hands.

7. And their Complaints grew exceedingly high, for they wot not what to do.

8. And behold a great Man, even the Man of Wisdom and Integrity,

and one of the Number of the Lawgivers in the great House of the great City, rose up, and seeing the Burthens and the Troubles of the People, cried out with a loud Voice!

9. Men and Brethren! Ye perceive the Things that I long forewarned you of, that they are now come to pass, and the Peoples Oppression become very grievous before our Eyes.

10. Aforetime have I spoken again and again, but you would not hear, neither listen to my Words, or to the Prophecies I foretold.

11. Therefore is this Evil come upon you, and the Children of the Land made to cry out, Fie! Fie!

12. For their Trade is now stopped, and their Merchandise (the Glory of the East, yea, also, and of the South) is become even as Nothing.

13. Therefore I say unto you, take off the Burthen from their Shoulders; for the Poor crieth out in the Streets, and the great Men of your Trade go mourning all the Day long.

14. Thus spake the good Man for the Children of the C_____s, and for the Merchants, and for the Poor of the Land of Britain; yea for three Hours did he speak, and he gained Applause.

15. But it came to pass that while he was yet Speaking, G_____e, the Son of B_____l, rose up, and uttered many Things against this good Man, and against the Words which he had spoken.

16. But his Tongue was as the Tongue of the Wicked, and he made no great Weight with the Clacking thereof.

17. Now it came to pass that after these Things, a Report spread in the great City, that the Tax which had been laid on the People, would shortly be taken away.

18. And the Words of the good Man were made known unto them, and they rejoiced greatly thereat.

19. (For in those Days there were Scribes, and Men who did cunning Work with Types, and there were also Devils, and they made a great Stir in the City and in the Col_____es abroad, even unto America.

20. And when they had heard all that was done, they were exceeding joyful, and Gladness appeared in their Eyes, and they spake forth their Praises with Tongues of Gladness.

21. And behold the Musick in the Steeples, and on the Cleavers, and on the Parchments, were heard through every Street, and every Alley and Court.

22. And the Instruments of Wind, and the Fiddle were also heard; but the Bagpipe was not heard all the Day long.

23. Now the Children afar off heard not of these Things by Reason of the great Distance across the Land, and across the Sea.

24. And behold they were exceeding wroth, and they laid hold of one Caleb, and John, and George, and another John; and they demanded the Papers with the Marks on the Corner thereof.

25. And their Number was very great, so that they dared not refuse: So they gave unto them the Things they desired.

26. And behold on the second Month, on the fourth Day of the Month, that they laid them in a Heap, and set Fire thereto, and they burned then even to Ashes, so that not one of them was left unburnt.

27. And they made Figures of Straw, and of Rags, and they called them Masters of Stamps, and they burnt them also.

28. And behold when they had burnt all they could get, they departed joyful each Man to his own Home.

A Resolution Concerning the Anglican Order of Worship

Virginia Gazette, July 20, 1776

In C O N V E N T I O N, *July 5,* 1776

RESOLVED, that the following sentences in the morning and evening service shall be omitted: *O Lord save the King. And mercifully hear us when we call upon thee.*

That the 15th, 16th, 17th, and 18th sentences in the litany, for the King's Majesty, and the Royal Family, &c. shall be omitted.

That the two prayers for the King's Majesty, and the Royal Family, in the morning and evening service shall be omitted.

That the prayers in the Communion service which acknowledge the authority of the King, and so much of the prayer for the church militant as declares the same authority, shall be omitted, and this alteration made in one of the above prayers in the Communion service: *Almighty and everlasting God, we are taught by thy holy word, that the hearts of all rulers are in thy governance, and that thou dost dispose and turn them as it seemeth best to thy godly wisdom; we humbly beseech thee so to dispose and govern the hearts of the magistrates of this commonwealth, that in all their thoughts, words and works, they may ever more seek thy honor and glory, and study to preserve thy people committed to their charge, in wealth, peace, and godliness. Grant this, O merciful Father, for thy dear son's sake, Jesus Christ, our Lord, Amen.*

That the following prayer, shall be used, instead of the prayer for the King's Majesty, in the morning and evening service: *O Lord, our heavenly father, high and mighty, King of Kings, Lord of Lords, the only Ruler of the universe, who doth from thy throne behold all the dwellers upon earth, most heartily we beseech thee with thy favor to behold the magistrates of this commonwealth, and so replenish them with the grace of thy holy spirit, that they may always incline to thy will, and walk in thy way; endue them plenteously with heavenly gifts; strengthen them that they may vanquish and overcome all their enemies; and finally, after this life, they may obtain everlasting joy, and felicity, through Jesus Christ, our Lord, Amen.*

In the 20th sentence of the litany use these words: *That it may please thee to endue the magistrates of this commonwealth with grace, wisdom, and understanding.*

In the succeeding one, use these words: *That it may please thee to bless and keep them, giving them grace to execute justice, and maintain truth.*

Let every other sentence of the litany be retained, without any alteration, except the above sentences recited.

EDMUND PENDLETON, President

(*A copy.*)

J. Tazewell, clerk of the Convention

Seasonable Reflections on the Conduct of the Puritans

The Royal Gazette, January 31, 1778

It must afford astonishment to the honest, and thinking part of mankind, that the conduct of those hypocritical fanatics, who brought the best of Princes to the block, should still find advocates among a generous and enlightened people. But that astonishment will cease, when we reflect that such as are now thus liberal in their censures of the unfortunate martyr, and are equally enthusastic in passing encomiums on his murderers, would in our days, from the like spirit, as is plainly evinced by their conduct, be as ready to dye their treacherous hands in the blood of their present sovereign.

A King, whose public and private virtues, are revered by all who are acquainted with his character, while from motives of venal opposition, blended with republicanism, in England, and ungrateful rebellious principles in the colonies, for the purposes of independency, ambition, fraud and rapacity; he is traduced with an appelation as ridiculous, as it is base. An appelation that tyrants only, who make their cruel sanguinary persecutions the test of justice, can apply to such a prince as George the third.

Taxation was the plea formerly—it is so now—But the great and primary source of rebellion at both periods, is to be ascribed to republican fanaticism. The multitude ever imposed on, merit our compassion. They are deluded, and inflamed to desperation and madness, by the puritanical trumpet of war: and the pulpit deum ecclesiastic. The humane therefore feel for their sufferings, but their leaders must excite indignation and resentment, in every loyal honest heart. By them the word of God is insiduously prophaned to promote persecution, desolation and distress, and to represent a prince conspicuous for his piety, as an object of divine wrath.

The good—the charitable, doctrines of the meek and humble Jesus, are impiously rejected, by pretended preachers of the gospel of Christ, while certain passages from the Old Testament are tortured to justify bloodshed, and to make the God of mercy, a pattern of rapacity, cruelty, and rebellion. To convince the public of the evil effects of puritanism and hypocrisy, I am warranted from history to observe, that these fanatics did all in their power to destroy the constitution as far back as the reign of Queen Elizabeth. Notwithstanding the patriotic zeal of that great Queen in defence of the Protestant religion, which depended almost entirely upon her for support. Notwithstanding her truly heroic spirit which has made the memory of Elizabeth dear to every honest Englishman, and revered by all good protestants, she repeatedly declared that she well knew how to please the Papists, but the Puritans she was sure neither God nor man could satisfy. The reason is obvious—It could not escape the pentration of an Elizabeth. She knew them to be

A Sect whose chief Devotion lies,
In odd perverse antipathies,
In finding fault with that and this,
And finding something still amiss.
                                        HUDIBRAS.

That Queen was honoured by them with the name of *Hell's Empress.*
Supreme offender. Most bloody opposer of God's Saints, and to compleat
the catalogue, *most vile and accursed tyrant.* A name which these
avowed enemies of monarchy, bestow as readily on an Elizabeth, or a
George, as on a Nero or a Caligula.

Such was the disquietude they gave to James the first, from their ran-
cour to Kings, and to episcopacy, that this judicious monarch, in the advice he gives to his son Charles, expresses himself in the following manner, "Take heed of all Puritans, for they are aspiring without measure,
and make their own imagination the square of their consciences." A trite
and just definition of the character of these fanatics, entirely agreeing
with the many witty lines thrown out against them in Butler's Hudibras.

A Poem that must render the memory of Puritans despicable to posterity, so long as truth shall find advocates, fanatical hypocrisy excite detestation, and wit and humour be admired.

In the reigns of Queen Elizabeth, and King James the first, these professed enemies to kingly government, were happily foiled in their base
and treasonable endeavours against the state. But the substituting a republic and calvinistical principles of religion on the ruins of the established government, being the grand object of their policy. An object
which could not be effected without the destruction of all that was held
sacred in the church and state. They were therefore determined to avail
themselves of cant and hypocrisy, which will ever prevail with the multitude, in a bigotted age, and by such base and iniquitous means, they at
length gained their end. Hence the martyrdom of that virtuous Prince,
Charles the first, and hence to the lasting infamy that must await on his
murderers.

A Prince, whose memory, when we allow for the difficulties he had to
combat, the undefined prerogatives of the crown, and the treachery of his
enemies, must be reverenced by the wise and the honest, whatever the
knave, the fool, and the deluded bigot may say to the contrary.

A rebellion, the evil effects of which, are alas! but too severely felt at
this time in America, from the pernicious influence of a fanatical priesthood; joined to the detestable machinations of designing demagogues,
whose ancestors, in the last age, deluged Great-Britain with blood, and
whose descendants are now, from the same motives, determined to rival
them, by introducing the like miseries in this once happy, but now truly
wretched country.

PACIFICUS

5

Disestablishment and Its Discontents

With independence from England came the need to find a way to create a united nation from 13 colonies, each with different needs, cultures and concerns. For the fledgling nation, what to do about religion was, perhaps, the most difficult question. Although philosophers of the era often linked religious and political freedom, the meaning and extent of that freedom became subjects for much public debate.

Some who supported the patriot cause firmly believed a common religion to be a necessity for peace, national unity and stability. In the essay from the *Massachusetts Spy* reproduced in this chapter, Worcestriensis argues that position most clearly. In the installment published in the next issue, he acknowledges the argument against an established religion, but finally concludes government has a duty to do what is necessary to promote national unity and protect people from error.

For others, safety and security seemed to lie in complete religious freedom and equality. Anything else was somehow un-American. In a satirical piece published in the June 1, 1776, *Pennsylvania Evening Post* over the names "Hutchinson, Cooper, Cato, &c. &c.," the authors give as two of 11 reasons for opposing independence from England:

> 7. The church will have no King for a head.
> 8. The Presbyterians will have a share of power in this country. N.B.
> These people have been remarked, ever since the commencement of our disputes with Great-Britain, to prefer a Quaker, or an Episcopalian, to one of their own body, where he was equally hearty in the cause of liberty.

Meanwhile, Virginia's representatives adopted a Declaration of Rights that, among other things, guaranteed religious freedom. The Declaration was duly published in the *Virginia Gazette* on May 24, 1776. It was reprinted on June 6, 1776, in the *Pennsylvania Evening Post,* where it became one more thing to consider by Pennsylvanians as they debated a new frame of government.

In installments that ran in the *Pennsylvania Evening Post* from October 10 through October 31, 1726, Orator Puff and Peter Easy debated every aspect of that new frame of government. The segment in this chapter presents arguments for and against removing religious tests for public office, which was among the most controversial of the proposed provisions. From June through October of that year, Philadelphia newspapers were filled with arguments supporting and opposing elimination of religious tests.

Although Pennsylvania was one of the few colonies that had never had an established religion, its laws had required that those serving in government be Christian. Rhode Island, founded on the principle of complete religious freedom by Baptists who had been driven from Massachusetts, was the most consistent supporter of complete freedom for Christians, non-Christians and nonbelievers alike. As early as January 11, 1733, the *Rhode-Island Gazette* carried essays making the case for a system like theirs where, "We have even no Terms of Reproach, and are burdened with no Establishment." After the state's convention debated the new Constitution for the United States, the *Newport Herald* of June 3, 1790, published the convention's sentiments, which included demands for "certain actual rights" including religious freedom. In the year before the Bill of Rights was finally adopted, Rhode Island papers published many exchanges like the one in this chapter between the Jewish community and President George Washington. As with an earlier petition from the Quaker community, published in the *Newport Herald* on October 29, 1789, the religious minority sought assurance their interests would be protected.

With the adoption of the First Amendment in 1791, debates over religious freedom temporarily died down. However, they quickly flared up again. The elections of 1798 and 1800 were among the most bitterly fought, dirty campaigns in American history. Religion, as much as politics, was the issue.

As war between England and France loomed, the federalists, who were in power, saw safety in siding with England. To them, the French Revolution appeared excessively violent and radical; they labeled the French, and the anti-federalists at home who generally sided with France, as atheists. In return, the anti-federalists accused the English-sympathizing federalists of wanting to restore the monarchy and establish the Church of England as the religion of the land.

In early salvos from New York, writers for the federalist *Gazette of the United States* launched attacks on Benjamin Franklin during late May and early June of 1796. Before providing a more complete defense of his grandfather's lifestyle and religious beliefs on June 15, Benjamin Franklin

Bache wrote in his Philadelphia *General Advertiser (Aurora)* on June 11, 1796:

> The private characters and conduct of men have never with propriety been dragged before the tribunal of the press; . . .
> . . . is a man to be judged incapable of sharing in the management of the finances of a country, because an infamous debauchee; or is another to be adjudged unworthy of an eminent station in a republic, because a brutal tyrant in his house?

But Bache was not above attacking his political opponents. Throughout the period, anti-federalist newspapers, and most notably Benjamin Franklin Bache's *General Advertiser,* kept up a steady stream of attack on the federalists. Their view that a vote for federalists meant a vote for a return to the monarchy and an establishment of religion can be seen most clearly in "Religious Tyranny Yet Practiced," which contains an extract from a work by the Quaker William Penn. When President John Adams, fearing the United States would soon be at war, called for a day of repentance and prayer, Bache devoted much of the March 30, 1798, issue to criticism of President Adams for his supposed monarchical tendencies and religious hypocrisy. While the item reproduced in this chapter comments more generally on public prayer in behalf of political interests, "A good Christian and Enemy to hypocrisy" wrote, in response to the president's proclamation:

> . . . to the President and Ministers *alone* can be applied these terrible words of the proclamation, that *the just judgments of God against prevalent iniquity are a loud call to repentance and reformation.* The good American people are only guilty of one fault . . . *it is that of having elected Mr. Adams their President.*

The federalist attacks on Thomas Jefferson for his unconventional religious beliefs are well known. Some examples can be found in July and August 1798 issues of John Fenno's *Gazette of the United States* and Noah Webster's *Minerva.* The article included in this chapter is somewhat unusual because it appeared in papers that are not usually associated with the party press of the era and because the writer attacks Jefferson's behavior with respect to religion as much as his religious beliefs.

The Need for a Common Religion with Limited Tolerance for Others

The Massachusetts Spy, August 21, 1776

For the MASSACHUSETTS SPY.
American Oracle of Liberty. NUMBER III.

"A serious attention to obtain in all our action the approbation of an infinitely wise being cannot fail of producing excellent citizens. For rational piety in the people, is the firmest support of a lawful authority. It is in the rulers heart, the pledge of the people's safety, and produces their confidence."   *VATTEL'S LAW, &c.*

To the Hon. LEGISLATURE *of the* STATE *of* MASSABHUSETTS [sic] BAY.

FROM the observation of stubborn facts we have undeniable proof that the practice of virtue and religion has a direct tendency to increase the felicity of a Nation or State.

By the word *religion* we are to understand the knowledge of divine things relative to the *other* world, together with a practice conformable thereto, and conscientious observance of the rites and ordinances of that worship which is best calculated for, and expressive of the honor and glory of the *great Governor* of the Universe.

In my last I endeavoured to prove the great utility and absolute necessity of establishing the means of good *education* in the State.

This must preceed the knowledge of religion, if we would begin at the right end. The knowledge of our duty must be obtained before the practice of it can take place. Next to *that,* it is incumbent on the conductors of a state to use the most probable means of instilling religious sentiments into the people under their care and direction. Every individual member of the State is indispensibly bound to obtain an acquaintance with the *Supreme Being,* and the relation he stands in to him, and also to maintain sentiments worthy of the dignity *of his* nature, that so proper homage love and submission to his will may be exhibited.

Now if every member is thus bound, the whole state of course must be under the same obligation. Hence the *rulers* of a people, above all others, ought to be continually under the influence of religion. On them is the public *eye* and their example is destructive, or beneficial proportunately as they are vicious, or virtuous. "Ye masters of the earth (says Vattel) who acknowledge no superior here below, what assurance can your subjects have of your intentions, if they do not see you filled with respect for the common father and lord of men and animated with a desire to please him?

Hereby they will not only secure to themselves the felicity resulting from the peace of their own minds, but also will much facilitate the performance of the duties of their office, by being patterns and examples of a rational and regular deportment.

So far as the religion of Subjects comes within the jurisdiction of public authority, the rulers of the State are indispensibly bound to exercise their utmost care and vigilance in the establishment and support of it. Rulers were appointed to promote the happiness of the people: This design respects their internal as well as temporal State, the felicity of a State results, in part, from the regularity and good orderance of its *internal police.* Therefore religion ought to be propagated and promoted, in as much as it causes men to yield a more chearful submission to good and wholesome laws; to act with fidelity in their dealings with their neighbour, and renders them "more firmly attached to their country." The rites and ordinances of religion very much affect the manners of men, and of consequence the felicity of the State. In respect of the eternal happiness of mankind, religion is of infinite importance, and therefore of right comes under cognizance and claims the protection and support of the directors of the common wealth.

Where there is no religion, there society is destitute of its strongest cement: Without it oaths have no solemnity nor force; a horrid train of consequences ensue, which have a most malignant influence upon Society.

But while we recommend to the conductors of this State a strict attention to the promotion of religion, we intend not, we deprecate a zeal not according to knowledge. A rational religion, void of fanaticism and superstition, alone ought to be countenanced. When narrow Principles and a persecuting spirit prevail, miserable is the State of that people among whom they display their horrid Glare.

But it must be remembered that it is only the External part of religion that comes under the legal cognizance of the State. We are entirely independent in matters which concern our consciences; our belief and worship are not under the controul of human power; we are answerable to the Deity only for our faith, to our own master we stand or fall.

For "every mans private persuasion or belief (as the Learned Dr.

FURNEAUX observes in answer to BLACKSTONE) must be founded upon evidence proposed to his own mind; and he cannot but believe, according as things appear to himself, not to others; for his own understanding, not to that of any other man. Conviction is always produced by the light which is struck into the mind; and never by compulsion, or the force of human authority."

Hence it follows that the Legislature of a State have no controul over the minds of men, in regard to their religious principles and belief. Therefore it is consistent with the best Policy, and is the most equitable proceedure, to give an universal TOLERATION of all religions, the principles and practice of which do not operate to the disadvantage and ruin of the Common wealth.

The reason why any particular religion should not be tolerated is not because *we,* or our *Rulers* may think it unscriptural or absurd; but because it militates with, and has a direct tendency to sap and undermine the foundation of State government.

The Romish Catholic religion is disallowed and proscribed, not so much because it contains a *Farrago* of Monstrous absurdities and contradictions, as because it is professedly and practically a distinguishing tenet, principle, and characteristic of the papists, that the ecclesiastical is above the civil power, that the *Church* is authorised to depose *evil rulers* at pleasure; and that to kill and destroy all, who differ from them in religious Sentiments, is no crime.

Properly to discuss this important Subject, opens a wide Field, and must be our business in another paper.

WORCESTRIENSIS.

(To be continued.)

A DIALOGUE between Orator *Puff* and *Peter Easy,* on the Proposed Plan or Frame of Government

The Pennsylvania Evening Post, October 15, 1776

Peter. Will not the people, and especially the clergy, be exceedingly alarmed to think in the midst of so dreadful a war, that we have, *by the public authority* of so great a State passed such strongly implied censures of contempt on our holy religion, and *weakened the securities of it by law establishment,* while, at the same time, we are continually imploring the assistance of heaven in supplications and form of that religion. Is not this hypocrisy? The former qualifications required by law was a positive, clear, direct, *"profession of the Christian faith."* It admitted of no gloss or equivocation. How can we ask or expect success, while we thus deliberately, in the face of the whole world, are undermining the religion graciously delivered to us by Heaven, with such amazing circumstances of mercy? I tremble at the thought. I most fervently hope this article will be altered when the new Assembly meets, that is to be chosen next *November.*

Orat. I tell thee it is impossible. That Assembly will have no powers but what are assigned to them by the Frame of Government; and the power of *altering* any part of the Constitution is not assigned to them, but is positively reserved to the Convention alone, that may be called *nine years hence.* If the Assembly could alter *one* part they might alter *another,* and so undo all the labors of our leaders; but they were too wise to leave that door open, and have thoroughly guarded against such an evil. Here—read the last lines of the preamble to the Declaration of Rights, &c. where the last Convention says, "We do, by virtue of the authority vested in us by our constituents, ordain, declare, and *establish* the following *Declaration of Rights* and *Frame of Government* to be the CONSTITUTION of this commonwealth, and to *remain in force therein forever,* except in such articles as shall hereafter, on experience be found to require improvement, and which shall by the same authority of the people, fairly *delegated* AS THIS FRAME OF GOVERNMENT DIRECTS, be amended," &c. that is by a Convention, called by a Council of Censors, which *cannot* be till *nine years* hence, as is *expressly* provided by the last section of the Frame. Again, in the *ninth* section, the Conventions says *positively* in mentioning the powers of the Assembly——"But they shall have *no power* to *add* to, *alter, abolish, infringe any part* of this Constitution." Indeed, I hope the late Convention has used words of such force that no Assembly or Convention to the end of time will have power to alter the *grand alteration* [t]hey have made; for they have used words on this point of *religion* which they have not on any other article. See the *tenth* section, where they say "and no *farther* or *other* religious test shall *ever hereafter* be required of any civil officer or magistrate in this state." This Frame is so calculated to coax the people, and it is to be so speedily carried into execution, that it cannot be opposed; and at the end of nine years, if we are successful, people will think religion is of no consequence in military operations. Now, *Peter,* however amazing these alterations in the qualifications of officers, and consequently this new RELIGIOUS FOUNDATON for our new commonwealth, are, yet, supporting one thing, thou must acknowledge the ingenuity and courage of our statesmen deserve admiration, if not esteem.

Peter. How so?

Orat. Why, suppose some of our statesmen do not like the religion profest in this country; suppose they do not think it *simple* enough, and they should be afraid that *their sentiments on this subject are well known*; how confoundedly must they have been gravelled, if they had not made this change?

Peter. What difficulty would they have been under?

Orat. Why, if the ancient declaration of *"faith"* were to be taken by every Member of Assembly, &c. such men must either refuse to take them, and thereby throw themselves out of power, or else take from time to time as often as required, and so by frequently and solemnly affirming to believe in a religion of which they did not believe a thing, draw down upon themselves the reproaches and detestation of all worthy men, who should *know their real sentiments.* Whether this is the case, I leave thee to judge from facts. Certain it is, that those inhabitants of this state, who do not believe the *Christian* religion, would have been very well off, if they had only been allowed a TOLERATION, and been permitted to live undisturbed; and therefore they are under the greatest obligation to our statesmen, who have put it into their power to hold the *highest offices* in the government, and both to *make* laws and to *execute* them. The *Christian* religion, *Peter,* has subsisted near eighteen centuries—*Peter,* near eighteen centuries—a long while—a very long while. Time alters opinions, *Peter,* thou knowest—as the poet says.

"We think our fathers *fools,* so wise *we* grow;
Our wiser sons no DOUBT will think us so."

Peter. However, there seems to be no great likelihood of any large number of persons getting into offices of power, who do not believe our religion, as long as the inhabitants in general continue *Christian.*

Orat. Ah, *Peter,* that is true; but thou art no politician—thou dost not comprehend the *mighty influence* which the FOUNDATIONS of a frame of government, as to religion, gradually produce in the minds of men. In a few years men may argue in this manner—"What could induce the *patriotic* and *wise* Convention of *Pennsylvania* that modelled this commonwealth in the year 1776, in so *wonderful* a manner as to excite the *astonishment* of all *America,* what could persuade that *learned, illustrious,* and *venerable* body, to alter the *old religious regulations* as to offices in government, and to put the *Christian, Jewish,* and *Mahometan* religions with respect to them on the same footing? Is no regard due to those *enlightened fathers* of their country? And must not they have had convincing reasons to have urged them to pass so slightly over the *Christian* faith? Must not they have been persuaded, that the *public welfare would be best promoted* by this surprising INNOVATION? Why else would they have acted in this manner? And if the public welfare will be *best promoted* by this extraordinary political refinement, can it be prejudicial to our souls? *That* is impossible: For the establishment that *best promotes the public welfare,* must be *best* in every respect." May not this lead people, *Peter,* to think with more indifference of the *Christian* religion than they used to do? Oh, *Peter,* great things may arise from this step of our Convention. They are, many of them, bright men—They see far into futurity. It must be acknowledged that the *Christian* religion some how or other discourages many bold exertions of the human mind. *Rome* and *Athens, Peter,* were not *Christian* commonwealths.

[*To be continued.*]

The Jews of Rhode Island Welcome the President, with Reply from George Washington

The Newport Herald, September 9, 1790

AN ADDRESS.

To the PRESIDENT *of the* UNITED STATES *of* AMERICA.

SIR:

PERMIT the Children of the Stock of Abraham to approach you with the most cordial affections and esteem for your person and merits—and to join with our fellow-citizens in welcoming you to Newport.

With pleasure we reflect on those days—those days of difficulty and danger, when the GOD of Israel, who delivered David from the peril of sword—shielded your head in the day of battle:—And we rejoice to think, that the same spirit, who rested in the bosom of the greatly beloved Daniel, enabling him to preside over the provinces of the Babylonish Empire, rests and ever will rest, upon you, enabling you to discharge the arduous duties of CHIEF MAGISTRATE In these States.

Deprived as we heretofore have been of the invaluable rights of free citizens, we now (with a deep sense of gratitude to the Almighty Disposer of all events) behold a Government, erected by the MAJESTY OF THE PEOPLE—a Government which to bigotry gives no sanction—to persecution no assistance; but generously affording to ALL liberty of conscience and immunities of citizenship—deeming every one, of whatever nation, tongue, or language, equal parts of the great governmental machine. This so ample and extensive Federal Union, whose basis is philanthropy, mutual confidence, and public virtue, we cannot but acknowledge to be the work of the GREAT GOD, who ruleth in the armies of heaven and among the inhabitants of the earth, doing whatsoever seemeth good.

For all the blessings of civil and religious liberty which we enjoy under an equal and benign administration, we desire to send up our thanks to the Ancient of Days, the great Preserver of men—beseeching him, that the Angel who conducted our forefathers through the wilderness into the promised land, may graciously conduct you through all the difficulties and dangers of this mortal life; and when like Joshua, full of days and full of honor, you are gathered to your Fathers, may you be admitted into the Heavenly Paradise to partake of the water of life, and the tree of immortality.

Done and signed by order of the Hebrew
Congregation *in* Newport, *Rhode-Island,*
August 17, 1790.

MOSES SEIXAS, Warden

The PRESIDENT's ANSWER

To the HEBREW CONGREGATION *in Newport,* Rhode-Island

GENTLEMEN:

While I receive with much satisfaction, your Address replete with expressions of affection and esteem, I rejoice in the opportunity of assuring you, that I shall always retain a grateful remembrance of the cordial welcome I experienced in my visit to Newport, from all classes of citizens.

The reflection on the days of difficulty and danger which are past, is rendered the more sweet, from a consciousness that they are succeeded by days of uncommon prosperity and security. If we have wisdom to make the best use of the advantages with which we are now favored, we cannot fail, under the just administration of a good government, to become a great and happy people.

The citizens of the United States of America, have a right to applaud themselves for having given to mankind examples of an enlarged and liberal policy—a policy worthy of imitation. ALL possess alike liberty of conscience, and immunities of citizenship. It is now no more that toleration is spoken of, as if it was by the indulgence of one class of people that another enjoyed the exercise of their inherent natural rights. For happily the government of the United States, which gives to bigotry no sanction—to persecution no assistance, requires only that they who live under its protection, should demean themselves as good citizens, in giving on all occasions their effectual support.

It would be inconsistent with the frankness of my character not to avow, that I am pleased with your favorable opinion of my administration, and fervent wishes for my felicity. May the Children of the Stock of Abraham, who dwell in this land, continue to merit and enjoy the good will of the other inhabitants; while every one shall sit in safety under his own vine and fig-tree, and there shall be none to make him afraid. May the Father of all mercies scatter light and not darkness in our paths, and make us all in our several vocations useful here, and in his own due time and way everlastingly happy.

GEO. WASHINGTON

Religious Tyranny Yet Practiced in Certain Parts of the United States

The General Advertiser (Aurora), November 4, 1796

For the AURORA.

The friends of undefiled religion and especially those, who have suffered grievous persecutions *for conscience sake,* ought to be particularly serious at this juncture. We are about to choose a Chief Magistrate and it is due to our Divine Maker himself, as well as to our Fellow Men, that we have a watchful, serious care of religious liberty.—Isaac Backus, a minister of the Baptist society in Massachusetts government, published *in June last* a continued account of many religious sufferings and impositions in that quarter, down to the present year, 1796.—Such things at this time of day would not be credited upon common authority; but certainly we must yield our sorrowful belief to facts openly stated in a volume of 300 pages in Boston, with the author's name about the impiety of the laws of that state, in imposing religious taxes and compulsions. At this time a single extract (page 302) must suffice. The book requires the reading of every good and prudent freeman of America.

EXTRACT.

"But as this has restrained our legislature from making any certificate law to exempt the dissenters from the congregational denomination from taxes to the worship, and they have put the whole power into the hand of the majority of voters in each town or parish, this iniquity has no covering left among us. For ministers are supported by worldly men, who act without any sort of religious qualification, and therefore there is no religion in their doings. And they now violate the most essential rule of all civil governments which is, that the majority of every civil community is the body politic, and that the minority is not the body. Therefore Mr. ELLIS, was never elected as pastor of the first parish in Rehoboth, from whom many thousands of dollars have been taken for him; neither was Mr. Nathan Underwood ever elected the pastor of the second parish in Harwich, by the body of the parish, who have been all taxed to him.

"But Mr. ELLIS'S great success appears to have emboldened Mr. UNDERWOOD, and his collector seized six men who were Baptists, on the first day of December, 1995 [sic], and carried them as far as Yarmouth, where one of them was taken so ill, being old and infirm before, that he saw no way to save his life but to pay the tax and costs, which he did, and the other five were carried to Barnstable prison, where they also paid the money, rather than to lie in a cold prison all winter. And these things moved many to pay said tax, rather than to be strained upon. Tho' as all did not do it, their collector went with aid to the house of one of the Baptists, when he was not at home, Jan. 8, 1796, and seized a cow for a tax to said minister; but his wife and daughter took hold of the cow, and his wife promised to pay the money, if her husband did not, and they let the cow go, and she went to Mr. UNDERWOOD the next day, and paid the tax and costs, and took his receipt therefor.

"Yet 4 days after, the woman and two daughters, one of whom was not there when the cow was taken, were seized and carried before authority, and fined seven dollars for talking to the collector and his aid, and taking hold of the cow while they had her in possession, so that they let her go. These things we have had very distinct accounts of, and if there is the least mistake therein, let them point it out in welcome. Another instance in the County of Plymouth is similar to these in one respect, though not in others. The minister of a Parish lately incorporated, was never chosen by the majority of the inhabitants therein, nor by many who are taxed to him, one of whom was lately seized to be carried to prison, but he paid the money, and others are threatened with like treatment.

"Before this distress was made for the salary of said minister, he got several Baptist ministers to preach in his pulpit, and seems to be in earnest to draw them into compulsive measures also. Yet the line of his parish was extended eight or nine miles from this meeting, in order to take in two valuable lots of ministerial lands, which lie near a Baptist meeting, where a Baptist minister is settled.—These are a few of the evils which have come from the practice of confounding the church and world together, about the government of the church, and the support of religious ministers. Whereas if the civil government would protect all its subjects impartially, without supporting any ministers by tax and compulsion, all true believers would lead a quiet and peaceable life in all godliness and honesty, and the power of other men to oppress them on religious accounts would be taken away."

Brethren—It is not good or safe to chuse a President from out of such a state while such a breach of duty to God and of justice towards men is suffered to dishonor the Government of Massachusetts. —If Evil should hereafter come of it let Pennsylvania keep their conscience clear of the mischief of having called a President from thence. Phocion, an abuser of THOMAS JEFFERSON, insinuates that there was no need of the law introduced by him in Virginia many years ago to repeal all religious impositions and establish liberty of conscience. Ponder all these things in your minds together.

WILLIAM PENN

Commentary on Prayer in Time of War

The General Advertiser (Aurora), March 30, 1798

An author of more than usual merit, after declaring that war is, 'a state in which it becomes our business to hurt and annoy our neighbour by every possible means; instead of cultivating, to destroy; instead of building, to pull down; instead of peopling, to depopulate; a state in which we drink the tears, and feed upon the misery of our fellow creatures;' briefly comments on the methods by which the European governments have contrived to associate it with the religion of Jesus. Their prayers, says this ingenious writer, 'if put into plain language would run thus; God of love, father of all the families of the earth, we are going to tear in pieces our brethren of mankind, but our strength is not equal to our fury, we beseech thee to assist us in the work of slaughter. Go out, we pray thee, with our fleets and our armies; we call them christian, and we have interwoven in our banners, and the decorations of our arms, the symbols of a suffering religion, that we may fight under the cross upon which our saviour died. Whatever mischief we do, we shall do it in thy name; we hope, therefore, thou wilt protect us in it. Thou, who hast made of one blood all the dwellers upon the earth, we trust thou wilt view us alone with partial favour, and enable us to bring misery upon every other quarter of the globe.' Whether supplications, which have ideas similar to these for their genuine import, and which the members of the different hierarchies are so often compelled to utter, are or are not in direct opposition to the benign spirit and the pacific precepts of the gospel, are questions which its most unlettered reader can feel no embarrassment in answering.

Jefferson the Infidel

The Boston Gazette and *Weekly Republican Journal,* August 13, 1798

From *The New-York Daily Gazette*

I have read with pain and indignation the account of a public dinner given to Mr. Jefferson, the Vice-President of the United States, on the Sabbath day, at Fredericksburgh in Virginia.—While I heartily approve of honor being paid to the officers of our government, and reprobate all just and indiscriminate abuse, I think the conduct of Mr. Jefferson and his friends merits severe reprehension. The account which I have seen is accompanied with some remarks, particularly on the impropriety of a high officer countenancing disrespect to the government of his country; immediately too on leaving his seat in the senate, where decisive measures had been taken to oppose an ambitious and rapacious enemy; but what I mean principally to remark is the open and horrid profanation of that day which is holy unto the Lord. It is the first instance of the kind I have ever heard of in this country, and from the time and circumstances must shock every serious mind.

As one of the toasts was "May the press be as free as the circumambient air that we breathe," so the gentleman cannot consequently, blame me for the freedom I now take, at the same time, let them be assured that the press shall never be used, intentional, by me, to propagate sentiments unfavorable to morality and the happiness of mankind. I use it at present to reprove what aims a deadly blow at both these, to hold up their conduct for the execration of my countrymen, and no name, and no consequence shall *deter me from my purpose*. There is a wide difference between misrepresentation and a fair discussion of measures, between calumny and the proof of facts notorious and flagrant. Against the latter there ought to be no bar in a free government. Let "the press be free as the circumambient air."

Why was this dinner made on the Lord's day? Mr. Jefferson arrived on Saturday. Was his business so pressing that he could not stay until Monday? If so, he ought to have travelled on Sunday. It is evident by his staying to partake of the convivial repast that his conscience did not forbid him to travel on that day, and that his business could not be so very pressing. But admitting that it was, then the dinner ought to have been omitted. It was not a work of either necessity or mercy, and consequently a direct violation of the divine commandment.

Was this day chosen in order to show publicly their disregard of it, that they adopted the principles of the French, and joined with them in their impiety? There is too much reason to believe that it was. The sentiments breathed in the toasts are in exact unison with a contempt of the precepts of the Christian religion. There is the more reason to believe that it was the intention, from the known opinions of him for whom the feast was made. And yet one would think a grain of prudence or decency might have taught him that, whatever his speculative notions were, and if even initiated in the society of the Illuminati his conduct would be censured as unbecoming the officer of a Christian nation; that though he regarded not the law of God, yet he ought to regard the law of his country, and enforce it by a good example.

I bless God that the people of America are not yet so far contaminated with the Atheistical principles of the French, as to view the transaction I blame with indifference, or think the Sabbath an unnecessary institution. No, they generally consider it as a moral and wise institution, the observance of which is intimately connected with the peace and order of society, as well as the spiritual and eternal interests of men. Their eyes are more and more opened on this subject by the awful miseries of France, and they deprecate her sins, lest they should partake of her plagues. They esteem the blessing that providence hath given them at this moment a Chief Magistrate who professes the Christian religion, and adorns it by his example. They will be grieved and think it inauspicious to find an opposite behaviour in any in whom they have reposed confidence, especially at this juncture when war is waging not only against the rapine, but the abominable principles of France.

CENSOR MORUM

---

* The Printers in the United States, who wish well to morality, and the prosperity of their country, will please to give a place to the above.

PART 2

Personal Journalism
for a Protestant America

After having successfully fought the Revolutionary War and then the War of 1812 against England, Americans quite naturally assumed that their nation had been blessed by God. From the beginning of the 19th century until well into the 20th century, a spirit of optimism prevailed as Americans set about making of their nation the "shining city on the hill" they believed it was meant to be. But it was an optimism tempered with concern.

In 1812, about 10 million people lived in the United States; by 1850 the population had more than tripled. Where once President John Adams had assumed it would take a thousand years, the steam engine and improved transportation led to an economy based on manufacturing in less than 50. In 1800 there were 15 farmers for every person living in a city; by 1850 the ratio of farmers to urban dwellers had been cut to something like 5.5 to one.

New industries were a magnet for immigrants. In the first wave, many of those new immigrants came from Ireland. To those already in the United States, the Roman Catholic religion the Irish brought with them seemed to be a direct threat to their vision of a Protestant America. But the problem was not just Catholic immigrants. For Protestant churches whose organization and values centered on the kind of community found in small towns, the growing industrial cities represented a source of temptation and licentiousness that would undermine the moral fabric of the nation. And if the cities were bad, the frontier was no better. The Louisiana Purchase opened up vast expanses of land that seemed beyond the reach of civilization.

Seeing the changes in their New Jerusalem brought about by geographic expansion and economic development, the churches responded with recurring calls for revival, religious renewal and reform, first of individuals and then of society. From the Second Great Awakening at the dawn of the 19th century through the 20th century crusades of evangelists such as Dwight Moody, Billy Sunday and then Billy Graham, the emphasis was on saving souls. But just behind that goal was, as theologian/historian Martin Marty points out in his 1984 book, *Pilgrims in their Own Land,* "the dream of one kingdom"—a Protestant America that would be the "shining city on the hill."

In their efforts to create that shining city, the Protestant churches had help from the American press. During the 19th century, newspapers proliferated. National circulation magazines sprang up and became immensely popular sources for information and entertainment. During that period, journalism changed; so, too, did the way the media covered religion. In some ways, journalistic practices were very much like those of the modern era. But in other ways, they held much in common with the ideological journalism of the early years.

When Benjamin Day started the first penny newspaper in New York City in 1833, there were 65 newspapers in the United States with a combined circulation of about 78,000. Thirty years later, there were more than 350 papers having a combined circulation of 1.5 million. Instead of having just a few hundred subscribers, individual papers now counted thousands of readers.

Urbanization and industrialization put large numbers of readers within newspapers' reach, but appealing to the urban masses meant redefining news. Benjamin Day promised readers "all the news of the day." To that mix, James Gordon Bennett's *New York Herald* added local coverage of churches and religious organizations, including the Bible, tract and missionary societies that grew out of the revival and reform movements.

The new mix attracted readers that in turn attracted advertising. That, in turn, gave newspapers the resources to hire staffs of reporters who could actively cover the news. New technologies and better communication and transportation made it possible to send reporters into the field as well as to band together with other newspapers to bring in news from the far reaches of the country in a more timely manner. In spite of Sunday blue laws and over clergy opposition, many papers began publishing on Sunday in response to the growing demand for news during the Civil War.

Until well into the 20th century, publications were individually owned and bore the stamp of their owners. Over the years, journalism became increasingly professionalized; news gradually became separated from opinion. However, journalism remained personal and sometimes polemical.

With most towns of any size having several papers, one paper might be

Whig or Democrat in politics and another Populist. But in religion, most were unabashedly Christian—either because of the convictions of their owner/editors or out of deference to the sensibilities of a majority of their readers. When other religions were covered, it was usually from a mainstream Protestant perspective with mainstream Protestant churches and their allied organizations getting the bulk of the coverage, and both newspapers and magazines unabashedly supporting their causes. By the 1880s some newspapers began setting aside space, most often on Monday, for reports of church meetings and Sunday sermons. By the 1920s, many papers had a church page on Friday or Saturday for coverage of church meetings and announcements of Sunday sermon topics and another one on Monday for reports on sermons from influential churches. By the middle of the 20th century, however, routine coverage of sermons disappeared from most newspapers, leaving Friday and Saturday as the most common days for church pages.

The stories reproduced in the chapters in this section deal with episodes that show how religion helped define American politics and culture from the early 1800s through World War II. Chapter 6 treats the early years of the 19th century when the mainstream Protestantism responded to the challenges of a growing and changing nation with an outpouring of missionary zeal. Chapter 7 provides examples of religion news coverage by James Gordon Bennett, whose work marks the beginning of the transition from religious journalism to religion journalism.

Chapters 8 and 9 illustrate the conflict between the dominant culture and two religious minorities, the Roman Catholics and Latter-day Saints. Chapter 10 includes stories that illustrate religious arguments surrounding the Civil War, while chapters 11 through 14 deal with the recurring calls for revival and reform in the years between the Civil War and World War I. Chapter 11 is devoted to examples drawn from the Rev. Charles Sheldon's attempt to create a mass-circulation Christian newspaper; Chapter 12 deals with revival movements while chapter 13 treats reform efforts more closely allied with the emerging social gospel movement that emphasized reforming society to make it more God-pleasing and thus more conducive to saving souls. That social gospel movement both grew out of and helped promote interest in science and all things scientific; it also represented a split within Protestantism that was at the heart of the Scopes trial, which is the subject of chapter 14.

The stories in chapter 15 represent the end of an era of personal journalism for a Protestant America. They document efforts to cope with disparate and sometimes dissident religious voices in the context of the threat to national security posed by World War II. As such, the stories signal the end of the vision of a Protestant America and the beginning of a more inclusive society.

6

The Missionary Spirit

With the passage of the First Amendment, America officially became a nation without a religion. But instead of spelling doom for religion and religiosity as many had feared, churches responded to the new order by launching what theologian/historian Martin Marty has described as a "soul rush."

At the beginning of the 19th century, evangelists set out to save souls. In the process, they also churched the nation and shaped its culture. As in the First Great Awakening, there were revivals and camp meetings. But the real influence of this Second Great Awakening came from the missionary, tract and Bible societies that sprang up as churches banded together to civilize and Christianize the cities and the frontier. The scope of these new voluntary associations can be seen in an item from the *Harrisburg Chronicle of* June 5, 1826, which reported:

> There are 3000 Bible Societies in the world founded all within twenty years. Their annual receipts are about 1,000,000 ($4,500,000) and more than three millions of Bibles have been distributed over the globe, in 148 different languages.

These new para-church organizations had the support of most newspapers. From the early 1800s on, papers regularly carried stories about them whenever they met. Many of those stories were little more than minutes of meetings; others, like "The Missionary Cause" reproduced in this chapter, capture the fervor of those involved in the cause. That story is a typical example of newspapers' use of contributions from readers to cover the news.

As the writer of that article suggests, foreign missionaries were the heroes. Missionaries in the United States had less prestige, but their efforts to civilize and Christianize those who were "different" influenced politics and shaped the culture.

The editorial, "Our Own Family," concerning missions to the Indians reproduced from *Niles' Register* is somewhat unusual for the period because it suggests that, in the long run, example is more effective than overt efforts at conversion and because it gives respectful voice to a Native American perspective.

Like most Americans of the era, the federal and state governments generally supported missions to the Indians. However, states sometimes kept close watch on missionaries lest they foment Indian uprisings. When that fear led the State of Georgia to charge and then convict Samuel A. Worcester and Elizur Butler for unauthorized missionary activity among the Cherokees, the legal battle over states' rights went all the way to the Supreme Court. The story played out in newspapers around the country.

Beginning on January 12, 1832, the *Vicksburg Advocate and Register* brought the story to Mississippi. Mississippians were, at the time, wrestling with the question of how to deal with the Cherokees who, having been driven from their homes, were passing through Mississippi on their way to the Oklahoma territory. On April 12 and 19, 1832, the Vicksburg paper published the full text of the Supreme Court decision written by Chief Justice John Marshall. Although that decision went against Georgia, the state refused to pardon the missionaries for over 100 years. News of the pardon can be found in the November 11, 1992, *New York Times*.

Efforts to Christianize the slaves raised fears, too, but those efforts also had widespread support. An item in *Niles' Register* on April 21, 1821, documents the kind of laws Southern states frequently passed to prevent such work. At the same time, southern support can be seen in the missionary's letter, reproduced from the *Charleston Mercury*.

The fact that many slaves became Christian gave southerners an excuse for portraying slavery as a benefit. It also spawned efforts, through the Colonization Societies that sprang up around the country, to use those converts to Christianize and civilize Africa. Stories about the Societies appeared in many papers including Rhode Island's *Newport Herald* of March 1, 1787, the *Daily National Intelligencer* of May 25, 1826, and the New Orleans *Daily Picayune* of May 1, 1847. A protest by "free people of color" against the colonization scheme can be found in *Niles' Register* for November 28, 1819.

As Martin Marty points out in his 1984 book, *Pilgrims in Their Own Land,* the goal of the missionaries was "to fill up the American landscape with their own kinds." For the Protestant majority, that meant filling it up with Protestants. Catholics presented the major challenge to that goal; in later years, Mormons were equally suspect. Coverage of the relations between those minority faiths and the Protestant majority is in chapters 8 and 9.

Although Jews suffered less discrimination, they were no more welcome than were other religious minorities. The editorial "Christian Missionaries" from *Niles' Register* illustrates the desire of many to bring the Jewish minority into the mainstream by making the Jews "one of their own kind," even as it perpetuates common anti-Jewish stereotypes.

Because of that kind of thinking, New York newspaper publisher M. M. Noah approached the New York State legislature in January 1820 with a plan to convert Grand Island in the Niagara River into a safe haven for the Jews of America. The *Albany Gazette* reported the plan; *Niles' Register* supported it in a January 29 story. Although the plan went nowhere, the dream stayed alive for almost 30 years through advocacy in Noah's newspapers, the *New York National Advocate* and later the *Courier & Enquirer,* and through frequent attacks from his rival, James Gordon Bennett, editor of the *New York Herald.*

The Missionary Cause

Meeting of the American Board at Portland

New-York Daily Times, September 20, 1851

BOSTON, Saturday, September 13, 1851

MY DEAR R:

While stopping at Boston for a few hours, I comply with your request to throw together some impressions and general views of the Missionary Cause, as exhibited at the recent important meeting in Portland, Maine. Details of what I saw and heard you will not expect me to give, except so far as these illustrate the general character and aspects of the meeting; of that a three days' observation of the acts and sayings of the Board, and some personal acquaintance with their leading men, qualify me to speak; as to particulars, the papers will be full of them to satiety.

1. *The hold which the Missionary movement now has on the general mind,* every thoughtful observer must admit on mingling with the great concourse which has just been gathered from all parts of the Union in the city of Portland. The American Board is a *National* Society. It is governed and controlled by a corporate board consisting of 200 gentlemen residing in all the States that have manifested any interest in the

work of Missions. The great West is represented in it, and next year the Society will meet at Cincinnati, Ohio; this week it has met together in the far East, and no more beautiful spot could be found for such a purpose, and none, surely, more hospitable than the well built and prosperous town of Portland. I suppose that five or six thousand persons were added to the population for the time being, and more than 2000 of these were the guests of the citizens during the three days of session; the other thousands went in and out day by day from the country adjacent. There was John Neal opening a Missionary meeting with a short speech, just to start the meeting, as he said; when I last heard this gentlemen he was preaching to New-Yorkers in the Tabernacle, 12 years since, "a new Gospel," upon the words "Him whom you ignorantly worship, Him declare I unto you"—the introduction to a Lecture on gymnastic training; and there stood up an excellent Missionary who had lived for 30 years among the Choctaws,—he thought it very strange that people should ask him so often, if the Choctaws were *civilized*; they paid their debts, without making long talks about it, and at one stroke had appropriated $24,000 annually, for twenty years, to the support of common schools— this was done just after receiving a government annuity; besides, had not the Choctaws utterly prohibited the sale of intoxicating liquors, by laws as stringent and summary as those of Maine herself? All classes and descriptions of men were represented in this convocation. Lawyers, judges and chancellors; generals, merchants and mechanics; doctors of medicine and of divinity; sailors and seamens' chaplains; makers of books, farmers and college professors; and of noble and notable women not a few. Is there any middling class in this country of sovereigns?

If it were constitutional to affirm its existence, I should say that the body of the great assemblies gathered at Portland belonged to the very best portion of this class, intelligent-looking, well dressed, well-mannered men and women, the salt of New-England, in numbers sufficient to fill those large churches.

The tone and complexion of the debates showed that it is becoming more and more a settled thing that this Missionary movement must go on to its consummation. It is well known that this state of things has been brought about in part by great dilligence in spreading the facts of the case before the public; these distinct publications have been issued during the year, with an average monthly circulation of 18,000, 41,000 and 55,000, respectively. Men in every department of life expressed with much earnestness of feeling their determination to give this cause a large place in their business plan. One of your New-York lawyers, besides largely increasing his individual contributions, means to keep a book in his office, labelled "American Board," and intends asking everybody that steps in to put down something; his friends must look out for this gentleman.

2. *Confidence in the official management of the Board* was strongly marked at the meeting. The executive power of the Society resides at Boston, consisting of a Prudential Committee, and three Secretaries for correspondence. The reputation of these gentlemen for successful management of the affairs committed to them, stands very high in the commercial world; no business house has better credit or sustains a fairer name. The sum of $300,000 is annually collected by their agents in this country, and disbursed at their missionary stations throughout the world.

3. *The character of our Missionaries,* as men of rare qualifications, and of rare success in their labors, is matter of commendation on all hands. There could hardly be higher or more valuable testimony on this score than a remark of the late distinguished Dr. Arnold who spoke of the American Missionaries in the Mediterranean and elsewhere, as by all accounts surpassing those of other nations, and of our country as going far before Great Britain in this enterprise, to *their* great reproach, he added.

They are unquestionably, as a class, men of intellectual vigor and of power; they have the strength, akin to the inspirations of genius, which comes from whole-souled devotion to a great cause. I have never heard better speaking, in the true elements of persuasive discourse, than the earnest speeches of some of these gentlemen, straight from the heart. The Missionary, Spaulding, of Ceylon, had a remarkable power of giving a picture by a word; when I heard him on his last visit to this country, he seemed, as he began to speak, to have but "few words of English speech;" but the right word always came at the right moment, and every word weighed a pound—it shone clear and and [sic] bright, like a coin fresh from the mint. Mr. Goodell, for thirty years resident at Constantinople, made repreated addresses at the late meeting, racy and spirit-stirring; a quaint, strange diction, the language of patriarchs and prophets come to life again. Full of strong, deep feeling was the soul of the excellent Byington, from Stockbridge, Mass., but during 31 years a Missionary among the Choctaws. The experiment of civilizing the Indians has succeeded well in the instance of that nation; there is no need, apparently, of their wasting away before the advance of civilization, as has been often asserted respecting those tribes. The Choctaws desire education, and they are now providing it for themselves; more than 1,200 of them are Church members, and in their country just laws are strictly and impartially enforced.

Yesterday morning we listened to the farewell speeches of several Missionaries. One would not say farewell; he told us he was not going far, and soon we should meet again. You are employed about the same work, he told us; occupied in the same field with us; while busy on your farms, at your merchandise, in every part of this country, we are all laborers together, and my word to you is, "ALL HAIL!" This salutation of Mr. Walker, Missionary at Gaboon, Western Africa, was a cheering and reviving word. Rev. Mr. Wood, of Constantinople, expressed briefly and happily his deep thankfulness at the welcome he had found in so many homes and hearts during his recent visit to America; and the joy he felt in the prospect of soon returning to his work abroad, where he had spent the happiest years of his life.

Missionaries gave great interest to this anniversary meeting. At two or three different times they assembled together with their families and friends—those who have returned and those, also, who are soon to go forth for the first time. On these occasions one would rise and another, from Africa, Asia and the Islands; and with a simple expression of pious feeling, or by a brief narrative of events, make himself known to the brethren of the several missions, or throw out some valuable thoughts for those that stay at home. These were among the most delightful reunions; men from various countries, and, in fact, representatives of the Church as existing among many different nations, all here speaking one language and declaring the wonderful works of God. Of those Missionaries, their families and immediate relations, there were present perhaps 100 persons.

With regard to the extent of the Society's operations, the work already done and their future promise, I must cut short my account, or I could name a multitude of interesting particulars.

Nearly four hundred missionaries, sent out from the United States, are now in the service of this Society; and in the churches which they have organized there are twenty-four thousand communicants. Africa has forty of these missionaries, and from their posts on the western and southern coasts of the continent, they are endeavoring to penetrate the interior, which thus far has been unexplored. At Athens, Greece, Dr. King fires away at the superstitions and vices of modern Athenians. In

Western Asia, a spiritual reformation has made cheering progress; and this formed the subject of earnest discussion at the recent meeting. Dr. Beman, of Troy, read a strong paper respecting the *Armenian* (not the *"American,"* as some newspapers have it), Reformation, and the encouragement afforded by it to increased labor in that most interesting country. To that region, the cradle of the human race, Americans are now bearing back the light of a pure gospel. Professor Thobeck, of Germany, says that he looks upon none of our labors with so much interest as upon those which are now bestowed upon the Western Asiatic nations, the centre of the World. To the Protestants in that nation the Sultan has recently granted an ample charter, conferring on them all the privileges possessed by his other subjects. The privileges guaranteed by this instrument are now enjoyed by 1500 Protestants.

A Mission has been established at Mosul Assyria, near which are the remarkable ruins of ancient Ninevah. Among the mountains of Persia, forty-five schools have been established for the instruction of Nestorian children and youth, and the missionaries are encouraged to hope for the conversion of this entire people.

In India, five Missions are maintained, with their complement of schools, seminaries and churches. At the Sandwich Islands hardly a man of the native population is now unable to read and write, and during the last year, $43,000 were expended upon schools, $32,000 of which were the gift of the Government. Far beyond these islands the missionaries are now urging their way, and very soon a company will proceed on an exploring expedition west and south, with the design to plant teachers and preachers on those distant groups.

At the beginning of the meeting the Society was in debt to the amount of $44,000; at the close of the meeting pledges had been received covering nearly half of this sum. A good meeting has been held, deepening and extending the interest felt by thousands of churches, and hundreds of thousands of believers in the missionary cause.   M.

Our Own Family

Niles' Register, April 14, 1821

"He that does not provide for his own family is worse than an infidel." The truth of this saying comes directly to the senses and he must be a bad member of society, indeed, who does not feel and acknowledge it.

While our country is inundated with societies, based on the best affections of the heart and aiming at the most sublime results to do good to *foreigners*—to send our missions to the *East Indies,** to disseminate the scriptures in the South-sea islands, &c—when we are infested with wretches playing on our charity for the relief of christian slaves in Algiers to repair damages occasioned by an overflowing of the Rhine,† and build churches, for what I know, on the eternally snow capt summit of Caucasus, &c—while we feel ready to give money to relieve the distresses of those lately burnt out in the *moon,* by the bursting of a volcano recently discovered therein, provided a good story could be told us *as how* the news of such distress could be received here, and *as how* the offerings of our credulity [the gifts of lunarians to *the* Lunarians] were to be transmitted there,—the following brief account of the progress of improvement among the Cherokee Indians, must afford great pleasure to the really charitable heart. It is not the business of these worthy people, who have taken up their abode in the wilderness, to "spy out the nakedness of the land" and point the path by which the destroyer shall advance on his prey: but, influenced by the spirit of truth, they TEACH the gospel instead of *preaching* it, and exhibit its benefits in a harmless life devoted to good works—inviting the poor Indian to civilization, as the only means of preserving his race from annihilation, and of preparing him for an adoption into the great American family, on an equal footing with his white brethren, in due season. These excellent people are quietly proceeding in their work: content in their honest endeavors and regardless of fame; and appear to have "began their business at the right end." Their schools have long been highly spoken of, and the proof of the advantages of them is in the fact, that the Cherokees (resident east of the Mississippi) are remarkable for civil improvement and domestic virtue.

It has always been our earnest desire that some, even one, of the Indian tribes should be won to an incorporation with the nation, for the sake of humanity—for the honor of our country. We know that there is an honest zeal existing to ameliorate their condition and confer upon them some of the advantages of civilization, to lessen the misery which the approaches of a white population heaps upon them—that such is the desire of the government and earnest wish of thousands of philanthropic individuals, but the wishes and the labors of both have been generally defeated by the intrigues and crimes of base men seeking an unfair and destructive trade with the Indians, to supply them with rum in exchange for their skins and lands—to keep them in the hunter-state, though that evidently leads to their utter extinction—if in the vicinity of settlements of white people: but we want something, one solitary fact to point at, that will "tell well in history," and shew the sincerity of our endeavors to do good to this injured people. Their habits and manners, it must be admitted, renders the task exceedingly difficult—they cannot brook dictation or restraint, and must be delicately dealt with. Long accustomed to regard white men as intruders upon them, and generally subjected to additional sufferings and privations as our settlements extend,—oftentimes cheated and basely deceived, it is difficult for them to apprehend that any person really comes among them disinterestedly, for their good: and this is not to be wondered at, seeing that we find so few persons among ourselves that are truly capable of giving up their private interests to a performance of the virtues. Self-interest is our leading star, and even on the very brink of the grave, we see that many are grasping at the goods of this world. Those then, who are permitted to reside among the Indians with a view to their improvement, should be of humble spirits, patient and forbearing—*working* persons, as farmers, smiths, carpenters, &c. thus making themselves useful and productive; not consumers of the scanty supplies of the inhabitants of the woods.‡ The axe and the plough, the hammer and the saw, should precede preaching, and in handling these the means of comfort which the Great Spirit affords, will be better illustrated to the Indians, than by the most learned dissertations on texts of scripture. Some attempts have been made in this way by the Quakers, and at Wapakanetta and other places, which have measurably succeeeded, though much interrupted by intruding whites, who lead the Indians astray. The establishment of schools [i]s of the highest importance—not schools to learn reading and writing only, but to lead the boys to a love of farming, smithing, &c. and the girls to spinning, knitting, sewing, &c. which we understand is the practice at Wapakanetta, Brainard, &c. If a regard for these things can be established in their minds, and they once feel the advantages that result, from a practice of them, all else that is needful will naturally follow.

Extract of a letter from a gentleman, one of the mission family at Brainard, in the Cherokee nation, to his friend in the city of New London, dated January 18, 1821.

"Our school continues to prosper—we have between eighty and ninety fine children—they are improving as fast as could be expected—

there is an increasing desire among the natives to have their children educated—the nation is rapidly increasing in civilization—at their last council they divided their country into eight districts, appointed circuit judges, sheriffs, constables and justices, and laid a tax on the people to build a court house in each district. They begin to pay very considerable attention to cultivating their land—there are many good persons among them.

It no longer remains a doubt whether the Indians of America can be civilized—the Cherokees have gone too far in the pleasant path of civilization to return to the rough and unbeaten track of savage life."

---

*The *bible* is too often used in the East Indies as the precursor of the sword. It has more or less been the practice of all the nations who have had much to do with the desolation of India, to send our priests as spies—the word of life on their lips and the dagger concealed in their bosoms! I recollect to have seen a letter from some canting scoundrel, who, after relating the kind manner in which he had been treated by the Indians, how attentively they listened to his discourses, &c. concluded with a description of the riches of the country, saying it furnished "a fine field for his majesty's arms!"—that is, his Britannic majesty's. The British in India have been the immediate cause of the death of not less than fifty millions of the human race in fifty years; and a sense of this destruction probably led to the determination of one of the native princes, as thus given in a Calcutta paper of the 14th of July last.—

"The missionaries at Rangoon, repaired to the capital on the accession of the present monarch, in order to congratulate him and solicit his protection; when he returned for answer that they might freely profess their own religion within his territories and preach as they pleased; but if any Birmans quitted the religion of the country to join them, he would decapitate the apostates."

†In the 19th, or last volume of the REGISTER, page 210, we inserted a notice from the mayor of Philadelphia, of the discovery of a nest of wretches who, under pretence of redeeming captives in Algiers, building churches, &c. were swindling the people out of their money, as charitable gifts for such purposes. They were well furnished with various documents of their own manufacture. One of this nest, or at least a fellow engaged in the same business, has been caught in Indiana. He had a great variety of documents *in blank,* to fill up at his discretion, as he chose to assume a new character, and about three thousand dollars in good money! He was permitted to pass after destroying his documents and papers, and compelling him to return the money which he had collected in the neighborhood.

‡The famous Seneca chief, *Red Jacket,* lately sent a letter, or talk, to governor Clinton, of New-York, complaining of many trespasses upon the Indians. Among other things he says—

"Our great father, the president, has recommended to our young men to be industrious, to plough and to sow. This we have done, and we are thankful for the advice, and for the means he has afforded us of carrying it into effect.—We are happier in consequence of it. But another thing recommended to us, has created great confusion among us, and is making us a quarrelsome and divided people; and that is the introduction of preachers into our nation. These black coats contrive to get the consent of some of the Indians to preach among us: and whenever this is the case, confusion and disorder are sure to follow; and the encroachments of the whites upon our lands, are the invariable consequence. The governor must not think hard of me speaking thus of the preachers. I have observed their progress, and when I look back to see what has taken place of old, I preceive that whenever they came among the Indians, they were the forerunners of their dispersion, that they always excited enmities and quarrels among them; that they introduced the white people on their lands, by whom they were robbed and plundered of their property; and that the Indians were sure to dwindle and decrease, and be driven back, in proportion to the number of preachers that came among them.

"Each nation has its own customs, and its own religion. The Indians have theirs, given to them by the Great Spirit, under which they were happy.—It was not intended that they should embrace the religion of the whites, and be destroyed by the attempt to make them think differently on that subject, from their fathers.

"It is true, these preachers have got the consent of some of the chiefs, to stay and to preach among us; but I and my friends know this to be wrong, and that they ought to be removed. Besides, we have been threatened by Mr. Hyde, who came among us as school-master, and a teacher of our children, but has now become a black coat, and refuses to them any more, that unless we listen to his preaching, and become christians, we will be turned off our lands, and not allowed to plague us any more; we shall never be at peace while he is among us.

"We are afraid too, that these preachers, by and by, will become poor, and force us to pay them for living among us."

Mission to the Slaves

Charleston Mercury, August 28, 1860

To the Editor of the Mercury:

From the would-be friends of the colored people, whose philanthropy is of the most suspicious and dangerous character, and whose interference has done those people a great injury, it is pleasant to turn to the kind attention of the many Christian masters, whose philanthropy is of a very different kind, not in words (as the prating of Abolitionists), but in deeds of kindness, both physical and spiritual, to the people whom Providence has placed under their particular care. And it is refreshing, to know that the people, many of them feel that their masters are their very best friends. I was especially impressed with this idea on last Sunday, while attending to my duties on the Mission in St. John's Parish. My plan has been, when we have implicit confidence in a member of the church, and whose piety is not doubted, to occasionally call upon such a one to close the services by prayer, as my labors on the Sabbath are generally severe, as was the case on last Sunday, having to preach four times, administer the Sacrament twice, and baptize some seven persons, and ride serveral miles in attending the appointment. Several of the owners of the plantations I visited being absent, travelling for their health, the burden of the prayers was for the safe return of their masters and for their families. If some of those persons who are so loud in their opposition to the institution, could see the affection existing between the owners and their slaves, especially between the nurses and the children (that word *mauma* comes so sweetly from the little one's lips), they would soon change their opinion, I think, if they are not so completely prejudiced as not to believe their own eyes.

Those missions to the slaves are accomplishing more than I fear some of the planters are willing to acknowledge. My own opinion, which is based on an experience of many years in this particular field of labor, is that the leaven of the Gospel seed sown in their hearts is working silently, but surely; and I think our congregations, for good order and propriety, can compare very favorably with any others, either in the city or country. It does seem to me that the true interest of the masters should be to encourage this good work among their people, by putting up proper buildings for the worship of God, and by contributing more liberally to the support of those missions, and occasionally to be present (as some have done) and worship with their people, to encourage them. While the Southern people are liberal in giving of their means to Foreign Missions, they should be more liberal in their contributions to Home Missions.

A MISSIONARY.

Christian Missionaries

Niles' Register, November 13, 1819

Many well disposed persons, in most parts of the Christian world, are deeply exercised to spread the light and benefit of the gospel to the uttermost parts of the earth, and give their time and money freely for the support of missions and missionaries; and, in respect to some of the latter, though we do not approve of their general manner of proceeding, it is impossible to withold our admiration of the patience and perseverence with which they meet and sustain themselves under the multitudinous hardships and privations to which they are liable.

Without reference to any particular case, we apprehend that the work of conversion is commonly *began at the wrong end.* The Christian dispensation, unpolluted by religious factionists, is, of all others *infinitely* best calculated for the government of man in the highest possible state of improvement that mortals can aspire to; and, as improvement advances and society becomes polished, the *necessity* of obedience to its leading precepts becomes more and more manifest. Without a feeling of this necessity, the labors of the missionaries among the heathen must continue to be profitless. Missions also are too often bottomed on political views—and the converts, instead of being "set free" by the gospel, are made slaves by the sword—in other cases, they are vexed by *parties,* and rather become worshippers of men than of God.

If it is desired that a people shall be converted to Christianity, let them be prepared by teaching them the use of the plough and the hammer—by instructing them in the agricultural and mechanic arts, through the agency of discreet workmen, who may practically shew them the benefits of industry, temperance, forbearance, &c. with a reverence for the Giver of all good gifts, as the base of our religion. If these proferred advantages are embraced, the teachers of righteousness may expect to reap a bountiful harvest. But it ought to be considered as high treason against common sense, for any one to deal in the dogmas of his sect—to extol one *mode* of worship and condemn another. The really pious man may do all that is appointed to him, without introducing the confusion of faction into the mind of his disciple, where all should be harmony. A *partizan* preacher should not be suffered any more go out as a missionary to teach the gospel to the heathen, than a tyger be sent to them as emblematic of mercy.

These brief remarks occurred by seeing in the newspapers an account of a "converted Jew," who is travelling through the Russian dominions, under the patronage of the emperor, to distribute Hebrew Testaments and religious tracts among the Jewish people, who are very numerous in some parts of the empire; and we have thought that, even as to the Jews themselves, the emperor would be most apt to succeed in the design of making Christians of them, if he were first to convert them into agriculturalists and mechanics, which it is within his power to do. This people have been so much and so long persecuted by pretended Christians, that they do not seem to have a *home* any where; and hence, in our opinion, it is, that so few of them are manual laborers. They are nearly all of them money-changers or dealers—and multitudes of them are continually travelling from place to place, buying and selling. Perhaps, not one in a hundred of them *produces* any thing useful by his own hands. We never knew of one that regularly *worked* for his living. It is not in the nature of man to act thus, nor is it the condition on which society exists—but this sect has been thrown into the *unproductive* class by oppression; and their religion itself is doubly endeared to them by the persecutions which they suffer on account of it. If they were treated like *men*—no one can hesitate to believe that in a few generations they would assimilate with, and, for all useful purposes become *national* in the countries wherein they might be located; and fall into the common manners and habits of the society in which they resided.

Had Napoleon Bonaparte restrained himself so as to have kept possession of the throne of France, no event, perhaps, would have marked his reign more strongly than a regeneration of the Jews—i.e, from wandering tribes of pedlars, or stationary money-changers and traffickers, he would have converted them into *Frenchmen*—by the powerful liberality which he extended towards them.

7

The Birth of Modern Religion Reporting

Although historians such as Michael Schudson have characterized James Gordon Bennett as "a man of little religious feeling," it was Bennett who captured for history the religious fervor of early 19th-century America. In the process, he forever changed the way newspapers approached religion. Where earlier newspapers had provided a kind of "religious journalism," Bennett introduced "religion journalism."

Newspapers had always covered religion, but their coverage consisted primarily of letters and essays written from an insider's perspective to defend or promote a particular religion. In contrast, Bennett wrote from the perspective of an outside observer. His religion coverage emphasized behavior, not beliefs. Bennett rarely used the Bible to argue the correctness of one religious belief over another. He did, however, use both examples from the ministry of Jesus and the U.S. Constitution to scrutinize beliefs and behaviors for their consequences on individuals and on society.

Although much has been made of the irreverent, satirical and sometimes sensational tone of much of the news in the early *New York Herald,* much of that came from Bennett's fascination with and coverage of religious hypocrisy and the interconnections among religion, money, politics and power. In covering those subjects, Bennett paved the way for hard news coverage and investigative reporting about religion. However, his work also provided the model for the traditional church page with its emphasis on church histories, religious events, worship services and individual examples of charitable and moral behavior.

In the *Herald* there were tasteless and tacky fillers, satires, more serious editorials and commentaries, straight news and news analyses. The stories reproduced in this chapter illustrate the kinds of coverage of religion for which Bennett became both famous and infamous. Other examples that illustrate Bennett's concern for religious liberty and for the rights of religious minorities can be found in chapters 8 and 9.

Although he published only two excerpts from what he admitted was a work of fiction, the first excerpt from the "Awful Disclosures by Maria Monk" illustrates the kind of sensational attention to religion that made

Bennett infamous and that, over time, led clergy, business leaders and rival editors to foment a Moral War against him. However, in spite of the criticism he received, Bennett never shied away from covering real news of sexual improprieties on the part of the clergy. One of the more noteworthy examples is the August 1, 1844, publication of court testimony from the Rev. Joy Fairchield, who was on trial for having an affair with one of his parishioners.

"Holy Evergreens" is an example of Bennett at his satirical best. That satire also illustrates his fascination with the corrupting power of money. The reference to Anneke Jants both alludes to earlier coverage of Trinity Episcopal Church's claim to her estate at the expense of her family and foreshadows subsequent attention to Trinity's vast wealth and political influence.

"Religion and Salvation" is Bennett's classic defense of his own independent and somewhat idiosyncratic allegiance to Roman Catholicism. In the words "judge . . . what their acts may justify," Bennett provides the clearest and most succinct summary of his approach to religion reporting.

Although Bennett made his name first by providing sensational and satirical attention to religion, one of his most lasting contributions to the field of religion reporting came from his serious and systematic attention to the annual meetings and activities of both major denominations and the para-church organizations that sprang up during the Second Great Awakening.

The story about the Bible Society that is included in this chapter is very short by Bennett's standards. However, in other respects it is typical of the many stories of annual meetings published in the *Herald* each May and June. Like those longer stories, it is a blend of the scene-setting description and detailed, factual reporting that made Bennett's reporting so appealing to a mass audience.

Initially Bennett wrote most of the news himself, but as his paper prospered, he was able to hire reporters to cover simultaneously occurring local events and bring him news from around the country. "Religious Intelligence" is an early example of the roundup column that subsequently became a staple on and off the church page. As in the Bible Society story, the imbedded commentary provides hints of Bennett's interest in the interplay between religion and politics.

"A Revival in Saratoga Springs" once again documents the mixture of piety and hypocrisy that Bennett found in most religions. In that story, the correspondent employs Bennett's writing style to create a rather unflattering but probably relatively accurate description of one of the many revivals that were a regular feature of religious life in the years after the Second Great Awakening.

From "Awful Disclosures by Maria Monk"

New York Herald, January 19, 1836

> *Taking the Veil.—Interview afterwards with
> the Superior.—Surprise and Horror at the
> Disclosures.—Resolution to Submit*

I was introduced into the Superior's room in the evening preceding the day on which I was to take the veil, to have an interview with the Bishop. The Superior was present, and the interview lasted about half an hour. The bishop, on this as on other occasions, appeared to me habitually rough in his manners. His address was by no means prepossessing.

Before I took the veil, I was ornamented for the ceremony, and was clothed in a rich dress belonging to the convent, which was used on such occasions; and placed not far from the altar in the chapel, in the view of a number of spectators, who had assembled, in number, perhaps about forty. Taking the veil is an affair which occurs so frequently in Montreal, that it has long ceased to be regarded as a novelty; and, although notice had been given in the French parish church as usual, only a small audience had assembled, as I have mentioned.

Being well prepared with a long training, and frequent rehearsals, for what I was to perform, I stood waiting in my large flowing dress, for the appearance of the Bishop. He soon presented himself, entering by the door behind the altar; I then threw myself at his feet, and asked him to confer upon me the veil. He expressed his consent; and then, turning to the Superior, I threw myself prostrate at her feet, according to my instructions, repeating what I had before done at rehearsals, and made a movement as if to kiss her feet. This she prevented, or appeared to prevent, catching me by a sudden motion of her hand and granted my request. I then kneeled before the Holy Sacrament, that is, a large round wafer held by the Bishop between his fore-finger and thumb, and made my vows.

This wafer I had been taught to regard with the utmost veneration, as the real body of Jesus Christ, the presence of which made the vows uttered before it binding in the most solemn manner.

After taking the vows, I proceeded to a small apartment behind the altar, accompanied by four nuns, where was a coffin prepared, with my nun name engraved upon it:—

"SAINT EUSTACE."

My companions lifted it by four handles attached to it, while I threw off my dress, and put on that of a nun of Soeur Bourgeoise; and then we all returned to the chapel. I proceeded first, and was followed by the four nuns; the Bishop naming a number of worldly pleasures in rapid succession, in reply to which I as rapidly repeated—"Je renonce, Je renonce, Je renonce,"—[I renounce, I renounce, I renounce.] [Translation in original.]

The coffin was then placed in front of the altar, and I advanced to place myself in it. This coffin was to be deposited, after the ceremony, in an out-house, to be preserved until my death, when it was to receive my corpse. There were reflections which I naturally made at that time, but I stepped in, extended myself, and lay still. A pillow had been placed at the head of the coffin, to support my head in a comfortable position. A large, thick, black cloth was then spread over me, and the chanting of Latin hymns immediately commenced. My thoughts were not the most pleasing during the time I lay in that situation. The pall, or Drap Mortel, as the cloth is called, had a strong smell of incense which was always disagreeable to me, and then proved almost suffocating. I recollected also a story I had heard of a novice, who, in taking the veil, lay down in her coffin like me, and was covered in the same manner, but on the removal of the covering was found dead. When I was uncovered I rose, stepped out of my coffin, and kneeled. Other ceremonies then followed, of no particular interest; after which, the music commenced, and here the whole was finished.—I then proceeded from the chapel, and returned to the Superior's room, followed by the other nuns, who walked two by two, in their customary manner, with their hands folded on their breasts, and their eyes cast down upon the floor. The nun who was to be my companion in future, then walked at the end of the procession. On reaching the Superior's door, they all left me, and I entered alone, and found her with the Bishop and two priests.

The Superior now informed me, that having taken the black veil, it only remained that I should swear the three oaths customary on becoming a nun; and that some Explanation would be necessary from her. I was now, she told me, to have access to every part of the edifice, even to the cellar, where two of the sisters were imprisoned for causes which she did not mention, I must be informed that one of my great duties was to obey the priests in all things; and this I soon learned, to my utter astonishment and horror, was to live in the practice of criminal intercourse with them. I expressed some of the feelings which this announcement excited in me, which came upon me like a flash of lightning; but the only effect was to set her arguing with me, in favor of the crime, representing it as a virtue acceptable to God, and honorable to me. The priests, she said, were not situated like other men, being forbidden to marry; while they lived secluded, laborious, and self-denying lives, for our salvation. They might, indeed, be considered our saviours, as without their services we could not obtain pardon of sin, and must go to hell. Now it was our solemn duty, on withdrawing from the world, to consecrate our lives to religion, to practice every species of self-denial. We could not become too humble, nor mortify our feelings too far; this was to be done by opposing them, and acting contrary to them; and what she proposed was, therefore, pleasing in the sight of God. I now felt how foolish I had been to place myself in the power of such persons as were around me.

From what she said I could draw no other conclusion, but that I was required to act like the most abandoned of beings, and that all my future associates were habitually guilty of the most heinous and detestable crimes. When I repeated my expressions of surprise and horror, she told me that such feelings were very common at first, and that many other nuns had expressed themselves as I did, who had long since changed their minds. She even said that on her entrance into the nunnery, she had felt like me.

[To be continued.]

Holy Evergreens

New York Herald, December 14, 1836

MR. BENNETT

Do not you think that the amount of money expended for Christmas Greens to dress up Churches with, could be better laid out? There are between twenty and thirty Episcopal Churches in the city, that pay from five to fifteen dollars each for evergreens. Now if this money were paid for fuel or clothing for the poor, how much relief it would give! If you get this done, you will be the poor man's friend.

HARRIETTE SMITH.

ANSWER.—I doubt, my dear Miss Harriette, whether I can be a poor man's friend in this case. The property of the Episcopal Church in this city is immense, and it will continue to be immense till the descendents of Anneka Jants get their own. It is utterly impossible to get rid of the property, or to bring the revenue within the limits of law, unless we expend it in every way that can be devised.

The purchase of beautiful evergreens at the very highest prices, not only helps to get rid of this surplus revenue of the Church, but it also circulates money during the present pressure, and furnishes, besides, a very fine relief to the eye when you enter church, to say your matins or sing your vespers—*Sancte Maria*—or otherwise thank Heaven that the Court of Errors (blessed be their errors) have not yet decided against you. It is true, the poor might be much aided by a few hundred dollars, as suggested by kindly Harriette Smith, but Eliza, her sister, says that the poor are so much accustomed to hunger and want, that pinching is necessary for their health and spirit at this season of the year.

Be that as it may, I do love to see God's holy churches look cheerful and evergreen on Christmas and New Year's days. It is a picture of the beauty and verdure of religion. If we might be permitted to imagine how the spirits of the just decorate Heaven on Christmas day, we would array its thrones, altars, columns of gold and pyramids of alabaster, with the freshest and purest evergreens taken from the trees of Paradise, where they are spreading freshness and fragrance along the banks of the clear stream of Eden eastward. If Trinity Church, or St. Pauls, or St. Thomas, or all the other Saintly Churches in the Episcopal calendar, are not beautifully and elegantly decorated, we shall give them one of the severest paragraphs they ever had. They ought to rejoice, if for nothing else, that they are still enjoying the vast property of Anneke Jants, and that many of her children's children are wandering pennyless around the Union as very useful examples to teach patience and resignation under misfortune and the law's delay, as well as give a lively example of sagacity of churchmen in holding on to what they get with a miser's grasp.

Let the best evergreens be got that Long Island can afford. The poor we have always with us—cheap and plenty. We must get rid of the church surplus in some way. It is as troublesome as Gen. Jackson's. We must be religious, elegant, expensive, and even buy evergreens for Churches! Why not decorate every parlor in which company is received on New Year's day with wreaths of evergreens? How beautiful a beautiful woman looks, surrounded with fragrant evergreens! Let it be done.

Religion and Salvation

New York Herald, December 14, 1838

I have received several letters, begging me to turn my attention to the state of my soul, expressing an opinion that my salvation is in a precarious condition, and entreating me to bestow a little time on the merits of the Episcopalians, if I could be induced to change my ancient faith for a modern. It is also mentioned that Dr. Wainwright of St. John's, Dr. Hawks of St. Thomas', or Dr. Schroeder, of St. Paul's, would be able to set my mind right in true religious opinions.

I have often thought of this subject, and have heard Dr. Wainwright with some pleasure, but little or no profit. In the Doctor's preaching it always appeared to me that he did not heartily believe in the doctrines he put forth. In matters of faith, I am an enthusiast. I believe in the Virgin and all that belongs to her—and if such an intelligent clergyman as Dr. Wainwright does not equally believe in those delicious and charming mysteries, I can only set him down as an infidel to the holy petticoat, and all that it contains. Religion—true religion—consists not in eating or drinking—not in high salaries—not in hanging round the apron strings of rich old women—not in presuming to judge the opinions of others beyond what their acts will justify. Neither does true religion—or real Christianity consist in believing the dogmas of any church—or the *ipse dixit* of any set of men. The Bible is before me. Have I not a right to read that book—to draw out from it religious opinions—and to create a belief and a church of my own? Perhaps Dr. Wainwright may think that the Trinity Church Corporation ought to have a monopoly of religion and roast beef, as it has of certain vast estates, which belong to other individuals.

On the whole, I begin to think, from what I hear of the clergy of the Episcopal Church, of their recent "sayings and doings"—that a gradual and thorough reform is wanted in that quarter. Their immense estates have created a similar state of morals which have characterized the loco-

focos and sub-treasury men. More of this by and by. Surplus revenue of
any kind, is a dangerous thing.

Bible Society Anniversary

New York Herald, May 23, 1836

Bright and beautiful did the sun rise yesterday morning. The sky was
pure—the air serene—and all over New York—the fragrance breathed as
if it had just been imported direct from Paradise. Our numerous religious
strangers rose early and said their prayers just loud enough to be heard
on high. The youth and beauty of the city began to stir at nine o'clock.
The pious, the philanthropic, the wise, the Christian all started together,
and by ten minutes past ten, one of the most splendid congregations had
assembled in the great Tabernacle that ever graced that magnificient
habitation of the holy.

It was the Anniversary of the Bible Society.

The Bible—what can we say of that book? It has revolutionised the
world. It yet contains the seeds of a thousand conflicts with Satan and
two thousands of religious intellectual movements in society. Talk to us
indeed of Homer's Poems—of the Sybilian Leaves—of the Institutions
of Menu! Were the Scriptures but a human production, they have already
produced more effect on the human race than all the other works in the
world.

The Tabernacle was full from top to bottom—from floor to ceiling.
Parsons, preachers, widows, old, young, single, married, sinners, saints,
all mingled together in one mass—piled up on each other like bundles of
blessedness in the granneries of Paradise. Behind the pulpit, which rises
in the centre like the glory of another Cherubim, were seated, file by file,
the whole host of stranger clergymen who are now wandering through
our city spelling the signs and inquiring for the scene of Ellen Jewett's
awful murder. Elsewhere nothing was to be seen but bonnets, feathers,
ostriches plumes, birds of paradise, and towering head dresses. Possibly
lovely female faces were under these canopies, but as to that we cannot
positively swear to.

Mr. Dunlap of Maine was speaking. He was formerly a politician of
our school—the Jackson school—now he is a saint. Jackson politics
always end in a spirit of devotion. Like the celebrated age of Louis XIV,

politics lead to devotion—so does a member of the Kitchen become always the best saint of the day. Mr. Dunlap was eloquent and powerful. He pictured forth in high colors the beauties of the Bible. He exhibited its effects on society—he carried conviction to all. The meeting was also addressed by half a dozen Reverends from various parts of the country, and wound up with a spirited speech from Peter A. Jay. During the last year $45,000 were appropriated to the dissemination of the Scriptures in the following way:

English Bibles,	63,160
English Testaments,	150,018
German Bibles,	1,996
German Testaments,	1,818
French Bibles,	593
French Testaments,	756
Spanish Bibles,	169
Spanish Testaments,	213
Modern Greek Testaments,	3,646
Portuguese Bibles and Testaments,	51
Welsh Bibles and Testaments,	66
Arabic, Syriac, Swedish and Dutch Bibles and Testaments,	56
Italian, Polish, Danish, Gaelic and Indian,	73

Making in all, 221,694 copies, and an aggregate since the formation of the society of 1,989,430.

Religious Intelligence

New York Herald, July 27, 1840

The Rev. Mr. Beatty of the Dutch Reformed Church, late of New Utrecht, Long Island, is about establishing a church in Buffalo. He is a gentleman of great erudition and piety, and as a logician and sound preacher is not surpassed, and we believe not equalled by any other clergyman of that persuasion in this country. We have this information from a gentleman of high standing in New Utrecht, and who is thoroughly competent to judge. We wish his undertaking every success.

The Rev. Dr. Cox, in a series of communications called the "Hexagon," (six doctrinal points,) is handling the Old School Calvinists without mercy. The doctor is an exceedingly popular preacher, and has a very peculiar mind. His style and language are different from every other writer; he often uses words which are not to be found in any dictionary. He is a fine classical scholar, and a good theologue. His communications in "The Evangelist" deserve the serious perusal of Presbyterians and Baptists in general.

There has been for some time in the village of Auburn, quite an interesting revival of religion. It commenced under the labors of the Rev. Mr. Orten, Presbyterian, and has extended itself to the different denominations. Many have been added to the Rev. Mr. Hopkin's church.

The Rev. Mr. Whitaker, pastor of the Universalist congregation in Duane street, the oldest of this denomination in the city, has declared, in a letter to the trustees, that he can advocate the doctrine of universal salvation *no* more. He therefore resigns his office, and begs them to renounce the doctrine immediately.

Probably no man has done more to convince the Universalists of the error of their ways, and the falsity of their hopes, than Professor Stuart has by his able and candid articles upon this subject.

It is but recently that the Rev. Mr. Smith, Pastor of the Universalist Church in Hartford, has renounced his former views, and has since received a license to preach from the Orthodox Congregational Association of Salem. How much more important are such conversions, than the conversions to Van Burenism and Harrisonism.

A Revival in Saratoga Springs

New York Herald, May 15, 1840

SARATOGA SPRINGS, May 5, 1840

JAMES GORDON BENNETT, Esq.

Dear Sir:

This place whose immortality may be dated from the publication of your first Saratoga letter, is sadly in want of your kind admonitions to regulate its affairs. You are received here by many, as the oracle of Fashion, Science, Fun and Trade, and your advice would be received and obeyed with more attention and alacrity, than even the thunders of pulpit orater. In our disputes of Literature and Commerce, the Herald is the umpire, and by a reference to it they are settled.

We have just awakened from a six month's slumber, and expect the sight of new faces, and a renewal of life to this now dull scene. This is certainly a beautiful and pleasant place, but the impressions formed from reading your letters have given me, as it were, new eyes to the comprehension of its beauties. The rides, the rambles in the woods, the calm mild scenery in the vicinity, the tall pines nodding and bowing to the breeze around the serpentine walk; all forming a scene of as quiet beauty as can well be found, and appear to have a charm that either the opening spring, or new impressions have given it—The frolics of the villages have been confined to a few balls, and the tamest and dullest of all village parties. In fact, the only relief to the tedium of experience has been a great revival in the Baptist church. It is a curious feature in the practice of this church, that it seizes the coldest weather to commence its operations, and their zeal appears to increase with the fall of the quicksilver,— at freezing, it is fever heat, and at zero it is boiling. There never was any thing to compare in excitement with this last revival; great has been the falling off from the kingdom of Satan, and he has been seen lying in in [sic] the gutter with a jug by his side, his tail wrapped around its neck to keep it from freezing, bemoaning the losses and defects he has met. First and greatest Elder Knapp. When he spoke of that worthy, he is reported to have laughed heartily and said, "Oh, that Bennett! Oh that picture!" There was one of Knapp's Albany proselytes, a young woman, who, seized with a deep conviction of her unworthiness, and the still greater unworthiness of her neighbors, called on the Deacons of the church and told them they were all sinners, and neglecting God's work, &c. &c. They examined the thermometer, and concluding it to be a favorable time, set to work, hammer and tongs, dealing out damnation and cold water baths with unsparing bounty. The Elder worked night and day, used any quantity of white handkerchiefs, and spoiled the stiffening of divers shirt collars with the reeking perspiration of holiness that poured from his face in a stream which must have been extremely gratifying to the sight and olfactories of the saints. The groaning and sighing, the pushing, jamming, pinching and squeezing, was horrible, the odor of holiness was delightful, especially in the vicinity of the more darkened part of the congregation. The vials of wrath were poured out; the watch dog of the flock backed the sheep into the fold, the stray doves of the Ark were lured into its cover by the promises of salvation; till night after night the "anxious seats" were filled to overflowing. Their "experience" or reasons for their hope, were very interesting—one dreamed that his head was a cabbage head, and that Jesus came in the shape of a spotted cow and bit it off; this opened his eyes to his lust and dreadful state inasmuch as the former part of it was so near the truth, and he became a convert. One "weary rev'rend" Elder who can vie with Knapp in making awful faces, and who has been preaching the Gospel for the last seven years, has just awakened to a deep conviction that he has been a hypocrite and a sinner, and has never known Jesus. The female experiences were very interesting, interlarded with pious ejaculations. "I feel I am a lost sinner." "God is too good to look at an evil creature like me." "I have a hope in a Saviour"—"I aint ashamed to own my Jesus," &c. &c. The sweet angels nearly filled the anxious seats, without aid from he creatures. Sunday after Sunday the cold bathing process was going on much to our amusement, and no doubt the salvation of those who were dipped. God knows they deserved it. The Elder stood up to his middle in the water, singing and crying for more to come to glory; it was curious to witness the efficient manner of their going and coming to the pool; they were passed down like empty buckets and handed out like full ones, when two of the sisters or brothers seized and supported the dipper to a house near by. There seemed, however, a very christian wish that some of them should have a full measure of salvation, one in particular, a sturdy knight of the sledge hammer appeared to need the ablution morally and personally so much, that when he was immersed, there was a general cry from the multitude of "hold him under!" There were at least fifty, some say sixty, brought into the fold of Christs lambs; of course there is some backsliding, but none of note except the false step of one of the most immediate brothers, with a dearly beloved sister; the hero, who is a Santrado in appearances and profession had been administering to the wants of a widowed sister, and is now burthened with a little responsibility. The church are up in arms to defend him and the old sisters were about endeavering to prove that it is impossible for one of the elect to commit a *faux pas*; the young ones only smile and say it originated in *hate of* Christ's children.

There are many things worthy of note I would wish to communicate, but am fearful that I have already trespassed too long.

Dear Bennett, yours ever.   M.

8

Anti-Catholicism in 19th-Century America

Like similar stories published in the *Boston Gazette* in 1834, the "Awful Disclosures by Maria Monk," reproduced in the previous chapter, reflected and fueled Protestant fascination and fears that predated the Revolution.

During the First Great Awakening, the Rev. George Whitefield filled his audiences with tales of the "swarms of monks" the Pope was planning to unleash on an unsuspecting and unrepentant America. His contemporary, the Rev. Jonathan Mayhew, denounced Rome as a filthy prostitute and mother of harlots. In spite of support for the Revolutionary War from Catholic France, Samuel Adams characterized the Church as the "whore of Babylon" in unsigned essays for the *Boston Gazette.* John Adams described it as both Hindu and cabalistic.

As noted in chapter 5, those sentiments fueled the political disputes between the English-supporting federalists and the French-supporting anti-federalists at the turn of the century. With the election of Thomas Jefferson as president, religio-political disputes diminished for a time, but anti-Catholicism lingered and then broke out with renewed fury in the 1840s in the wake of Irish Catholic immigration. Rabidly anti-Catholic white Protestants, calling themselves "Native Americans," banded together against the rising tide of Catholic immigrants.

On his visit to America in 1844, Alexis de Tocqueville gathered the impression of America as a land of religious tolerance. But while he was visiting, riots broke out between the Native Americans and the Roman Catholics living in the working-class Kensington district of Philadelphia.

For almost two weeks, the *Herald* provided extensive coverage of the riots. So heavy was that coverage that on May 10, 1844, Bennett apologized that riot coverage had forced postponement of coverage of many annual church meetings. Most of the riot coverage took the side of the Catholic minority.

"Riots in Philadelphia" and "The Philadelphia Riots" show the depth of feeling on both sides. As journalism, they illustrate the increasing emphasis on active newsgathering, factual reporting and vivid writing. At the same time, the second story shows the easy commingling of opinion and news that characterized journalism in the 1840s. In it, the author first comments on the social implications of the riots before adding updated and new information about them.

Together, the Philadelphia riot stories illustrate how newspapers covered and updated breaking news. They also show the speed with which a story could be published in one city and then picked up and republished in another. Although first published in Philadelphia newspapers, they can be found in the more readily available *New York Herald,* from which they are reprinted. "Riots in Philadelphia" was reprinted in a 3 p.m. extra edition. "The Philadelphia Riots" also arrived in New York in time for the 3 p.m. edition.

In the wake of the riots, Bennett published his own commentaries on the riots and the danger of mixing religion and politics on May 9, 11 and 22. He also published the full text of New York Catholic Bishop John Hughes's pastoral letter on the riots on May 22. However, he continued to criticize the Roman Catholic Church and Bishop Hughes for meddling in congregational affairs, for attempting to make Catholic teachings part of the public school curriculum, and for encouraging Catholics to form their own voting block. Noteworthy examples of that coverage of Catholicism in America can be found in the *Herald* on stories on May 24, May 25, June 4, July 12 and December 23.

On August 7, 1844, Bennett printed an open letter to candidates for president and vice president calling on them to renounce the Native American platform and the use of religion for political purposes. Despite his admonitions, the mixing of religion and politics persisted, causing Bennett to write the bitter commentary, "The Bible in the Election."

Although the Native American, or Know Nothing Party as it came to be called, did not capture the presidency; by the 1850s the Know Nothings controlled most governments in Pennsylvania. As Protestant fears that the growing number of Catholics in America would be loyal to the Pope rather than to America grew, efforts intensified to use public schools to indoctrinate Catholic children in Americanism, that is Protestantism.

In the editorial "Dr. Cheever on the Bible in Schools," Horace Greeley reproduces arguments on both sides of that question that remain relevant today. However, in spite of opposition from leading papers such as the *Tribune* and *Herald,* for decades the Protestant majority remained intent on using the schools to promote Protestantism. One such effort is documented in "Trouble in the Wigwam" reproduced from the church-owned

Deseret News in Salt Lake City; Latter-day Saint leaders had their own reasons for concern.

Riots in Philadelphia

The Kensington Riots—Renewed Hostilities and Awful Destruction of Life and Property—The Native Americans and Irish Catholics

Spirit of the Times, May 8, 1844

Our city is a general scene of alarm and confusion—Kensington is the theatre of an unprecedented riot, of conflagration and bloodshed—the fruits of the quarrel between the Native Americans and the Irish Catholics. We have only room to continue the account of death and devastation commenced yesterday, confining ourselves to the facts as we can gather them, without comment.

During the forenoon of yesterday the scene of Monday's disturbance was remarkably quiet for the time and circumstances, most of the poor Irish were leaving their houses, and moving what they could of their property. At the corners and in the squares around the battle ground were collected crowds of Native Americans, conversing with much excitement upon the doings of Monday, and ready at a moment, to join in a general riot.

About ten o'clock a large party of Native Americans assembled at Second and Master streets, and marched in procession through the district of Kensington, passing the Market House where the fight took place on Monday evening and last night. In the procession was carried the large flag which had been raised on Monday, and which was considerably torn. Preceding this was a banner borne by one man, and having upon its front this inscription:

> THIS IS THE FLAG THAT HAS BEEN
> TRAMPLED UPON
> BY THE IRISH PAPISTS!

The procession moved down Third street to the heart of the city, and cheered at some of the newspaper offices—groaning others.

In the afternoon the Natives assembled in Independence Square, numbering from two to three thousand. A meeting was organized, and the crowd was addressed by Mr. C. J. Jack. From thence they proceeded in procession to Kensington, headed by Mr. Jack, and marched to Second and Master streets, then to the Washington street market, where the fights had occurred on Monday. Here they again organized a meeting, and Mr. Jack again mounted the stage to address them. It was then about 5 o'clock P.M.

Immediately after the organization of the meeting, a scene of extraordinary riot commenced, and which, it is alleged, by the parties was commenced, some say, by the Irish—others say by the Natives. We give the account as accurately as possibly, without any wish to side with either party. Some boys who were in the crowd at the market, commenced throwing stones at the Hibernia hose house opposite on Cadwallader street. Some exhibitions of a general outbreak were apparent, and in a few moments a volley of stones and brickbats were thrown by both parties. There were several small wood houses adjoining the hose house, occupied by Irish people, and at and into the windows these stones and other missiles were thrown. The riot now increased with fearful violence, and one or two guns were fired. It is said that the first shot was from the house at the corner of Master and Cadwallader streets. A rush was made at the Hibernia hose house, and the Hibernia hose carriage, and an old carriage belonging to the Washington hose company, were taken out and carried off—both afterwards broken up.

About this time a volley was fired by the Irish from the corner house named above, and one or two men were shot. The rioting then broke up in extraordinary confusion. During the first of the riot an Irishman rushed out of a house half a square above the scene of destruction, ran down to within some five to ten rods of the mob and fired, killing one man dead. At this time the mob had, it is believed, no arms, and all fled precipitately, leaving a boy with the flag, which was borne off by him and a man who came to his assistance.

The mob then placed the flag up before a house at the N.E. corner of Second and Master, and, after getting a number of muskets, again repaired to the market house, headed by Peter Albright, who had been shot in the hand. They then paraded on the space west and south of the market house, exposed to the shots of the Irish in the houses opposite. A general and bloody skirmish now took place. The natives numbered from thirty to sixty armed men, and they were all who came into the bloody arena. The rest—numbering from five to eight thousand, blocked up every avenue and street leading to the market.

As soon as the armed men appeared in front of the Irish houses, volley after volley was fired into them, and the fire was returned, but with little effect, as the assailed were in a great measure sheltered. This lasted nearly an hour, during which upwards of twenty men of the Natives were shot—probably near half that number killed. Several of the Irish were wounded, but it is not known how many, or whether any of them were killed. Several times, they sallied out in small numbers, and fired upon the Natives, retreating immediately into the houses.

One daring fellow named John Taggart, rushed out of a house, and fired several times upon the Natives—it is said, killed two or three men. A rush was made upon him, and he was captured, though fighting like a madman, and just in the act of shooting a fourth gun. The weapon was wrested from him by a citizen named Bartholomew Baker, and the infuriated mob rushed upon him, knocking him down, and stamping his face almost to shapelessness. Some of the more humane got possession of Taggart, and took him to the ofice of Ald Boileau, in Second street above Beaver—Several times on the way, and even at the office, the infuriated Americans rushed on the Irishman and beat and stamped him most unmercifully. Ald. B. made out a commitment for Taggart, on a charge of murder, and he was given into the hands of citizens to be sent to the Mayor's office of the N. Liberties. They had not proceeded far, however, when another rush was made—those who had charge of him were beaten off, and a most revolting scene followed. The prisoner was kicked and stamped until hardly a feature was discernable; then dragged, by a rope tied round his neck, down the street to the Second street market above Brown. Here the mob attempted to hang him up, but citizens interfered, and after some delay he was borne off to the office of Mayor Cannon, still breathing.

While this was going on, the Natives had been fearfully industrious at the scene of terror. About 6 o'clock, almost every attempt at opposition ceased, and they had it all their own way. The frame house at the corner of Master and Cadwallader streets was broken open and set fire to, and the flames soon spread to the Hose House on Cadwallader street, and several frame houses on Masters street. The armed Natives patroled the streets in front to prevent any attempt to extinguish the flames, and every now and then a gun was fired from the burning buildings and the fire was returned trebly by the crowd.

We left the scene of destruction at at [sic] half-past 7 o'clock P.M. At that time six or eight buildings were in flames and the fire was rapidly spreading. The scene was awfully terrible, and there was a dreadful silence in that vast mob of thousands—broke only by the roar of the flames, the discharges of musketry, and now and then a hoarse hurrah! at some new success of the Natives—that was more alarming than the tumult of battle. The fire balls had been tolling for an hour, and several companies had repaired towards the conflagration, but were all stopped three or four squares off.

We hasten towards the close of this soul-sickening detail—hardly half relating the events of the last ten hours. The following are the names of the killed and wounded, which our reporters have gathered up to this time. They are yet at the scene of carnage, and their return may swell the list.

Charles Rinedollar, ship carpenter, lived in Front st., near Green. Shot in the back of the left shoulder—ball came out of right breast. Died almost instantly.

George Young of Southwark—shot through the left breast—supposed to be mortally wounded.

Augustus Peale, dentist, lives at 176 Locust street, left arm broken by a ball.

Mathew Hammet, ship carpenter, lived in Crown street, Kensington, over 50 years of age, shot through the head, and died instantly. He was fighting desperately at the time.

C. Salisbury, residence not known, shot in the arm.

Charles Stivel, aged about 23, rope maker, lived in Carpenter street above Fifth, Southwark, shot in the neck from above, the ball passing through his lungs and heart—died instantly.

Henry Heiselbaugh, keeper of the Hand-in-hand Tavern, Third and Poplar streets, shot in the fleshy part of the hand.

James Whittaker, lives in Front street, below Spruce, shot in the thigh, the ball striking the bone—bad wound.

Charles Orte, lives in Apple street, near Brown, shot in the head with a slug—very bad wound, not considered dangerous.

John Loeser, lives in Shackamaxon street, Kensington, shot through the left breast—mortally wounded.

Lewis Grebble, lived in Christian street, Southwark, shot in the forehead, brains literally dashed out.

William H. Hillman, turner, lives in Kose Alley, back of School street, Northern Liberties, shot through the body, dangerously wounded

Wright Artiss, ship carpenter, shot through the thigh, badly wounded.

S. Abbott Lawrence, Massachusetts, struck in the breast by a ball; life saved by a penny which was in his vest pocket. The penny was much bent, and he was stunned by the blow. He was merely a spectator.

Willis H. Blaney, ex-Lieut. of Police—shot in the heel—slight wound. P. Albright, of Kensington, shot in the hand—slight wound.

A large man, six feet or more high, was carried off very badly wounded, name not ascertained.

A keeper of a dry goods store in Second street below Pine, shot in the leg, flesh wound; name understood to be Perry or Pierry.

A lad, half grown, shot in the groin, bad wound; name not ascertained.

Another lad shot through the lower part of the abdomen, killed instantly; name unknown.

Another lad, name not known; struck in the breast by a spent ball; flesh wound.

These are all we have heard of up to this time, but there are doubtless more. It is said that three Irishmen were shot and burned in their house; we are not sure of the fact.

The First Division of the Military, under command of Gen. Geo. Cadwallader, and the Sheriff's posse, proceeded to the scene of riot.

NINE O'CLOCK P.M.—We have just left the dreadful yet picturesque scene. The market houses are all in flames and quite a row of brick and frame dwellings whose frighted occupants have fled in all directions for safety and for life. The dark red clouds are lighting up with a horrid glare the blue and quiet sky. Rolls of bright smoke taking fantastic shapes thicken the air, while here and there through the dense crowd the flame tongues of living light may be seen licking with fire some new building preparatory to its destruction. In front may be seen congregations of excited men, shouting, talking, arguing, blustering, and tossing their arms in the air with vehement agitation. Beyond on that open space the plumed heads of glittering swords of the cavalry are waving and glancing in the lurid light, while the heavy tread of men, and the ringing clank of muskets betoken the near presence of the infantry. The adjacent streets are deserted. The houses are closed and abandoned. Since the approach of the military all is still, save that here and there the shriek of a child, or the sob of a woman, or the deep oath of a man break the solemn stillness.

Dim figures move suspiciously in the shade as if seeking concealment, while wretched looking beings driven from their abodes, houseless and homeless, are stealing off with beds, pillows, chairs and tables upon their shoulders, looking for some distant place of deposit. Hark!—a shot!—a scream!—a rush of the soldiers!—and another victim is borne away for surgical assistance. A solitary one horse cart, as we leave, is turning away, and in it are a woman, two girls, a boy, and an infant, all crying. It contains some furniture, and by its side walks a man, who turns back to waste one lingering gaze on the burning pile at hand; and with a groan of intense agony, exclaims, "the toil of twenty years all gone in one moment! My God! have I deserved this!" The cart drove on, and we heard no more. We walked homeward thinking can it be possible that this is a land of Freedom, a land of Laws, a land of Christianity.

TEN O'CLOCK P.M.— We have just learned that an Irish weaver named Joseph Rice, a dweller in one of the houses assaulted in Cadwallader street, but who is said to have taken no part in the contest, was shot through the head while looking over the fence to see how the riot progressed. We looked at the corpse as it lay mangled on the floor of its late habitation, with none save a weeping widow and two fatherless children, sitting in agony beside it. It was a shocking picture.

A man named John S. Fagan, an American, was shot through the shoulder, the ball coming out at his back. A young man, 22 years of age, named John Shreeves, a painter, living in Front above Green street, was shot through the head, and instantly killed. He was an American, and had only been married three months. A man named Deal was shot in the arm. About 7 o'clock P.M.. a young man returning from his work and passing the scene of action, was badly wounded. A great many others were shot, and several killed, whose names we could not ascertain.

The military arrived on the ground about 8 o'clock, P.M. They consisted of the companies of the first brigade, under Gen. Cadwallader. The Sheriff was also on the ground with a small civil posse. As the military approached the market house, they were fired upon from a house on Washington street, but nobody was hurt. Those who fired the gun—some seven or eight Irishmen—principitately fled, and were not captured. The presence of the military had the effect of restoring an almost immediate quiet.

The military occupied all the vacant ground at the scene of destruction. They were stationed along Master, Cadwallader, and Washington streets, and the Germantown road, with cannon planted at every commanding point. A regular guard was set, and patrolling parties kept in constant motion. About 10 o'clock several of the most active of our fire companies arrived on the ground, and protected by the military went into service, and in about an hour succeeeded in arresting the conflagration. They went quietly to work, and did immense execution. They merit all praise.

ELEVEN O'CLOCK—A few guns are being discharged at intervals in Master street. Military in motion, but no rioters discovered. It is said that from 20 to 30 houses altogether have been consumed, located on Cadwallader, Master and Washington streets—some large handsome dwellings, but generally poor buildings. Nohing is left of the Market house but the brick pillars, with which the standing chimneys of the dwellings look like blackened monuments of anarchy. It is thought that many dead bodies of the Irish were consumed in the burning houses.

MIDNIGHT.—All quiet. The military are on the ground. The fires are all extinguished, and the firemen returning home. We have just learned that about nine o'clock, a group of men standing at the corner of Franklin and Second street, was fired upon by a party of Irishmen who came through Perry street, and under cover of the darkness, discharged their guns at them across the lot, wounding a butcher in the Wharton Market, named Taylor, in the eye, and several other persons seriously.

One of the Irish who fired on Monday night at the School House, at the time young Wright was killed, lost his thumb by the bursting of his musket. The thumb and fragments of the gun were picked up yesterday morning. He was tracked by his blood, but could not be found. The man Taggart who was dragged with a rope and hung until apparently dead, was, it seems, simulating death. When taken to the Northern Liberties police office, he quite recovered, and was able to walk with the officers to Moyamensing prison.

Mr. Hillman has just deceased.

The Philadelphia Riots

The Riots in Kensington—The Irish and the Native Americans

Philadelphia Times, May 9, 1844

The late riots in Kensington between the Native Americans and the Irish Roman Catholics—for the feud is now a *religious* one entirely, conceal the fact as we may—have filled out city with excitement, and every thoughtful mind with deep reflection. What are we coming to? Are the people forgetting at once the elements of Republicanism, viz: tolerance of opinion, freedom of thought and action, and obedience to the laws, or can any man engaged in these disgraceful broils believe that he is aiding by such conduct, however provoked, in carrying out the principles of civil and religious liberty?

As a Protestant and a Native born citizen, we protest against this unnatural admixture of religion and politics. In the whole history of the human race, we find the bloodiest pages those in which are recorded the contest of the Church; are we willing to introduce this fire-brand of destruction and desolation into the midst of our peaceful and happy country? Have we a mind to rival Europe in our chronicles of inhuman massacre and slaughter, or shall we bathe our hearth-stones in blood, and make our homes charnel-houses, because of differences of opinion, the entertainment of which is guaranteed to every American citizen, whether Native-born or Naturalized, by our glorious Constitution?

We are opposed to the political sentiments of the Native Americans, but we respect their sincerity, and would be the last to stand silently by and see them insulted; to see their peaceable assemblies broken up by an unfuriated multitude, and see them or any other set of men, whether right or wrong in their views, waylaid and assaulted for promulgating their political notions. We are too much of a Republican, and have too much genuine American feeling for this; but, we are equally opposed to the introduction of religious abuse into political orations; we entertain a very contemptuous opinion of the wisdom, the law-and-order-loving dispositions, and the *real* Christianity of those demagogues who do it to accomplish, by the fearful public orgasm which must follow, their own selfish ends.

We give up to n[o] man in our respect for the Bible, and our zeal for its dissemination. We up to no man in our love for our beloved country, its unparalleled institutions, its mighty and intelligent people, and above all its freedom for that curse of Europe, an union of Church and State. But, in tenaciously reserving for ourselves and our children the right to peruse the Bible, we should be the first to rebel against any attempt to coerce others into its perusal; in jealously watching to prevent the political dominance of any other religious persuasion, we should be among the first to denounce any attempt at such dominance contemplated by the members of our own.

These are the dictates of patriotism; nay more, they are the dictates of

Christianity. Without pretending to take any side in this unfortunate controversy—without pretending that the Roman Catholics are right or wrong, or that the Native Americans are right or wrong, for we concive [sic] both to have committed a grievous error in appealing under any circumstances to physical force or to arms,—let us ask, is such conduct characteristic of either Freemen or Christians? Is it the part of a true republican to thrust his opinions upon others, and to picture all those who differ from him as fit subjects for immolation; or did the great prototype of the Christian church when on earth set his followers such a belligerent example? Was not the language of the latter always "peace? peace?" Was not his course exemplarily pacific? Did he turn even on his revilers and persecutors? Did he not take every occasion to teach his disciples forbearance, and radically subdue in them the slightest impulse towards retaliation?

If so, we are bound to follow the example as well as the advice of the head of the Universal Christian Church! And in doing so, we at once carry out the principles of good government, for republicanism and christianity are identical, and the very spirit of the one, is incorporated into and animates the other. Let us have *peace* then. Cease these wicked contentions. And in order that they may cease, stop at once this mingling together of religion and politics. Away with it. It is an unhallowed, an iniquitous, and an incestuous union. The issue must be a monster, misshapen and deplorable, inimical to liberty, repulsive to tranquil government, and ever associated with but anarchy, discord, murder, and civil war.

The mob then insisted that he should dismiss every Irishman from the city police. He said he had made no appointments except of naturalized citizens, &c, according to law. If there was any fault it was in the law. The First City Troop under Capt. Butler then came up, and after parading around, retired towards Kensington. Quiet ensued for a moment—then the mob rushed at the police, drove them back—pelted the church windows with stones—then lifted two boys over the iron railing who climbed into the buildings by a window that had been broken, and while one set fire to the curtains with a match another cut the gas pipe thus putting the church into a blaze in a few moments!

The police then rallied, and made several arrests. The two boys were captured, but immediately rescued by the Natives. So were the rest. The police were severely beaten in the attempt to retain the prisoners. One of the night police, named Long, was much injured by a brick bat. A pistol was wrested from the hands of another officer. An immense crowd soon gathered. The firemen arrived and played on the adjoining houses, some of which were partially burned. The church burned slowly, lighting up the whole city with its blaze, while thousands from all quarters stood gazing on calmly at the work of destruction.

11 O'CLOCK, P.M.—St. Augustine's Church is entirely consumed, and the multitude dispersed. St. Mary's, St. Joseph's, and St. John's churches have been filled with armed men, and as their demolition is threatened, people are gathering around them and in them waiting for the assault. The two first churches are guarded outside by three companies of the 2d brigade, under Col. Goodman. The troops occupy Fourth street, from Walman to Spruce. A party of the Philadelphia Greys have just brought to the Mayor's office, arrested at Kensington, a boy named Hess, taking in the act of communicating fire to a house.

The City Councils have just met.

Order it is said, have been sent down to Fort Mifflin for U.S. soldiers. The City is all in confusion. Nothing but vigourous efforts which cannot be expected from the Volunteers, or the Civil posse will prevent Philadelphia from becoming a prey to the mob, and preventing a general conflagration!

12 o'clock.—The Governor is said to have just arrived in town, and to have declared the City of Philadelphia under MARTIAL LAW!

THURSDAY MORNING, 1 o'clock.—The Catholic Churches throughout the City are now protected by Companies of Volunteers. The whole of the First Division has arrived from Kensington leaving that District to the care of two Companies of Germantown Volunteers. The citizens of Kensington are in great alarm in consequence, and are sending down to the city for aid. Gen. Cadwallader and the First Brigade are at St. John's Church. Military patrols walk the streets, and every thing wear the aspect of war. The City Councils are still in secret session with the Sheriff.

TWO O'CLOCK A.M.—The Mayor, in the melee at St. Augustine church last night, was struck in the abdomen with a brick bat, and rendered insensible for an instant. The only person who stuck to him was a thief.

The mob were dispersed from St. John's church by the military— Gen. Cadwallader giving them but five minutes to leave the ground, at the peril of being fired upon. The artillery are now guarding St. John's church, the State arsenal opposite, and the Orphan Asylum, Chestnut street, Market, Thirteenth and Chesnut streets are full of the artillerists and their field-pieces.

The infantry are at the other churches. Private Hartnett, of the State artillery, was accidentally shot through the leg while marching up to Kensington in the afternoon.

The Bible in the Election

The New York Herald, December 27, 1844

The party at present in the ascendency in the corporation are preparing to sustain themselves in the election next spring. Their policy is very curious and very amusing. During the last few months that they have been in office, they have abandoned with the utmost coolness and impudence every single principle of reform to which they solemnly pledged themselves before the election. They have increased the city taxation enormously—they have refused us police reform—they have kept the streets in an alarmingly filthy condition—they have continued all the old corrupt system of job work—in a word, they have proved themselves to be the most worthless, inefficient and imbecile rulers whose burden the city has ever been called to endure.

But the dominant party in the corporation have, it appears, a weapen to employ, by the help of which they are confident of retaining power, and being enabled to impose upon the community for another year. They are going to make a great noise about "the Bible"—they are going to bring that holy volune into the polluted arena of the dirty politics of this city. If any one complains of increased taxation, they will call out in reply—"the Bible! the Bible!" If we talk about the dirty streets, they will silence us with—"the Bible! the Bible!" If we ask for a good police, they will shout out—"the Bible! the Bible!"—All this will not avail men who have been false to every promise. The Bible teaches men to abide by the truth, and to fulfil their engagements; and it also warns us to beware of those who have once deceived us. The people will soon discover that they are quite prepared to discover a practical adherence to this maxim of the Bible, at least.

Dr. Cheever on the Bible in Schools

New-York Daily Tribune, February 28, 1854

The Education of the Whole People, everywhere most important, is, in a Democracy an imperative necessity. To be led by the blind among treacherous pitfalls, over dizzy hights [sic] and beside unfathomable chasms, involves perils only less formidable than those of unlimited Despotism. Whatever elements of weakness or mischief may be discovered in our political system flow directly from the incompetency of a portion of our people for the momentous duties thereby devolved on them; and we cannot remember an instance where our Government has been popularly impelled into a wrong course wherein it was not manifest that the mischief had been done by a large majority of our uneducated voters overruling a majority of those who had enjoyed the advantages of at least rudimental instruction. If the education of every child were inexorably required and enforced, and each adult migrating to our shores were subjected to a similar requisition as a qualification for voting, in lieu of the present exaction of five years' residence, the basis of our political fabric would be as nearly perfect as Humanity in its present estate will permit.

Now the Education of the Whole People otherwise than by a comprehensive, State-supported system of Common Schools, has been abundantly proved impracticable. They who assert that the Education of Children devolves on the Church, or should be left to the care of the parents respectively, cannot controvert the general fact that, just so far as Education has been cared for by the State, has it been general and efficient, while wherever the State has left it to individuals, voluntarily associated, or to clerical impulse and guidance, a very large proportion of the children of the poor and powerless have been suffered to grow up in ignorance. If there be an exception to this rule, we are not aware of it.

The Patriot, the Liberal, the Philanthropist, the Conservative, the Devotee, would seem to be equally inerested in demanding that the State shall make careful and ample provision for at least the elementary Education of All. For though the Devotee, of whatever creed, cannot hope to have the tenets of his faith expounded and commended to the children attending Common Schools under a Government which is wisely interdicted from the establishment of a State Religion, he should nevertheless be satisfied in view of the fact that the Common School plows up the ground and prepares it for the seed which it is his or his Church's duty to sow. The modern Sunday School, as at first established, was devised by a Christian philanthropist for the purpose of teaching the children of the poor to read, so that they might afterward be indoctrinated in the great truths of religion. The Common School has since superseded this use of the Sunday School, so that the latter is now devoted exclusively to the direct inculcation of religious and moral lessons. And this seems to us the natural and proper solution of the great problem of Universal Education in communities where radical diversities of faith exist. Let the Common School, for thirty hours of each week, instruct the children in Reading, Writing, Grammar, Geography, Arithmetic, &c. and let these children, thus qualified to receive and apprehend religious truth, be instructed in religion on Saturday, Sunday, or during any other than school hours on other days, by such clerical or other teachers as their respective parents or guardians may prefer and indicate.

But shall there be no religious exercises in Common Schools? Our choice would be that a brief prayer should be offered and a select portion of Scripture read by the teacher and a hymn of praise to the Father of All sung by the entire school; perhaps the two former at the beginning, the latter at the close of the day's lessons. But we recognize the Rights of Conscience as above all considerations of choice or convenience, and we should most strenuously protest against these or any other religious exercises in any school where they would grate on the religious convictions, sensibilities, or if you please, prejudices of any portion of the pupils or their natural guardians. Rather let every exercise of a religious nature be remitted to other occasions than have one parent feel that the faith he cherishes is endangered or undermined by the inculcations or disciplines of the Common School. Whenever this shall become the school of a predominant Church, or of a local Majority, then will its usefulness be fatally undermined and its hold on the confidence of the people be seriously weakened.

The Reverend Doctor George B. Cheever holds a theory very different from this. In his view, those who desire to have certain religious exercises in Schools have as good a right to insist on their introduction as those who object to such exercises, and whose faith would be assailed thereby, have to require their exclusion. In other words, if there were a sect who made pork-eating a part of their religious exercises, and they were a majority, it would be perfectly right for that majority to force their pork-eating into a common school where a minority of the children were Hebrews, and insist that those children should swallow the pork or be kicked out of school. Nay: if we do not misapprehend the Doctor, he believes the pork-eating majority, if they were orthodox in their faith, would have a *better* right to make pork-eating a common school exercise than the minority would to resist it. Hear him:

"The case stands thus: You either know this book to be the Word of God, or you do not; if not, then you are engaged in a solemn farce in teaching it any where as God's Word. But if you do know it to be God's Word, then you have no right to put a book of fables on an equality with it;—you have no right to permit the plea of another man's conscience as against it, to prevent you from violating it, wherever you have the proper opportunity and the power. If you know this book to be the Word of God, you cannot, without a glaring inconsistency, which is fatal to the claims of God's Word, admit the conscience of a Mohammedan or Pagan as of equal authority with the conscience of a man instructed out of God's Word. The conscience which commands the worship of idols is not to be treated with the same respect as the conscience which commands the worship of God. If you say that it is, you are instantly driven to the most dreadful conclusions, fatal to the very existence of Christian society."

Surely, no one can fail to see that here is the assumption of an Established Religion already existing in the land, whose adherents have rights under our laws superior to those of all dissenters. And Mr. Cheever proceeds to quote Judge Story as authority for the assertion that it is the duty of our Government to foster and encourage the diffusion of Christianity among all our citizens, and to aid in setting forth "the great doctrines of religion," among which he enumerates a *future* "state of rewards and punishments." We take this as an illustration of the dangerous and utterly un-American tendency of Mr. Cheever's project. We believe that men will suffer in a future state of being on account of the evil they have done in this life; but some of the purest men and best Christians we have ever known understand the Bible to teach that all sin is limited to this life, and that all sin here committed is here inexorably punished. By what right—on what principle consistent with our Constitutional guarantee that "Congress shall make no law respecting the establishment of religion, or prohibiting the free exercise thereof," with the corresponding provisions in all or most of our State Constitutions—shall money be taxed out of these citizens for the support of schools wherein their children are to be taught theological dogmas which they earnestly regard as borrowed from ancient Paganism and at war with the fundamental basis of Christianity? If a small minority may be thus treated, who can feel secure in the immunity hitherto enjoyed by *his* religious convictions? If today the Common School may teach that the punishment of sin committed here is wholly or partly postponed to another life, may they not to-morrow be engaged in the inculcation of Roman Catholic or Lutheran, Trinitarian or Socinian, Baptist or Methodist tenets, as the majority may see fit to prescribe? And how much longer will they deserve the name of *Common* Schools?

True, Mr. Cheever seems to be animated by a special hostility to the Catholics, against whom his batteries are generally pointed, while he is professedly pleading only for the unqualified use of the Bible in Schools; but one must be blind indeed who does not see that the scope of his argument is far broader, and tends virtually to the recognition of a legally established Religion, to be based, as nearly as practicable, on his own ideas of what the State Religion should be. To such an establishment we are sure a large majority of the American people are sternly opposed, and not even the cry of "No Popery!" potent as that is, will suffice to swerve them from their settled convictions.

No one can need to be told that our religious views differ widely, radically, from those of the Roman Catholics, with whose Hierarchy the march of events in Europe has involved us in a conflict which the future is likely to aggravate. Roman Catholics as a class do not take THE TRIBUNE, and we presume they never will; they do not vote with us, and that we suppose will generally if not always remain so. We mean to deserve their respect, with that of all other citizens, by speaking the truth fearlessly and standing firm for Equal Rights to All: but their favor and patronage is neither sought nor expected by us. Yet it is but simple justice to say that Mr. Cheever's incessant representations that Roman Catholics dread the Bible, fear the Bible, or as he says on page 36, *"hate* the Bible," are in our view false and calumnious. The only Catholic family wherein we ever lived had an open Bible in its parlor throughout our stay in it; and this was more than twenty years ago, before any collision with regard to the Bible in schools had been developed in this City. In almost every Catholic journal we glance over, we see editions of the Bible advertised for sale, and commended to Catholics by their Archbishops and Bishops; and these facts are to our mind utterly inconsistent with the assumption that they either hate the Bible or dread its dissemination.

That they may object to the use of the Bible as a school reader, especially if a version be used which their Church has condemned as erroneous and heretical, by no means justifies Mr. Cheever's imputations, which seem only calculated to fan the fires of sectarian bigotry and increase the bitterness of religious hatreds.

It is in this view that we ask the attention of all earnest, intelligent friends of Universal Education to the doctrines and spirit of Mr. Cheever's book. Surely, no discerning person can fail to see that this spirit, if allowed to dominate, will prove fatal to all hopes of the maintenance of Common Schools. We hear it asserted that the Catholic priesthood are hostile to our Common Schools, and mean to withdraw the Catholic children therefrom as fast as possible. If such be the fact, Mr. Cheever is helping them efficiently, and only needs to become sufficiently influential with Protestants to insure the meditated consummation. For whenever the spirit which animates his book shall predominate in the management of our Common Schools, Catholic parents will be driven, by self-respect if nothing else, to take their children away, and give them such education as they can find elsewhere. Ignorance is a calamity, and to pay twice for an education a hardship, but better even this than to submit tamely to insult, misrepresentation, and a wanton attack on profoundly cherished convictions respecting the most momentous theme that can fix the attention of Man.

Trouble in the Wigwam

Deseret News, March 18, 1855

[Correspondence of the *Evening Post*]

BOSTON, January 12, 1855

Our Legislature is hard at work to convince its constituents that Popery and foreigners are to receive no quarter at its hands. Already several orders have been introduced bearing against the Catholics.

There was an order adopted on Wednesday, instructing the Judiciary Committee to consider the expediency of reporting a bill making convents, or nunneries, and Roman Catholic schools as open and free to public visitation and inspection as Protestant institutions.

The Committee on Education, the same day, was instructed to inquire

into the expediency of altering laws, so as to provide that every child between the ages of eight and fourteen, whether of native or foreign birth,
be compelled to attend the public schools at least twelve weeks in the
year.

This last proposition, however, will hardly come to anything, as it is
calculated to play the very deuce with the truest and bluest Protestants in
the state. The passage and enforcement of a law containing such a provision would break up all the private establishments for education in Massachusetts, so far as they are attended by children between the ages of
eight and twelve years.

The interference which this order contemplates on the part of the
state, in the private affairs of families, may be suited to the latitude of
Prussia; but it will not answer for this bleak part of the world.

The reformers will find much difficulty in hitting Catholics hard without cutting down five times the number of Protestants.

Perhaps it is as well that it should be so, in order to prevent us from
becoming rampant.

A third order contemplates the daily reading of the common English
version of the Bible in all of the public schools of the state, or at least of
restricting the school fund appropriation of the state to such schools, and
only such, as shall comply with such daily practice. This is bringing up
of an old question, and one out of which the whigs made a great deal of
capital in 1853, when the new constitution was voted down, principally
because the Irish Catholics did not like a provision providing against the
public support of sectarian schools, and which was not in the body of the
instrument. It is a queer sight to see that of a gentleman who called upon
the Catholics to vote against the provision named, now demanding that
such people shall be excluded from voting, and be compelled to send
their children to Protestant schools. Their opinion and their practice have
been wonderfully changed. Perhaps they are resolved to keep his Excellency strictly in countenance.

Yesterday the Judiciary Committee were ordered to consider the expediency of reporting an amendment to the constitution, providing that any
man owing allegiance to any foreign power, either civil or ecclesiastical,
shall not be eligible to any office in Massachusetts. The object is to place
the Catholics on the same footing that they now occupy in New Hampshire.

The signal given by the Governor for war upon the Catholics has been
heartily responded to. We seem to be on the eve of civil and religious

troubles like those of which we have read in history, without deeming it possible that such things would ever threaten the peace of an American state.

The reports of Mr. J. R. Lowell's lecture in the 'Daily Advertiser' are made from the author's manuscript, by a distinguished literary gentleman of Cambridge, and can therefore be depended upon for correctness and finish. The first lecture was admirable, and the whole course will probably be of the same character.

9

The Mormon Question

The Second Great Awakening unleashed a wave of religious fervor that once again divided families and split churches and paved the way for new ones. Some of those new churches were well within the Christian tradition; other religious movements were not. For mainstream Protestants, however, the most troubling and perplexing of the upstart religions was that of the Church of Jesus Christ of Latter-day Saints.

The Church traces its origins to 1821 when its founder, Joseph Smith, first claimed to have had visions that included a visit from a messenger of God, Moroni, who revealed to him a hidden book of golden plates and special stones through which Smith could read and translate the writings. Those writings, the *Book of Mormon,* told of America as a special place. They also gave to those who accepted the new revelation an important role in furthering God's plan for the world.

Smith's message that those who believed were saints and would rule struck a responsive chord, particularly among the poor and disadvantaged. Others, however, saw the Mormon religion as a dangerous heresy with the potential to undermine traditional Christianity. As the new religion attracted converts, fears of it grew. The Mormons were driven from New York to Ohio, Missouri, and then to Nauvoo, Illinois.

In Illinois, the tightly knit Mormon communities prospered, but they invited envy and raised fears that the Mormons, voting as a block, would influence elections and establish a theocracy. When Joseph Smith announced in 1843 that he had received a new revelation sanctioning plural marriage and then in 1844 that he would seek the presidency, those fears escalated. On the night of June 27, 1844, a mob marched on the Nauvoo jail. There, someone shot Smith, who was being held on charges related to destruction of a printing press that had been used to publish anti-Mormon sentiments.

Before his death, Smith and his followers had received scattered and mixed attention in the *New York Herald* and other major newspapers. The murder was a major story, but it, too, produced mixed coverage. In "The Mormon Massacre," James Gordon Bennett takes the side of the threatened religious minority, just as he took the side of the Irish Catholics in the Philadelphia riots. In "The Mormon Massacre," he once again describes the combining of religion and politics, mixed with jealousy and prejudice as the root causes of the massacre. Although Bennett used the occasion to again attack other newspapers for their role in inflaming public opinion, he also opened his paper to other viewpoints. News from "Carthage" begins by mimicking Bennet's style. However, in contrast to Bennet's opinion about the massacre, the correspondent from Illinois attacks the eastern press as he justifies the massacre.

Shortly before his death, Joseph Smith had written that the Mormons should "secure a resting place in the mountains, or some uninhabited region, where we can enjoy the liberty of conscience guaranteed to us by the Constitution of our country." In 1846, under their new leader, Brigham Young, the Latter-day Saints set off for Utah, where their community once again flourished.

On his trip west in 1859, Horace Greeley, one of the most influential newspaper editors of his time, provided readers of his *New-York Daily Tribune* with on-the-scene reports from the Mormon territory. The first of those, "Two Hours with Brigham Young," is one of the first, if not the first, examples of the question-answer format for reporting on an interview. In it, Greeley tries to give a faithful, accurate account of Mormon theology. At the same time, the questions reveal as much about Greeley's interests and concerns as those of the Mormons.

The critical commentary Greeley appended to the transcript of the interview captures the prevalent view that the Mormon practice of plural marriage threatened morality and the social order. That view persisted even after renunciation of the practice paved the way for Utah statehood. In January 1900, Congress refused to seat Brigham H. Roberts as Utah's duly elected representative because he had refused to abandon his wives. Accounts of the debate in the House of Representatives can be found in many papers, including the *Topeka Daily Capital,* which published many speeches and Roberts's final statement on January 26.

"Polygamy, Politics, and the Union Pacific Railroad," the final article in this chapter, provides another glimpse of attempts to tame Mormon influence and Mormon counterefforts to protect and preserve their culture. The piece once again points to the kind of Mormon business acumen that so often inspired envy and fueled anti-Mormon prejudices.

The Mormon Massacre

New York Herald, July 12, 1844

Accounts confirmatory of the fact that Joe Smith and his brother were actually massacred—murdered in cold blood, continue to reach us from the West. There can be no doubt that political feeling entered largely into the popular excitement in that region against the Mormons. It was feared by the Whigs that the Nauvoo people would give material aid to Polk. This affords another and most melancholy illustration of the pernicious, demoralizing, brutalizing influence of the party presses, which are daily influencing the passsions of the people by the vilest and most incendiary tirades against their respective opponents.

Besides, Nauvoo was very favorably situated, and from its natural advantages combined with those created by the Prophet, under his singular government, was very rapidly increasing in population and trade, which excited the jealous and envy of the people of Warsaw, a business place a little below Nauvoo. The people of Carthage, also, another trading village or town in the interior, were stimulated by the same feelings to oppose the Mormons. These feelings of enmity arising from accursed envy and avarice, were constantly inflamed by a blackguard paper in Warsaw called the "Signal."

The conduct of the people of Illinois and Missouri towards the Mormons has been brutal and detestable in the extreme, and discovering the same spirit that burned the witches at Salem and the Convent at Boston.

Carthage

The Mormons and their Leader—His Crimes,
Character, and Massacre—Pleas in Palliation—
Anti-Mormon Defence.

New York Herald, September 2, 1844

CARTHAGE, August 11th, 1844

DEAR SIR:

Since I had the pleasure of seeing you, last winter, in your sanctum sanctorum, from whence editorial genius spreads its brightening rays and illuminates the civilized world, I have been playing the cosmopolite, but at last returned to the country of Joe Smith notoriety in time to witness the scenes— the glorious and inglorious achievements of the Mormon war in Hancock county—and as many uninformed correspondents have written for the eastern papers, whose statements are erroneous, in many particulars, in relation to the causes of the death of the Smith's at Carthage, while also many editors are severely rebuking the old citizens of Hancock county, a portion of whom are supposed to be among the perpetrators of the offence, leaving the impression upon the public mind that they are a vindictive set of cut throats, and guilty of one of the foulest murders recorded in the annals of crime, I will relate to you a few facts, being a few of the prominent causes which induced the old citizens of the surrounding country to arise in their indignation and strike the blow which cut off the head of an evil, which to them, and to every freeman within the sphere of its baneful influence, had become intolerable.

First, sir, let me promise that I shall not attempt to justify the course of the perpetrators, but to palliate their conduct by showing the circumstances by which they were surrounded. I know, sir, that the spirit of mobocracy which results in the infliction of summary vengeance or justice is dangerous in its tendency; that it generally rushes beyond the convictions of the community; that it disarms men of reason; that it unbridles and gives free exercise to the baser portions of our nature; but I have been unwillingly convinced of one lamentable fact—that, on the border settlements of our free republic, beyond the influence of a high degree of virtue and refinement, such as exist in older settlements in a new country, where so many bankrupts, in honor and character, are found, who are willing to foster and cherish crime, a case has arose where the slow, uncertain and obstructed operation of the law was not adequate to redress the grievances of an injured and an oppressed community—where the old and honored citizens of the country must either yield as slaves and bow submissive to the will of a despotic, pretended Prophet of the Lord, or grasp the sword of retributive justice, and execute the decree which emanates from the heart of every patriot.

You, doubtless, are acquainted with the past history of the Mormons—how the imposter Joe Smith commenced his pretended divine mission in the State of New York, where he was known as a lazy, idle, thick-headed boy; that he gathered around him a few loafers there, and soon became so obnoxious to the inhabitants there, that they employed means to rid the State of his presence; that from there he went to Kirt-

land, Ohio, and in a few years gathered a considerable number of proselytes; that he there commenced his swindling operations on quite an extensive scale, at a time when the banking system was popular; he successfully demonstrated the proposition that paper currency was unsafe,
after committing outrages there which the good citizens of Ohio were
not disposed to submit to. They gave him a few strikes, which induced
him to pack up and lead his motley crew to the Western borders of the
State of Missouri; there he carried on such a series of agitations which
brought on a bloody war, and resulted in the total extermination of the
Mormons. From there they fled to the hospitable shores of Illinois. Upon
their arrival here, they sung the plaintive song of persecution and oppression for their religious opinions, and being in a state of abject poverty,
the citizens of Illinois contributed liberally for their relief, and established for them a home in their midst. The legislature granted them a
charter for their city, expecting from them professions that they would be
a valuable acquisition to our young populace, little thinking that they
were cherishing a viper that would sting them the moment he was
warmed into life and power.

Let us enquire what has been the situation of the old citizens; the kind
entertainment of a band of strangers; and what the conduct of Joe Smith
and his followers, the recipients of not only kindness and hospitality, but
even honors, from the hands of their new neighbors. They, the Mormons,
instead of adopting principles of action comporting with their professions of Christianity, have outraged every principle of the Christian religion. Joe Smith, assuming the character of a religious reformer, was
practically, a public blasphemer, who often shocked the moral sense of
the christian with his heaven daring declarations of his intimacy with
Deity. Charges were preferred against him and many of his followers, of
being guilty of almost every crime known to our laws, both moral and
municipal, and those charges are susceptible of the most indubiable
proof. Credible witnesses can be had who lived in Nauvoo, some who
were in the confidence of Smith, to whom he would make admissions
and solicit their aid in the destruction of female virtue, and in swindling
his deluded victims out of their property, under pretence that it was the
Lord's will they should yield to the wants and desires of God's Holy
Prophet, or jeapordize their eternal salvation. Other persons in the city
who are unconnected with the Mormon church, have been close observers of Smith's conduct during the existence of the city of Nauvoo,
who are acquainted with a chain of circumstances which fixes guilt of

the deepest dye upon him as unerringly as though the knowledge had been derived through the medium of the senses. Still the apologists of the Mormons appear to think the charges against the Mormons are amply disproved by the senseless declarations of a few itinerant news-gatherers, who seem to think they are the cause of the world preserving its proper equilibrium, by their attending to the business of others and reporting upon the state of the public mind in the different quarters of the globe—they come to Nauvoo, anxious to ascertain for themselves the facts in relation to the Mormons; they of course would go to the source of Mormon truth, Joe Smith. He immediately sees they are strangers, and shrewdly suspects their business; he treats them politely, takes them in his carriage, shows them the curiosities of the city, the exhibitions of industry among the citizens; speaks of his persecutors; says the true church always was persecuted; appeals to God that he is innocent of crime and free from all unrighteousness. The stranger, if he does not go down to the water and be baptized, he goes away satisfied that the poor Mormons are an injured people, and those who are opposed to them are maddened by the demon of prejudice. Of course, those astute philosophers, to become satisfied of the truth of the charges made against Smith and his adherents, would expect them to confess their crimes to them and practice their iniquities at noon-day, in the presence of strangers. I hope some of the institutions of the East will note those gentlemen benefactors of the age, and reward them with a leather medal apiece.

The citizens in the immediate neighborhood of the Mormons are not destitute of intelligence. It is to them the people must look for correct information in relation to their own difficulties; either they or the Mormons must tell the tale. It is a question of veracity between them—that question can be settled by viewing the circumstances. The old citizens of Hancock have always heretofore enjoyed an enviable reputation. How does the case stand with the Mormons? Let their past history answer! Can it be possible that a large portion of the people of New York, Ohio, Missouri and Illinois, are unworthy the appelation of American citizens, and that Joe Smith was a true prophet, and a paragon of excellence? The historian of our country may answer the question.

The question will be asked, why was not the Smiths punished by law? I am obliged to answer briefly, as my sheet is nearly full. Joe Smith had the power and the will to defeat entirely the ends of justice in Hancock. He could have a Mormon jury—he could have Mormon witnesses, who were bound by the severest penalties to deliver him from danger, if required the commission of perjury, or murder—he could then with impunity, as he did do, imprison men to gratify his malice,—attack and beat men in the street, for daring to do their duty—virtutally disenfranchise the old citizens of the country, and abuse and vilify them if they dared to say a word against him. He slandered and libelled the character of those in Nauvoo, who established a press to defend themselves, which press was destroyed by Smith's order; he refused to be brought to justice for the offense, for which reason the militia of the State had to be called out at an expense of some $20,000; the people after draining the cup of endurance to the very dregs, arose in their indignation and struck home to the traitor's heart.

THE SPIRIT OF THE NAUVOO EXPOSITER

Two Hours with Brigham Young

New-York Daily Tribune, August 20, 1859

SALT LAKE CITY, Utah, July 13, 1859

Mr friend Dr. Bernhisel, M.C., took me this afternoon, by appointment to meet Brigham Young, President of the Mormon Church, who had expressed a willingness to receive me at 2 P.M. We were very cordially welcomed at the door by the President, who led us into the second story parlor of the largest of his houses (he has three), where I was introduced to Heber C. Kimball, Gen. Wells, Gen. Ferguson, Albert Carrington, Elias Smith, and several other leading men in the Church, with two full-grown sons of the President. After some unimportant conversation on general topics, I stated that I had come in quest of fuller knowledge respecting the doctrines and polity of the Mormon Church, and would like to ask some questions bearing directly on these, if there were no objection. President Young avowed his willingness to respond to all pertinent inquiries, the conversation proceeded substantially as follows:

H.G.—Am I to regard Mormonism (so-called) as a new religion, or as simply a new development of Christianity?

B.Y.—We hold that there can be no true Christian Church without a priesthood directly overmissioned by and in immediate communication with the Son of God and Savior of mankind. Such a church is that of the Latter-Day Saints, called by their enemies Mormons: we know no other that even pretends to have present and direct revelations of God's will.

H.G.—Then I am to understand that you regard all other churches professing to be Christian as the Church of Rome regards all churches not in communion with itself—as schismatic, heretical, and out of the way of salvation?

B.Y.—Yes, substantially.

H.G.—Apart from this, in what respect do your doctrines differ essentially from those of our Orthodox Protestant Churches—the Baptist or Methodist, for example?

B.Y.—We hold the doctrines of Christianity, as revealed in the Old and New Testaments—also in the Book of Mormon, which teaches the same cardinal truths, and those only.

H.G.—Do you believe in the doctrine of the Trinity?

B.Y.—We do; but not exactly as it is held by other churches. We believe in the Father, the Son, and the Holy Ghost, as equal, but not identical—not as one person [being]. We believe in all the Bible teaches on this subject.

H.G.—Do you believe in a personal devil—a distinct, conscious, spiritual being, whose nature and acts are essentially malignant and evil?

B.Y.—We do.

H.G.—Do you hold the doctrine of Eternal Punishment?

B.Y.—We do; though perhaps not exactly as other churches do. We believe it as the Bible teaches it.

H.G.—I understand that you regard Baptism by Immersion as essential.

B.Y.—We do.

H.G.—Do you practice Infant Baptism?

B.Y.—No.

H.G.—Do you make removal to these valleys obligatory on your converts?

B.Y.—They would consider themselves greatly aggrieved if they were not invited hither. We hold to such a gathering together of God's People as the Bible foretells, and that this is the place, and now is the time appointed for its consummation.

H.G.—The predictions to which you refer have usually, I think, been understood to indicate Jerusalem (or Judea) as the place of such gathering.

B.Y.—Yes, for the Jews—not for others.

H.G.—What is the position of your Church with respect to slavery?

B.Y.—We consider it of Divine institution, and not to be abolished until the curse pronounced on Ham shall have been removed from his descendants.

H.G.—Are any slaves now held in this Territory?

B.Y.—There are.

H.G.—Do your Territorial laws uphold Slavery?

B.Y.—These laws are printed—you can read for yourself. If slaves are brought here by those who owned them in the States, we do not favor their escape from the service of their owners.

H.G.—Am I to infer that Utah, if admitted as a member of the Federal Union, will be a Slave State?

B.Y.—No; she will be a Free State. Slavery here would prove useless and unprofitable. I regard it generally as a curse to the masters. I myself hire many laborers and pay them fair wages; I could not afford to own them. I can do better than subject myself to an obligation to feed and clothe their families, to provide and care for them in sickness and health. Utah is not adapted to Slave Labor.

H.G.—Let me now be enlightened with regard more especially to your Church polity: I understand that you require each member to pay over one-tenth of all he produces or earns to the Church.

B.Y.—That is a requirement of our faith. There is no compulsion as to the payment. Each member acts in the premises according to his pleasure, under the dictates of his own conscience.

H.G.—What is done with the proceeds of this tithing?

B.Y.—Part of it is devoted to building temples and other places of worship; part to helping the poor and needy converts on their way to this country; and the largest portion to the support of the poor among the Saints.

H.G.—Is none of it paid to Bishops and other dignitaries of the Church?

B.Y.—Not one penny. No Bishop, no Elder, no Deacon, or other church officer, receives any compensation for his official services. A Bishop is often required to put his hand in his own pocket and provide therefrom for the poor of his charge; but he never receives anything for his services.

H.G.—How, then, do your ministers live?

B.Y.—By the labor of their own hands, like the first Apostles. Every Bishop, every Elder, may be daily seen at work in the field or the shop, like his neighbors; every minister of the Church has his proper calling by which he earns the bread of his family; he who cannot or will not do the Church's work for nothing is not wanted in her service; even our lawyers (pointing to Gen. Ferguson and another present, who are the regular lawyers of the Church), are paid nothing for their services; I am the only person in the Church who has not a regular calling apart from the Church's service, and I never received one farthing from her treasury; if I obtain anything from the tithing-house, I am charged with and pay for it, just as any one else would; the clerks in the tithing-store are paid like other clerks, but no one is ever paid for any service pertaining to the ministry. We think a man who cannot make his living aside from the Ministry of Christ unsuited to that office. I am called rich, and consideer myself worth $250,000; but no dollar of it was ever paid me by the Church or for any service as a minister of the Everlasting Gospel. I lost nearly all I had when we were broken up in Missouri and driven from that State; I was nearly stripped again when Joseph Smith was murdered and we were driven from Illinois; but nothing was ever made up to me by the Church, nor by any one. I believe I know how to acquire property and how to take care of it.

H.G.—Can you give me any rational explanation of the aversion and hatred with which your people are generally regarded by those among whom they have lived and with whom they have been brought directly in contact?

B.Y.—No other explanation than is afforded by the crucifixion of Christ and the kindred treatment of God's ministers, prophets and saints of all ages.

H.G.—I know that a new sect is always decried and traduced—that it is hardly ever deemed respectable to belong to one—that the Baptists, Quakers, Methodists, Universalists, &c., have each in their turn been regarded in the infancy of their sect as the offscouring of the earth; yet I cannot remember that either of them were ever generally represented and regarded by the older sects of their early days as thieves, robbers, murderers.

B.Y.—If you will consult the contemporary Jewish accounts of the life and acts of Jesus Christ, you will find that he and his disciples were accused of every abominable deed and purpose—robbery and murder included. Such a work is still extant and may be found by those who seek it.

H.G.—What do you say of the so-called Danites, or Destroying Angels, belonging to your Church?

B.Y.—What do *you* say? I know of no such band, no such persons or organizations. I hear of them only in the slanders of our enemies.

H.G.—With regard, then, to the grave question on which your doctrines and practices are avowedly at war with those of the Christian world—that of a plurality of wives—is the system of your Church acceptable to the majority of its women?

B.Y.—They could not be more averse to it than I was when it was first revealed to us as the Divine will. I think they generally accept it, as I do, as the will of God.

H.G.—How general is polygamy among you?

B.Y.—I could not say. Some of those present [heads of the Church] have each but one wife; others have more: each determines what is his individual duty.

H.G.—What is the largest number of wives belonging to any one man?

B.Y.—I have fifteen; I know no one who has more; but some of those sealed to me are old ladies whom I regard rather as mothers than wives, but whom I have taken home to cherish and support.

H.G.—Does not the Apostle Paul say that a bishop should be "the husband of one wife?"

B.Y.—So we hold. We do not regard any but a married man as fitted for the office of bishop. But the Apostle does not forbid a bishop having more wives than one.

H.G.—Does not Christ say that he who puts away his wife, or marries one whom another has put away, commits adultery?

B.Y.—Yes; and I hold that no man should ever put away a wife except for adultery—not always even for that. Such is *my* individual view of the matter. I do not say that wives have never been put away in our Church, but that I do not approve of the practice.

H.G.—How do you regard what is commonly termed the Christian Sabbath?

B.Y.—As a divinely appointed day of rest. We enjoin all to rest from secular labor on that day. We would have no man enslaved to the Sabbath, but we enjoin all to respect and enjoy it.

———————————

—Such is, as nearly as I can recollect, the substance of nearly two hours'conversation, wherein much was said incidentally that would not be worth reporting, even if I could remember and reproduce it, and wherein others bore a part; but, as President Young is the first minister of the Mormon Church, and bore the principal part in the conversation, I have reported his answers alone to my questions and observations. The others appeared uniformly to defer to his views, and to acquiesce fully in his responses and explanations. He spoke readily, not always with grammatical accuracy, but with no appearance of hesitation or reserve, and with no apparent desire to conceal anything, nor did he repel any of my questions as impertinent. He was very plainly dressed in thin summer clothing, and with no air of sanctimony or fanaticism. In appearance, he is a portly, frank, good-natured, rather thick-set man of fifty-five, seeming to enjoy life, and be in no particular hurry to get to heaven. His associates are plain men, evidently born and reared to a life of labor, and looking as little like crafty hypocrites or swindlers as any body of men I ever met. The absence of cant or snuffle from their manner was marked and general, yet, I think I may fairly say that their Mormonism has not impoverished them—that they were generally poor men when they embraced it, and are now in very comfortable circumstances—as men averaging three or four wives apiece certainly need to be.

If I hazard any criticisms on Mormonism generally, I reserve them for a separate letter, being determined to make this a fair and full exposé of the doctrine and polity, in the very words of its Prophet, so far as I can recall them. I do not believe President Young himself could present them in terms calculated to render them less obnoxious to the Gentile world than the above. But I have a right to add here, because I said it to the assembled chiefs at the close of the above colloquy, that the degradation (or, if you please, the restriction) of Woman to the single office of child-bearing and its accessories, is an inevitable consequence of the system here paramount. I have not observed a sign in the streets, an advertisement in the journals, of this Mormon metropolis, whereby a woman proposes to do anything whatever. No Mormon has ever cited to me his wife's or any woman's opinion on any subject; no Mormon woman has been introduced or has spoken to me; and, though I have been asked to visit Mormons in their houses, no one has spoken of his wife (or wives) desiring to see me, or his desiring me to make her (or their) acquaintance, or voluntarily indicated the existence of such a being or beings. I will not attempt to report our talk on this subject, because, unlike what I have above given, it assumed somewhat the character of a disputation, and I could hardly give it impartially; but one remark made by President Young I think I can give accurately, and it may serve as a sample of all that was offered on that side. It was in these words, I think exactly: "If I did not consider myself competent to transact a certain business without taking my wife's or any woman's counsel with regard to it, I think I ought to let that business alone." The spirit with regard to Woman, of the entire Mormon, as of all other polygamic systems, is fairly displayed in this avowal. Let any such system become established and prevalent, and Woman will soon be confined to the harem, and her appearance in the street with unveiled face will be accounted immodest. I joyfully trust that the genius of the Nineteenth Century tends to a solution of the problem of Woman's sphere and destiny radically different from this.

H. G.

Polygamy, Politics and the Union Pacific Railroad

Ohio State Journal, November 6, 1882

The Mormons, doubtless encouraged thereto by expected Democratic victories, are growing bolder and more outspoken in regard to their peculiar institution. Hon. George Q. Cannon, an ex-Congressional delegate, and one of the Twelve apostles of the Mormon Church, is making speeches in advocacy of polygamy, and blaming the non-polygamic Mormons with being the immediate cause of all the trouble which has come upon the church. He admonishes the brothers and sisters who are not living in polygamy that they are not to be "the saviors of the Latter day saints." "If this people are saved it will be through the men and women who have obeyed this divine command, and this is as true as if spoken by any angel from heaven." The logical sequence of such a creed is followed up in this manner: "If we cannot obey the laws of our country and God, better far for us to obey God. Let us go from this Conference and obey the revelations we have heard better than we have heretofore."

By the "laws of our country" Apostle Cannon of the course alludes more particularly to the Edmunds law, which is now being put in force in Utah, and by "the revelations" he means the injunction to practice polygamy.

But Mr. Cannon goes further still in his defiance and tells his followers that "if we had obeyed the counsels of the prophets of God we would have kept these people from getting a foothold here. We have warmed a viper in our bosom, and it has stung us," and in this he doubtless has reference to the customs of the Mormons, in the days before the completion of the Pacific railroad, when Gentiles were fewer, and communication with the United States much less expeditious than now. In those palmy days the "avengers of blood" could very easily rid the community of an obnoxious interloper, and no questions were asked. The brutal murder of Dr. Robinson in the streets of Salt Lake City, and the Mountain Meadow massacre, were illustrations of how the church attempted to prevent the vipers from getting a foothold there.

And this horrible, unrepublican system is now more active in its propagandism than ever before. Its emissaries are scouring the countries of Europe and the remote portions of our Southern States, openly recruiting for their infernal purposes, and defying every law, human and divine, while the United States Commission is in Utah endeavoring to enforce laws which shall put a stop to the system.

In 1867, when Mr. Sam. Bowles wrote that the extension of the Pacific railroad through Salt Lake City would be the solution of the Mormon question, he little appreciated the devotion of that people to their system, and the skill of the Mormon leaders in taking advantage of the new relations which the railroad would place them in toward the Gentile world. Brigham Young had the sagacity to make the best of the situation, and to control it for his own purposes. He took the contract to build the railroad in his Territory, and himself built the branch from the main line at Ogden to Salt Lake City, making a large profit in the operation. Bishop Sharp, a Mormon official, has been a Director in the Union Pacific road ever since it was built, and has been shrewd enough to make a great deal of money out of its securities. The completed road offered increased facilities to bring recruits from distant lands, and the growth of the church from immigration has been greater than ever before. The audacity of that people would seem to be so rapidly growing that Congress will be driven to such extreme measures as will put an effectual quietus on their operations.

10

A Nation Divided

From the very beginning, the institution of slavery presented Americans with a dilemma that was both religious and political. As a religious question, divergent views, all firmly rooted in the Bible, provided the moral underpinnings both for those who supported slavery and those who opposed it. As a political question, it provided a focus for diverse views about the scope and meaning of the freedom for which people fought and died in the Revolutionary War. At the same time, slavery also raised serious constitutional questions about the authority of the federal government and the meaning of states' rights.

All of those concerns came to the fore and intermingled with each other and with more mundane considerations of economic and regional self-interest as the young nation grappled first with terms for admitting western territories into the union and then with the Civil War itself. The articles reproduced in this chapter illustrate the ways in which religious and political beliefs intertwined with purely pragmatic concerns to shape views on slavery, abolition and the Civil War.

The "Petition from Baptists in Missouri Concerning Slavery and Statehood" is a typical remonstrance arguing against slavery, yet opposing federal intervention in that question on constitutional grounds. "Mr. Douglas on the Preachers" begins with a remonstrance sent to Congress by New England clergy who argue that slavery is wrong on moral grounds. However, the Mormon-owned *Deseret News,* from which the version in this chapter is taken, coupled that protest with an attack on clergy meddling. The themes of northern duplicity and hypocrisy in that attack figure even more prominently in news coverage from southern papers and from the Copperhead press in the North.

Both "Praying for the Union" and "Morals of the North" ran in the *Charleston Mercury,* but "Praying for the Union" first appeared in the *New York Herald.* Although Bennett generally sided with the underdog, he consistently opposed abolition and the Civil War, at least partly out of concern that cheap labor from freed slaves would undermine the already precarious economic position of Irish Catholic immigrants. As early as September 11, 1835, Bennett published commentary critical of abolitionists. On March 21, 1854, the *Herald* attacked the well-known antislavery clergyman, Henry Ward Beecher, for delivering from the pulpit a political speech opposing the Nebraska Bill that Bennett supported; seven days later Bennett produced an essay likening abolitionists to the Native American Party.

"Morals of the North" is typical of Southerners' states' rights beliefs. Like Bennett's commentary, it also portrays Northerners as opportunistic and hypocritical meddlers. But however much Southerners may have condemned their foes for enlisting God in their cause, they also turned to God for support. As secession led inevitably to war, prayers and sermons supporting the cause became increasingly common features in southern newspapers. A typical sermon can be found in the *Charleston Mercury* on December 14, 1860.

Perhaps the most influential paper in support of the northern cause was the *New-York Daily Tribune*. Horace Greeley's concerns about slavery can be seen in the questions he asked Brigham Young in the interview reproduced in chapter 9. In January and February of 1854, Greeley published important exchanges between the Rev. Henry Ward Beecher and his critics. As an open letter to President Abraham Lincoln, Greeley's "Prayer of Twenty Million," published in the *Tribune* on August 20, 1862, both reflected and helped shape northern opinion. Lincoln's reply to that impassioned argument for emancipation, along with Greeley's response to Lincoln's reply, can be found in the paper on August 25. However, in contrast to those religio-political items, the "Church and State" column reproduced in this chapter speaks to the divisive effects of arguments over slavery and the Civil War on the churches. As a roundup of church news, it illustrates the use of religious publications as news sources.

A Petition from Baptists in Missouri Concerning Slavery and Statehood

Niles' Register, November 27, 1819

From the *Missouri Intelligencer*

To the senate and house of representatives of the United States of America, in congress assembled.

The delegates from the several baptist churches of CHRIST, composing the Mount Pleasant association, holden at *Mount Zion* meeting-house, Howard county, and territory of Missouri, on the 11th, 12th and 13th days of September, in the year of our Lord one thousand eight hundred and nineteen,—having finished the business for which they convened together, and viewing with deep concern the present situation of our beloved country,—take the opportunity, being thus assembled, to declare;—

That, as a people, the *baptists* have always been republican, they have been among the first to mark, and to raise their voice against oppression, and ever ready to defend their rights, with their fortunes and their lives: in this they are supported as well by the principles which organized the revolution, and secured our independence as a nation, as by those recognized in our bill of rights, and that constitution which as citizens we are bound to support.

Viewing the constitution of the United States, as the result of the *united* experience of statesmen and patriots of the revolution, and as the sacred palladium of our religious as well as civil liberty, we cannot without the most awful apprehension look on any attempt to violate its provisions, and believing that the vote of a majority of the last congress, restricting the good people of this territory in the formation of their constitution for a state government to be in direct opposition thereto; we would enter our most solemn protest against the principles endeavored to be supported thereby. Because, our government is a solemn covenant entered into between the citizens of the United States, pledging our fortunes, our persons, and our lives, to defend and protect to each other, the enjoyment of the privileges intended to be secured; and altho' with *Washington, Jefferson,* and every other person, we regret the existence of slavery at all, and altho' we feel it our duty to alleviate the situation of the unfortunate beings who are its subjects among us, and anxiously look forward to the time when a happy emancipation can be effected consistent with principles of safety and *justice*—

Yet, we believe that "the powers not delegated to the United States by the constitution, nor prohibited by it to the states, are reserved to the states respectively, or to the people."

By the treaty of cession, "The inhabitants of the ceded territory, shall be incorporated in the union of the United States, and admitted as soon as possible, according to the principles of the federal constitution, to the enjoyment of *all* the rights, advantages, and immunities of citizens of the United States; and in the mean time they shall be maintained and protected in the free enjoyment of their liberty, property, and the religion which they profess."

The 3d sec. of the 4th article of the constitution provides that, "No person held to service or labor in one state under the laws thereof, escaping into another, shall, in consequence of any law or regulation therein, be discharged from such service or labor, but shall be delivered up, on claim of the party to whom such service of labor may be due."

The necessity of these provisions grew out of the political situation of the states forming the constitutions, as explained in the words of our beloved Washington, in his letter to the president of the congress.

The constitution does not admit slaves to be freemen; it does admit them to become *property*, and guarantees to the master an ownership, which his fellow-citizens, living in another state holding other principles, cannot legislate from him: and as under the constitution, a sister state cannot emancipate those slaves who flee to its jurisdiction, and as the power is not expressly delegated to congress, they cannot emancipate a slave, for the right is reserved to the people.—And if they cannot emancipate a slave in a state, and it be lawful to hold slaves in this territory, congress neither have the right to emancipate our slaves whilst we live in a territorial form, nor under a state government; for, by the treaty of cession, congress are not only bound to admit us into the union, but are bound to protect us in the free enjoyment of our liberty and property— and therefore, not only our right to admission into the union, but our right to hold slaves is secured by the treaty of cession, which is ratified by the president and senate, and also by several acts of congress.

With awful apprehensions we view the principle involved in this question; we are bound to hope that many are conscientious in endeavoring to enforce the proposed restriction—and we believe that they are carried away by a blind zeal and mistaken philanthropy, with due deference we would ask, if the same *zeal* that would trample on the said provisions of the constitution to emancipate a slave, if actuated by ignorance and prejudice, and stimulated by policy, would not violate a provision still more dear to us as Christians. To enslave the conscience in the establishment of a religion—from the violation of the sacred rights of property, and the still more sacred rights of conscience is but one step. Withness the attempt made in Virginia, the birth place of *Washington.*

Relying on the wisdom of God, we hail with Christian gratitude those manifestations of his providence, which tend to lessen the burden imposed on the unfortunate slaves, and hope that not only we, but all who profess the religion of *Jesus* will always aid any measures tending thereto. And believing that the policy proposed in the restriction will not only cause jealousy, foment discord, and shake the foundation of our government, but by confining them to one small district, will increase the task, augment the pains and rivet the chains of the slaves, we warn you in the name of humanity itself to beware.

The time has arrived when it is possible to admit us into the union—we have all the means necessary for a state government. And believing that the question of slavery is one which belongs exclusively to the state to decide on, we, on behalf of ourselves, our fellow citizens, and of the most solemn faith of the nation, claim admission into the union on the principles of the *federal constitution*—on an equal footing with the other states.

Praying that God, who grants so many blessings to us as a nation, to guide and direct you not only in this, but in other questions; that he will make you wise to the preservation of all our rights, with the most sincere and ardent attachment to the principles of our government, we subscribe ourselves your fellow citizens.

Signed by order and on behalf of the association.

EDWARD TURNER, *Moderator.*

Geo. Stapleton, clerk.

Mr. Douglas on the Preachers

Deseret News, May 24, 1854

Our readers have been advised that the Ministers of New England, sent a protest against the Nebraska Bill to the Senate. Mr. Everett presented it. It was in the following words:

> To the honorable the Senate and House of Representatives of the United States in Congress assembled.

The undersigned clergymen of different denominations, in New England, hereby, in the name of Almighty God, and in his presence, do solemnly protest against the passage of what is known as Nebraska bill, or any repeal or modification of the existing legal prohibitions against slavery in that part of our national domain which it is proposed to organize into the territories of Nebraska and Kansas. We protest against it as a great moral wrong—as a breach of faith eminently injurious to the moral principles of the community, and subversive of all confidence in national engagements—as a measure full of danger to the peace, and even existence of our beloved Union, and exposing us to the righteous judgments of the Almighty—and your protestants as in duty bound, will ever pray.

Dated at Boston, this 1st day of March, A.D., 1854.

Mr Douglas arose as soon as the memorial was read, and immediately pitched into the preachers—Among other things, he said:

"It protests against our action as being a breach of faith, as involving a moral wrong, as destructive of all confidence, and as subjecting us to the righteous judgment of the Almighty. It is presented, too, by a denomination of men calling themselves preachers of the gospel. It has been demonstrated in debate that there is not a particle of truth in the allegation of a breach of faith or breach of confidence—It has been demonstrated so clearly that there is no excuse for any man in the community who believes it any longer. Yet here we find a large body of preachers, perhaps three thousand, following the lead of a circular which was calculated to mislead and deceive the public. They have here come forward with an atrocious falsehood and an atrocious calumny against this body, and prostituted the pulpit, prostituted the sacred desk to the miserable and corrupting influence of party politics.—[Ex.]

Praying for the Union

Charleston Mercury, December 20, 1860

The efficacy of prayer has been admitted by so many generations and in so many different creeds that it would be a work of supererogation to deny it at this late day. It is, however, a curious fact that the cruelty of a nation increases in the exact ratio of its piety. Probably the hardest praying people that the world has ever seen are the Hindoo Brahmins and the Arab Sheiks. The time which they do not occupy in their devotions, or in the ordinary affairs of every day life, is taken up for the devising of plans for the cutting off of heretics and infidels. When the Spanish inquisitors put a poor trembling wretch upon the rack, *aves* and *paters* without number were thrown in free of charge. That Queen of England known as "Bloody Mary" was rarely away from her oratory, and James the Second was as pious as he was mean, which is saying a great deal. Nor were the Dissenters much better. Cromwell never prayed that the hearts of the cavaliers might be turned from the error of their ways, but he asked that the arms of the Covenanters might be strengthened so that they could smite the friends of the man Stuart, even as the children of Israel overthrew the Midianites.

This fanatical spirit seems to have been transmitted in the blood of the Puritans, and disseminated throughout New England and some parts of the North. With a few honorable exceptions the Northern clergy has labored zealously to draw down Divine vengeance on the South. In every New England village sermons have been preached against the "sins" of the South. Without doubt this this [sic] tendency of the pulpit has aided greatly in the abolitionizing of the North. The people of New England are naturally a pious, God-fearing, praying and preaching race. They have, both in State and Church, a bad way of jumping at the conclusion that they are right, and every body else necessarially wrong; and, therefore we are not surprised to find them in the attitude of utter hostility to the South.—*N.Y. Herald.*

Morals of the North

Charleston Mercury, December 29, 1860

Our beloved brethren of the North, the men of ideas and philanthropy, and virtuous abstractions, have but one great grief in this Confederacy—that their consciences suffer because of the degree of responsibility which is theirs, as connected with a Confederacy in which slavery exists. One would think that a short process could be found by which to relieve their consciences of this dreadful moral responsibility—simply by quitting the connection. But the hypocrisy exposes itself the moment the Slave States propose to relieve them by their own withdrawal from the Union. And then they ignore their own peace and philanthropy doctrines by insisting upon carrying war and carnage into the South, to compel the continuance of that very Union which was their loathing and horror. Mr. LINCOLN and the Union savers all, allege that they have no design against the peace, the safety, or the institutions of the South; and all they ask of the South is, simply, that they should have a trial, only to prove how innocent they are. Excellent Christians! Admirable politicians! Virtuous philanthropists! They curse slavery, threaten its destruction, and use all their energies to acquire the power to destroy it. And when they think they have got this power and are exulting in it, they suddenly abjure it. The victim struggles. They did not think that—for hypocrites are always fools as well as knaves. He may free himself, perhaps, before his throat is cut. If we now can only persuade him to be quiet! There's the rub! Who shall we look to? DOUGLAS CRITTENEEN, WINTER DAVIS, BOTTS—by, BOTTS!

These tender consciences should be relieved from the moral hurt which they suffer from connection with Slave States.

We quit them accordingly. We release them.

These world-wide philanthropists, peace men and innocents, repudiate war, and strife, and all bad passions.

We propose to quit them in peace, after a fashion prescribed in the Scriptures—"You go your ways; we go ours."

Why will these Innocents, who loath the Union with the slaveholder, still insist upon it, even at the risk of war? Alas, brethren! They wish, *themselves,* to become slaveholders; not of the negro, but the white races of the South! They have long since cheated brother ESAU, who was a simple herdsman, of his mess of pottage. They would now sell him into Egypt, and reduce him to brick-making, without straw, that they should build themselves mighty pyramids. Their weapons will not prevail. But what a fearful power have they in their cunning! How dextrously do they mask their faces with ESAU'S hair, and approaching our poor benighted brethren, the Patriarchs, BELL and CRITTENDEN, and others, persuade the poor blind men that they are the favorite brothers, the best friends, the true heirs; while, with cormorant appetites, they devour the pottage; and, with irreverant scorn, they mock the blessing. But the great God of the world still governs it; and His eyes are not blind to the acts of the wicked. In His own good time, He will rebuke the cunning hypocrites; the pottage shall be as poison in their throats and bowels; and the blessing shall become the curse.

Church and State

New-York Daily Tribune, August 23, 1862

—The boldest encroachments ever attempted by the Pro-Slavery Churches of the South upon the territory of the Free States of the Union was the organization of congregations and conferences of the Methodist

Episcopal Church South in California and Oregon. Each church, school, paper and member of these conferences was an agent for preparing the way for the introduction of Slavery into these States. It is one of the many blessings of this war that the Methodist Episcopal Church South in the two Pacific States is now threatened with extinction. The many and persevering efforts which have been made to establish it upon a permanent basis have all failed. Dr. Jesse Boring, the first founder of Southern Methodist congregations on the Pacific, spent some $20,000 of his private funds on account of his church in San Francisco, and was never reimbursed. Some five years since, the Southern Conference resumed the work, as they thought under better auspices. A new paper was started, a metropolitan church edifice was projected for San Francisco, to cost some forty or fifty thousand dollars; a book depository was established, Oregon was occupied, a college enterprise was started, and all departments of the work of building up the denomination were pushed with vigor approaching desperation. But what has been the result? The paper suspended some months since, the editor having worked three years without salary, and expended $6,000 of his private funds to keep it afloat. The book depository is about to close, with no purpose of attempting to reopen it. The college is no more than a small preparatory school. In Oregon, the race of the church is nearly run. In short, the cause of Southern Methodism on the Pacific Coast is generally collapsed, and will soon cease to exist.

—The American war will furnish some additional material for the science of canonical law. Two disloyal members of the Second Presbyterian Church of Nashville having usurped the control of the church edifice and parsonage, and ousted the loyal pastor thereof, the United States military authorities at Nashville have restored the church to the direction and control of the loyal portion of the congregation.

—One of the foremost theological scholars of the slave power, Dr. Thomwell, died at Charlotte, N.C., Aug. 8. He was until the outbreak of the Rebellion one of the leading men of the Old School Presbyterian Church, and few men have done more than he to pervert the views of the Southern churches respecting Slavery.

—Nearly all the freedmen of South Carolina are under the ministration of Baptist missionaries, who derive their support from the American Baptist Home Missionary and the American Baptist Publication Societies. The missionaries are active and efficient, and speak encouragingly of the progress of their labors. Large numbers of the colored population have been baptised, after giving satisfactory evidence of their religious condition.

—*The Southern Lutheran,* in Charleston, S.C., a rabid Secession sheet, publishes the following sentiment by the Rev. Dr. Bachman, one of the most aged clergymen of Charleston, and author of a book on the Unity of the Human Race, in which he maintained that negroes are human beings, and descended from Adam:

"You may fetter the arms and bind a freeman in chains—you may lay him in a dungeon, and place a gag in his mouth, *but the moment he breaks his shackles, he will rise up a man,* AND THEN WO[E] TO HIS OPPRESSORS."

Of course, in the opinion of the author, this is meant only for the benefit of the white Secessionists; but if the slaveholders should ever allow their slaves to learn how to read, sentences like the above might teach the slaves a very dangerous lesson.

—The editor of *The Central Christian Advocate* of St. Louis has learned from Col. Bussey that two of the three missionaries of the Methodist Episcopal Church in Arkansas have been murdered, and that the church herself is now extinct. The editor thinks that little or nothing can be done in that State for several years, and that it will take one or two generations to replant it in that region.

—It seems that the military laws of Ohio do not exempt ministers from drafting. *The Evangelical Messenger,* of Dayton, O., thinks that ministers of the gospel must go as substitutes for the negroes whom the Government refuses to accept.

—The Rev. J.B. Himes, who has so many times fixed upon the year in which this present world is to come to an end, is starting out on a new mission to give himself "entirely to the work of preaching these things"—the coming of the Lord in 1867 or 1868.

—The French Court of Perigneux has recently decided the great question of the marriage of priests. An ex-priest, Mr. Bron de Lauriores, has, in spite of the doctrine of the Catholic Church, that holy orders are indelible, professed to throw them off and claim the right of contracting a civil marriage. Whether such marriage can be legally contracted in France, has been long a controverted point, and from several decisions like that of the Court of Cassation in 1833, it became the habit to refuse marriage to persons renouncing the priesthood. It was, however, only a habit, for there is nothing in the French laws which says that it ought to be so. This is what the decision at Perigneux has admitted, and it has done so with a clearness of views which can leave no doubt on the subject.

—Alarming revelations are made on the increase of suicides in France. In the space of thirty-two years from 1827 to 1858 inclusively, 92,622 suicides were committed in France, being an average of 2,895 in the year. The suicides of males, which have only been kept distinct since 1836, amount to 56,562, and of females to 18,548—the yearly average for the former being 2,450 and for the latter 807. The difference is only to be explained by the fact that the religious sentiment sets more powerfully on women than on men. It is proved by the official returns that the most religious provinces present the fewest suicides, and that the proportion of suicides increases as we approach Paris, where it attains the maximum. Old age even does not seem to allay the furore for self-destruction: the proportion constantly increases from childhood to the age of eighty when it begins to decline.

—The agitation in Switzerland against the emancipation of the Jews seems to be successful. In the canton of Aurgan, which is the only one that has a Jewish population of any amount, the people have been called upon to vote on the dissolution of the Grand Council (the House of Representatives,) which had decreed the emancipation, and has decided by 25,000 votes against 16,000 in favor of the dissolution. As the law of emancipation was the only ostensible reason for which the dissolution of the Grand Council was demanded, the repeal of the law by a new Grand Council seems to be certain.

11

The "Jesus Newspaper"

By the end of the 19th century, newspapers had come to rely on professional reporters to gather local news and the telegraph to transmit it from the scene of action to papers around the world. They began to emphasize the new and unusual. Many papers adopted or adapted the news formulas of the "yellow press." To compete with each other and satisfy public demand for news, they published on Sunday in spite of blue laws and clergy protests. Although those changes were generally popular, they also raised questions about the influence of the "yellow press" and the proper practice of journalism.

In that climate, the Rev. Charles E. Sheldon, clergy author of the still-popular *In His Steps,* proposed a plan to protect public morals and improve the practice of journalism by creating a daily newspaper edited the way Jesus would edit it. In response, the *Topeka Daily Capital* gave him complete editorial control of the paper for one week, March 13–19, 1900.

Sheldon accepted the offer and the *Capital* announced the experiment with great fanfare on January 23, with a front page devoted entirely to hyping Sheldon and the "Jesus Newspaper." "Unique Idea in the History of Journalism" provides the background for the experiment. "The Topeka *Capital* This Week," taken from the first Sheldon edition, describes Sheldon's press philosophy; "The Saturday Evening Edition" tells of Sheldon's plan to replace the Sunday paper with an extra Saturday edition devoted to material "suitable for Sunday reading."

Newspapers around the country and the fledgling *Associated Press* commented on the experiment and reported its progress. Subscriptions poured in. The March 11 *Daily Capital* reported:

> The subscription list to the Capital for Sheldon week yesterday passed the 300,000 mark. The subscriptions have come from forty-eight states and twenty-seven foreign countries . . .

On March 17, the ever-skeptical *Atchinson Daily Globe* reported:

> The Sheldon edition of the Topeka Capital has grown to such size that it has been necessary to arrange for its publication in New York, Chicago and Kansas City as well as in Topeka.

But the *Globe* also noted dissatisfaction among regular subscribers and advertisers and delightedly took potshots at Sheldon's refusal to carry ads for corsets, patent medicines and "secret societies," as well as at the paper's lack of "telegraphic dispatches" and real local news. During the first four days of the experiment, the *Globe* published these irreverent comments as the one-line quotes under its masthead:

> Children Soon Learn That On Nights When They Forget To
> Say Their Prayers, Nothing Terrible Happens.

> If You Do Not Practice Honesty, Justice, Truth and
> Industry, the Church Cannot Keep You Out of Hell.

> The Men Guilty of the Hold-Ups in Kansas City, Should
> Know That During Lent, Their Conduct Is Improper.

> The Women's Sign of Spring, the Violet, Is Not Here, but the Men's Favorite
> Sign Is: Bock Beer.

On March 17, "The Disciples of Brer. Sheldon Are Now Engaged in a Row That Will Add to the General Merriment" appeared under the masthead. As the top story, the *Globe* published the *Associated Press* account, which is included in this chapter, of dissension at the *Capital* under the headline "The Devil at Topeka."

In spite of its popularity, ultimately most observers concluded the "Jesus Newspaper" had failed as journalism. In "The Sheldon Edition of the Capital," reproduced in this chapter, the editor, who had never endorsed Sheldon's experiment, reflects on lessons learned from the experiment and offers thoughtful commentary on the proper role for religious publications and publications intended for a mass audience. From March 20 through March 25, the paper published both favorable and unfavorable comments about the experiment from clergy and newspapers including the *Chicago Tribune, Commercial-Appeal, Kansas City Star, New York Times* and the *New York World.*

Unique Idea in the History of Journalism

Its Birth and Development Into a Far-Reaching Plan to Elevate the Press

The Topeka Daily Capital, January 23, 1900

THE CAPITAL this morning makes an announcement that is unique in the history of journalism. Rev. Charles M. Sheldon, author of "In His Steps," will, on March 13 next, assume the entire editorial and business control of this paper. For six days he will be its absolute owner. Unhampered, he will dictate its policy; edit its news columns; control its advertising. In a word, he will embody his idea of what a Christian daily newspaper should be.

CRADLED AT DETROIT IN JULY

This conception was cradled at Detroit last July. It took form in a query which startled one of the largest assemblies of Christian workers ever gathered. Mr. Sheldon asked this question, "In this day, when philanthropy munificently endows our institutions of learning, is there here a man who, recognizing the potency of the public press to make or mar our civilization, will contribute a million dollars to establish a daily Christian newspaper?"

ITS SIGNIFICANCE AND GROWTH

The significance of this suggestion received instant and widespread recognition. It went at once from the great Christian Endeavor convention, in which it was uttered, to the world.

Why?

The press is the vanguard of civilization. The daily paper is its vitality.

This is an age of government by newspaper.

The press convenes law-making bodies, marshals armies, builds navies. It declares wars and dictates the terms of peace. It is the die in which opinion is cast. It is the force which makes opinion effective.

GIVING EFFECT TO THE PLAN

Responding to the interest aroused by what has come to be known as the Sheldon idea, the Topeka Daily Capital, a modern daily newspaper, the leading journal of dignity and importance of the state in which Mr. Sheldon resides; equipped with every mechanical facility to give effect to the plan, made tender of its plant, franchises, contracts and property to the experiment. With a deep appreciation of all that is involved, it is prepared to abdicate its news, editorial and business interests to Mr. Sheldon and his aides, that he may demonstrate his idea of the needed reform in the daily press by tendering to the country an example of a Christian daily newspaper. Accompanying it is a realization of what may be the tremendous significance of a reform in this respect. Sheldon's idea is charged with prodigious possibilities. It may inject the Christianizing ethics of a higher civilization into the coming generation. It may put a new complexion of morality, thought and human conduct upon the growing age. Its ramifications may be infinite.

Mr. Sheldon himself fully realizes the gravity of the trust he has assumed and is content reverently to make himself the conspicuous mark of this effort.

He will call to his assistance the best minds and the best exemplars of modern Christian thought, and, confident of the far-reaching effect of what he may accomplish, the Topeka Capital commits the Sheldon idea to the considerate judgment of all mankind.

The Topeka *Capital* This Week

The Topeka Daily Capital, March 13, 1900

Last December the owners of the Topeka Daily Capital asked me to assume entire charge of the paper for one week and edit it as a distinctly Christian daily.

I have accepted the invitation on condition that I receive no financial compensation and that a share of the profits be used for some benevolent work, and named the week beginning Tuesday, March 13, 1900, as the week for the experiment. With the hearty co-operation of every person connected with the paper and with the help of the wisdom that I have prayed might be given me from Him who is wiser than any of us, I shall do the best I can.

If a thousand different Christian men who wished to edit Christian dailies should make an honest attempt to do so, the result might be a thousand different papers in very many particulars. In other words, these Christian editors might arrive at different conclusions in the interpretation of what is Christian. It is, of course, the farthest from my purpose to attempt to show in a dogmatic way what is the one thing that Jesus would do in every case. The only thing I or any other Christian man can do in the interpretation of what is Christian in the conduct of this paper is to define the term Christian the best that can be done after asking for divine wisdom, and not judge others who might with equal desire and sincerity interpret the probable action of Jesus in a different manner.

With this understanding of the conduct of the paper this week, I will state in part its general purpose and policy.

1. It will be a news paper. The word "news" will be defined as anything in the way of daily events that the public ought to know for its development and power in a life of righteousness. Of necessity the editor of this paper, or of any other with this definition of "news," will determine not only the kind, but the quantity of any particular events that ought to be printed. The importance of one kind of "news" compared with another kind will also determine the place in the paper where matter will be printed. If it seems to the editor that certain subjects representing great causes that belong to the profoundest principles of human life are the most important, they will be given the first page of the paper whether they are telegraphic items or not. It might easily become the settled policy of a permanent paper similar to this one, to consider the detailed account of an unusual battle as of less importance to the reader than an account of the usual daily destruction being caused by liquor. The first page of the Capital this week will contain what seems to the editor to be the most vital issues that affect humanity as a whole.

2. The paper will be non-partisan, not only in municipal and state politics, but also in national politics. I do not mean to say that a Christian daily can not be partisan. This is simply my interpretation of Christian as applied to this part of the paper's life.

3. On the liquor question the paper will advocate the prohibition of the whole liquor business from Maine to California and all around the globe. By prohibition I mean the total extinction of the curse of making, selling, buying and drinking intoxicating liquor; its extinction by legal enactment, by personal total abstinence, and by every form of state, home, church and school education that Christians can devise.

4. The great social questions of the age will be given prominance. The selfishness of mankind in every form of greed, commercially or politically, will be considered as of more serious consequences to us as a people than many other matters which too often engage the time and attention of mankind.

5. The paper will declare its abhorrence of war as it is being waged today not only in Africa but in the Philippines and everywhere else.

6. On matters of "finance" or "tariff" or "expansion," matters of public concern which have to do with measures of this character, the editor has personal opinions which may or may not be voiced in this paper. If he gives expression to them it will be in no dogmatic or positive manner, as if he knew what the whole Christian truth was concerning them. In regard to many of these questions I do not know what is the Christian answer to them. In regard to others, my study of them has not yet resulted in convictions that are strong enough to print. I do not wish to declare through this paper a policy concerning certain political measures which are not clear in my own mind.

7. The main purpose of the paper will be to influence its readers to seek first the Kingdom of God. A nation seeking the Kingdom of God first of all, will in time find right answers to all disputed questions and become a powerful and useful nation.

8. Editorial, and other articles, written by reporters, will be signed by the writers. The exceptions will be small items and such local and telegraphic news as in its nature does not require signature.

9. There will be no Sunday paper, but instead a Saturday evening edition suitable for Sunday reading.

I wish to take this opportunity to thank the many friends everywhere who have sent me words of encouragement. It has been impossible for me to answer them personally. I also wish to express to the host of Christian correspondents who have sent me assurances of their prayers for this week's work, my deep acknowledgement of the source of whatever strength I have felt in preparing for a task which lies beyond the reach of any merely human effort.

May God bless the use of this paper to the glory of His Kingdom on the earth.

CHARLES M. SHELDON

The Saturday Evening Edition

The Topeka Daily Capital, March 17, 1900

We read in the Bible that God rested after the work of the creation, then declared that this rest period was to be observed by the human race.

The great wisdom of this divine command has never been questioned by the most thoughtful men and women. The reasons why we need a regular, recurring period of rest for body and mind are so many and so sensible that they are practically self evident. Disobedience to the command has always resulted in loss to nations and individuals. Obedience to it has always resulted in blessing to nations and individuals.

It is with a very profound belief in the value of this one day out of seven that this particular issue of the Capital has been published. One of the greatest blessings connected with Sunday ought to be the opportunity it affords for a change of thought and a rest for mind and soul. On this account there is no news of the world published in this issue. The human race can be just as happy and useful and powerful it it does not know every twenty-four hours the news of the wars and the sports and the society events of the world. Let us give God a fair opportunity to reach our souls by turning from the six days of our earthly struggles which we call history, and letting our religious natures have a whole day in which to grow and express themselves. For we are religious before we are intellectual or artistic. Our souls are of more importance than our bodies. Let us give one whole day to God and to heaven, and to our Christian relations to our neighbor. We shall not lose anything if we do not know until Monday or even the next day what the world has been doing. It is not fair to shut out of our lives so much Him who made us to live to His glory on earth.

It is entirely possible for Christian civilization to be a great deal more powerful, useful and intelligent, if every one would take one whole day in seven to read what he does not read the other days of the week, to think what he does not think during the week, to rest, and pray, and commune with God, as he does not during the week. We have too much humanity if that is all we are willing to have. We need more divinity to make our lives complete.

It is hardly necessary for me to say that this particular kind of a paper for Sunday use might be varied in such a way as to bring to its readers each Saturday night a quantity of reading matter of great value. I have used the Bible for this one issue as an illustration of what might be done for every week in the year. I would have a different paper each time. The one thing kept in view each time would be to give the public something entirely different from the other issues of the paper. The editor of a daily paper ought not to be afraid to give the readers one paper during the week that would be distinctly religious. A special editor to take charge of this one number could find plenty of good material for the fifty-two weeks in the year and the amount of good that might be done by that last issue of each week is incalculable. The same plan could be pursued with an evening as with a morning paper. It would, however, be easier to do this with an evening instead of a morning paper. On that account if I were in charge of a Christian daily of my own I would choose an evening paper.

There has been no Sunday work done on this paper. The press and mailing work stopped before midnight of Saturday. The carriers were instructed to deliver their papers in time to reach home themselves before Sunday. There will be no papers sold or delivered on Sunday with the approval of the editor.

May God bless the use of the press of the world to the glory of His Kingdom on earth.

CHARLES M. SHELDON

The Devil at Topeka

Owners of the Capital Newspaper in a Row, With Brer. Sheldon Against Joe Hudson

Atchinson Globe, March 17, 1900

By *Associated Press*

TOPEKA, March 17—The *Capital* management is in a tremendous row over the future conduct of the paper. The directors are now holding an excited meeting. Popenoe, who favors its continuation as a religious daily, seems to have a majority of the directors in his favor. J. K. Hudson, the editor, and Dell Kizer, the business manager, strongly oppose the proposed idea. Mr. Hudson says emphatically he will not consent to run anything but a secular partisan newspaper. Mr. Kizer threatens suit against Popenoe for announcing a change of policy.

Dell Keiser, a director in the Topeka *Capital* company, president and business manager of the paper, announced to-day that the paper will not be continued according to Mr. Sheldon's plan. He says he will prevent the continuation of the venture by legal proceedings if necessary.

General J. K. Hudson, the editor in chief, announces that he will not be editor of anything but a secular partisan newspaper.

"I have never been in sympathy with the idea of a religious daily newspaper," said Gen. Hudson to-day. "There has been no secret about this. A year ago I said so editorially, and recently have said so to Mr. Sheldon and in interviews. I don't believe such a paper as Mr. Sheldon has made the *Capital* this week fills the bill of this day and age. What the present demands is a newspaper that gives all the news every day in the week, and reaches sinners as well as saints. The editorial page of a daily newspaper may be whatever the people in charge desire to make it, but the news columns should be devoted to the news of the world.

"I could no more edit a Christian newspaper than I could edit a populist or Democratic newspaper. It would be hypocrisy for me to attempt to edit such a paper as Mr. Sheldon has made the *Capital,* the same as it would be hypocrisy for me to attempt to edit the Kansas City *Times* along the principles it now advocates. I have my ideas as to what a daily newspaper should be, and I am too old to change them."

Hudson has a contract, with a number of years to run, as editor-in-chief in charge of the editorial policy of the *Capital* at a salary of three thousand dollars a year.

———————

There is little joy in the Topeka *Capital* office. A Chicago *Record* dispatch from Topeka says: "Dell Keiser, the business manager, for the first time since Sheldon took hold, realized to-day that the real trouble would begin after the preacher had yielded his editorial chair. General Hudson, editor-in-chief, who was never in favor of the induction of Sheldon or his methods, said to-night that he was more than ever convinced of the futility of the Christian daily run as Jesus would run it, and he gave it as his opinion that, except from a financial standpoint, the thing was a failure. Even the money gain may be wiped out if the discarded advertisers choose to make their experience basis for suits at law. The fraternal organizations, many of whose "ads" were repudiated by Editor Sheldon, are

very angry, and foreigners who did not like his attack this morning upon
the methods and morals of the Bohemians, are asking what has become
of Editor Sheldon's announcement that he would attack no race and no
creed, but would deal as kindly with all people as he expected them to
deal kindly with him.". . . F.O. Popenoe, principal owner of the Topeka
Capital, announced last night that the *Capital* would continue as a Christian daily "indefinitely." This decision was arrived at after a conference
between the *Capital* owners and Mr. Sheldon. Mr Sheldon gave it as his
opinion that the paper could acquire a circulation of 100,000 if run on
the Christian plan. The management will modify the Sheldon policy
somewhat by printing more or less current news. All details concerning
the future policy of the paper will be determined at a conference Monday afternoon. Mr. Sheldon will not remain in charge of the paper. His
services could not be obtained at this time. However, he will be a frequent contributor and will lend the enterprise every encouragement possible. . . . Major J. K. Hudson will hold the position of editor-in-chief.
The announcement that "Fighting Joe" will edit a Christian daily is causing much amusement here. Harold T. Chase will continue as associate
editor. August Babize, of the *Times-Herald* of Chicago, who has bought
stock in the *Capital,* will be news editor, having complete control of the
news service. Mr. Popenoe says that the paper will advocate Republican
principles, but will not say harsh things about political opponents, either
in its own party or the opposition party. . . . Rev. Chas. W. Savidge, of
Omaha, and Councilman C. C. Lobeck went to Topeka to interest Rev.
Charles M. Sheldon in the work of the People's church at Omaha, of
which Dr. Savidge is pastor. The church does work of a missionary character among the lower classes, and for that reason help was expected
from Mr. Sheldon, but the visitors were disappointed. They were told
there was no available space. Both men were very much disappointed,
and Mr. Lobeck said: "I don't believe that Jesus would have turned us
down after we had come 250 miles."

The Sheldon Edition of the *Capital*

The Topeka Daily Capital, March 20, 1900

The Topeka Daily Capital again assumes its sphere and work as a Republican daily newspaper. The experiment tried by Rev. Charles M.
Sheldon from March 13 to March 18 in making a Christian daily is a

matter of history. It has deeply interested millions of people. With the zealously religious people, at least with many of them, there is a sincere belief that the experiment will be a benefit in arousing interest in higher standards of journalism, while a large majority of people will refuse to see anything in it but the great zeal or an earnest evangelist in a strange field of labor.

The vast number of people who have read the Sheldon edition have been attracted to Mr. Sheldon's newspaper work because of his books, especially "In His Steps." The suggestion of Mr. Sheldon at the national meeting of the Endeavor society last year that some one give a million dollars to establish a Christian daily was the beginning of the experiment tried last week. One week was not long enough to test the idea, but it has aroused a discussion in every school district in the nation out of which much good will come to the readers as well as the publishers of newspapers, imperfect as the lesson of one week has been.

Running through the national comment, east and west, north and south, there is much harsh criticism. Mr. Sheldon is not spared, and as to this the Capital can only reiterate what it has heretofore said regarding the author of "In His Steps." No matter how widely one may differ from him regarding the experiment he has tried or the work he has done, all who come to know him recognize his intense earnestness, his unsullied integrity, his modesty and lack of all pretense. What he does is from a high conscientious sense of duty to which he addresses himself regardless of praise of [sic] criticism. Their [sic] is neither vanity or self-exaltation about the man, and the writer, who has seen Mr. Sheldon come and go here in Topeka in his work for years, can not but believe in his usefulness and that he is only upon the threshold of his life work.

The estimate placed upon Mr. Sheldon's experiment will generally be that it was a failure as a newspaper, and not above the average as a religious paper. The legitimate work of a newspaper is above all else to give the news. It may have a rich miscellany, a broad and intelligent editorial survey of the topics and issues of interest, but if it fails to give the general news from all parts of the world, as well as local and state news, without emasculation and censorship, it fails primarily in giving the people what they want, and have a right to have. The religious weeklies and monthlies of the country are edited by able men, and they offer in good form religious news and discussions of subjects appropriate for their columns that fully satisfy the general demand for special religious reading. On the other hand, the secular daily press in large cities is supported by unlimited capital and employs the ablest writers and best trained men for every department. Men equipped for news gathering and the treatment of any literary, scientific, military, educational or religious topic the world has ever seen. There are also a vast number of class papers covering every field of human labor in education, law, literature, science, reforms of all kinds, agriculture, trade and commerce in infinite variety. The daily and weekly newspapers fill fields entirely different and in no wise conflicting with illustrated weeklies, monthlies, critical reviews or class papers. The secular daily paper, whether partizan or independent, is not made for a class or a sect or a part of the people, but for all the people, and as such must offer its readers a paper free from sectarian religious bias.

Whether a daily paper is Republican, Democratic or Populist in politics it is made for all religious denominations, the Jew as well as the Methodist, the Catholic as well as the Presbyterian, and for the man who has no belief. That it should stand for all that builds a community, for all that makes good citizens, for clean municipal government, for honest political methods, for schools and churches and libraries, for the good name of the city, the state and the nation requires no argument. The press of the country today is on the side of law and order, it is against crime, it is for fairness and justice and as ready as any profession to champion the weak against the strong and to demand honesty and fair dealing.

The editor of the Capital has heretofore said in these columns that there is no field for the "Christian daily" and that there is no demand for such a publication. In the great centres of population with ample capital such a paper might be made self-sustaining in time, but it is gravely to be doubted. The Capital will in the future go forward upon the lines it has worked in the past as a Republican newspaper, improving all its departments from year to year, desirous of maintaining the confidence and good will of the people of Kansas for whom it labors.

12

Revivalism

The years following the Civil War saw rapid changes in transportation, communication, business and industry. The transcontinental railroad, the telegraph and finally the automobile bound the nation together, but also led to profound changes in the social fabric. With the means for acquiring raw materials and then shipping finished products throughout the country assured, manufacturing boomed, setting off a new wave of immigration and migration to the cities.

The changes affected even those who remained on farms or in the many small towns and villages. Mass production led to brand-name advertising. That, in turn, supported truly national mass media and led to market-driven local media. Increased dependence on commercial advertising for economic support produced changes in media content that made the comforts and culture of city life seem within easy reach of people everywhere.

While many embraced the changes, others greeted them with suspicion. Fear of the effects of city life and the new consumerism lay just below the surface as the Rev. Charles Sheldon started his "Jesus Newspaper." Although the end of the 19th century has never been labeled a third Great Awakening, it was an era of intense religious activity. Protestant churches and itinerant clergy renewed their efforts to weld the newly reunited states into a Protestant Christian nation. As in the Second Great Awakening, evangelistic campaigns and revivals kept many within the Protestant mainstream. But the religious fervor also paved the way for new responses, both within Protestantism and outside its fold.

In spite of the Rev. Sheldon's concern that newspapers were not giving proper attention to religion, stories of church activities and support for their revivals and other causes were staples of news coverage. *McClure's Magazine* routinely published Bible commentaries, accounts of trips to the Holy Land and other articles contributed by clergy authors; *Godey's Ladies Book* carried articles designed to help women create a Christian home.

However, as newspapers came to rely less on contributors and more on their own professional reporters, news style changed. The "First State

Convention of the Y.M.C.A. of Ohio" tells of the efforts within one state to revitalize one of the most influential of the 19th-century organizations for ministering to the needs of those who moved to the cities. As was common for the period, the story unfolds in chronological order, giving to it the character of minutes of a meeting. "Moody's Start" is a later example of the use of a story that was picked up from another paper. In contrast to that story, told in the first person by the noted evangelist, "Aged Missionary's Tour" illustrates the new emphasis on colorful writing and narrative; "Billy Sunday on the Rampage at Columbus, Ohio" mixes the inverted pyramid form with the journalist's commentary. "A New Mission," about the first worship service held by Nazarenes in Los Angeles, illustrates the emerging news style with its emphasis on precise names, facts and figures as well as the developing trend toward using staff reporters to cover Sunday worship services and other meetings of religious organizations that was typical from about 1880, when church pages were introduced, until the mid-1900s.

While popular evangelists such as Dwight Moody and Billy Sunday became national figures and media darlings at the turn of the century, their old-style revivalism appealed more to the middle class than to others. On March 18, 1897, the *Ohio State Journal* published a story documenting early efforts to organize and promote a turn-of-the-century kind of New Age spirituality. In "Weird Babel of Tongues" reproduced in this chapter, choice of language and detail provide a vivid word picture of the birth of Pentecostalism, but the same choices that make the story so compelling also illustrate the tendency of outside observers to impose mainstream judgments on unconventional religions.

First State Convention of the Y.M.C.A. of Ohio

The Morning Journal, November 9, 1867

Columbus, Friday, October 8

A number of delegates to the Convention being in the city, a meeting was called at 11 o'clock A.M., at the Congregational Church, for devotional exercises, preparatory to entering upon the regular business of the Convention this afternoon—H. Thane Miller, of Cincinnati, in the chair. The meeting was opened by singing, after which Hon. C. N. Olds read a Scripture lesson from the 2d chapter of the 1st Epistle of John, beginning at the 7th and ending with the 17th verse. An hour was spent in in [sic] singing and prayer and remarks by various members of the Convention.

2½ O'CLOCK, P.M.

The Convention met according to previous arrangement, and was called to order by H. W. Cheever, of Cincinnati, and joined in singing, "Ask and ye shall receive," after which prayer was offered by Rev. G. S. Chase, of this city.

Hon. C. N. Olds, of Columbus, was elected temporary chairman.

Mr. Olds, on taking the chair, stated that in obedience to resolutions passed by the Convention of the Young Men's Christian Associations of the United States and British Provinces, held in Montreal in June last, State Conventions had been called in various States of the Union and were yet to be called in others. In obedience to a call by delegates to that Convention, from this State, this Convention meets to-day.

Bro. H. J. Rowland of Cincinnati was then elected temporary Secretary.

On motion of H. J. Sheldon, of Toledo, a committee of five were appointed to nominate permanent officers to consist of a President, four Vice Presidents and two Recording Secretaries. The following Committee was appointed by the Chair:

H. J. Sheldon, of Toledo; Samuel Chester, of Cincinnati; Woodward Awl, of Columbus; J. J. Wilson, of Cleveland; M. M. Saunders, of Painesville.

During the absence of this Committee, the Convention spent a few moments in devotional exercises.

The Committee on Permanent Organization then made the following report:

For President—H. Thane Miller, of Cincinnati.

For Vice Presidents—Rev. A. J. Lyon, of Sandusky; Rev. P. C. Prugh, Xenia; Rev. W. C. Tisdale, Painesville; C. E. Bolton, Cleveland.

For Secretaries—R. S. Fulton, Cincinnati; H. A. Sherman, Cleveland.

On motion, the report was adopted.

ADDRESS OF WELCOME.

Upon the President elect taking the chair, Capt. Wm. Mitchell, of Columbus, made, on behalf of the Young Men's Christian Association of Columbus, the following address of welcome to the delegates from abroad:

MR. PRESIDENT AND BRETHREN: It becomes my pleasant duty, this afternoon, on behalf of the Young Men's Christian Association of this city—and I believe I may speak on behalf of the Christian community in general, and not only of them but of all well-wishers of the public good—in behalf of these brethren of the Association, and our christian brethren in the city in general, and on behalf of all good citizens of our city, I bid you a welcome among us. We come together as fellow workers in the vineyard of the Lord. The field is a large one and the harvest is an immense one, but we may say as one said of old truly, "the laborers are few." We have our churches, the light of the world, a city set on its hill, but it appears as though in this Young Men's Christian Association there is something akin to that plan sometimes adopted by military forces when the strongholds of the enemy are to be taken, and it is necessary often to penetrate within their lines. They sometimes organize a "forlorn hope" composed of soldiers from different regiments and battallions and corps to force the enemy from his works, so from the different churches we have organized our forces for a special work, and I believe it is our duty often to penetrate within the lines of the ememy and to lay our plans of attack upon the enemy. The work truly is a great one. We hope, as residents of this city, for much good from your coming among us. We have here a great field, and a great work to do; but we feel like going forward and doing all we can to accomplish this great work. We hope we will be greatly strengthened and helped in this glorious work by your coming among us. We hope that your coming up from different parts of the State, with zeal in your hearts, and with your good counsels while among us, will kindle such a fire in our hearts as shall greatly interest us, and that our young men, in the light of this fire, will be induced to lead lives of holiness, happiness and usefulness.

I bid you into our midst, to our homes, and to our hearts, a heartfelt and earnest welcome.

REPLY OF THE PRESIDENT, H. THANE MILLER OF CINCINNATI.

Brethren of the first State Convention of the Young Men's Christian Association of Ohio:

I need not assure you that I consider it a very great honor that has been conferred upon me in electing me President of a Convention like this. I shall not dwell upon that, but I want, on behalf of this Convention to express the gratitude with which we receive these words of welcome. They are not unexpected by us. When the invitation was given for us to meet here, it was made so cordially, with such warmth of heart, that we knew when we came we should find these hearts and these homes all open. Besides, it seems to me that Columbus is a place where you have so many Conventions that you must always be ready to entertain strangers.

We hope our coming, as has been expressed, may be a good to Columbus, not because of the men who come, but because Jesus Christ, the great Head of the Young Men's Christian Association, is in our very midst; because those who came up, may come with love for this dear Savior; because we come to talk of Him; because we come to gather around Him more closely.

We have come to you, brethren of Columbus, with the most earnest prayer that our coming together may be with very great spiritual profit. We hope that we may here catch such a spirit from Heaven that we shall go away strengthened, and with more zeal, more fervent love, and a greater spirit of self-consecration to the Master. These gatherings, or Conventions, which we have had within the past few months, seem like getting to the mountain top and looking over the fields of the past.

As we gather here, we hope it may prove a Pisgah's top to our souls.

Looking back, we see that years ago this State was blooming with its Young Men's Christian Associations. They were active, zealous, and very successful, but the war coming on with its desolations, our young men left their homes, and the Associations, for the want of those who had with so much vigor prosecuted the work, sickened and died. We find on looking back over those past years, that souls in great numbers were converted to God by the aid of these associations. Since the war, in God's infinite mercy, has been brought to an end, these associations here and there are springing up again, and the membership of those that continued in existence greatly increased.

But, dear brethren, while we are thankful to God for the past, it is more needful that we look from the mountain top into the valley, where we shall have to work. There we find fields ready to be entered upon by the laborer, and from this view here we should see the demand that we go down into these fields and engage in this work.

Dear Brethren, it is by coming to the mountain springs, to the mountain hight [sic], that we shall catch anew [sic] and fresh life and as we go down may we carry this spiritual blessings with us, and may they result in good works to the honor and glory of God, and the salvation of souls.

We have come here, dear brethren, not only to look upon the past, but in order that we may understand our defects, and perfect our plans for the future. Oh, what a blessed thing it is, if we can only hear that Scriptural injunction, which says, "If any man lacks wisdom, let him ask of God, who giveth liberally, and upbraideth not." Let us, then during the association, pray very much; pray during the discussions, and during our sojourn in these delightful homes, and oh, may God hear and answer our prayers, that we may devise liberal things and may God's blessing be upon us, and may we gather strength as we gather around Christ and there learn the sacrifice he was willing to make for us. If we could hear from those lips of His, we would hear Him say, "Learn of me." God help us to learn lessons that shall enable us when we go to our home to know better how to work, and may we carry home some of the first fire we expect to receive, and may the whole State feel the influence, then shall we not have come together in vain; then shall our meeting be fruitful in honor and glory to God, our Savior.

Maj. Lloyd, of Cincinnati, moved that a committee of three, on enrollment, be appointed, and Maj. H. P. Lloyd of Cincinnati, Prof. J. P. Patterson and H. Early, of Columbus, were appointed on the committee.

On motion of E. S. Taylor, of Columbus, a committee of five were appointed to make the necessary arrangement for business and devotional exercises during the continuance of the convention. E. S. Taylor, of Columbus, Judge S. F. McCoy, of Chillicothe, Rev. J. H. Cheever, of Cincinnati, and J. J. Wilson of Cleveland, were appointed members of this committee.

The first topic for discussion was taken up, viz: What field of work can be most effectively occupied by the Association in our smaller towns and villages.

The discussion was opened by Rev. Bro. H. J. Sheldon, of Toledo, and was participated in by Brothers Smith, of Akron, White, of Columbus, and Miller and Cheever, of Cincinnati, in five minute speeches.

The time for adjournment having arrived, the further discussion of this topic was postponed until the evening session, and after uniting in singing and prayer, the Association adjourned till 7 o'clock P.M.

EVENING SESSION—7 O'CLOCK P.M.

After spending a half hour in devotional exercises, the discussion of the first topic was resumed, and short speeches were made by Bros. Witt, of Indianapolis, Floyd, of Cincinnati, Wilson, of Cleveland, Lyon, of Sandusky, Saunders, of Painesville, and Miller, of Cincinnati.

Rev. Mr. Goodwin, of Columbus, who had been appointed to offer a resolution at the close of the discussion expressive of the sense of the Association on the topic, offered the following:

Resolved, That this Convention recommends to the Associations in the smaller towns and villages, that while they keep ever foremost as their great aim, the conversion of young men, they make use of every means they can to secure through intellectual social and moral improvement; and as among such means it recommends, wherever practicable, systematic visitation, union prayer meetings, mission Sabbath schools, street preaching, neighborhood meetings, Bible classes, lyceums, reading rooms, courses of lectures, and over all, much prayer and great faith.

The fifth topic was then taken up: What relations should exist between the associations and the Church of Christ?

Rev. Mr. Rowland, of Mt. Auburn, opened the discussion, and was followed by five minute addresses by Bros. Tisdale, Eaton, Cheever, Witt, White and Patterson.

Rev. Mr. Chase, of Columbus, who had been appointed to offer the resolution, gave the following:

Resolved, That the relation between the Young Men's Christian Association and the Church should be that of Christian paternal sympathy and support, and of earnest inward cooperation, of combined whole-hearted consecration to the apostolic work of casting—in obedience to Christ—the net on the right side of the ship and drawing within the circle of Christian influence and within the pale of the church, that vast multitude of young men who are at present out of the one, and virtually beyond the reach of the other.

A number of questions were then read, which had been handed in and answers given, by persons designated to answer them.

The Association then joined in singing and prayer, after which it adjourned until 9 o'clock A.M. to-morrow.

ORDER OF EXERCISES FOR SATURDAY AND SUNDAY
NOVEMBER 9TH AND 10TH

Saturday, 9 o'clock A.M., Devotional exercises conducted by E. C. Bolton of Cleveland.

9:30 A.M. Discussion of the 6th topic:—What should the members of the associations do for young men coming to their rooms as strangers? To be opened by L. Sheaff of Cincinnati.

11 A.M. Essay on the "Use and abuse of amusements," by Wm. Mitchell of Columbus.

2:30 P.M.—Devotional Exercises, led by Judge S. M. McCoy, of Chillicothe.

3 P.M.—Discussion of topic No. 2, "What means shall be used to promote the organization of new Associations? The discussion to be opened by John H. Cheever, of Cincinnati, Corresponding member of the Executive Committee.

7 P.M.—Devotional Exercises, led by Mr. Lyon, of Sandusky.

7:30 P.M.— Discussion of topic No. 7, How can Woman's Talent be best Employed in aid of these Associations?

The discussion to be opened by Rev. Dr. Reid, of Cincinnati.

On Sunday afternoon, Children's Mass Meeting will be held at the Town Street M. E. Church, and at the Congregational Church.

Sunday 7 o'clock P.M., a farewell meeting of all the delegates, and all interested in the work of the Young Men's Christian Association.

Moody's Start
How He Came to Take Up the Great Work of His Life

The Topeka Daily Capital, January 27, 1900

From the Northwestern Christian Advocate

Mr. Dwight L. Moody thus relates how he came to give up what promised to be a successful business career and devote all his time and energy to evangelistic work:

"The way God led me out of business into Christian work was as follows:

"I had never lost sight of Jesus Christ since the first night I met him in the store in Boston. But for years I was only a nominal Christian, really believing that I could not work for God. No one had ever asked me to do anything. When I went to Chicago I hired five pews in a church and used to go out on the street and pick up young men and fill these pews. I never spoke to those young men about their souls; that was the work of the elders, I thought.

"After working for some time like that, I started a mission Sabbath school. I thought numbers were everything, and so I worked for numbers. When the attendance ran below 1,000 it troubled me; and when it ran to 1,200 or 1,500 I was elated. Still none was converted; there was no harvest.

"Then God opened my eyes. There was a class of young ladies in the school, who were without exception the most frivolous set of girls I ever met. One Sunday the teacher was ill and I took that class. They laughed in my face and I felt like opening the door and telling them all to go out and never come back.

"That week the teacher of the class came into the store where I worked. He was pale and looked very ill.

"'What is the trouble?' I asked.

"'I have had another hemorrhage of my lungs. The doctor says I can not live on Lake Michigan, so I am going to New York state. I suppose I am going home to die.' He seemed greatly troubled, and when I asked him the reason, he replied: 'Well, I have never led any of my class to Christ. I really believe I have done the girls more harm than good.'

"I had never heard any one talk like that before and it set me thinking. After a while, I said: 'Suppose you go and tell them how you feel. I will go with you in a carriage, if you want to go.' He consented and we started out together. It was one of the best journeys I ever had on earth. We went to the house of one of the girls, called for her and the teacher talked to her about her soul. There was no laughing then! Tears stood in her eyes before long. After he had explained the way of life he suggested that we have prayer. He asked me to pray. True, I had never done such a thing in my life as to pray God to convert a young lady there and then. But we prayed and God answered our prayer.

"We went to other houses. He would go up stairs and be all out of breath, and he would tell the girls what he had come for. It wasn't long before they broke down and sought salvation. When his strength gave out I took him back to his lodgings. The next day we went out again. At the end of ten days he came to the store with his face literally shining.

"'Mr. Moody,' he said, 'the last one of my class has yielded herself to

Christ.' I tell you, we had a time of rejoicing. He had to leave the next night, so I called his class together that night for a prayer meeting, and there God kindled a fire in my soul that has never gone out. The height of my ambition had been to be a successful merchant, and if I had known that meeting was going to take that ambition out of me I might not have gone. But how many times I have thanked God since for that meeting!

"The next evening I went to the depot to say good-by to that teacher. Just before the train started one of the class came, and before long, without any pre-arrangement, they were all there. What a meeting that was! We tried to sing, but we broke down. The last we saw of that dying teacher he was standing on the platform of the car, his finger pointing upward, telling that class to meet him in Heaven.

"For some days after the greatest struggle of my life took place. Should I give up business and give myself to Christian work or should I not? I have never regretted my choice. Oh, the luxury of leading some one out the darkness of this world into the glorious light and liberty of the gospel!"

Aged Missionary's Tour

Rev. Corydon Millard Will Travel Around the World

Atchinson Globe, March 9, 1900

A tall, gray haired, gray bearded old man, keen eyed and erect, stood near the south approach to the Rush street bridge in Chicago early the other morning and looked around him doubtfully. Three dingy traveling bags were on the sidewalk where he had dropped them because they were so heavy. A rainy wind from the lake whipped the skirts of his long coat about his legs and made him gasp for breath. He waited there half an hour, and as no one came to meet him he trudged off alone, stopping every few steps to rest his tired arms.

The old man was Rev. Corydon Millard of Milwaukee. The traveling bags contained a little clothing, a Bible and some tracts. Mr. Millard had come down on the morning boat, and the Rush street bridge was the end of the first stage in a missionary trip around the world. The aged traveler has lived 82 years, but he is as enthusiastic, as any evangelist can be.

"This is the best period of the world's history," said the old missionary to a reporter of the Chicago Post. "Now is the time to do good, and I feel that I am not too old to do my share. After a few days in this big city I shall go south to Cuba to hold services among the soldiers and the natives. Then I shall go to the City of Mexico to work awhile. There I will get my instructions about the rest of my journey, for I never do anything until I get my orders from the Lord.

"Eighty-two years old I am, and I don't feel half of it. I was born in the best part of the world, New York state, and in the nick of time, so that I was old enough to answer Lincoln's first call and to serve until the end of the war as chaplain in the Fourth United States Heavy artillery. That's why I like to work among the soldiers. If the Lord lets me, I shall visit all the countries of the globe, carrying his message to all peoples."

Mr. Millard is a first cousin of President Millard Fillmore and is proud of it. Although he is a Methodist, he says he isn't a strict sectarian and proved it by making a bee line toward Dr. Dowie's Zion. This is his second trip around the world.

Billy Sunday on the Rampage at Columbus, Ohio

People Converted by the Thousands—Rumsellers Kick and Squirm All Around

The New Republic, January 24, 1913

Columbus, Ohio, January—There is weeping and wailing and gnashing of teeth in this old capital. There are those who go mourning all the day long, who see blood on the stars and who are afraid for the terror by night, the arrow that flieth by day, the pestilence that walketh in darkness and the destruction that wasteth at noonday.

Said weepers, wailers, gnashers, mourners and blood-detectors are the saloonkeepers, brewers, wholesale liquor dealers, white slavers, madames, red-light habitues and vice protectors.

Said terror, arrow, pestilence and destruction are the Rev. William Ashley Sunday, D.D., Presbyterian clergyman, more familiarly known as "Billy, the Baseball Evangelist."

There is good reason for the aforesaid weeping, wailing, etc., etc. Billy Sunday has been conducting an evangelistic campaign here, in the largest tabernacle ever erected for such a purpose, seating more than 12,000 persons, and the results are clearly manifest. During the three weeks and a half he has been preaching, with two meetings every day except Monday, three on Sunday and scores of side assemblies, more than three thousand persons have hit the sawdust trail. The invitation to the trail was given less than two weeks ago. The prospects are that the evangelist's record of conversions for Columbus will be 20,000 or more. Thousands of eager persons are turned away from each service for lack of room. Some of the wiser ones who have time go to the tabernacle and wait outside for two or three hours before the time of service, in order that they may get in.

The men's meetings, especially, have been helpful, and at each one of them scores of men of all ages and conditions come forward or raise their hands as indicating their desire to lead better lives. There are sixty-two churches co-operating in the revival, and one notable result is that the churches of Columbus and for thirty or forty miles around have been revived by the evangelist's own work and that of his helpers. Before the second week of the meetings had closed some of the saloons here were forced to turn off their bartenders and the proprietors to don the white aprons, to save money, because of the decrease in the sale of liquor. The vice sections, too, have felt the influence. Drunkenness has fallen off to a remarkable extent. Among those who have hit the sawdust trail have been saloonists and bartenders. One saloonist became converted and quit the business.

Of course the booze dispensers are howling, for they have been hit. Billy Sunday, without disparagement to any other reform worker, is able to land the most deadly solar plexus blows of any man on the American platform. He is delivering the goods. He has hurled a lot of stones among a bunch of curs, and, of course, the ones that have been hit hardest have howled loudest.

Billy is striking at all forms of sin, but the liquor business is so hateful in his eyes that he reserves for it his most bitter denunciation, most powerful vials of wrath and most scathing arraignment. As a consequence he is drawing the fire of the unholy bunch back of the liquor business and its companion ungodly vices.

The evangelist will preach his celebrated booze sermon on the afternoon of Sunday, January 26, as an opener for the Anti-Alcohol Congress.

One good feature of the campaign is that Billy Sunday has the backing of every daily newspaper in this city. The only sheet that tries to oppose him is the Liberal Advocate, issued by the liquor interests. This vicious sheet has been almost frantic since it was announced that the ministers of this city had invited the former baseball player to help clean up the town. The editor, Brother Kemmler, is said to be sitting up till long after midnight, and rising at the cock-crowing in order to con his dictionary in an effort to find words mean enough to fit the situation, and there is dense gloom around the quarters of the local liquor dealers.

"Been to hear him yet?" That's the question on all sides. The questioner never has to specify who is meant, for everybody knows: Even the weekly calendar has been revised, and every day is Sunday in Columbus now.

A New Mission

Opening Service of the Church of the Nazarene

Christ the Infallible Head of Christian Church—The
Gospel a Guide-book—The Kingdom of God Is Within
You—Influence of Lives for Good or Evil—An Historic Fact
That Christ Came into the World to Save Sinners—Gospel
Meeting—Rest and Unrest—Religious Notes

Los Angeles Daily Times, October 21, 1895

The new "Church of the Nazarene" was organized yesterday with a membership of eighty-two, and the opening service was held in the hall at No. 317 South Main street, the present home of the new church, which is devoted to city mission work.

The morning service was taken by Dr. Widney, who preached from Christ's words to Peter in Matthew iv, 19: "Follow Me." The sermon gave a picture of the hard, toiling life of Peter and the change which this call brought to him. The after portion of the discourse was especially devoted to an explanation of the new movement, its plans and its object.

In speaking of the meaning of the command "Follow Me," the speaker said: "Notice that Christ does not say: Accept the creed which I frame. Observe the church forms or rituals I devise or, join the church which I found. He only said, 'Follow Me.' It was as though He had said, 'Come, live My life with Me.' What does it mean? It means that Christianity is not a creed; not an ecclesiasticism; not a ritual; but a life.

"Christ had no church edifice for His service; gave no forms save a simple prayer that a child may repeat; framed no formal creed. The nearest to a creed was when he was asked, 'Master, which is the great commandment in the law?' And the reply was: "Thou shalt love the Lord thy God with all thy heart, and with all thy soul, and with all thy mind." And the second is like unto it, "'Thou shalt love thy neighbor as thyself. On these two commandments hang all the law and the prophets.'

"Add to these, as comment and completion, the Christ life, for Christ himself says that He came not to destroy to law, but to fulfill, and you have the essence of Christianity, the religion which Christ came to live, and to bequeath to the world. It is this simple Christ life which the world hungers for, and which gives birth to the cry that goes up from all lands, 'We are tired of forms and creeds. Let us go back to Christ.' It is this Christ life which leads Tolstoly to abandon position, social standing, wealth, and to go back to his Russian village to take up with his people the toiling life of a peasant. And it is this Christ life which we are to take out with us, and teach and live, in this city mission work which is our chosen field.

"Yet the question has been asked, 'Why not do this work under present church lines with their machinery, instead of forming a new organization for it?' The question contains its own answer. It is because of the machinery. Somehow the churches are failing to hold the hearts of our cities and are steadily retreating from the field. The fact is so apparent that it is a matter of public discussion in the church papers. Why is it so? We can hardly admit it is the fault of their teachings. We can only hold that in some way the defect must lie in the methods, the machinery. With this fact staring us in the face it was not deemed wise to take the machinery and the methods which have already been tested, and found in the same way to be inadequate to the work, which is undertaken in no spirit of rivalry.

"The name, the Church of the Nazarene, seemed especially to express the toiling, lowly mission of Christ, the name which he used of Himself, the name which was used in derision of Him by His enemies, the name which above all others links him to the great toiling, struggling, sorrowing heart of the world. It is Jesus, Jesus of Nazareth, to whom the world in its misery and despair turns that it may have hope."

Weird Babel of Tongues

New Sect of Fanatics Is Breaking Loose—Wild Scene Last
Night on Azusa Street—Gurgle of Wordless Talk by a Sister

Los Angeles Daily Times, April 18, 1906

Breathing strange utterances and mouthing a creed which it would
seem no sane mortal could understand, the newest religious sect has
started in Los Angeles. Meetings are held in a tumble-down shack on
Azusa street, near San Pedro street, and the devotees of the weird doctrine practice the most fanatical rites, preach the wildest theories and
work themselves into a state of mad excitement in their particular zeal.

Colored people and a sprinkling of whites compose the congregation,
and night is made hideous in the neighborhood by the howlings of the
worshipers, who spend hours swaying forth and back in a nerve-racking
attitude of prayer and supplication. They claim to have "the gift of
tongues," and to be able to comprehend the babel.

Such a startling claim has never yet been made by any company of fanatics, even in Los Angeles, the home of almost numberless creeds. Sacred tenets, reverently mentioned by the orthodox believer, are dealt with
in a familiar, if not irreverent, manner by these latest religionists.

Stony Optic Defies

An old colored exhorter, blind in one eye, is the major-domo of the
company. With his stony optic fixed on some luckless unbeliever, the
old man yells his defiance and challenges an answer. Anathemas are
heaped upon him who shall dare to gainsay the utterances of the
preacher.

Clasped in his big fist the colored brother holds a miniature Bible
from which he reads at intervals one or two words—never more. After
an hour spent in exhortation the brethren present are invited to join in a
"meeting of prayer, song and testimony." Then it is that pandemonium
breaks loose, and the bounds of reason are passed by those who are
"filled with the spirit," whatever that may be.

"You-oo-oo?? under the bloo-oo-oo?" shouts an old colored
"mammy," in a frenzy of religious zeal. Swinging her arms wildly about
her she continues with the strangest harange ever uttered. Few of her

words are intelligible, and for the most part her testimony contains the most outrageous jumble of syllables, which are listened to with awe by the company.

"Let Tongues Come Forth"

One of the wildest of the meetings was held last night, and the highest pitch of excitement was reached by the gathering, which continued in "worship" until nearly midnight. The old exhorter urged the "sisters" to let the "tongues come forth" and the women gave themselves over to a riot of religious fervor. As a result a buxom dame was overcome with excitement and almost fainted.

Undismayed by the fearful attitude of the colored worshiper, another black woman jumped to the floor and began a wild gesticulation, which ended in a gurgle of wordless prayers which were nothing less than shocking.

"She's speakin' in unknown tongues," announced the leader, in an awed whisper. "Keep on, sister." The sister continued until it was necessary to assist her to a seat because of her bodily fatigue.

Gold Among Them

Among the "believers" is a man who claims to be a Jewish rabbi. He says his name is Gold, and claims to have held positions in some of the largest synagogues in the United States. He told the motley company last night that he is well known to the Jewish people of Los Angeles and San Francisco, and referred to prominent local citizens by name. Gold claims to have been miraculously healed and is a convert of the new sect.

Another speaker had a vision in which he saw the people of Los Angeles flocking in a mighty stream to perdition. He prophesied awful destruction to this city unless its citizens are brought to a belief in the tenets of the new faith.

13

The Spirit of Reform

The years after the Civil War marked a turning point within American Protestantism. While saving souls remained paramount, the lessons learned in the struggles over slavery produced a growing awareness of and willingness to take on other political and social problems. Out of the problems of the era was born a spirit of reform within churches.

Where revivalism sought to bring about the Kingdom of God on earth by converting individuals, the reformers sought the same end through efforts to make the nation's social and structural arrangements more God-pleasing and, therefore, more conducive to Christianity. That social gospel movement, based on the writings of the Baptist Walter Rauschenbusch, dovetailed nicely with Methodist perfectionism. Together, they tapped into and gave to the progressive politics of the era their moral and religious underpinnings.

The November 13, 1897, *Cleveland Plain Dealer* reported relief efforts on behalf of Cuban victims of the Spanish-American War. The March 22, 1900, *Topeka Daily Capital* noted Kansas Methodists' concern about the Boer War in South Africa and their educational efforts "for the benefit of the Negroes" in the South.

McClure's Magazine regularly published Bible commentaries and articles about missionaries as well as Ray Stannard Baker's exposé of New York City churches as slumlords. It also published Theodore Roosevelt's "Reform through Social Work." That article, reproduced in this chapter, nicely captures both the synergy between the social gospel movement and progressive politics and the kinds of efforts engaged in by churches committed to the social gospel movement. A similar article, noting the role of churches in combating crime, can be found in the *Arkansas Gazette* for June 28, 1925.

As the stories in chapter 12 illustrate, both those who banded together to create the Young Men's Christian Association and those who joined the Church of the Nazarene did so at least partly because of their concern over the problems associated with urban life. Even evangelists such as Dwight Moody and Billy Sunday, whose primary goal was to save souls, engaged in crusades to change laws in order to make conversion easier and society more God-pleasing. Thus, throughout the era, revivalism and reform reinforced each other as American Protestants remained committed to the dream of building their "shining city on the hill."

"Against Cigarettes" reports one of the many efforts aimed at individual and social reform in which churches cooperated with secular organizations. While smoking and other unhealthy practices were concerns, alcohol was the problem that united both revivalists and reformers. Newspapers regularly reported and promoted the work of temperance and prohibition societies. Examples can be found in the *Topeka Daily Capital* on March 13, 1900, and *Public Opinion* on January 14, 1909, and May 25, 1916.

By the second decade of the 20th century, prohibition efforts merged with and sometimes overpowered other issues. "Sunday Preaches to Record Crowds" illustrates the interconnectedness of Protestant thinking about war, alcohol and women's suffrage. From a reporting standpoint, those stories illustrate the increasing attention to attribution and to the inclusion of alternative perspectives, as well as the continuing use of lengthy quotes from sermons or other official statements in reporting about religion.

Stories documenting Jewish thought on suffrage and the war effort appeared in the *New York Times* for April 29 and October 16, 1917; Catholic perspectives on suffrage can be found in the December 21, 1919, *New York Times*. A Baptist call for government intervention to alleviate the threat to morality posed by alcohol and by movies can be found in the *Cleveland Plain Dealer* for June 1, 1930.

With passage of the Eighteenth Amendment on January 16, 1919, revivalists and reformers realized their fondest dream. However, within a few years, many from the mainline and reform wings of Christianity quickly had second thoughts about the wisdom of prohibition. According to an August 20, 1928, *New York Times* article, a national poll of 1805 clergymen from the Protestant Episcopal church showed that almost three-fourths of them considered prohibition a failure.

Yet support for prohibition remained strong; taking the "dry" position in favor of prohibition or the "wet" position against it came to define party, class and religious lines. As the historian/theologian Martin Marty explains in his 1984 book, *Pilgrims in Their Own Land*:

> Dry men were native Americans who were serious about religion; they were small-town professionals, parents of children, farmers who kept high moral

standards when they moved to the city. The Wets were immigrant new-comers, supporters of the great city machines; they were infidels and heathens who violated Sabbath laws. . . .

That mixture of antialcohol and anti-Catholic sentiments coalesced when Alfred E. Smith, the "wet" Catholic governor of New York, had the temerity to run for president of the United States. Articles published in the *New York Times* on January 3, February 1 and March 2, 1927, pointed out that Smith was a good governor, but they also warned his candidacy would divide the Democratic Party. On May 21, the *Times* reported that, in convention, Southern Baptists had voted, with only one dissent, for a resolution "pledging their church, in effect, to vote against Smith if he is nominated." A December 2 headline warned the "South Will Fight Smith on His Religion."

In its April 1927 issue, the *Atlantic Monthly* published an open letter to Smith, over the name of Charles C. Marshall, which raised all the old Protestant fears about Catholic patriotism. Although Smith tried his best to answer those concerns in a May 1927 reply, published in the same magazine, the widespread belief that a Catholic president would be the Pope's puppet did not disappear even after a June 28, 1928, *New York Times* article revealed that Charles Curtis, Republican nominee for vice president, had been baptized Catholic. In fact, so influential was the *Atlantic Monthly*'s open letter that it resurfaced in 1960 when John F. Kennedy ran for president.

Reform through Social Work

Some Forces That Tell for Decency in New York City

Theodore Roosevelt, *McClure's Magazine,* March 1901

Any one who has a serious appreciation of the immensely complex problems of our present-day life, and of those kinds of benevolent effort which for lack of a better term we group under the name of philanthropy, must realize the infinite diversity there is in the field of social work. Each man can, of course, do best if he takes up that branch of work to which his tastes and interests lead him, and the field is of such large size that there is more than ample room for every variety of workman. Of course there are certain attributes which must be possessed in common by all who want to do well. The worker must possess not only resolution, firmness of purpose, broad charity, and great-hearted sympathy, but he must also possess common-sense sanity, and a wholesome aversion alike to the merely sentimental and the merely spectacular. The soup-kitchen style of philanthropy is worse than useless, for in philanthropy as everywhere else in life almost as much harm is done by soft-headedness as by hard-heartedness. The highest type of philanthropy is that which springs from the feeling of brotherhood, and which, therefore, rests on the self-respecting, healthy basis of mutual obligation and common effort. The best way to raise any one is to join with him in an effort whereby both you and he are raised by each helping the other. This is what has been done in those factories in Cleveland, Dayton, Pittsburg, and elsewhere, in which the betterment of working life has been aimed at and partially achieved, through measures beneficial alike to employer and employed.

Any man who takes an active part in the varied, hurried, and interesting life of New York must be struck, not only by the number of the forces which tell for evil, but by the number of the forces which tell for good. Of course most of these are not, in the narrow sense of the term, philanthropic forces at all; but many of them are, and among these there is the widest variety. In this paper it is only possible to touch upon a very few of the ways in which philanthropic work of worth is being done in New York City. It is necessary to speak of individuals, because otherwise it would be impossible to emphasize the widely different kinds of work which can thus be done. These individuals are mentioned simply as typifying certain phases, certain methods. There are countless others who could be mentioned; it merely happens that these particular men have occupied to advantage certain widely different parts of the great field of usefulness.

Much can be done in downright charitable work, and there are great fragments of our social life in which the work must be in part or in whole charitable. The charity workers do an amount of good which in some cases is literally inestimable. Yet, on the whole, it becomes ever increasingly evident that the largest opportunity for work along the lines of social and civic betterment lie with the independent classes of the community—the classes which have not yielded to the many kinds of downward pressure always so strong in city life. Sometimes this work may take the form of an organized effort to secure greater equality of opportunity. Sometimes the best way to work is the oldest and simplest; that is, by trying the effect of character upon character.

Political and social conditions are often closely interwoven, and always tend to act and react upon one another. It is impossible to have a high standard of political life in a community sunk in sodden misery and ignorance; and where there is industrial well-being there is at least a chance of its going hand in hand with the moral and intellectual uplifting which will secure cleanliness and efficiency in the public service. Politics have been entered by a good many different doors, but in New York City Mr. F. Norton Goddard is probably the only man who ever entered on the career of a district leader by the door of philanthropy. Mr. Goddard, feeling he ought to do something serious in life, chose a quarter of the East Side for his experiment, and he entered upon it without the slightest thought of going into politics, simply taking a room in a tenement house with the idea of testing his own capacities and to find out if he was fit to do what has grown to be known as "settlement work." He speedily became very much interested in the men with whom he was thrown in contact, and also became convinced that he personally could do most by acting, not in connection with others, but for his own hand. After a few weeks he joined a small club which met at first in a single room. From this one room sprang in the course of a couple of years the Civic Club at 243 East Thirty-fourth Street, than which there exists in all New York no healthier center of energetic social and political effort. Very speedily Mr. Goddard found himself brought into hostile and embarrassing contact with that huge and highly organized system of corruption, tempered with what may be called malevolent charity, which we know as Tammany. Every foe of decency, from the policy player to the protected proprietor of a law-breaking saloon, had some connection with Tammany, and every move in any direction resulted in contact of some sort with a man or institution under Tammany's control. Mr. Goddard soon realized that organization must be met by organization; and, being a thoroughly practical man, he started in to organize the decent forces in such fashion as would enable him to check organized indecency. He made up his mind that the Republican party organization offered the best chance for the achievement of his object. As it then was, however, the Republican organization of the district in question served but little purpose save to deliver delegates in conventions, and was under the control of men who, although some degrees above the Tammany leaders, had no conception of running things on the plane which Goddard deemed necessary. There were three courses open to him: He could acquiesce helplessly; he could start an outside organization, in which case the chances were a thousand to one that it would amount to nothing; or he could make a determined effort to control for good purposes the existing Republican organization. He chose the latter alternative, and began a serious campaign to secure his object. There was at the time a fight in the Republican organization between two factions, both of which were headed by professional politicians. Both factions at the outset looked upon Goddard's methods with amused contempt, expecting that he would go the gait which they had seen so many other young men go, where they lacked either persistency or hard common sense. But Goddard was a practical man. He spent his days and evenings in perfecting his own organization, using the Civic Club as the center. He already had immense influence in the district, thanks to what he had done in the Civic Club, and at this, his first effort, he was able to make an organization which, while it could not have availed against the extraordinary drill and discipline of Tammany, was able overwhelmingly to beat the far feebler machine of the regular Republican politicians. At the primary he got more votes than both his antagonists put together. No man outside of politics can realize the paralyzed astonishment with which the result was viewed by the politicians in every other Assembly district. Here at last was a reformer whose aspirations took exceedingly efficient shape as deeds; who knew what could and what could not be done; who was never content with less than the possible best, but who never threw away that possible best because it was not the ideal best; who did not try to reform the universe, but merely his own district; and who understood thoroughly that though speeches and essays are good, downright hard work of the common-sense type is infinitely better.

It is more difficult to preserve the fruits of a victory than to win the victory. Mr. Goddard did both. A year later, when the old-school professional politicians attempted to oust him from his party leadership in the district association, he beat them more overwhelmingly than before; and when the Republican National Convention came around he went still further afield, beat out his opponents in the Congressional district, and sent two delegates to Philadelphia. Nor was his success confined to the primary. In both the years of his leadership he has enormously increased the Republican vote in his district, doing better relatively than any other district leader in the city. He does this by adopting the social methods of

Tammany, only using them along clean lines. The Tammany leader keeps his hold by incessant watchfulness over every element, and almost every voter, in his district. Neither his objects nor his methods are good; but he does take a great deal of pains, and he is obliged to do much charitable work; althout it is not benevolence of a healthy kind. Mr. Goddard was already, through the Civic Club, doing just this kind of work, on a thoroughly healthy basis. Going into politics had immensely helped with the club, for it had given a great common interest to all of the men. Of course Goddard could have done nothing if he had not approached his work in a genuine American spirit of entire respect for himself and for those with whom and for whom he labored. Any condescension, any patronizing spirit would have spoiled everything. But the spirit which exacts respect and yields it, which is anxious always to help in a mood of sincere brotherhood, and which is glad to accept help in return—this is the spirit which enables men of every degree of wealth and widely varying social conditions to work together in heartiest good will, and to the immense benefit of all. It is thus that Mr. Goddard has worked. His house is in the district and he is in close touch with every one. If a man is sick with pneumonia, some member of the Civic Club promptly comes around to consult with Goddard as to which hospital he shall be taken to. If another man is down on his luck, it is Goddard who helps him all through the hard times. If a boy has been wild and got into trouble and gone to the penitentiary, it is Goddard who is appealed to to see whether anything can be done for him. The demands upon his time and patience are innumerable. The reward, it is to be supposed, may come from the consciousness of doing well work which emphatically was worth doing. A very shrewd politician said the other day that if there were twenty such men as Goddard in twenty such districts as his, New York City would be saved from Tammany, and that in the process the Republican machine would be made heartily responsive to and representative of the best sentiment of the Republicans of several districts.

The University Settlements do an enormous amount of work. As has been said, they demand on the part of those who work in them infinitely more than the sacrifice of almsgiving, for they demand a helping hand in that progress which for the comfort of all must be given to all; to help people to help themselves, not only in work and self-support, but in right thinking and right living. It would be hard to mention any form of civic effort for righteousness which has not receieved efficient aid from Mr. James B. Reynolds and his fellow-workers in the University Settlement.

They have stood for the forces of good in politics, in social life, in warring against crime, in increasing the sum of material pleasures. They work hand in hand, shoulder to shoulder, with those whom they seek to benefit, and they themselves share in the benefit. They make their house the center for all robust agencies for social betterment. They have consistently endeavored to work with, rather than merely for, the community; to cooperate in honorable friendship with all who are struggling upward. Only those who know the appalling conditions of life in the swarming tenements that surround the University Settlement can appreciate what it has done. It has almost inevitably gone into politics now and then, and whenever it has done so has exercised a thoroughly healthy influence. It has offered to the people of the neighborhood educational and social opportunities ranging from a dancing academy and musical classes, to literary clubs, a library, and a children's bank—the clubs being administered on the principle of self-management and self-government. It has diligently undertaken to cooperate with all local organizations such as trade unions, benefit societies, social clubs, and the like, provided only that their purposes were decent. The Settlement has always desired to cooperate with independent forces rather than merely to lead or direct the dependent forces of society. Its work in cooperation with trade unions has been of special value both in helping them where they have done good work, and in endeavoring to check any tendency to evil in any particular union. It has, for instance, consistently labored to secure the settlement of strikes, by consultation or arbitration, before the bitterness has become so great as to prevent any chance of a settlement. All this is aside from its work of sociological investigation and its active cooperation with those public officials who, like the late Colonel Waring, desired such aid.

Healthy political endeavor should, of course, be one form of social work. This truth is not recognized as it should be. Perhaps, also, there is some, though a far lesser failure to recognize that a living church organization should more than any other be a potent force in social uplifting. Churches are needed for all sorts and conditions of men under every kind of circumstances; but surely the largest field of usefulness is open to that church in which the spirit of brotherhood is a living and vital force, and not a cold formula; in which the rich and poor gather together to aid one another in work for a common end. Brother can best help brother, not by almsgiving, but by joining with him in an intelligent and resolute effort for the uplifting of all. It is towards this that St. George's

Church, under Dr. W. S. Rainsford, has steadily worked. The membership of St. George's Church is in a great majority composed of working people—and young working people at that. It is a free church with a membership of over 4,000, most of the members having come in by way of the Sunday-school. Large sums of money are raised, not from a few people, but from the many. An honest effort has been made to study the conditions of life in the neighborhood, and through the church to remedy those which were abnormal. One of the troubles of the East Side is the lack of opportunity for young people, boys and girls, to meet save where the surroundings are unfavorable to virtue. In St. George's Church, this need is, so far as can be, met by meetings—debating societies, clubs, social entertainments, etc., in the large parish building. Years ago the dances needed to be policed by chosen ladies and gentlemen and clergymen. Now the whole standard of conduct has been so raised that the young people conduct their own entertainments as they see fit. There is a large athletic club and industrial school, a boys' battalion and men's club; there are sewing classes, cooking classes, and a gymnasium for working girls. Dr. Rainsford's staff includes both men and women, the former living at the top of the parish house, the latter in the little deaconess-house opposite. Every effort is made to keep in close touch with wage-workers, and this not merely for their benefit, but quite as much for the benefit of those who are brought in touch with them.

The church is, of all places, that in which men should meet on the basis of their common humanity under conditions of sympathy and mutual self-respect. All must work alike in the church in order to get the full benefit from it; but it is not the less true that we have a peculiar right to expect systematic effort from men and women of education and leisure. Such people should justify by their work the conditions of society which have rendered possible their leisure, their education, and their wealth. Money can never take the place of service, and though here and there it is absolutely necessary to have the paid worker, yet normally he is not an adequate substitute for the volunteer.

Of course, St. George's Church has not solved all the social problems in the immediate neighborhood which is the field of its special effort. But it has earnestly tried to solve some at least, and it has achieved a very substantial measure of success towards their solution. Perhaps, after all, the best work done has been in connection with the development of the social side of the church organization. Reasonable opportunities for social intercourse are an immense moral safeguard, and young people of good character and steady habits should be encouraged to meet under conditions which are pleasant and which also tell for decency. The work of a down-town church in New York City presents difficulties that are unique, but it also presents opportunities that are unique. In the case of St. George's Church it is only fair to say that the difficulties have been overcome, and the opportunities taken advantage of, to the utmost.

Aside from the various kinds of work outlined above, where the main element is the coming together of people for the purpose of helping one another to rise higher, there is, of course, a very large field for charitable work proper. For such work there must be thorough organization of the kind supplied, for instance, by the State Charities Aid Association. Here, again, the average outsider would be simply astounded to learn of the amount actually accomplished every year by the association.

A peculiar and exceedingly desirable form of work, originally purely charitable, although not now as exclusively so, is that of the Legal Aid Society, founded by Arthur von Briesen. It was founded to try to remedy the colossal injustice which was so often encountered by the poorest and most ignorant immigrants; it has been extended to shield every class, native and foreign. There are always among the poor and needy thousands of helpless individuals who are preyed upon by sharpers of different degrees. If very poor, they may have no means whatever of obtaining redress; and, especially if they are foriegners ignorant of the language, they may also be absolutely ignorant as to what steps should be taken in order to right the wrong that has been done them. The injuries that are done may seem trivial; but they are not trivial to the sufferers, and the aggregate amount of misery caused is enormous. The Legal Aid Society has made it its business to take up these cases and secure justice. Every conceivable variety of case is attended to. The woman who has been deserted or maltreated by her husband, the poor serving-maid who has been swindled out of her wages, the ignorant immigrant who has fallen a victim to some sharper, the man of no knowledge of our language or laws who has been arrested for doing something which he supposed was entirely proper—all these and countless others like them apply for relief, and have it granted in tens of thousands of cases every year. It should be remembered that the good done is not merely to the sufferers themselves, it is also a good done to society, for it leaves in the mind of the newcomer to our shores, not the rankling memory of wrong and injustice, but the feeling that, after all, here in the New World, where he has come to seek his fortune, there are disinterested men who endeavor to see that the right prevails.

Some men can do their best work in an organization. Some, though, they occasionally work in an organization, can do best by themselves. Recently a man, well qualified to pass judgment, alluded to Mr. Jacob A. Riis as "the most useful citizen of New York." Those fellow-citizens of Mr. Riis who best know his work will be most apt to agree with this statement. The countless evils which lurk in the dark corners of our civic institutions, which stalk abroad in the slums, and have their permanent abode in the crowded tenement houses, have met in Mr. Riis the most formidable opponent ever encountered by them in New York City. Many earnest men and earnest women have been stirred to the depths by the want and misery and foul crime which are bred in the crowded blocks of tenement rookeries. These men and women have planned and worked, intelligently and resolutely, to overcome the evils. But to Mr. Riis was given, in addition to earnestness and zeal, the great gift of expression, the great gift of making others see what he saw and feel what he felt. His book, "How the Other Half Lives," did really go a long way toward removing the ignorance in which one-half of the world of New York dwelt concerning the life of the other half. Moreover, Mr. Riis possessed the further great advantage of having himself passed through not a few of the experiences of which he had to tell. Landing here, a young Danish lad, he had for years gone through the hard struggle that so often attends even the bravest and best when they go out without money to seek their fortunes in a strange and alien land. The horror of the police lodging-houses struck deep in his soul, for he himself had lodged in them. The brutality of some of the police he had himself experienced. He had been mishandled, and had seen the stray dog which was his only friend killed for trying, in dumb friendship, to take his part. He had known what it was to sleep in door-steps and go days in succession without food. All these things he remembered, and his work as a reporter on the New York "Sun" has enabled him in the exercise of his profession to add to his knowledge. There are certain qualities the reformer must have if he is to be a real reformer and not merely a faddist; for of course every reformer is in continual danger of slipping into the mass of well-meaning people who in their advocacy of the impracticable do more harm than good. He must possess high courage, disinterested desire to do good, and sane, wholesome common sense. These qualities he must have; and it is furthermore much to his benefit if he also possesses a sound sense of humor. All four traits are possessed by Jacob Riis. No rebuff, no seeming failure, has ever caused him to lose faith. The memory of his own trials never soured him. His keen sense of the sufferings of others never clouded his judgment, never led him into hysterical or sentimental excess, the pit into which not a few men are drawn by the very keenness of their sympathies; and which some other men avoid, not because they are wise, but because they are cold-hearted. He ever advocates mercy, but he ever recognizes the need of justice. The mob leader, the bomb-thrower have no sympathy from him. No man has ever insisted more on the danger which comes to the community from the lawbreaker. He sets himself to kill the living evil, and small is his kinship with the dreamers who seek the impossible, the men who *talk* of reconstituting the entire social order, but who do not *work* to lighten the burden of mankind by so much as a feather's weight. Every man who strives, be it ever so feebly, to do good according to the light that is in him, can count on the aid of Jacob Riis if the chance comes. Whether the man is a public official, like Colonel Waring, seeking to raise some one branch of the city government; whether he is interested in a boys' club up in the country; or in a scheme for creating small parks in the city; or in an effort to better the conditions of tenement-house life—no matter what his work is, so long as his work is useful, he can count on the aid of the man who perhaps more than any other knows the needs of the varied people who make up the great bulk of New York's population.

Half a dozen men have been mentioned, each only as a type of those who in the seething life of the great city do, in their several ways and according to their strength and varying capacities, strive to do their duty to their neighbor. No hard-and-fast rule can be laid down as to the way in which such work must be done; but most certainly every man, whatever his position, should strive to do it in some way and to some degree. If he strives earnestly he will benefit himself probably quite as much as he benefits others, and he will inevitably learn a great deal. At first it may be an effort to him to cast off certain rigid conventions, but real work of any kind is a great educator, and soon helps any man to single out the important from the unimportant. If such a worker has the right stuff in him he soon grows to accept without effort each man on his worth as a man, and to disregard his means, and what is called his social position; to care little whether he is a Catholic or Protestant, a Jew or a Gentile; to be utterly indifferent whether he was born here or in Ireland, in Germany or in Scandinavia; provided only that he has in him the spirit of sturdy common sense and the resolute purpose to strive after the light as it is given him to see the light.

Against Cigarettes

Enemies of the Coffin Nails to Begin Crusade in Topeka

The Topeka Daily Capital, March 11, 1900

Miss Lucy Page Gaston, of Chicago, general superintendent of The Anti-Cigarette league, and the Rev. Wallace R. Struble, lecturer in the same organization, are in the city. They will remain here throughout the coming week, working in the interests of the league.

Great interest is being shown in their work in this city by the churches, young people societies, women's clubs and other organizations, and a united effort will be made to further the interests of the anti-cigarette campaign.

In speaking about the Anti-Cigarette league yesterday, Miss Gaston said:

"I believe that there are thousands of boys going to destruction because there is no other very interesting place for them to go. Now is the time to save the boys.

"Our hope is to inaugurate a movement in Topeka similar to the one in Chicago, and I believe we shall have necessary help. People generally realize the destructiveness of the cigarette habit, but can think of [no] way to stop it.

"The method that we has pursued has been very successful. You would be surprised, if you knew what wonderful things have resulted from our work. It is amazing to witness the eagerness with which boys in the large cities come into this league. They see at a glance its great worth, and we have not the slightest difficulty in getting them interested."

This morning Miss Gaston will speak in the Sunday school of the First Presbyterian, and the First Congregational churches, and at the First Methodist Sunday school this afternoon.

At 4:15 this afternoon, Miss Gaston will conduct a woman's mass meeting in the First M.E. church. Mothers and teachers are especially invited.

She will address the First Congregational church Y.P.S.C.E. at 6:30 and will attend the evening service at the Rev. C. M. Sheldon's church. The Rev. Mr. Struble will also be present at the Central church, and both will take some part in the service.

On Wednesday night, the Rev. Mr. Struble will lecture in the First
M.E. church on the subject, "Burning His Brains."

Miss Gaston and Mr. Struble will make a strong point of the enforcement of law during their stay here. There is a law on the statute books of
Kansas forbidding the sale of cigarettes to children, and an agitation will
be started to secure a strict enforcement of the law.

The Anti-Cigarette league was organized in Chicago by Miss Gaston
about three years ago. It was originally an organization within the con-
fines of the Chicago schools, but has now become national in scope. The
league occupies fine quarters in the Woman's Temple, Chicago, and employs a large number of people to carry out the principles for which it
was organized.

Over 6,000 Chicago boys are enrolled as members of the league. All
these are active workers. They distribute cards and invitations, and gain
many new members.

The pledge each boy takes on becoming a member of the organization
is as follows:

"I do hereby pledge myself upon honor to abstain from smoking cigarettes and using tobacco in any form at least until I reach the age of 21
years, and to use my influence to induce others to do the same."

The representatives of the league expect to make a campaign in many
other of the leading cities of this part of the country. They expect to create an influence in Topeka against the cigarette habit which will spread
throughout the state.

Sunday Preaches to Record Crowds

More People Than on Any Previous Week Day Hear
Him Praise Mayor's Saloon Lid—DENIES HE'S A
PLAGIARIST—Will Give Away Receipts from Free-Will
Offering in Coming Chicago Campaign

New York Times, April 19, 1917

The biggest crowds that have yet attended the Billy Sunday revivals
on a weekday turned out yesterday, afternoon and evening, to hear his
sermons on the home. The address was full of homely advice to parents,
and it reiterated again and again the necessity of their living as examples
to their children, pointed out the effect of godless home surroundings

upon the rising generation, and was diversified with a declaration for woman suffrage and denunciation of birth control and the European plan hotel.

Sunday was much heartened in the morning by learning of Mayor Mitchell's abolition of all-night licenses, and declared that before the war was over the saloons of New York would be closed for good. At the same time announcement was made in Chicago, where Sunday will conduct a three months' revival next Winter, that all the personal offering made to him on the last day of the campaign—a contribution which will presumably amount to thousands of dollars—would be donated to the Pacific Garden Mission, where Sunday was converted nearly thirty years ago.

Reports that this gift, following the determination to give the money received in New York to the work of the Red Cross and the army Y.M.C.A., indicated Sunday's decision to take no more money for his services, but to give it all to philanthropic purposes, were denied by Mrs. Sunday last night. The contribution of the New York offering for patriotic purposes was inspired by Mr. Sunday's patriotism, and especially, it is said, by the fact that being too old to go to the front himself he wanted to help financially since he could not in person. As for the Chicago contribution, there are special reasons for that. Sunday played baseball in Chicago, he was converted there, Mrs. Sunday lived there all through her early life, and the two met in Chicago, were married in Chicago, and lived there for years afterward. It was only a natural sentiment, according to Mrs. Sunday, that prompted the gift to the Pacific Garden Mission. What shall be done with the offering in any other city will be decided when the time comes according to circumstances then prevailing.

The crowd at the afternoon service was estimated at 13,000, about two-thirds of the capacity of the tabernacle, showing that friends of the movement have taken to heart the exhortation of Homer Rodeheaver, that those who can come in the afternoon do so, and thereby leave more room for people who cannot attend services except at night.

Last night the tabernacle was packed with as many people as the Fire Department regulations would allow, and great numbers were turned away.

There were a large number of special delegations, headed by a group of several hundred employes of the New York Telephone Company. A body of more than 100 sailors from the New York Navy Yard sat on the platform and were cheered long and loudly by the audience, and Rodeheaver, in welcoming them, told how he had fought for his country in the Spanish war.

One of those in the front of the tabernacle, was the Rev. Dr. Stephen S. Wise, who has preached a number of sermons denouncing Sunday. The Rev. Dr. Ladd Thomas, head of the committee arranging the Chicago meetings, was on the platform, and the Rev. Dr. Paul Rader of the Moody Church, in that city, offered prayer before the sermon.

"We thank Thee, O Lord, for the bravery of this man," he said. "We thank Thee for his open mouth that no man can shut. O Lord, drive on: may the slain of the Lord be many in this place."

When the collection toward the expenses of the local campaign was being taken up Rodeheaver reminded the audience that contributions were not coming in as fast here as they had in Detroit or Buffalo. "We hear talk enough about what you do over here," he said, "but we haven't seen it yet." There is still nearly $90,000 to be raised on the budget of $150,000.

Sunday began with a denunciation of persons who have charged him with plagiarism, and his remarks were taken to apply particularly to the charge that he plagiarized extensively from Ingersoll in a Declaration Day address delivered in a Pennsylvania town in 1912.

"I am indebted to a friend of mine," he said, "for some of the thoughts in this sermon. I've skimmed through English literature for illustrations and analogies; I owe something to nearly every editor from the Atlantic to the Pacific. I've had a wagon load of clippings sent me by various people for use in my sermons. Everybody does it. I know a preacher in this town who hires two men to do nothing but read for anecdotes and illustrations and clip them out for him to use. Yet the whiskey gang goes up and down the land saying that I'm a thief.

"Nobody else is a thief but me, because nobody else hits their business like I do. That dirty, stinking bunch of moral assassins hires men to sit in the audience and hear me, to write down what I say and then try to find some author who said something like it, and accuse me of having stolen my ideas.

"I know that $30,000 was offered a man in New York City to write a series of articles attacking me. All right, if you know anything about me that you want to publish, go to it. Everything they say about me is a dirty, stinking, black-hearted lie. The whole thing is a frame-up from A to Izzard. I'll fight them till hell freezes over, and then borrow a pair of skates. By the grace of God I've helped to make Colorado and Nebraska, and Iowa, and Michigan, and West Virginia dry, and I serve notice on the dirty gang that I'll help to make the whole nation dry.

"My text tonight is Genesis, 18:19—'I know him for he will command his children and his household after him.' The proper or improper settlement of the home question—and it is never settled right till it is settled first that you as a father or a mother will be a follower of Jesus Christ—means weal or woe to more boys and girls than any other influence. Sixty-five per cent of the boys and girls in the reform schools come from homes where the parents are divorced.

"What can you say of the homes where the parents indulge in wines and champagnes, the most costly vintages of France and California? What can you say when women loan their presence to vaudeville, they have it in their homes, they indulge in gambling and drinking, they know more about poker chips than English literature, and more about expensive champagnes and wines than about the word of God?

"The biggest monstrosity in the world is a mother with children playing around her knee and not teaching them the religion of God. A stepmother would be a godsend if she had religion.

"The normal way to get rid of drunkards is to get rid of the dirty, rotten, stinking hellholes that make drunkards. It always makes my blood boil to see a cop pinch a drunkard and take him away to the police station while he throws the protecting arm of the law around the hellhole that made him." [Cheers.]

"Let's do something to save the families in New York which are blasted by drink and vice; to put the smile on the face of those pale, wan, weak, anaemic boys and girls when their daddy walks home sober from the sawdust trails [Applause.]

"Woe betide the nation when we sink down to the level of brutes. What would the world be if the beasts had birth control? There'd be no milk to drink, no meat on the table; the chickens would refuse to lay eggs, seeds would refuse to produce, and we'd all starve to death.

"I have no faith in a woman who talks of heaven while she makes her home a hell. If I wanted to investigate your piety I'd ask your cook.

"I believe in blood. Blood tells [applause]—good blood and bad blood. Scotch blood means prudence, Danish blood love of the sea, Welsh blood love of religion and God. English blood stands for reverence of ancient things as shown by the fact that England spent fifty million dollars to put the crown on George's block.

"According to our standards of gold and silver, Abraham was worth a

billion dollars, David three billion, Solomon five billion. David could
have hired John D. Rockefeller as his chauffeur." (John D. Rockefeller,
Jr., who sat on the platform, joined in the laughter at this.) "Solomon
could have hired Carnegie for a butler and J.P. Morgan to mow his lawn.

"Neither law nor gospel can make a nation great without home authority and home influence. The sneering use of the phrase, 'tied to his
mother's apron strings,' will make over a fairly decent boy into a tough
with the tastes of a wharf rat. I notice the boy tied to his mother's apron
strings, who can't tell four aces from a load of hay, is the one who
comes in with the blue ribbon when there are forty applications for the
job.

"What your children learn at your knee will last when they hobble on
the crutches of decrepitude and take their teeth out to clean them in the
sink. (Laughter.) 'How old are you, little boy?' 'Five at home, 6 at
school, 4 on the street car.' Is it any wonder the child grows up a liar?

"It's disgraceful the salaries we pay school teachers and preachers. I
never aspired to but one office—the School Board; and if I were on it I'd
raise the teachers' salaries and pay them twelve months in the year.
(Applause.)

"A woman with seven noble sons was asked how she raised them.
'With prayer and a good hickory stick,' she said. There are homes that
need the hickory stick with the motto hanging above it, 'I Need Thee
Every Hour.'

"Don't drive the children into the street to play. If you want to ruin
the home let the children understand that mirth and merriment must stay
outdoors. If they don't get recreation at home they'll get it in the haunts
of vice.

"The average little sissy not yet separated from short skirts knows
more about the devil and the shady side of sin than her grandmother did
at 75. Twenty-five years ago you couldn't find a decent woman that
would drink in a public place. You could hardly find a European plan hotel in America. Now you can hardly find one on the American plan. Go
downtown and you'll see women drinking beer, champagne, wines, and
cocktails, and smoking cigarettes. [Applause.] Some of you that hit your
hands together on that do it with a bad conscience. Probably your hide's
full of rotten booze right now. God help your husband and children.
You'll never save New York or any other city while you run a barroom in
your own home.

"This nation has no better friend than the mother who teaches her boy or girl to pray, no worse enemy than the woman who teaches her children to sneer at religion. Ingersoll said: 'A hundred men make a company, but one woman makes a home.' [Applause.] If George Washington's mother had been like Happy Hooligan's, George would have run around with a tin can on his head.

"When the nation refuses the mothers the right to defend the home by refusing the right to vote then it is sure of oblivion. If you have not manhood enough to defend your mother, your wife, your children against the assaults of the evil iniquitous, vile, damnable whisky traffic then put the ballot into their hands and they'll drive it into hell."

Sunday finished with a story of the state funeral of John Howard Paine, holding the name till the very last, and when he finally shouted, "It was John Howard Paine, who wrote—" Rodeheaver and the chorus, alert to the instant, cut in with the final strains of "Home, Sweet Home."

This morning Mr. Sunday will address a gathering at the home of John D. Rockefeller, Jr., at 10 West Fifty-fourth Street. There will be a number of outside meetings, already announced, and the usual tabernacle services at 2:00 and 7:30.

When he was told yesterday morning that the Mayor had decided to close all night cafes and saloons till the war was over Mr. Sunday was much pleased.

"The Mayor has done well," he said. "It is tangible evidence of his patriotism and shows that he wants to help the country. He feels that in curbing the saloon he is helping recruiting. I approve most heartily for the saloon undoubtedly breeds slackers.

"Oh, the devil is growling and grinding his teeth, you may be sure. He doesn't want the saloons closed, even for a little while. He wants them open every minute of the twenty-four hours. But a man cannot be efficient who drinks booze. This is only the first step. No doubt before long another step will be taken, until finally all saloons will be closed during the period of the war. And when the people once see what that means they will rise up and close them for good."

14

Faith, Science and Scripture

The technological and industrial revolutions of the 19th century brought with them a new emphasis on the practical and the demonstrable. With the 1862 passage of the Morrill Act granting public land for the establishment of educational institutions, state universities devoted to "science and the useful arts" sprang up. Elite colleges such as Harvard and Yale, which once had been devoted almost exclusively to training clergy, opened up whole new programs devoted to "practical learning" while simultaneously segregating theological training into divinity schools.

The science of the age undergirded and promoted progress, but it also opened up new ways of knowing that affected religion and religious understanding. When word of Charles Darwin's *Origin of the Species* reached the United States, scientists and clergy greeted the possibility of evolutionary change with skepticism. But gradually, as the ideas became more widely accepted by scientists, clergy and laity alike found themselves dividing into two camps in response to evolution and to science itself.

Those who came to call themselves "traditionalists" or "fundamentalists" reacted much as the Anglicans in colonial New England had reacted to the smallpox vaccination. For them, science had the power to subvert the natural order by offering to people powers of control over nature that rightly belonged only to God. For modernists, however, science was a gift from God that, far from undermining faith, opened up new possibilities for creating a more God-pleasing world. Theologically, they tended to agree with Horace Greeley, who wrote in the New York *Tribune* on April 20, 1875:

> Take from the whole Bible the idea of special, infallible inspiration which we have so long attached to it, . . . Admit freely the probability of errors. . . . Nothing can take from us the life, the living example, and the precepts of Christ. . .

However, "the living example" alone was not enough for the fundamentalists. In contrast to the modernists, they saw anything less than an infallible, unerring Bible as a threat that would lead inexorably to the destruction of Christian faith. In response to modernist inroads in public discourse through the media and, especially in public education, they passed laws such as the one in Tennessee that provided the excuse for the trial of John Scopes for teaching evolution in a public high school.

Although those who supported the Tennessee law were serious about protecting the faith of their children, the Scopes trial was conceived as a way to garner publicity for the little town of Dayton, Tennessee. But the trial itself took on a life of its own, becoming in the process a media event. A thorough account of the trial, as well as references to many news stories and commentaries about it, can be found in Edward J. Larsen's award-winning 1997 book, *Summer of the Gods.*

By the time of the Scopes trial, most northern and big city media had adopted the modernist perspective. When *Time* magazine started its religion section in April 1923, its sympathies were clearly with the modernists. The articles reproduced in this chapter show that sympathy. At the same time, they clearly outline the theological differences that divided modernists and fundamentalists in the 1920s and that still divide Christians today. They also provide background on the division within the Presbyterian Church that made William Jennings Bryan, populist spokesman and frequent presidential candidate, so eager to take on the cause of the antievolutionists.

Writings by social commentator and critic H.L. Mencken, many of which were published in the *Baltimore Sun* and are readily available in collections of his work, fueled the widespread impression that the media were antireligion. Trial coverage was heavy and sometimes sensationalistic, but it was also more diverse than critics on both sides sometimes acknowledge.

"Why the Anti-Evolution Law Was Introduced" explains the fundamentalist perspective. That article, republished from the *Arkansas Gazette,* also profiles John W. Butler, the author of the law. Butler also wrote trial commentaries that were published primarily in southern newspapers.

"Evolution Case Serious Matter to Older Folk" written by *Sun* reporter Frank R. Kent illustrates the kind of bright writing that could simultaneously be entertaining, informative and offensive. Like his other work, that story shows the influence of secularization theories that dominated the sociology of religion for much of the 20th century, but also gives evidence of a reporter striving to understand what, for him and for many of his readers, was a foreign culture.

In addition to publishing stories by Mencken and Kent, the *Baltimore Sun* also published lengthy, thoughtful analyses of constitutional issues on July 10 and 12, 1925, that provide a sharp contrast to Butler's consistent characterization of the law as championing taxpayers' rights and local control of public education.

Other stories provide a thorough analysis of the modernist and fundamentalist perspectives. Examples of stories that counter the notion of the trial as one between the forces of religion and irreligion can be found in a *Chicago Tribune-New York Times* special published in the *Arkansas Gazette* on July 15, 1925. On July 19, the *Gazette* also published a story by Harriette Ashbrook noting parallels to the trial of Galileo.

Who Is Fundamental?

Time, May 19, 1923

The General Assembly governs the Presbyterian Church. It is now in annual session at Indianapolis. It is the scene of a significant conflict of opinion over modernism in general and Dr. Harry Emerson Fosdick in particular.

On the one side are the so-called Fundamentalists; on the other are Liberals or Modernists who believe that they are more fundamental than the Fundamentalists.

The Fundamentalists. In 1643 was written the Westminster Confession, the constitution of Presbyterian faith. It substituted the authority of the Bible for the authority of the Roman Pope, and it held that the Bible is "the only infallible rule of faith and practice." But who shall decide what the Bible means? One group today insists on a literal interpretation. They are Fundamentalists. They claim that not one jot or one tittle of the Word of God can be wrong. And they seek to oust Liberal preachers who interpret the scriptures in the light of modern thought.

Liberals, like Dr. Fosdick, claim that the age-long experiences of religion remain, but that the interpretation changes with the time. He rejects the biblical ideas of science, and accepts modern conclusions. In a sermon last summer Dr. Fosdick pointed out the many similarities between the story of the Virgin Birth and the stories told of the founders of other religions. This now famous sermon, entitled *Shall the Fundamentalists Win?* made the conservative Presbyterians of Philadelphia attack Dr. Fosdick's right to preach in the pulpit of the First Church, New York. The

Fundamentalists hold that the Bible is proved by prophecies which have come true, and miracles like the Virgin Birth, which demonstrate the Divinity of Christ, and the absolute superiority of Christianity over all other religions. Dr. Fosdick points out the similarities between Christian miracles and those of other religions, and declares that the might of Christianity is in its Christ, not in the prophecies or miracles which have clustered about Him.

Liberals believe themselves to be more fundamental than the Fundamentalists, because their religion does not center on smaller matters of scripture like unscientific geography or unproved miracles, but on a Being who was so Divine that men could see God in Him. While the Fundamentalists see their whole scheme of salvation slipping if science and higher criticism of the Bible are accepted, the Liberals see the whole scheme of salvation rendered ridiculous if unscientific (and to them stories non-essential) in the Bible are held to be prerequisite to Christianity. Both sides of the controversy are interested in science, one claiming ideas like evolution and the reign of law as revelations that can be made friendly to the truths of Christianity, the other holding them to be irreconcilable with Christianity as taught in the Bible.

The conservatives have a strong leader in William J. Bryan. Dr. Fosdick, who, although a Baptist, has been preaching in a Presbyterian Church, is one of the few liberals who has produced real devotional literature, such as his books on "The Meaning of Prayer," "The Second Mile" and "The Meaning of Service." If he is ousted, it will show that the fourth largest Protestant denomination in the United States, caught between the two horns of a dilemma, has chosen to impale itself upon scriptural infallibility rather than leave the interpretation of the Bible to individual conscience, which is too prone to be affected by modern science.

Fosdick

Time, June 4, 1923

William J. Bryan and a slight majority of the governing body of the Presbyterian Church know how Jesus Christ was born. Dr. Harry Emerson Fosdick and many leading Presbyterian ministers do not know. The difference is typical of all differences between Christian "Conservatives" and Christian "Liberals."

At the General Assembly of the Presbyterian Church Dr. Bryan lost his fight to keep evolution out of the schools, but won his fight to condemn sermons delivered by Dr. Fosdick (a Baptist) in a New York Presbyterian Church.

The anti-Fosdick resolution adopted by the Assembly provides that if Dr. Fosdick continues to preach, he shall conform to the following doctrines:

1. The men who wrote the Bible made no mistakes because the Holy Spirit guided them.

2. Jesus Christ was born of Mary, a Virgin.

3. He went to His death "to satisfy divine justice and to reconcile us to God."

4. He rose from the dead with the same physical body with which He died, and He is now sitting on the right hand of His Father, making intercession.

5. He worked miracles.

All of these doctrines, votes the Assembly, are "essential."

Dr. Henry Sloane Coffin, a leading Presbyterian of New York, sharing Dr. Fosdick's views, declares that none of the aforementioned doctrines are essential.

Dr. Coffin's attitude:

1. The Bible is not without error. It is the Word of God only in so far as it accords with the Word made flesh in Christ.

2. "I do not know how our Lord was born, and I certainly refuse to teach the Virgin birth as essential doctrine."

3. Christ died for our sins, but no single interpretation of the Cross is adequate.

4. Death did not conquer Christ, but the Scriptures do not teach a physical resurrection.

5. Jesus did not consider faith in His miracles essential.

Dr. Coffin teaches that loyalty to Christ is the one essential.

In agreement with Dr. Coffin is Rev. William P. Merrill, of the Riverside Presbyterian Church and Rev. John Kelman of the Fifth Avenue Presbyterian Church. Thus, the four leading Presbyterian Churches of New York City are absolutely opposed to the reactionary theology which the General Assembly would like to force upon them.

An analysis of the Presbyterian Church indicates that it is divided into two groups: the ultra-conservatives and the "tolerants." The "tolerants" include both conservatives and liberals, who, while differing in their views, do not believe that these differences justify a refusal to work together for greater common purposes.

One subtle point remains to be recorded: the Presbyterian Church, by condemning Dr. Fosdick, took its stand on old conservative theology, but previously, by rejection of Bryan's anti-evolution program, it also took its stand in favor of modern science.

Baptists

Time, June 4, 1923

The session of Northern Baptists at Atlantic City was calm. Dr. John Roach Straton was hissed, but that was soon forgotten. (He had fulminated against liberal Baptist college presidents such as Faunce of Brown and Burton of Chicago.)

The so-called "Fundamentalists," lacking a Bryan, fared badly, and protested against machine politics at the convention. Their fight will be carried on through a new-formed Bible Union which has flatly denounced Dr. Woelfkin of New York.

Seventeen thousand baptisms by foreign missionaries in the last year were reported—a record.

Science Serves God

Time, June 4, 1923

A great and glorious manifesto of liberalism has been issued. It says to the world that there is no warfare between science and religion. It is signed by Secretaries Hoover and Davis, and by 40 other distinguished Americans of various denominations, who include: Bishops Lawrence, Manning and McConnell, President Angell of Yale and President Burton of Chicago, Dr. William J. Mayo, Frank O. Lowden, Admiral Sims, Julius Kruttschmitt, Frank A. Vanderlip, Victor Lawson, Henry Van Dyke, Professor Henry Fairfield Osborn.

The manifesto:

"We, the undersigned, deeply regret that in recent controversies there has been a tendency to present science and religion as irreconcilable and antagonistic domains of thought, for, in fact, they meet distinct human needs. And in the rounding out of human life they supplement rather than displace or oppose each other.

"The purpose of science is to develop, without prejudice or preconception of any kind, a knowledge of the facts, the laws and the processes of nature. The even more important task of religion, on the other hand, is to develop the consciences, the ideals and the aspirations of mankind. Each of these two activities represents a deep and vital function of the soul of man, and both are necessary for the life, the progress and the happiness of the human race.

"It is a sublime conception of God which is furnished by science, and one wholly consonant with the highest ideals of religion, when it represents Him as revealing Himself through countless ages in the development of the earth as an abode for man and in the age-long inbreathing of life into its constituent matter, culminating in man with his spiritual nature and all his Godlike powers."

Why the Anti-Evolution Law Was Introduced

Arkansas Gazette, July 14, 1925

"I believe that the teaching of evolution as the origin of man is contrary to the teachings of the Bible and to the law of God as expressed through His Word, the Bible. That is why I introduced a bill making it illegal to teach evolution in the schools and colleges of Tennessee. There were enough other men in the legislature who believed as I do to pass this bill, making it a law, and I am satisfied that their action will pass the test of any court.

"For some time it has been against the law of Tennessee to teach the Bible in the public schools or to allow the teaching of any system of religion, although the Bible can be read in such schools without comment. If this law can be upheld, I am satisfied that a law which, in my opinion and those of thousands of other Tennessee parents, would tend to prevent the making of infidels of our children can be equally enforced."

Sitting on a bench in the courtyard in the little town of Fayetteville, Tenn., his nearest postoffice, John W. Butler, author of the bill which has aroused so much excitement throughout the country and has directed the eyes of the world toward Dayton, Tenn., where a school teacher is to be tried for breaking this law, thus spoke his mind to an interviewer for the New York Times.

A huge bulk of a man, with a kindly eye, he fairly exudes sincerity and honesty. His neighbors believe in him and have confidence in him. His word is his bond and, once given, will not be broken. He has a reputation for keeping it.

To get at the environments that produced the measure it is necessary to tell something of the town and of the man.

Lafayette (pronounced Lafay-ette in Tennessee) is a little town of a few score inhabitants, situated about 65 miles from Nashville, and 16 miles from the nearest railroad, which in turn is a little branch that runs from the N., C. & St. L. at Gallatin, Tenn., the nearest "big" town. A few big cars make the trip between Hartsville, the terminal of the branch road, and Lafayette daily to meet the one train. The rest of the travel is in small cars of a popular make, which are the only kind of vehicle that will traverse the so-called roads of most of that section.

Away from everybody and having no railroad, the inhabitants run on what they term "sun time," varying their clocks and watches with the change of the sun. The automobile is the only change in the methods of separating town and travel since the days of the Revolution.

Three miles beyond this town John W. Butler has his home. His house was built by his grandfather 50 years ago and Mr. Butler was born in Macon county, raised there, married there, and has five children, three boys at home on the farm, two daughters married and four grandchildren. He is 49 years old.

"We are poor folks in this section of the country," he said, as, with the interviewer, he drove out to his home in his Ford. He explained, as he cranked it, that economy had forced him to buy one without starter or demountable rims. "But we believe in God and we believe in the Bible. We feel that we have the right to say what our children shall be taught in their schools. If we haven't, we want to know who has.

"I am not opposed to the teaching of fundamental facts of science," he continued. "It is when the school teacher begins to interpret certain scientific theories as facts and to teach them as facts to the children that I commence to object.

"The law is plain. It forbids the teacher hired with the Tennessee taxpayers' money from teaching the children of those taxpayers that they are descended from monkeys or other inferior forms of animal life. It has been violated, according to my information and the violator will be tried the same as if he had violated any other state law.

"I don't believe that I am descended from a monkey. I don't believe that I or my neighbors have gradually evolved from some inferior form of animal life. I consider it a direct denial of the Bible, on which our government is founded, to teach any such theory as a fact, and my law was designed with the approval of my neighbors and thousands of other Tennesseans, to prevent such teachings."

Mr. Butler wrote out the following statement in support of his position:

"I have been asked why I introduced Tennessee's anti-evolution law and the purpose of that law.

"In the first place the Bible is the foundation upon which our American government is built and the teaching of any theory which denies the Bible will, I believe, destroy the principles which have made our nation what it is and for which our soldiers have fought and shed their blood from Bunker Hill to the battlefields of France.

"The law is not directed against evolution, which has for its object the improvement of plants and animals but against evolution which denies the Bible story of creation and teaches that man has descended from a lower order of animals and did not come into existence by a creative act of God, as stated in the Bible.

"The text-book 'The Story of Mankind,' which has been used in the Tennessee schools for more than two years, teaches that man's first man-like ancestor was half ape and half monkey, and that this state was reached by evolution through the jellyfish and different reptiles, and other forms of animal life.

"Darwin says that man is an off shoot of the Old World monkeys and so his theory denies the Bible story that God created man in His own image. The teachings of this theory of evolution breaks the hearts of fathers and mothers who give their children the advantage of higher education in which they lose their respect for Christianity and become infidels.

"The evolutionists against whom the law is directed deny the immortality of the soul, the virgin birth of Christ, the resurrection of the body, and that the Bible is the inspired Word of God. If we are to exist as a nation the principles upon which our government is founded must not be destroyed which they surely would be if we became a nation of infidels, and we will become that very thing, a nation of infidels, when we set the Bible aside as being untrue and put evolution in its place.

"To uphold the law is to uphold the government and Christianity; to destroy the law is to attempt to destroy Christianity and to say that a state has no right to control its own schools.

"Believing that the law would check the growth of atheism and infidelity and that the principles upon which our government stands would be safeguarded thereby, I introduced the bill which is Known as House Bill 185.

"It passed the House without debate by an overwhelming majority. I talked to the members of the House privately and they were almost unanimous in their support.

"The measure met with some opposition in the Senate, but passed by a good majority when it came up for final reading, although Senators Evan and Sims made a desparate fight to defeat it.

"Governor Peay's office was flooded with telegrams urging him to veto the measure, but he signed it with his approval and also sent a nice message back to the House with the signed document.

"Tennessee law does not permit the Bible to be taught in its public schools nor does it allow any system of religion to be taught, but the Bible can be read without comment, and as the Tennessee law does not permit a doctrine to be taught the purpose of which would be to make Christians then I maintain that it is not fair to the people who pay the taxes to support the schools to be forced to send their children to schools where they will be taught a doctrine which causes them to become infidels and have no respect for Christianity. This, I maintain, is what the teaching of evolution does for our children.

"Christians believe that the Bible is the inspired Word of God. They believe that it is true. They believe that after death their bodies will be resurrected and that they will live again in a beautiful place called heaven, where there will be eternal grace and joy."

Mr. Butler is proud of his farm, his children and his wife. He is proud of the business he has built up as a thresher. Although he raises tobacco among his other diversified crops, he does not use the "weed" in any form. Indeed, there is a singular lack of smoking among the inhabitants of Lafayette, although tobacco is grown in large quantities in that whole section.

There is a surprisingly strong sentiment in favor of the evolution bill throughout the state. I talked to prominent ment. [sic] including bankers, farmers, merchants, lawyers and newspaper editors and almost to a man they displayed the same attitude that the evolution question was one for Tennessee to settle and that outside interference was resented.

They do not like the idea of the so-called celebrated men from other states coming in to meddle in their affairs and feel that such men as Darrow, Colby, Bryan and others have no business entering the case in any capacity.

Evolution Case Serious Matter to Older Folk

Kent Finds Religious Sentiment Silences Jeers at Dayton Case—Bulk of Citizens Cling to Bible—Flooding of Light on Subject Seen as Justifying Proceedings

Frank R. Kent, *The Baltimore Sun,* July 9, 1925

CHATTANOOGA, TENN., July 8

IT is easy enough to come out here and make fun of this evolution trial, but when you get here you do not want to do it. Not that there are not plenty of funny features: not that there are lacking loads of people to laugh about it, or that it does not abound in cheap and clownish color and was not casually conceived as a publicity effort—it does and was.

YET, in spite of all these things, few could fail to sense that back of the whole business, disconnected with the principals and disassociated from the boomers and jokers, there is a sincere something at which it isn't pleasant to jeer. What it is, of course, is the religious sentiment of the people—not the people you meet around town here or those who drive you out from Chattanooga, show you the place and explain the background of the case, but the quiet people, the inarticulate people back in the country, in the mountains, on the farms and in the towns, too, whose lives center around the churches and who are past middle age.

EVERYBODY here agrees that from three-fourths to four-fifths of the citizens of Tennessee do not believe in the theory of evolution and do believe in the biblical story of the Creation. It is also agreed that Tennessee people in this respect are not an isolated folk, but typical, and that what is true here is true largely of most of the other States of the country.

Whether these people are on the right track or are misled and uninformed, whether they are bright or blind is beside the mark. The fact is
that in this State and in other States the great bulk of the population are
church-going people who unshakably believe in the Old as well as the
New Testament, who want to believe and not to think.

IF the evolutionary theory is sound it will win its way ultimately and
the generations to come gradually will accept scientific truth and adjust
their religious beliefs to the facts. But it is not to be expected that the
older generation of the present day will do so.

The justification for this trial, even if it degenerates into a farce, is not
only that it opposes a backward step by a State, but that it will flood the
whole great subject with light and force people to read and think, which
things, however commically garbed, sweep toward truth.

But that makes it none the less hard for the countless thousands of
men and women no longer young and who do not want to think, whose
years are numbered and who, sliding down hill toward the inevitable
end, grip closer to them the rigid faith implanted in their youth as the
one thing that braces them against the approach of death.

IT is in the years following fifty that the tendency to become rigidly
religious strengthens. It is the period of repentance, the time when the
immoral begin to become moral, the crooked go straight, the reckless acquire caution. The elemental biblical belief in the hereafter is seized with
a new tenacity and the yearning for something solid and simple in the
shape of soul insurance grows intense. Fear of the dark unknown from
which we are so happily free in youth seizes the souls of those who feel
themselves slipping. They hold on to hope and don't want to argue about it.

THAT is why in Tennessee the sentiment behind the anti-evolution
bill was so strong in the State. The legislators, who do not believe in it
were afraid to vote against it. That is why in Tennessee and everywhere
else it is those on the sunny side of fifty who largely laugh at the Garden

of Eden tale and approach and embrace evolution with open and eager minds, while those on the other side of fifty pull down their intellectual shutters and resent the effort to shake their foundations. It is the older generations that are the firmest fundamentalists; it is the young, the red-blooded and vigourous who laugh about the monkeys and apes.

ATTEMPT to convince the elderly fundamentalist against his will is a futile thing. It isn't worth while to explain that evolution does not take away from his religion and his hope of immortality. To believe that, he has to build all over again from the ground up, has to reorganize himself mentally and spiritually, and he is too stiff. It can't be done.

With the birthdays rolling swiftly by, his joints stiffening, his youth gone, he wants to hold what he has and is afraid of what he has not. No amount of argument, no array of acts avail with the older church-going generations which have absorbed the Biblical teachings from the start.

THAT is the situation in this State, and in all the others, and that is why, whatever the outcome of this trial to begin on Friday, so far as they are concerned, nothing will be changed. Whatever the verdict, those who believe in the Bible literally and reject the evolution theory as an abhorrent and irreverent thing will not weaken in their convictions any more than the upholding of Mr. Scopes will cause evolutionists to concede themselves in error. Beliefs will not be changed by the trial. No one will convert anyone else.

The real result will be upon the generation now in the schools and those to follow. It is not a battle, as Mr. Bryan believes, in which his side can crush the other because God is with it. Nor, as those on the other side are convinced, will the scientific facts render untenable the belief of the majority. The real effect is upon the children and upon the children's children. Whether the Tennessee law is knocked out or sustained is not particularly important. The vital thing is that as the generations pass the inevitable adaptation of religion to the facts will proceed and the world gradually get nearer the truth, and this Dayton discussion helps a little toward that end.

SO that it makes little difference whether the disposition of the Dayton people to commercialize the trial and advertise their town and the disposition of the metropolitan newspaper men here to magnify that disposition makes a farce of the thing or not. It still will have its effect upon the future.

However, when you reflect upon the whole business it isn't a funny thing at bottom.

15

Pulling Together

World War II marked a turning point. For nearly three centuries, most Americans saw their country as a Protestant, or at least a Christian, nation. Even the Supreme Court had confirmed that vision in countless court cases, including the highly influential 1811 case of *Ruggles v. Williams* in which the court, with the words "we are a Christian people," ruled that blasphemy against the Christian God, but not other gods, is a punishable offense. But the threat of war and then its reality suddenly made it necessary, as never before, to promote national unity and gain wholehearted support from everyone, not just from those in the cultural and religious mainstream.

The first challenge was the Jews. As persecutions in Germany became known, there was a general fear that anti-Semitism in the United States would thwart efforts to enlist American support to combat the Nazi threat. To offset prejudice against American Jews and to prevent the kind of reprisals against German-Americans of all faiths that had occurred during World War I, government leaders urged tolerance and forbearance, reminding Americans of the Bill of Rights's guarantees of freedom and justice for all. But when Japan attacked Pearl Harbor, those guarantees did not extend to the Japanese-Americans who saw their property confiscated as they were rounded up and relocated to camps where they became virtual prisoners of war.

In spite of protests from some Christian churches about the treatment of Japanese, most churches considered World War II a just war and gave to the war effort their wholehearted support. The "peace churches," which opposed all war, and the occasional clergy who spoke out against war or against particular military actions were, with some exceptions, tolerated in the interest of distinguishing American democracy from German and Japanese totalitarianism.

However, religions or religious leaders who interfered with recruitment efforts or whose allegiance to America seemed problematic were a different matter. Of those religions, the most troublesome were the Jehovah's Witnesses, who throughout the 1930s and early 1940s were frequently singled out for persecution and arrest, first for their proselytizing activities and then for their refusal, on religious grounds, to pledge obedience and allegiance to any earthly power. In response, the Witnesses fought back through appeals of their convictions that ultimately resulted in Supreme Court rulings that greatly enhanced constitutional protection for unpopular religious and political groups and their opinions.

The stories in this chapter trace World War II-era efforts to bring minorities into the mainstream from the early calls for tolerance of Jews through the 1943 Supreme Court case, *West Virginia State Board of Education v. Barnett,* protecting the right of Jehovah's Witness children to refuse to recite the Pledge of Allegiance.

Throughout the late 1930s, news stories from Europe mentioned Nazi persecution of Jews. On November 11, 1938, the *New York Times* carried the story of Kristallnacht—the night of broken glass—when German Nazis and Nazi sympathizers vandalized and destroyed Jewish homes and businesses. Two months later, Gov. Herbert H. Lehman of New York used his inaugural address to explain the meaning, purpose and value of religious freedom for all. The *New York Times* published the full text of that speech on January 13, 1939. A year later, it also published the full text of Attorney General Frank Murphy's speech as a sidebar to the story, "Bigotry Imperils All, Murphy Says" reproduced in this chapter because it includes information on early support for a Jewish homeland as a "solution to the Jewish problem."

Throughout the period church pages regularly reported on sermons, many of which encouraged support while also reassuring church members that God would protect them and bless their efforts. A week after the bombing of Pearl Harbor, on December 15, 1941, a page one headline in the *Rocky Mountain News* proclaimed "Clergymen of City Back War Effort." Among the many stories of that genre that appeared on the same day, the one reproduced in this chapter from the *New York Times* church page is noteworthy for its reminder of the equality of all in the eyes of God and under the laws of the nation.

As government restrictions on Japanese-Americans progressed, those same pleas for acceptance, along with protests of government action, became common themes in mainline religious publications. However, little of that found its way into daily newspapers. "War Ban on Liquor Urged by Women," is one exception, but as was typical it buried the protest of treatment of the Japanese-Americans among other church concerns.

In general, however, churches encouraged unquestioning support for wartime endeavors. A December 15, 1941, *New York Times* story, for example, reported that the Right Rev. Henry Knox Sherill, Episcopal Bishop of Massachusetts, had launched a drive to raise $500,000 to support "Army and Navy Men." On December 24, 1941, the *Rocky Mountain News* reported that the Rev. Frank E. Eden, Pacific Coast director for the Northern Baptist Convention and former pastor of a Denver congregation, had encouraged women to support the war effort by knitting and sewing garments for soldiers during church services.

Some clergy and some churches did speak out against war or particular military operations. A December 15, 1941, *Rocky Mountain News* story, picked up from the *Associated Press,* reported that the Rev. John Haynes Holmes, pastor of the Community Church in New York City, had resigned from the ministry because he could not condone using the church "to bless, sanction or support war." The *Associated Press* story in this chapter, reproduced from the *Rocky Mountain News,* notes clergy protests over saturation bombings of European cities. For comparison purposes, a very much shortened version of the same story can be found in the rival *Denver Post.*

An October 5, 1940, *New York Times* roundup of church news reported that there would be a "Christian Loyalty Parade" in the Bronx the next day, but also that 21 conscientious objectors had registered with the United Lutheran Synod of New York. On December 1, it reported Quaker efforts to organize alternative service opportunities for pacifists. In contrast to those stories, "Sect Members Ask Draft Exemption," reproduced in this chapter, shows the suspicion directed toward Jehovah's Witnesses. That suspicion of groups that would not be conventionally patriotic led to the Supreme Court decision, reported in "Compulsory Salute to Flag Barred," protecting Witnesses' right to refuse to say the Pledge of Allegiance. Pro and con editorials on that decision can be found in the June 16, 1943, *Washington Post* and Washington *Evening Star* respectively.

Bigotry Imperils All, Murphy Says

Jews Only a 'Smoke-Screen,' He Tells Palestine Backers—Warns of 'Virus' Here

Special to the *New York Times*, January 8, 1940

WASHINGTON, January 7—"The world will make a grave mistake if it concludes that the revival of intolerance is primarily or peculiarly a Jewish Problem," Attorney General Frank Murphy said today, delivering before the National Conference of the United Palestine Appeal his first public address since his nomination to the United States Supreme Court.

Declaring that "the Jews are serving as a smoke-screen to conceal more aggressive designs of power-mad men," Mr. Murphy warned that "not guns nor battleships will ultimately preserve democracy."

"Democracy will be saved if as a people we are wise enough to know that if we do not respect others' faiths the day may come when other men will not respect our faiths."

Count Rene' Doynel de Saint-Quentin, the French Ambassador, and Alfred Duff Cooper, former First Lord of the Admiralty of Great Britain, were among the other speakers. The Ambassador declared that the solution of the refugee problem was one of the foremost war aims of the Allies. Mr. Duff Cooper called on his country to do more for the Jewish homeland.

Murphy Warns of Bigotry Here

Attorney General Murphy, after recalling that "America itself came into being at the hands of harried and homeless people searching for the blessings of peace and freedom," warned that there was a reason for this country as well as Europe in the rise of forces abroad which oppressed not only Jews but Catholics and Protestants, too, when the time was ripe.

"For the virus of anti-Semitism has made itself felt here as well as abroad," he declared.

"The purveyors of hatred" were laboring to bring to the United States the same conditions of group hatred and civil war that had destroyed the peace of Europe, all the while representing themselves as defenders of God, America, and the Constitution, he said. This "professional hate-mongering" would be combated by the government but, in the main, "American democracy must look for its defense to the wisdom of the people and their determination not to be led on to the paths that have taken other peoples to communism and fascism."

There might be honest differences of opinion on matters of national policy, Mr. Murphy continued, but if American democracy were to be preserved there could be no disagreement on one policy: "the creed of tolerance which for a century and a half has sustained civil liberty and representative government in this land."

Men Not "Cattle," Envoy Says

Count de Saint-Quentin declared that "we are no longer willing that hundreds of thousands or millions of people should be branded as outlaws by the country in which they had lived, often for several centuries, and should be thrown without resources and indeed almost without the barest necessities, on the highway of international charity."

"Nor do we approve those exchanges of populations which deal with men as they would with cattle and which create much havoc and impose such great suffering," he said. "Peace and the new order it will establish will make possible the voluntary repatriation of a certain number of refugees and the inevitable departure of those who have usurped their homes.

"As for Palestine, it will remain the very symbol of voluntary immigration by energetic men guided by their faith and their traditions."

Mr. Duff-Cooper evoked prolonged applause when he asserted that in view of the unprecedented and "ghastly persecution of the Jews, which is a disgrace and a branding shame not only to the countries that are taking part in it but to the whole of Europe and the whole of Christendom," it was now obligatory upon Great Britain to do more for the Jews in the rebuilding of Palestine than she "ever promised or intended to do before."

The policy of seeking to show no favoritism in Palestine, either to Jews of Arabs, he said, had failed because it was unworkable and called for a change in which the government must show "bias upon one side or the other." Since the Arabs already had a great domain which they were free to govern in their own way, Mr. Duff-Cooper suggested that if the Arabs wished no longer to remain in Palestine, "vast spaces of territory await their expansion."

A resolution appealing to the British government to open the doors of Palestine to unrestricted Jewish immigration was adopted by the conference.

Expert Lauds Palestine Farming

Dr. Walter D. Lowdermilk, assistant chief of the Soil Conservation Service of the Department of Agriculture, told the conference that the Jewish agricultural colonization of Palestine was "one of the most remarkable works of restoration and reclamation of waste lands that I have seen in three continents."

Senator King of Utah, speaking at the banquet tonight, warned that if the sweep of brute force were not halted 1940 might bring the complete disappearance of all small nations.

Dr. Abba Hillel Silver of Cleveland was re-elected national chairman, Dr. Stephen S. Wise, Louis Lipsky, Dr. Solomon Goldman of Chicago,

Dr. Israel Goldstein and Judge Borris Rothenberg of New York were named national co-chairmen, with Dr. Wise heading the executive committee and Mr. Lipsky the administrative committee.

Elected as honorary chairmen were Dr. Cyrus Adler of Philadelphia, Professor Albert Einstein, Governor Lehman, Judge Julian W. Mack of New York, Henry Monsky of Omaha, Nathan Straus of New York and Miss Henrietta Szold.

Arthur M. Lamport of New York was again elected national treasurer with Abraham L. Liebowitz and Louis Rimsky associate treasurers. Selected as vice chairmen were Dr. Barnett B. Brickner of Cleveland, Leon Gellman of New York, Rabbi James G. Heller of Cincinnati, Rabbi Edward L. Israel of Baltimore, Judge Louis E. Levinthal of Philadelphia, Elihu D. Stone of Boston, Joe Weingarten of Houston, Texas, and David Wertheim of New York. Charles Bess of New York was elected honorary secretary.

Use of Nation's Force in Spirit of Policing Urged by Sockman, Who Decries Hatred

New York Times, December 15, 1941

While as a nation we are now committed to the use of force, it should be used in the spirit of police putting down international lawlessness and not in the spirit of hatred, the Rev. Ralph W. Sockman declared yesterday in his sermon in Christ Church, Methodist, at Park Avenue and Sixtieth Street.

"We must not allow hatred of persons or peoples to poison the springs of our patriotism," he pleaded. "We must respect the personalities of the loyal American citizens whose ancestry belongs to nations now at war with us, but who are in no sense to blame for the actions of their ancestral governments. Some of our best citizens are of German, Japanese, and Italian descent.

"Let us remember that it is one of the glories of our country that it holds that all men are created equal regardless of race or class or creed. In winning the war, let us not lose the ideals which have inspired the American way of life, for what shall it profit a nation if she gain the whole world and lose her own soul?"

War Ban on Liquor Urged by Women

Drive Opened by Presbyterian Missionary Groups to Gain Return of Prohibition—PUBLICITY AIM STRESSED—Aid for Japanese Evacuees in West Also Asked by Church Conference

Special to the *New York Times,* May 19, 1942

Atlantic City, N.J., May 18—The Women's missionary organizations of the Presbyterian Church in the U.S.A., with a membership of 1,500,000, opened today a campaign to prohibit the sale and manufacture of liquor in the United States for the duration of the war.

The action was taken by 500 women delegates to the quadrennial session of the organization in the Hotel Dennis.

It took the form of a resolution, which said:

"Whereas in this time when our country is at war we are urged to deny ourselves unnecessary indulgence, to maintain physical fitness and to conserve material, we resolve that, in the interest of the conservation of both material and human resources, we desire the prohibition of the manufacture and sale of intoxicating beverages within the United States of America for the duration of the present emergency. We further resolve that we will undertake to promote public sentiment toward the proposition by seeking publicity for it in our local and church papers and by making it a topic of conversation."

Campaign Steps Outlined

Mrs. Paul Moser of Topeka, Kan., who was elected chairman of the new executive council of the organization, said she "would not be surprised if other church organizations took similar steps." Instructions of the procedure to be followed in the campaign will be mailed to the member groups within the next week, she added.

The Rev. Cameron P. Hall, Philadelphia director of social education and action of the board of Christian education in the Presbyterian Church, will be in charge of the campaign. He will present the plan to the meeting of the general assembly of the church in Milwaukee next week.

Copies of the resolution will be sent to members of Congress while the various synods are expected to work through the representatives of their respective districts in the State Legislatures.

The delegates adopted another resolution before adjournment petitioning Congress to enact Senate Bill 860, known as the Shepard bill, prohibiting the sale of intoxicating beverages within and near military bases.

Fellowship for Japanese

Another resolution in the form of a letter sent by Synodical groups bordering on the Pacific Ocean to those of the next line to the east into which Japanese evacuees are being moved urged that the evacuees be "encouraged by fellowship, consultation and practical assistance." Such action, the letter said, would "help them through this time of trial and strengthen the efforts of Christian Japanese to make this a time of great evangelistic ingathering of non-Christian evacuees." A similar message of encouragement was sent to the commissions on aliens and prisoners of war, which represents all Protestant interdenominational work among the interned.

Elected to the national executive committee with Mrs. Moser were members from the Pacific Area: Mrs. J.C. McClung, Los Angeles, and Mrs. James H Edgar, Ashland, Ore.; Central Area: Mrs. Thomas A. Jenkins, Knoxville, Tenn., and Mrs. Gerritt Labotz, Youngstown, Ohio: Eastern area: Mrs. Arthur V. Bishop, Carlisle, Pa., and Mrs. Horace Z. Goas, West Orange, N.J.

Clergymen, Writers Ask End to Bombings

Rocky Mountain News, March 6, 1944

New York, March 5 (AP)—Twenty-eight clergymen and writers have signed an appeal to Christians to "examine themselves concerning their participation in this carnival of death," John Nevin Sayre, co-secreatry of the American Fellowship of Reconciliation announced today.

The plea is contained in a foreword to the organization's publication of "Massacre Bombing," an article by Vera Brittain, British author, on what she calls the "obliteration bombing" of enemy-occupied countries of Europe, and purporting to detail effects of Allied bombings of 10 German cities.

"Apparently," said Sayre, " the same sort of bombing is in store for

Rome and other occupied cities unless public opinion can stop it."

The foreword said that in the first World War "some shreds of the rules of war were observed," but today warring countries "pay little heed to the former decencies and chivalry."

Sayre, in a postscript to the article, supported proposals for "open towns" or other non-military sanctuary areas, and expressed fear that the United Nations might be approaching use of poison gas.

Signers included Dr. George A. Buttrick, Dr. Allan Knight Chalmers, Dr. Harry Emerson Fosdick, Dr. John Haynes Holmes, all of New York; Dr. Henry H. Crane, Detroit; Miss Josephine Johnson, author; Dr. E. Stanley Jones, former Methodist missionary to India; Dr. Rufus Jones, Havorford College; Dr. Kenneth Scott Latourette, Yale Divinity School; Rt. Rev. W. Appleton Lawrence, Episcopal bishop of Western Massachusetts; Rt. Rev. Walter Mitchell, bishop of Arizona; Rev. Edwin McNeil Posteat, Colgate-Rochester Divinity School; Dr. Richard Roberts, United Church of Canada; Dr. Oswald Garrison Villard, former editor of the Nation.

Sect Members Ask Draft Exemption

Brooklyn Board Puzzled by 50 Jehovah's Witnesses
Who Object to Army Service

New York Times, January 10, 1941

Out of the 280 local draft boards in New York City a singular problem in one area yesterday plagued the men who are administering the Selective Service Act in New York. All of the eligible males of a religious sect known as Jehovah's Witnesses claimed exemption as conscientious objectors.

While 264 men were taken into the Army yesterday, for a year of training under the Selective Service Act, Colonel Arthur V. McDermott, city administrator, declared that no other board in the city presented the problem that has snarled Local Board 133 of Brooklyn, taking in an area that includes Brooklyn Heights.

It was learned that members of Board 133 have certified two of the sect for service, from which appeals have been taken. But David Moffat of 2 Montague Terrace, Brooklyn, chairman of the board, refuses to talk about it.

"If you give these people publicity you only increase the problems of the local board," he said. "This job is already a headache."

Fifty in Sect Involved

It was learned that at least fifty members of the sect have declared themselves as objectors, or, as they are known among selective service officials, CO's, and the status of many of them remains to be determined by what happens to the two who have appealed.

Under orders issued Jan. 3, the appeals go directly to the Department of Justice. There an effort will be made to determine when the registrants joined the sect. In any event the members of the group may be called for non-combatant service in cleaning of company streets and similar tasks.

While the problem of Jehovah's Witnesses remained unsettled yesterday, another snarl was straightened out, according to Colonel McDermott. Under a ruling that he said had come from the War Department, aliens who claim to have filed an application for their first papers as citizens will be accepted when they cannot produce papers. It was said that their answers on questionnaires served the purpose of affidavits as to their citizenship status.

Rejection Rate Rises

The city's two induction centers "processed" 342 men from the city yesterday. Of these, seventy-seven were rejected, bringing the rejection percentage upward to 22.51 for the day after a period in which the rate steadily declined. The men accepted went by afternoon trains to Fort Dix, N.J., and to Camp Upton at Yaphank, L.I.

Only one man was held over. He could not complete his physical examination.

The tabulation of the day's inductions follow:

Borough	Exam.	Acc.	Rej.	To Camp	Held Over
Manhattan	115	87	28	87	0
The Bronx	69	51	17	51	1
Brooklyn	86	68	18	68	0
Queens	72	58	14	58	0
Totals	342	264	77	264	1

Compulsory Salute to Flag Barred by High Court Decision

The Washington Post, June 15, 1943

By the *Assoicated Press*

Speaking out against the use of coercion to weld national unity, the Supreme Court held yesterday that States cannot compel school children to salute the American Flag.

"Compulsory unification of opinion achieves only the unanimity of the graveyard" said the court's 6-3 opinion by Justice Jackson, handed down as the Nation observed Flag Day.

"To believe that patriotism will not flourish if patriotic ceremonies are voluntary and spontaneous instead of a compulsory routine is to make an unflattering estimate of the appeal of our institutions to free minds.

"If there is any fixed star in our constitutional constellation, it is that no official, high or petty, can prescribe what shall be orthodox in politics, nationalism, religion, or other matters of opinion, or force citizens to confess by word or act their faith therein. If there are any circumstances which permit an exception, they do not now occur to us."

1940 Decision Overruled

The court thus overruled its 1940 decision upholding the constituionality of the Flag salute. It outlawed in the case before the court, a Flag salute requirement of the West Virginia Board of Education. In both cases, the Flag salute was challenged by members of Jehovah's Witnesses on grounds of religious freedom.

Justice Frankfurter, who wrote the majority opinion in 1940, dissented today with Justices Roberts and Reed. Frankfurter asserted that an act promoting good citizenship and national allegiance is "within the domain of Government authority, and is therefore to be judged by the same considerations of power and of constitutionality as those involved in the many claims of immunity from civil obedience because of religious scruples."

State Antisedition Law

At the same time, the court unanimously declared unconstitutional a Mississippi law prohibiting statements or the distribution of literature "which reasonably tends to create an attitude of stubborn refusal to salute, honor or respect" the Flag or Government of the United States or Mississippi."

Noting the court's decision in the Flag salute case, Justice Roberts declared that if the Fourteenth amendment bans enforcement of the salute it also prohibits the "imposition of punishment for urging and advising that, on religious grounds, citizens refrain from saluting the Flag."

The decision reversed the conviction of members of Jehovah's Witnesses charged with violating the law through statements criticizing the President for sending the army overseas and through the distribution of literature.

The West Virginia board of education has required school children to salute the Flag and repeat the oath of allegiance. Expulsion from school was the penalty for failure to do so. Parents of expelled children could be prosecuted on truancy charges.

Saying there was no question in this case whether officials may foster national unity by persuasion and example, the court declared the problem was "whether under our Constitution compulsion as here employed is a permissible means for its achievement." The opinion added:

"Probably no deeper division of our people could proceed from any provocation then [sic] from finding it necessary to choose what doctrine and whose program public educational officials shall compel youth to unite in embracing.

"Those who begin coercive elimination of dissent soon find themselves exterminating dissenters. Compulsory unification of opinion achieves only the unanimity of the graveyard. It seems trite but necessary to say that the first amendment to our Constitution was designed to avoid these ends by avoiding these beginnings."

Other Cases Before Court

Among other actions, before adjourning until next Monday, the court:

Refused to review the conviction of the Rev. Kurt E. B. Molzahn, pastor of the Old Zion Church in Philadelphia, of charges of conspiring to violate the Espionage Act by aiding an attempt to deliver military secrets to Germany and Japan.

Uphold in a 5-to-3 decision an Interstate Commerce Commission (I.C.C.) order permitting railroads to charge local rates for grain reshipped from Chicago to Eastern destinations after arriving by water over the Ilinois waterways.

Agreed to review a decision that Associate Industries of New York State, Inc., with a membership of 1356 persons, firms and corporations, had a right to test in the courts the validity of price-fixing orders of the bituminous coal division of the Interior Department.

Refused to review a decision that land granted by the United States to a State to be used for school purposes, and not to be disposed of except at public sale, may be obtained by the United States through condemnation proceedings.

Motion Picture Decision

Refused to review a decision that a 1940 motion picture entitled "We Who Are Young" had not infringed the copyright on a book with the same title published in 1936.

Refused to review a decision that the Chicago, Burlington & Quincy Railroad Co. had the right to acquire by condemnation proceedings a group of tracks serving industries located in the north Kansas City (Missouri) industrial district.

Refused to review a decision that "one conducting a business inseparably connected with gambling" may not recover under the Sherman Antitrust Act, for injuries resulting from "a competitions-squeezing combination of his competitors."

Refused the wage-hour administrator a review of a decision denying an injunction against violation of the Wage-Hour Act by T. Buettner & Co., Chicago, which was said to have already stopped the alleged offenses.

Bankruptcy Case

Refused review to Paul Douchan, convicted in the Federal District Court at Detroit of concealing from his trustee in bankruptcy real estate bonds with a par value of $26,200.

Refused to review a decision holding unconstitutional a section of the Federal Firearms Act providing that the possession of any firearm from which the manufacturer's serial number has been removed shall be presumptive evidence that the firearm was received from across a State line.

Agreed to review an Interstate Commerce Commission order denying the Chicago & North Western Railway Co. a certificate to operate a motor vehicle service between designated points as an auxiliary to the railroad.

Refused to review a decision that Ferdinand A. Kertess, identified as a German national, had no legal right to appeal from a decision by the Federal District Court at New York accepting a plea of nolo contendre from the Chemical Marketing Co. Inc., to charges of unlawfully exporting metals.

PART 3

Detached Journalism
in a Changing World

Theologians have written volumes about the effect of World War II on the collective emotional state of the nation. The atrocities of Hitler's death camps, the devastation of the atom bomb and the losses to families whose loved ones died in battle all left Americans with a sense of fear about the future, a knowledge of the extremes of human evils and a sobriety bought with tragedy. As America began the rebuilding of lives and businesses, the singleness of purpose that helped the nation be a strong defender in war created a spirit of cooperation during peace. The late 1940s and 1950s became a time of ecumenical foment, phenomenal Christian church growth and a sense of consensus around Judeo-Christian values and beliefs. Historian William G. McLoughlin Jr. noted in his 1959 book *Modern Revivalism* that World War II

> . . . brought a change in the inchoate pietistic movement, as it did throughout American life . . . the horrors of the war itself and the perplexities of a divided world in which America had, willy nilly, to assume a leading role in international power politics, climaxed the series of historical shocks which formed the background of America's fourth great awakening. The resurgence of neo-fundamentalism was merely one aspect of a theological and intellectual reorientation which affected the whole of American life more profoundly than any that preceded it.

Statistics on church membership for the decade after the war tell a tale of increasing attendance at religious institutions. Between 1944 and 1953, church membership climbed by 20 million to nearly 94 million in 1953. Large-scale religious gatherings, out-of-vogue since the 1920s, were suddenly popular again, with a 1945 Youth for Christ revival at Soldier Field in Chicago featuring a young Billy Graham reportedly drawing 70,000. Seminaries were packed with future clergy; colleges were expanding departments of religious studies and the nation's news magazines were putting religion on their covers.

This revival of religion necessarily affected the coverage of religion after World War II. The *Religion News Service,* founded in 1933, by 1950 boasted 16 full-time employees and 400 correspondents around the globe, producing up to 50 stories a day. The news service's radio scripts went to 100 radio stations each day. Trade publications began noting increased, better coverage of religion at the same time the recently established field of religious public relations led newly savvy information officers to grouse about the quality of coverage.

The changes affecting religion reporting were part of a transition occurring in the entire profession of journalism. Before World War II, the reporter's craft was often learned as a trade, through apprenticeships beginning on the street hawking papers or inside on the copy desk. But college degrees in journalism, first offered at the turn of the century, became more common for reporters from the 1950s on, and mandatory by the 1970s. Trade associations and clubs for reporters grew as part of this increased professionalization of journalism.

In an effort to professionalize their own lot, a dozen religion reporters met in 1949 to found the Religion Newswriters Association, to encourage quality coverage of religion in the secular press. A few years later the *Associated Press* named its first religion beat reporter—George Cornell— who stayed on the job for more than 40 years. Louis Cassels, who wrote about religion for *United Press* (later *United Press International*), became that wire service's first religion reporter a few years after Cornell's appointment.

Religion reporting was, for the first time ever, a hot beat. Hot enough, in fact, that several colleges set up courses in what they called "Religious Journalism." Many of the programs operated until the mid-1960s.

During the 1960s, religion reporters went from dutiful coverage of Sunday sermons to often turbulent peace and justice issues. More so than in the past, stories on the religion beat intersected with coverage of the courts, police, national politics and education.

Edward Fiske, former religion reporter for the *New York Times,* wrote about religion reporting during the 1960s for a 1973 issue of the *Religious Journalism Newsletter.* According to Fiske, it was in the 1960s that religion reporting became a "front-page phenomenon." Why the 1960s? Fiske reports:

Religion went through the sort of massive institutional upheaval that makes news no matter what the particular institution is. Protestants began talking of church mergers and in a few cases, actually doing it. The ecumenical movement went well beyond the light petting stage of putting a priest, rabbi and minister on the same podium and began to alter the way virtually every religious group saw itself and related to other institutions. And then, of course, there was the whole transformation of the Roman Catholic Church. The Catholic story of the 1960s was in many ways a journalist's ideal—a medieval institution suddenly confronting the modern world.

The whole crisis of faith symbolized most vividly in the "God is dead" controversy also brought religion reporting to the forefront. "In a technological society and a day of mind-boggling scientific advances, people began wondering whether it was either necessary or even possible to believe in God," Fiske recalled. After 1970, change was the norm, making it hard "to get any news mileage . . . out of a nun in a picket line."

In another change, by the mid-1970s debates over the demise of God had given way to a religious revival of sorts, especially among evangelicals. The protest strategies by liberals in the 1960s evolved for the religious right into shrewd legal and political agendas, so that by 1980, the religious right had developed a sophisticated and influential political machine. With the 1973 *Roe v. Wade* decision legalizing abortion, a different U.S. Supreme Court decision that strengthened the separation of church and state, and the sexual revolution all as fuel in the war, the religious right and televangelists—some of whom were closely tied to a political agenda—became the top religion stories of the 1980s.

The articles in chapter 16 summarize the emerging ecumenicism and shared perspective among religious groups in the 1950s. Chapter 17 represents a transition from these united core values to an era in the mid-1960s when some theologians would propose Christianity without a personal God. The Death of God controversy, as it became known, is in chapter 18. Chapter 19 gathers stories reflecting the social upheavals of the era and the responses by some faith groups. The rise—and for some, downfall—of the television evangelist industry, a major story of the 1980s, is reflected in the stories found in chapter 20. Many of the most famous television ministers also had strong political agendas. Stories about God and politics appear in chapter 21, closing out this third section.

16

Consensus Religion

In the 1950s, the dominant Protestant culture was elevated in a way that created what many have called a consensus of religion. Will Herberg, in *Protestant, Catholic, Jew,* argued that the United States was really a nation of a singular faith, a blend, of sorts, of Protestantism, Catholicism and Judaism. Some of this "consensus" was even institutionalized. In this era, for example, both the National Council of Churches of Christ, U.S.A., and the World Council of Churches were born. The National Council was a consolidation of 11 ecumenical agencies, uniting efforts by 29 denominations representing a purported 31 million believers.

But in those years after World War II, the United States battled a new threat: the ideology posed by communism. As the United States became enmeshed in the Cold War, voicing an adherence to Christianity was the easiest way for a person to assure he or she wouldn't face questions about an allegiance to democracy. At a 1950 gathering of Roman Catholics at New York's St. Patrick's Cathedral, thousands sang the "Star-Spangled Banner" and prayed for those under the influence of communism. But the change in the religious milieu of the 1950s was more than just a safeguard against political ideology. One of the most celebrated theologians of the century, Reinhold Niebuhr, responded affirmatively to his own question of, "Is there a Revival of Religion?" in a November 15, 1950, issue of the *New York Times*'s Sunday magazine. Similarly, *Newsweek*'s December 26, 1949, cover story proclaimed: "More millions are flocking to church."

Books by Norman Vincent Peale and Bishop Fulton Sheen were serialized. The *Chicago Daily News* ran a column by Fulton Oursler, author of the 1940s best-selling *Greatest Story Ever Told.* The columns made page one for 40 days.

Other religious "superstars" were being made as well. Not since Billy Sunday's flamboyant revivals or Father Charles E. Coughlin's anti-Semitic sermons had a single clergyman roused the masses the way evangelist Billy Graham did. The press generously covered his crusades, which drew thousands of faithful at every stop. But it was Graham's appearance in Los Angeles that is credited with propelling him into national celebrity status. Reports from the eight-week revival said more than 400,000 jammed into a circus tent during daily appearances. Hollywood elites, including actress Jane Russell, were among the converted. A reported 4,000 people were saved, at a cost of more than $106,000, covered by donations of more than $119,000.

Newspaper lore says press magnate William Randolph Hearst, impressed by a meeting with Graham, cabled his *Los Angeles Examiner* asking it to "puff Graham" during Graham's 1949 crusade. Evidence as to whether or not the message was ever sent is only anecdotal. But reprinted here are *Examiner* reports from the revival's sixth week—two weeks before it ended. Each article was the lead story of the day, with the text and two large accompanying photos comprising most of the above-the-fold space. *Associated Press* distributed a story nationwide using quotes and figures from the *Examiner*'s stories. *Life* magazine included a feature on the Los Angeles crusade in its November 21, 1949, issue. From then on, Graham crusades garnered front-page attention and coverage unheard of for a single religious leader.

Even when Graham was in his 70s and hampered by Parkinson's disease, his crusades continued to draw thousands of people. They also received phenomenal, special-section treatment by newspapers. For an example, see the *Charlotte Observer*'s October 1, 1996, special section called "Billy Graham Comes Home," recapping his September 26–29, 1996, crusade there.

During the period when Graham got his start, reporter George Cornell was just starting the religion beat at *Associated Press*. His 1951 three-part trend story about the state of religion in the United States, which is included in this chapter, documents church growth as well as the efforts toward unity among major faiths.

Great Religious Revival to Continue Sixth Week

Overflow, Tent Meetings Induce Evangelist Graham to Stay

Los Angeles Examiner, October 31, 1949

So great has been the religious fervor of the crowds nightly packing the huge tent at Washington Boulevard and Hill Street that it was decided yesterday to continue the Christ for Greater Los Angeles revival for another and sixth week.

This is the third continuation of what has been characterized as the greatest religious revival in the history of Southern California. The announcement was greeted with loud applause at both the afternoon and evening sessions.

Evangelist Billy Graham explained that while he had other commitments in the East the response to his preaching here has been so fervent he considered it a solemn duty to remain.

50,000 More

It is estimated that more than 200,000 persons have attended the 42 meetings held so far and there is prospect 50,000 more will be registered before the week ends.

The original seating arrangements were for 6000 but as the crowds grew it was necessary to add an additional 3000 seats. Despite this, the Rev. Mr. Graham, a young and forceful preacher, continued to be greeted by overflow audiences.

In the first 42 meetings more than 5000 persons, including doctors, lawyers, schoolteachers and a number of other business and professional people, publicly reached a "decision" to return to Christ.

Louis Zamperini

At tonight's meeting when the Rev. Jack Schuler, son of Dr. Bob Schuler, prominent clergyman, will substitute for Evangelist Billy Graham, Louis Zamperini, famous University of Southern California track star, will attest publicly his return to the teachings of Jesus Christ.

Almost unbelievable stories of salvation from misfortune, grief and misery have been told by the penitent in the smaller tent where those who reach "the decision" confer with personal workers of the revival group.

One of the most dramatic was that of a business man in his late 50s.

Hopeless

Through irreligious habits and practices he lost his family, self-respect and place in the community. He felt hopeless, he explained, until he attended the revival and heard the Rev. Mr. Graham's promises that Christ was eager to help him.

Leading him to the smaller tent, one of the campaign workers advised:

"We'll have someone assist you in prayer."

That "someone" turned out to be the wife he hadn't seen since she divorced him 10 years ago.

The are to be remarried soon.

Teenagers

One of the features of the revival has been the Youth for Christ Rallies held in the big tent on Saturday evenings, with the majority in the audience being of teen age.

At each of the rallies, the Rev. Mr. Graham has prepared special messages for the young folk and local clergymen attest attendance at their Sunday services has shown a remarkable increase.

Ordinarily Youth for Christ Rallies are held at the Church of the Open Door, Sixth and Hope streets.

At Saturday's meeting in the big tent Youth for Christ units from San Luis Obispo to San Diego joined the Los Angeles group in setting a new attendance record.

"The answer to the problems of youth, in fact, the problems of the entire world, can be found in Christ," the evangelist told them.

"Youth, as in all ages, is troubled yet they need not be. He, the Savior, is anxious to eliminate all your fears—fear of war, insecurity and the future. Just give Him the opportunity to bring peace to your hearts.

"Christ is why we are on this earth and if you'll only dedicate yourself to Him and His way of life you'll find the happiness on earth He promises in Heaven."

With this message and a sermon by the Rev. Bob Jones, Jr., several score youngsters, many of them accompanied by their parents, joined the long list of those who have already publicly announced their "decisions to accept Jesus Christ."

While the regular sessions are devoted to sermon and prayer the Youth for Christ Rallies have followed a pattern of entertainment, choir singing and specialties by well-known artists.

Saturday's rally featured two pianos and an organ with a trumpet solo by Bill Cundall; songs by Radio Singer Beverly Shea and numbers by the Collins Twins.

Following an appeal by Bob Pierce, vice president, Youth for Christ International, the offering was set aside to transport Dave Morken, former Los Angeles Youth for Christ director, from his missionary post in Communist China to Japan.

Thirty-five pastors of local churches were guests of Howard Townsend, acting Los Angeles YFC director, at the meeting.

Included among others on the platform were Edward Hard, executive vice president, Northwest School, Minneapolis; Mitchell Seidler, Chicago Youth for Christ executive; Cliff Barrow, master of ceremonies and song leader, and Evangelist Jack Shaler.

Revival Stirs "Colonel Zack"

Harvey Fritts, in Western Garb, Among Throngs at Rites

Los Angeles Examiner, November 3, 1949

Humbly and joyously, additional throngs of persons lifted their hands in testimony of their new acceptance of Jesus as Evangelist Billy Graham returned yesterday to the Christ for Greater Los Angeles revival.

After a single day's rest from nearly six weeks' nightly sermons, the 30-year-old Rev. Dr. Graham's message drew scores to the prayer tent for individual help.

There, on their knees in the sawdust, were people of every age and walk of life, joined in the single purpose of prayer.

Among them was Harvey Fritts, in the Western garb he wears as "Colonel Zack" in the starring role of his television show.

"As a young man I drifted away from the Bible," he testified. "A week ago a lady asked me to come here and hear Billy Graham.

"I still fought against being a Christian, but as he spoke I finally admitted to myself I could not oppose the will of God."

Like many others of the more than 5000 who have testified to their finding again the teachings of Christ in the big tent at Washington and Hill street, "things began happening" to Fritts.

From among the nearly 250,000 people who have attended the services, he found a cousin he had not seen in 25 years, and the cousin put him in touch with his own family, virtual strangers more than a dozen years.

With the nightly 7:30 o'clock meetings continuing indefinitely by public demand, the scene of fervent faiths was described by the Rev. Dr. Graham in his sermon:

"There are signs on every side that the great revival is on its way!"

Trends in American Religious Life (Part I)

George W. Cornell, *Associated Press,* January 31, 1951

American Churches today are pulling together. On a scale unprecedented in the nation's history, religious bodies have pooled their forces for common goals.

The pattern is writing an end to the old days of feuding and sharp rivalry among separate denominations.

Teamwork is the swelling theme.

"Cooperation among churches now unquestionably is at its greatest yet," said Episcopal Bishop Henry Knox Sherrill, president of the National Council of Churches of Christ in the U.S.A.

Shaken by the materialism of a peril-driven world, the churches have tightened ranks in seeking to fill the spiritual gap.

The movement marks a new stage of maturity in the sometimes helter-skelter religious life of America.

Its roots trace back to the early part of the century but only in recent years has it gained momentum and widespread impact.

"The efforts of farsighted men of a generation ago are now coming to fruition," one church leader said. "It has taken a generation for these proposals to be heard."

There still are points of sectarian tension—usually arising from differences on isolated issues or doctrinal emphasis.

But the general overall direction for the majority of U.S. churches is toward more unified efforts and cooperation.

The "age of consolidation" as some churchmen call it. Among religious scholars, it's known as the Ecumenical Movement.

It has brought this complete mingling of several major Protestant groups. More significantly it has given rise to church federations dedicated to broad joint programs.

First of these is the new National Council launched at the start of 1951 as the nation entered the 2nd half of the 20th century.

Analysts called this the most important religious event since the Reformation of the 1500s in Europe.

The council includes 29 denominations—25 Protestant and four Eastern Orthodox—with nearly 32,000,000 members and 11 previous separate inter-denominational agencies.

"In the providence of God," the preamble of the council's constitution begins, "the time has come when it seems fitting more fully to manifest the essential oneness of the Christian churches of the United States."

The alliance gives a majority segment of American religious adherents a unified voice, and the increased strength of collective prestige. It also combines their support behind a broad program of education, missionary work, service and toward guiding the ethics of society.

"Christianity—the cement that has held our social order together—is building a mutual rampart," said Dr. Samuel McCrea Cavert, the council's top administrative officer. "But we still know that the basic thing is where it has always been—in the heart of the individual."

Governing policies of the council safeguard the right of member bodies to worship as they please. There is no control over denominational organization, doctrine or customs.

"Cooperation with freedom" is the watchword.

While the council specifically does not foster organized unions, its development has come hand-in-hand with a growing tendency toward such mergers.

In the last 40 years, 14 major church unions have occurred, involving 29 previously separate denominations. Although numerous small sects have sprung up during that time, they represent a relatively small fragment of the overall picture.

Possibilities of mergers involving a dozen other church bodies are in the wind.

Bishop G. Bromley Oxnam, of the Methodist Church—largest united Protestant body in the nation—phrased the idea this way: "The identities that unite are more significant than the differences that divide."

Other key signs that mark the growing trend toward united church action:

1. In eight years, the number of states, cities and counties with interfaith councils has tripled. There were 336 of them in 1942; now the figure is nearing 1,000.

2. Community churches, without denominational ties, have blossomed across the nation, and now number more than 3,000.

3. New understanding among American clergymen of different faiths came during World War II, when thousands of chaplains served the religious needs of men in uniform without regard to specific faiths.

4. An increased proportion of ministerial students now are trained at

interdenominational seminaries—such as those at Yale, Harvard, Duke and Vanderbilt Universities, the University of Chicago and New York's Union Theological Seminary.

Unlike the bygone period of jealousies, it is now common practice for a minister of one denomination to occupy a pastorate in another. These so-called "supply pastors" ordinarily installed when a pulpit cannot be conveniently filled with a minister of its own denomination, often are kept by the congregation indefinitely.

One authority estimated that one-fifth of the churches in some denominations have pastors who belong to other Protestant faiths. Some eventually transfer their affiliation.

The general church-going public also has become less denomination-conscious.

"People don't worry much more about fine points of denominational differences," said Dr. Reinhold Niebuhr, one of the country's top theologians.

The custom of holding joint services on special occasions—such as Thanksgiving and Christmas—has gained wide usage.

The National Council itself includes 11 interfaith commissions, councils and federations, some of which pioneered the way toward closer church relations. Through the World Council of Churches, the national group is linked with 160 religious bodies in 45 countries.

"Diversity is giving away to the larger values," said Dr. Douglas Norton, administrative head of Congregational-Christian churches. "There is no reason why we have to think and act precisely alike to do a better, overall Christian job."

Only two of the larger Protestant bodies are not part of the national council. These are the Southern Baptists, with about 7,000,000 members, and the Missouri Synod of the Lutheran Church, with more than 1,700,000 members.

Although the big Missouri Synod is taking part in tentative steps to unite some of the 17 Lutheran branches, it has remained aloof from the national agency.

"Some of the churches in the council speak as we do; some do not," said Rev. Oswald C.J. Hoffman, a Missouri Synod spokesman. "We feel it would be impossible for such a nondescript organization to offer real concerned Christian testimony. In general, we consider it less of a problem not to be a member."

Lutherans traditionally have steered clear of most inter-faith activity, but the second largest Lutheran body, the United Lutheran Church, with 1,400,0000 members, last year decided to enter the new council.

"In this step, our churches crossed a very important meridian," said Dr. F. Eppling Reinertz, the church's general secretary. "So far as we are concerned, the last four years have seen a greater development in the sphere of interdenominational cooperation than the previous 40 years."

While three other Baptist denominations with a total of 3,500,000 members have joined the council, the ardently independent Southern Baptists feel they would lose some freedom if they did so.

Their administrative head, Dr. Duke K. McCall of Nashville, Tenn., said Southern Baptists view some council actions as "liberal" and feel the council is too highly centralized.

"The Southern Baptist Convention works toward decentralization, a sort of free cooperative enterprise," he said. "Each Southern Baptist Church is virtually an autonomous body."

Direct opposition to the council has come chiefly from another church federation, the American Council of Christian Churches, which represents 15 smaller denominations with a reported total of 1,500,000 members.

This group, espousing intensely fundamentalist doctrine, claims the National Council is a "Protestant hierarchy," including "pacifistic, socialistic and modernistic leaders."

America's multiplicity of religious bodies has been, for centuries, an amazing phenomenon to Christians of older Europe. In no part of the world have so many sects developed as in the U.S. Although 97 per cent of the U.S. Christians belong to the 50 larger denominations, there are more than 200 other Protestant bodies.

While the older, established churches are moving toward closer unity and kindred bonds of service, the small, fervently evangelistic sects continue to increase in number.

They manifest an individualistic spirit that characterized the frontier days in American religion, which has given away only in recent decades to the movement for integration.

Religious leaders of all faiths have joined increasingly in mutual projects.

The National Conference of Christians and Jews, which seeks to promote universal "brotherhood though faith in the fatherhood of God," has grown in its 20 years from a tiny nucleus of 500 supporters to a worldwide organization with offices in 250 U.S. cities, and more than a half million contributors.

"Many more top leaders of all faiths—Jewish, Protestant and Catholics—are working with us than ever before," said Allyn P. Robinson, head of the conference's religious organization division.

"But sometimes," he added, "I get the feeling that the situation is becoming better and worse at the same time. What is clearly evident is that there is a stronger will to find ways to erase religious friction."

Isolated issues, usually disassociated from mutual trust in God, have pointed up the still-existing tensions.

Protestant-Catholic differences underlined the debate over public aid to parochial schools; Protestant feelings also figured in opposition to naming of a U.S. envoy to the Vatican. Jewish-Protestant disagreement was apparent in discussions of released time in schools for religious instruction. The observance of Reformation Sunday, commemorating the Protestant break from the Catholic Church, has spread from six communities in 1946 to 160 in 1950.

Religious authorities trace the difficulties to three basic factors:

1. Protestant pride and resentment at the Catholic dogma that it is the "one true church."

2. Lack of general knowledge of Catholic pronouncements supporting free choice in religion.

3. Jewish opposition to actions that single out its members as followers of a minority faith.

There have been zealots on both sides, fanning sparks of dissension. But such activity is an old story, inherited by this generation from centuries of more intense religious strife.

Despite negative aspects still apparent, the ruling tide in the American religious stream has moved steadily toward creating unity of purpose.

Recognizing the broad scope of the "Ecumenical Movement," in the U.S., the Vatican last year instructed American prelates to give it "vigilant attention" and to "foster and guide it in order to assist its members in their search for truth."

Many Catholic priests have joined in interfaith programs in which participants do not officially represent their churches.

Dr. Benson Y. Landis, research officer of the National Council, said Catholics and Protestants indirectly work shoulder-to-shoulder in other ways.

"When they make separate statements on great social issues," he said, "you usually can't tell whether the statements come from Rome or from the Protestants."

Between Jews and Protestants, cooperation on an organizational plane is becoming more and more common.

"Compared to 75 years ago," said Dr. Bernard J. Bamberger, president of the Synagogue Council of America, "the contrast is incredible."

Dr. Bamberger, whose organization represents the Orthodox, conservative and reformed wings of American Judaism, added:

"There is an increasing sense of community to support the religious view as opposed to the views which bypass religion."

In some cities, joint Jewish-Christian services have become an annual occasion with some congregations. Institutes to give Christian leaders a better understanding of Judaism have been targeted in recent years. In the last three years, Dr. Samuel H. Goldenson, Rabbi Emeritus of Temple Emanuel in New York, has toured some 160 U.S. cities, speaking in churches or before other Christian audiences in all of them.

With the growth of interfaith good will, rabbis have been brought into community ministerial associations. In several cases, rabbis have been elected to office in predominantly Protestant areas.

The old style of openly vilifying the other fellow's religion has come into general disrepute. Once a successful political weapon, it seldom works anymore. Its gradual loss of respectability was hastened by Hitler's use of it. Communist persecutions further showed up its true label. Although subtle undercurrents of tensions persist, the sharp edge has worn off.

Retired Methodist Bishop Francis J. McConnell, 79, a top Protestant leader for a half century, summed it up this way:

"People used to get furious and talk as if it were treason for a man to quit one church and join another. They don't do that anymore. You'd rather a man would be a good Catholic than a poor Methodist."

Trends in American Religious Life (Part II)

George W. Cornell, *Associated Press*, February 1, 1951

With a Bible under one arm and a stack of pronouncements under the other, a new reinvigorated figure has stepped into the U.S. public arena.

He represents American churches.

Usually on the sidelines in the past, you'll find him today in the chambers of government, in the halls of labor and industry and sitting with the Council of Nations. In a strengthened voice, he states what he stands for.

He is a symbol of a new milestone in U.S. religious annals that has focused the basic creed of the churches on the conduct of the country.

Never before have churches moved on such a broad, allied front in seeking to inject the ethics of their faith into practical, working problems of society.

"Too often in the past the churches have not given expression to the Christian conscience of the nation and community," said Episcopal Bishop Henry Knox Sherrill, president of the National Council of the Churches of Christ in the U.S.A.

"Events of the world have made it essential for the church to speak out."

The concept itself is not a new one, but it is only in recent times that it has gained its present stature, and won the support of most denominations.

It has been a bit-by-bit thing, slowly gathering strength and now emerging with new force as the Earth resounds with ideological strife, and threats of new, scientific catastrophe. It has blended the once-sporadic, disconnected voice of American churches into a rising, more articulate chorus.

And what do the churches say?

"They proclaim," said Dr. O. Frederick Nolde, church expert on international affairs, "that moral law must become controlling, not only in the lives of men as influentials, but also in their corporate lives as nations."

While churches regard the individual as the bedrock of good and evil, most of them now also view the wider social order as a sphere where spiritual values must be reinforced.

Most religious bodies at present declare their interest in such fields as: economic practices, labor-management relations, foreign policies, racial problems, marriage and domestic matters, the United Nations and international justice, immigration measures, education and overseas relief.

Some denominations have shunned any part in considering such issues, feeling that to do so would bring their religion down to the level of secular controversy and politics.

But the majority of U.S. Protestant churches, as well as Jewish and Catholic leaders, now see not only man, but man's communal affairs, as their mission.

"Church people have come to realize," said the Rev. Charles E. Warren of the American Baptist Convention, "that man isn't saved just to sit around and wait to accept heaven. But that man has a responsibility here on Earth to fulfill the Lord's Prayer that 'Thy will be done on Earth, as it is in heaven.'"

To make the "Christian conscience" effective in government and society, the programs of the newly established National Council and that of many individual denominations embrace such actions as these:

Testimony before congressional committees, consultation with high government officials on major issues, presentation of views to the U.N. and other bodies, sponsoring of conferences, institutes, research and surveys on various subjects, and the broadcasting of the Christian stand via modern communication channels and literature.

In at least one instance last year, churches joined in filing a friend-of-the-court brief in behalf of a Negro student's efforts to enroll in the University of Texas.

Special nationwide observances—such as the annual "Labor Sunday," "Economic Life Week" and "Race Relations Sunday"—also point of the growing religious emphasis on social problems. Some denominations now maintain observers at the U.N. Many have begun sponsoring member visits to the U.N. and to the U.S. Capitol.

Through the National Council, most major Protestant and Orthodox faiths now can speak with wider impact than ever before.

In a modern era, whose large cities and fast communications have dissipated the influence of single denominations, the members have combined their weight in behalf of principles on which they are generally agreed.

At the same time, they retain their separate modes of worship.

All but two leading Protestant bodies are represented in the 29-denomination council, which drafts its conclusions through a democratic, consultative process that reaches down to the individual churches.

Dr. Walter Van Kirk, head of the council's Department on International Justice and Good Will, said the council avoids commitments on specific legislation, and concentrates on moral issues.

"We don't button-hole congressmen or threaten retaliation at the polls or take any steps contrary to the separation of church and state," he said. "Our purpose is to give utterance to the Christian idea, and make it effective in the actions of our society."

Impetus to this objective has stemmed from the rise of world communism, and the accentuated cleavage between religion, its stress on influential dignities and rights, and regimented materialism.

Most church leaders feel that a spiritual vacuum feeds the dynamics of communism. To overcome this force, they believe religion must become even more dynamic in bringing justice and fraternity into situations dominated by social conflict.

Against this backdrop, Catholics and Jewish groups, as well as Protestants, have become increasingly vocal on social issues. The efforts for a stronger, bolder religious strategy has repeatedly brought efforts joining and separate expressions from leaders of the three faiths.

"The simple, old-fashioned concept of the priestly role is no longer realistic," says an officially circulated Catholic article. "We must operate on the assumption that the faithful laity will enter a program of social action under the dynamic leadership of the social-minded priest."

Catholic labor schools have sparked new Catholic activity in trade unionism. Recent papal encyclicals have stressed the moral uses of economic systems.

The Rev. R.C. Hartnett, editor-in-chief of the official Catholic national weekly, America, said Catholic school curricula today puts "much more emphasis on the application of religion to economic and social problems."

Jewish organizations increasingly have stressed the relevance of Biblical teachings to current questions. On a recent Saturday in New York, a check of sermons in five synagogues showed that each had touched on international issues.

Jews and Protestants have joined in opposing the communist-inspired Stockholm Peace Petition, in urging Senate ratification of the anti-genocide convention, and in opposing discriminatory immigration policies.

Dr. Van Kirk said most debate over the propriety of the churches entering secular affairs has died out.

"Christians now see that they are so much involved in these affairs," he said, "that they cannot extricate themselves and live in an isolated self-defined kingdom."

Dr. F. Eppling Reinertz, a United Lutheran Church spokesman, said that a decade ago it was "almost inconceivable" for his church to consider making an overture to the President or Congress. It isn't anymore.

"We tended toward confusion of the separation of church and state with the separations of good citizenship and religion," he commented.

Some denominations not in the National Council also have enlarged their programs in the field of community and national affairs.

Consider the Missouri Synod of the Lutheran Church, one of the two major Protestant bodies outside the council. (The other is the Southern Baptist Convention.)

"While we regard the gospel of Christ as our primary mission," said Rev. Oswald C.J. Hoffman, a Lutheran spokesman, "we now recognize we have an obligation to see that moral law is upheld. This is a responsibility that in the past hasn't been carried out as it should have been."

The church has set up study programs in race relations, labor-management problems and economics. On occasions, it sends representatives to legislative hearings, and encourages a more active role by members, as Christians, in civic affairs.

Louis Minsky, managing editor of Religious News Service, said that "churches are realizing increasingly over the years that religion has to be applied to life and current issues, and they are expressing themselves more and more on those problems."

This activity by churches is the historical child of the old "Social Gospel" preached by crusading, individual ministers around the turn of the century.

It was carried on by the founders in 1908 of the Federal Council of Churches, which grew from a small beginning to form the foundation of the new national council.

In their present approach to social problems, the churches have sought to employ practical realism. While seeking to better the character of civilization and combat deep-seated social evils, they spurn the illusions of a world utopia, or sudden moral regeneration.

"The church can't prevent war now, if war's going to come," said Dr. Samuel McCrea Cavert, general secretary of the National Council. "But in the long run, it can. Not by itself, but by developing understanding and bringing an enlarged lesson to the people.

"The drives for power and preoccupation with material self-interest are tremendous forces, and their perils cannot be offset in a few months or years. It is a long gradual process."

Dr. Nolde, the tall, suave theological professor who directs the Commission on International Affairs of the World Council of Churches, said the churches seek "to begin where the thinking of government leaders stops."

"We don't follow the government, but try to lead the way, and give guidance in moral meanings and purposes.

"It is not being done to benefit the church, but to benefit the world. If what the churches are doing today is not worth while to all people, it is not worth while to Christians."

The job, he said, is not predicated on the "certainty of success or failure."

"Can it produce a better world? We believe it can. But win, lose or draw, it has to be done."

Trends in American Religious Life (Part III)

George W. Cornell, *Associated Press*, February 2, 1951

While the evidence doesn't show that the country as a whole is more devout, it does hint that organized religion is commanding new, wider attention.

A few of the clues:

1. Seminaries are packed and some of them for the first time are being forced to turn away applicants.

2. Bible sales have nearly doubled in the last decade, increasing between five and 10 per cent in the last year.

3. A radio network's broadcast on religion last month stirred the greatest letter response in the program's 16-year history.

4. The number of newspaper and magazine syndicates handling religious features has jumped from 17 to 45 in five years.

5. Church-building is at an all-time high.

6. Most colleges and universities across the country have expanded religious curricula to meet student demands.

7. Present-day touring evangelists have attracted near-record crowds.

8. American industry and advertising men for the third time are backing an unusual, nationwide religion-promotion program.

9. Church contributions and attendance (a basic gauge of church vitality) are considered by officials to be at a peak.

10. Religious and inspirational books in recent years have achieved a regular place on best-seller lists.

Close observers view the sharpened religious appetite of the country as a result of the insecurity of the times.

They also see it as a possible reaction against an age of intense scientific rationalism, and a resurgent conviction that materialistic advances can never fully cope with life's basic needs.

One minister, the Rev. Ira W. Langston, of the Park Avenue Christian Church here, offered this analysis:

"People have discovered that the things they counted on most are no longer dependable. The family structure is not what it once was 20 years ago. The absolute, positive assurance of U.S. invulnerability is gone. The value of money has fallen to pieces. To put it briefly, things are shaking, and the people are looking for something unshakable."

What is the result of this instability? Here are answers of some leading church authorities:

Theologian Dr. Reinhold Niebuhr: "There is a new receptivity toward the message of historic faith which is in marked contrast to the indifference and hostility of past decades."

Clarence Hall, managing editor of The Christian Herald: "Religious interest is at an all-time high. Churches are packed. People are going who had never been inside a church before."

Dr. Samuel McCrea Cavert, General Secretary of the National Council of the Churches of Christ in the U.S.A.: "There is a tremendously increased interest in religion, and I hope a steadying influence. Primarily it is a revival in interest, rather than in religion itself. People no longer are writing of religion as old-fogey and outmoded. This might be a prelude to a real revival religion."

Dr. Bernard J. Bamberger, president of the Synagogue Council of America: "Unquestionably there is a very much greater degree of affiliation and participation. Parents are demonstrating much greater concern for the religious training of their children."

Episcopal Bishop Henry Knox Sherrill: "The number going into the ministry and life vocations in the church has increased tremendously. The atmosphere in university and college circles is more friendly to religion than at any time in a generation. There are indications in my correspondence that more people are laying greater emphasis on prayer."

Monsignor Thomas J. McCarthy, of the National Catholic Welfare Conference, Washington, D.C.: "Particularly since the end of the war, there has been a notable rallying to the church. The tremendous struggle the Catholic Church is waging against communism has attracted a great deal of attention, not only to the church's historical position but to its teachings. The high percentage of converts being received into the church is witness to the growing interest."

Louis Minsky, managing editor of Religious News Service: "There is a very great spiritual upsurge in this country as a result of uncertainty and a growing realization that what is involved in the present crisis is an ideological struggle between the materialist and spiritual concept of society."

Southern Baptist Executive Secretary Dr. Duke K. McCall: "There is a very definite trend toward a revival of religious interest."

Rev. James E. Hoffman, executive secretary of the General Synod of the Reformed Church in America: "It's the best year we've ever had."

Dr. Jesse M. Bader, of the Disciples of Christ, and head of the National Council's Evangelism Department: "The churches in the last few years have made their greatest progress in history. Evangelism was never more healthy, vigorous and active than it is right now. This evangelism is not the spectacular kind, but it's down in the churches and parishes."

While church leaders applaud heightened concern with religion, they also note its potential dangers.

Since periods of stress, such as the present, usually spark wider religious inquiry, they say, the impulse is often partially due to fear, and possibly to psychological panic.

When this motive is great, they feel that many persons may be driven into erratic and unwholesome "fringe expressions" of religion such as weird cults and mysticism.

These activities, together with a host of strange psychological fads and mental-balm theories, have become a part of the modern scene.

The hope of church leaders is that men's present search for spiritual security can be channeled into stable areas, without extremism.

"If we make a sound ministry available to the growing sense of need," one churchman said, "then there is a real possibility of a tremendous upsurge in the basic religious life of America."

Concrete evidences of such a possibility appear on many fronts.

The interest that religion has stirred in purely business circles is reflected in the two-year-old, countrywide program, "Religion in American Life," which is planning increased work this year.

Backed by the Advertising Council, Public Service Agency of American Industry and Advertising Men, the program embraces all faiths. Last year, it put out hundreds of radio broadcasts, 8,000 newspaper advertisements and 94,000 bus and trolley cards to promote religion. It set up 5,000 billboards across the nation, saying: "Take Your Problems to Church This Week. Millions Leave Them There."

"The program is unique, the first time American business has done anything like it," said its national director, Rev. Earle B. Pleasant. "It evidences a growing interest in religion and the spiritual values of life the like of which [we] have not known for a long time."

On college campuses, spiritual matters are drawing more notice. In the last year, interfaith Evangelistic meetings were held at 48 universities and colleges, most of them attracting overflow crowds.

Although there are no tangible indications that students are more pious, it appears that religion is getting more consideration in dormitory "bull sessions."

Consensus of churchmen is that a once-modish inclination of students to dismiss religion as old-fashioned and unscientific has given away to a more open-minded attitude.

As a result, many colleges have broadened religious courses, and some in recent years have set up new departments in this field.

Religion—as an attention-getter—has outstripped other subjects on the "town meeting of the air," carried by the American Broadcasting Company.

Ruth Barash of Town Hall, Inc., said a religious forum last December stirred a mail response of 16,200 letters, highest ever. The previous record was a 15,510-letter response to a 1947 foreign policy discussion, the type of topic that in the past usually has sparked the biggest reaction.

Evangelism, both of the old revival-meeting type and of some newer varieties, is having a heyday.

Most of the headlines have gone to emotion-charged revivalists like Billy Graham, whose flailing arms, flashing eyes and "old-time religion" preaching have packed auditoriums in many parts of the country.

Others have had similar success. Anglican minister Brian Green of England has drawn huge crowds in appearances in Boston, Chicago, Cincinnati, Houston, New York, and other cities.

Methodist Evangelist E. Stanley Jones, who usually spends half of each year in India, switched his plans last year to devote a full 12 months preaching in the United States.

His schedule was part of a just-concluded, 15-month United Evangelistic Advance, backed by 38 denominations and featuring crusades across the country. These got big results.

In the Baltimore area, 400 guest preachers took to the pulpits, and in 10 days, won 4,000 church members. In the Syracuse-Rochester-Buffalo, N.Y., area, 600 guest preachers in 10 days gained 14,000 new members, more than the area's 300 churches had added in the past year. Similar affairs were held in 44 other areas.

As part of the campaign, projects were conducted in 77 areas to contact non-church residents, and give evangelism training. In 85 communities, special membership drives were made by personal calls by laymen.

Another long-term interdenominational evangelistic drive is being planned, through the National Council, to start next fall.

Ever since World War II, young men—and women—have flocked into the ministry. Seminaries are full, and flooding over into improvised facilities.

The Methodist Church, reporting larger enrollments than ever before in its theological schools, said it had to turn applicants away for the first time last year.

A Congregational-Christian Church spokesman said 75 men are now entering the ministry, where 15 were doing so a few years ago. "Only the cream of the crop is picked," he said. The United Lutherans expect 170 spring graduates, compared to a usual class of 90 to 105.

Some denominations, like Missouri Synod of the Lutheran Church, have purchased apartment buildings and improvised facilities to accommodate overflow seminary classes.

The Episcopal Church last year ordained 240 new priests, an increase of 43.71 per cent over the previous figure.

Elbert M. Conover, director of the interdenominational bureau of architecture, said church construction in the past year has surpassed any previous period in history.

He estimated $200,000,000 in new churches and additions went up in the past year, with another billion-dollars worth in the planning stage.

At Hillsdale, Mich., Dr. Harry S. Myers, secretary of the National Council's stewardship department, said the amount of church contributions has risen steadily since 1936, and last year toward the billion-dollar mark for 48 denominations for the first time.

The average per-capita yearly contribution by members last year was $30.53, compared to $27.43 for 1949.

The upswing in religious interest, in some ways, compares with the spectacular revivals just before the turn of the century, when the proportion of the population belonging to churches increased from 19.9 per cent in 1880 to 34.7 per cent in 1900.

In the present corresponding period, the proportion has climbed from 42.7 per cent to 54.2 per cent. The gain in actual numbers, about 30,000,000 is almost twice that of the previous 20-year period.

Total U.S. church membership last year stood at 81,862,328, including Protestants, Catholics and Jews. Although the 1950 figures will not be available until spring, gains by individual denominations indicate the total will exceed 33,000,000.

Although membership statistics are considered an inaccurate measure of religious life (because an unknown number of members are inactive, but still on the rolls) the figures show a clear pattern over the last half century.

Up to the mid-20s, the cycle moved up rapidly. Then came a slump in membership gains that lasted through the late roaring 20s, and the depression. For three years,—'32, '33 and '34—the proportion of the population on church rolls lingered at the 48-percent mark. About 1936, signs of the new growth appeared, steadily climbing toward the current resurgence.

17

Winds of Change

By the time Roman Catholic John F. Kennedy ran for president, 30 years had passed since Al Smith's 1928 doomed presidential candidacy sparked virulent essays spewing anti-Catholicism. Earlier in the century, Smith's opponents dubbed him "Al(cohol) Smith" for Smith's opposition to prohibition. The Ku Klux Klan issued a "Klarion Kall for a Krusade" opposing the Catholic candidate.

Despite a climate of less religious bigotry compared to earlier in the century, religion was still a controversy in the 1960 presidential campaign of Kennedy against Republican Richard Nixon. Kennedy met questions about his faith directly, notably in an April 1960 address to the American Society of Newspaper Editors. Said Kennedy:

> I am not the Catholic candidate for president.
>
> Do not expect me to explain or defend every act or statement of every Pope or priest . . . If there is bigotry in this country, then so be it—there is bigotry. If that bigotry is too great to permit the fair consideration of a Catholic who has made clear his complete independence and his complete dedication to separation of church and state, then we ought to know it. But I do not believe that this is the case.

West Virginia—a state of mostly Protestants—was a key battleground in the 1960 Democratic primary. The primary there followed the Wisconsin primary in which analysts attributed Kennedy's surprising and unexpected win to "the Catholic vote." In early May 1960, surveys showed West Virginians were wary of Kennedy's Catholicism and Minnesota Senator Hubert Humphrey was edging ahead of Kennedy. A defeat in West Virginia would be, as a May 2, 1960, issue of *Time* put it, Kennedy's "death notice." Kennedy hammered Humphrey during West Virginia campaign stops, attempting to refocus on the issue of poverty, not "where I go to church on Sunday." The strategy worked; Kennedy won West Virginia.

Nonetheless the Catholic issue wouldn't die, even after Kennedy won the Democratic nod. Conservative Christians, *The Power of Positive Thinking* author Norman Vincent Peale among them, voiced continued concern. Less than two months before the election, Kennedy addressed

Houston's ministerial association. Kennedy reiterated his view of the separation of church and state with one forceful addition: He pledged to resign from the presidency if the job required him either to violate his conscience or the national interest. The caveat seemed to be what voters wanted to hear, because critics of Kennedy's religion were mostly mute after that.

In this chapter, writer Helen Hill Miller explains to *New Republic* readers why the 1960 election reflected a different culture—politically and economically—from the 1928 election. Her two-part series in 1957, the first part of which is reproduced here, was among the earliest articles discussing Kennedy's faith as a campaign consideration. Her thorough review looks at Kennedy's voting record in light of his religion, the changing nature of Catholicism in the U.S., what type of voting block, if any, Catholics are, and other differences of the 1960 election compared to that of 1928. The April 12, 1960, issue of *Time* magazine also revisits the 1928 campaign.

One of the issues in the 1960 election was whether or not Catholics were indeed a voting block. Catholicism in the United States was undergoing change. It evolved from being a church of sometimes persecuted immigrants into a church of power and wealth. A series of historical gatherings—dubbed Vatican II—throughout the 1960s would transform the church even further and open it up to greater ecumenical involvement, increased roles for laity, liturgy in the vernacular, and many more "updatings." And unlike the Kennedy campaign, which was always a political beat reporter's story, Vatican II was clearly the burden of religion reporters. Along with other changes, Vatican II partially reformed relations between reporters and the Catholic church hierarchy.

The *Sun* in Baltimore, based in a city that was home to the country's first Catholic diocese, was known for its persistent coverage of Catholicism. While Religion Reporter Weldon Wallace's piece reprinted here displays the grandeur and spectacle of Vatican II, it obviously couldn't, at the start of the council, reflect the monumental changes that affect Catholic life today. His story is an example of the kind of pageantry writers today relay when covering the pontiff's travels abroad. Wallace's story ran on the front page with a large photo, but was accompanied inside by a verbatim reprinting of Pope John XXIII's opening address.

Reporting from the closely sealed Vatican II sessions throughout the next few years was notoriously difficult, with news media dependent on vague and brief summaries from church officials that were sometimes distributed selectively. Vatican II reporters were warned by influential U.S.

Bishop Fulton J. Sheen that "no journalist can understand a council of the church unless he has the spirit of Christ."

The October 26, 1964, issue of *Newsweek* noted difficulties of the 488 accredited reporters assigned to the Vatican. The *Sun*'s Wallace, a veteran of three Vatican II sessions by 1964, told *Newsweek* that reporters had to "burrow behind the scenes and get our own sources." Some reporters held dinners where key council clergy gave background. Others used bribes, "a time-honored Vatican reportorial technique," according to *Newsweek*. For its part, the Roman Catholic Church complained about trivial and sensationalistic stories from the first two sessions of the council. By the third council, the Vatican beefed up its briefings and more thorough stories ensued. The closed meetings practice of the Roman Catholic Church extended to National Conference of Catholic Bishops' gatherings until, after repeated protests by leaders in the Religion Newswriters Association, the bishops finally opened their general sessions to the press in 1972.

No significant story about the Roman Catholic Church today can ignore the impact of Vatican II. Peter Steinfels of the *New York Times* wrote a thorough four-part series on the health of the U.S. Catholic Church in the late 20th century that ran May 29 through June 2, 1994. Coverage of a different sort is found in the yearlong glimpse at a single Catholic parish by *Newsday* reporter Bob Keeler. Keeler's series, the first part of which ran in the paper's April 2, 1995, issue, won a 1996 Pulitzer Prize. A story by former Baltimore *Sun* reporter Diane Winston about the impact of Vatican II on one aspect of the church—the laity—can be found in Chapter 28.

A Catholic for President?

Part I—1960 Is Not 1928

Helen Hill Miller, *The New Republic,* November 18, 1957

If one of the major political parties, in 1960, should nominate a Catholic for the Presidency, to what extent would voters be influenced for him or against him by the fact of his religion?

With Sen. John F. Kennedy of Massachusetts clearly in the running on the Democratic side, and American Red Cross Director Alfred M. Gruenther frequently mentioned as a dark horse who might emerge from a Republican deadlock, the question acquires more pertinence than it has had since the campaign of Al Smith vs. Herbert Hoover in 1928.

During the intervening generation, the political and economic scene in the United States has changed so markedly as to make one thing sure: There will not be a repeat performance of the 1928 contest. One characteristic of the American Catholic remains unchanging: he is a faithful member of an hierarchically organized religious community which has spiritual concerns and secular interests, membership in many countries, and its center of authority vested in the Pope in Rome. But many other characteristics of the American Catholic population have altered appreciably over the past 30 years.

In 1928, to begin with, American Catholics were mostly immigrants; earlier Irish and German arrivals were being followed by a heavy influx from Southern and Eastern Europe. Congress, with bipartisan support, had just passed a series of immigration laws to hold down incoming numbers. The Irish were concentrated chiefly in the large cities of the Eastern seaboard; the Germans were clustered in the Ohio and Upper Mississippi river basin, from Cincinnati to Milwaukee to Bismarck to St. Louis. The Southern and Eastern Europeans supplied the low-paid labor in the mines, the steel mills, the garment industry. The only two states with long-term backgrounds of Catholic culture were Maryland and Louisiana. Elsewhere, the Protestantism of the founding fathers was pervasive and militant—a source of informed pride on the Atlantic seaboard among Pilgrim descendants in New England, Scotch and Scotch-Irish Covenanters in the uplands of the South, and a taken-for-granted assumption westward from the prairies to the coast. In the late 1920s, the Ku Klux Klan was in full revival—anti-Catholic, anti-Negro, anti-Jew— in circulation among the willingly ignorant was the assurance that if a Catholic became President, the Pope would build a communicating tunnel under the Atlantic affording direct access between the White House and the Vatican. The facsimiles of the avidly-circulated literature of hate presented by Michael Williams in his "Shadow of the Pope" illustrate contemporary extremes of bigotry.

In 1928, most Protestants outside the South were Republicans, and the Republican Party was in power. Prosperity had dried up many issues, but not the issue of prohibition. Voters in the Middle West and the Great Plains states found it easy to echo the slogan of 1984: "We are Republicans, and don't propose to leave our party and identify ourselves with the party whose antecedents have been Rum, Romans, and Rebellion." And in the South feeling about the rum and the Romans was so strong that six states did leave their party and help put Herbert Hoover in the White House.

All of this background was pertinent to the Smith campaign: Smith was a Catholic, but he was also a wet Tammany Democrat from the sidewalks of New York. (And what sort of hostess, went the gossip, would that wife of an immigrant's son make in the White House?)

Today, positive efforts to reduce intolerance have produced a climate very different from that of 1928. True, the White Citizens Councils and the Defenders of State Sovereignty and Individual Liberty are currently inciting the same elements as the Klan of the 1920s did, but their threat to the fabric of national tolerance is at present concentrated on the Negro. Current social mores take for granted a balanced representation of Protestants, Catholics and Jews on the directorates of a wide variety of American institutions—civic, cultural, charitable. Three national co-chairmen, and a board of 200, head the National Conference of Christians and Jews, founded after the 1928 campaign in response to a study of religious bigotry conducted by the Federal Council of Churches.

This civic organization, which started with an initial budget of $15,000 and one paid secretary, now has 62 regional offices across the country and an annual budget of $2¾ million; on behalf of "brotherhood," defined as giving to others the same rights, responsibilities and dignity that one wants for ones self, it acts through a wide range of organizations and through the mass media. Partly as a result of the missionary work of such organizations (the Anti-Defamation League of the B'nai B'rith is another of the more effective pro-tolerance organizations) almost any public reference to a politician's religion has come to be considered improper. (Indeed, while Abie's Irish Rose established a Broadway record in the 1920s, opinion now so frowns on the telling of stories on Negroes, Jews and Catholics that the only safe butt for this kind of humor is the traditional Scotsman.)

Today prohibition has been removed as an issue.

Today, outside the South, Catholics can no longer be regarded as a minority, or indeed as a readily-identifiable group. Available figures on religious affiliation are not too reliable—they are compiled from official counters by the various religious bodies. Methods of computation, particularly the age at which children are counted as members, differ from church to church. The last adequate government census of religious bodies was taken in 1926, and no attempt at enumeration has been made since 1936. (The propriety of inserting a question on individual religious affiliation in the 1960s census is a subject of current controversy—most Catholics, incidentally, would welcome it; a likely compromise solution would be to make a sample survey.) But such statistics as are at hand show that among those Americans—they constitute about half the population—who claim a religious affiliation, the Catholics predominate by nearly three to one in New England, five to three in the Middle Atlantic states. In the South, the ratio of Catholics to Protestants is only about one to four, but in the North Central area it is about five to seven; they come close to breaking even in the West, with a slight margin in the Catholics' favor on the Pacific coast. The percentage of Catholics outnumber that of Protestants in the population of 15 states; all six New England states, New York, New Jersey, Illinois, Michigan, Louisiana, Montana, New Mexico, California. In one state, Pennsylvania, the ratio is: Catholic 27.3 percent, Protestants 28.2 percent. In four other states—Ohio, Wisconsin, Maryland, Nevada—there is less than 6 percent difference between the two ratios.

During the first session of the current Congress, 95 Catholics served as members of the U.S. Senate and House of Representatives. Some came from states or districts with large urban centers but others—Mansfield of Montana, O'Mahoney of Wyoming—from rural areas. By no means do all of them rely solely on the votes of their co-religionists. Indeed the 1956 gubernatorial race in Louisiana indicated that on occasion religious lines can be crossed both ways. In defeating Catholic deLesseps Morrison, Protestant Earl Long obtained 70 percent of the votes in Evangeline Parish, where Catholics outnumber Protestants 20 to 1, while in Caddo Parish, where Protestants outnumber Catholics by 7 to 2 he polled only 38.8 percent.

Nor are all Catholics grouped under one party banner. Though in the past most of them have tended to be Democrats, both parties agree that there has been a movement to the Republican column reflected in Congressional elections after World War II and in the Presidential choices of 1952 and 1956. One estimate suggests the shift accounted for perhaps 7 percent of the 1952 vote for Eisenhower. (Should this trend continue, nomination of a Catholic on the Republican ticket in 1960 might produce a greater change than would result from a similar nomination by the Democrats.)

The shift in party allegiance is regarded as having been greatest among Catholic families whose recent history has included a move—a geographic move to the suburbs, and an economic move to a higher income bracket—in both cases a move to a Republican milieu.

Today, not only Tammany, but most of the big city Catholic machines have heard their last hurrah. As their former clients have increased in earning power, become entitled as of right to unemployment insurance and social security, and moved to the suburbs, the old political mechanisms have been left destitute. In some areas, too, what used to be a solid Irish Catholic vote has become complicated by ethnic complexity. Today's New England Catholic may be of Portuguese, or Italian, or French-Canadian ancestry quite as well as of Irish extraction. Asking one Irish Catholic to vote for another has a double pull, only half of which is available when the appeal is to Catholic voters for whom the old country is not the auld sod. With a diminution in power of the machine in a given city, a Catholic candidate from the area can dissociate himself from it and seek a broader constituency, even without action as overt as that of Senator Kennedy in 1947. Then, as a freshman member of the House of Representatives, alone among Democrats of the Massachusetts delegation, Kennedy refused to sign a petition of clemency for former Boston mayor James M. Curley, in prison for mail fraud. The incident was underlined by the fact that Curley was Kennedy's immediate predecessor as Representative of the 11th Massachusetts District.

But the most striking recent evidence of new power of a Catholic candidate to attract votes appeared in the enthusiasm for Kennedy among Southern delegations during the contest for the Vice Presidential nomination last summer. On the second ballot, eight Southern states—Arkansas, Georgia, Kentucky, Louisiana, Mississippi, South Carolina, Texas and Virginia—gave him their entire vote; Alabama gave him a majority of its delegation; North Carolina and Florida indicated sizable minorities in his favor. Of these states, a generation earlier, five had switched parties to support Hoover rather than Smith. True, their 1956 votes were closely related to the Stop-Kefauver movement, but political preferences always are largely determined by available alternatives. The noteworthy fact is that the preferred alternative was a Catholic.

Since that time, moreover, a liking for Kennedy for 1960 has been indicated by advance billing in a number of states. On the week-end of June 10, Senator Kennedy went to Georgia for a commencement address, a TV appearance, and a joint reception with Senators Russell and Talmadge for some 700 local leaders at Atlanta's Dinkler-Plaza; Georgia Democratic state chairman John Sammons Bell announced it "highly likely that the state's next Democratic delegation will support Kennedy." On August 4, Sen. John McClellan of Arkansas, on whose labor racketeering subcommittee Senator Kennedy is a member and his brother

Robert is general counsel, noted that "Kennedy has definite Presidential potential." In recent weeks, Kennedy has received ovations in the deep South from Gainesville, Florida, to Jackson, Mississippi. It looks as though some, at least, of the conservative Southern leadership searching for a candidate for whom local support might be available within the framework of the national Democratic party, have picked Kennedy as the least objectionable of the Northern contenders. Their liking, indeed, is sufficiently cumulative for Kennedy to be in some danger of appearing in the North as white supremacy's white-haired boy.

A parallel exists between Kennedy's support in the states of the Southeast, Georgia, in particular, and the support of Premier Maurice Duplessis in Canada's Province of Quebec. Over the years M. Duplessis, a Catholic, has enjoyed the backing not only of Quebec's Catholics, but also of the largely Protestants industrialists who have been rapidly installing a modern economy in what was formerly an agricultural region. In the decade and a half since the war, Montreal and Atlanta have both become centers of an expanding industry, much of which, in each instance, derives its capital and top management from the big industrial and financial centers of northeastern United States. In both cases, the industrial influx has been due to a combination of natural resources, abundant labor, and the developing markets resulting from their exploitation. While Catholicism in itself is not necessarily attractive to the management group who increasingly set the social tone of these areas, the conservatism normally associated with it is attractive; in the face of less conservative alternatives, an accommodation can be arranged.

Actually, Kennedy's voting record, unlike the predilections of M. Duplessis, hardly supports his acceptance as a conservative. In a compilation of Senate voting records by the Committee on Political Education of the AFL-CIO made on 20 selected issues of the 1946-56 decade, 11 of which occurred after Kennedy's election to the Senate, Kennedy is noted as having been absent in the hospital during one (on conflict of interest among government executives); voting wrong on another (flexible farm price supports); and voting right on the remaining nine—the Bacon-Davis amendment (on wages paid on federal construction), civil service, postal pay, unemployment compensation, offshore oil, public housing, social security, a $700 income tax exemption, natural gas, Dixon-Yates. (On the McCarthy censure motion, which came to a vote while he was away and which the AFL-CIO omitted from its list, Kennedy has not declared his stand.) Similarly, in a compilation of 12 roll-calls regarded as significant by Americans for Democratic Action during the first session of the current Congress, Kennedy was rated as voting liberal 83 percent of the time.

But conservatives find the Kennedy family background immensely reassuring. Over the years, patriarch Joseph Patrick Kennedy's economic and financial interests have been substantial and ubiquitous and his views—from isolation to McCarthyism barely distinguishable from the GOP Old Guard. His legal residence is in Palm Beach, Florida; his summer home in Hyannisport, Massachusetts; his office on Park Avenue, New York. His business connections range coast-to-coast—shipping, corporation finance, the movie industry. (It was Hollywood's Dore Schary who selected Jack Kennedy as narrator for the Democratic Party's 1956 convention film, *Pursuit of Happiness*.) Squarely in mid-continent is Chicago's Merchandise Mart, a $17 million Kennedy purchase whose manager, his son-in-law Robert Serwin Schreiber [sic], Jr., is showing marked signs of becoming an Illinois gubernatorial candidate. His [Kennedy's] seven children are Ivy League-Junior League in manners. They experienced diplomatic life in a foreign capital when their father served as this country's Ambassador to the Court of St. James in the years before World War II. One daughter married into the English aristocracy. In this country, occasional news items have announced feminine Kennedy jewel losses running into tabloid-sized figures.

Joe Kennedy has said that he and son Jack disagree on many issues, but when a Kennedy campaign is on, the entire family gets into the act, the father with fountain pen flowing. During Jack Kennedy's 1952 campaign for the Senate, "Coffee with the Kennedys" on TV and tea with the Kennedys in precinct after precinct gave Massachusetts voters a chance to see in person most of the highly personable tribe. Together they defeated incumbent Republican Sen. Henry Cabot Lodge, Jr., by 69,000 votes at a time when President Eisenhower carried the state by a margin of 208,000—and thereby revenged the 1916 defeat of their maternal grandfather by Henry Cabot Lodge, Sr., who nosed out Boston's former mayor John F. (Honey Fitz) Fitzgerald by 33,000 to return to the Senate and make world history.

So since 1928, many of the circumstances surrounding a Catholic candidacy for top federal office have changed.

Ecumenical Meeting in Rome Opens

Weldon Wallace, *The Baltimore Sun,* October 12, 1962

ROME, OCT. 11—Giving the opening address of the twenty-first Ecumenical Council, Pope John XXIII stated in clear terms today that the council contemplates no change in doctrine.

He said, however, that modern times call for new forms of expression for the ancient beliefs.

From his throne at the main altar of St. Peter's Basilica the Pope looked out upon some 2,700 richly robed dignitaries of the Church, who had come from all over the earth, the greatest gathering of its kind in Catholic history.

In surrounding areas were arranged officials of special missions sent by numerous governments; the massed clergy of Rome; observers from other Christian faiths; news and television personnel, and special groups of many other kinds.

"Pure and Integral"

The Supreme Pontiff spoke at the end of ceremonies that had started more than four and a half hours earlier with a procession from the Vatican palace.

In a strong voice, the 80-year-old Pope declared that the council "wishes to transmit the doctrine; pure and integral, without any attenuation or distortion, which throughout twenty centuries . . . has become the common patrimony of men."

"The Church," he said, "should never depart from the sacred patrimony of truth received from the fathers."

However, he continued, authentic doctrine "should be studied and expounded through the methods of research and through the literary forms of modern thought."

He drew a distinction between "the substance of the ancient doctrine" and "the way in which it is presented."

"Salient Point"

"The salient point of this council," Pope John said, "is not a discussion of one article or another of the fundamental doctrine of the Church, which has been repeatedly taught by the Fathers and the ancient and modern theologians and which is presumed to be well known and familiar to all. For this a council was not necessary."

But while never departing "from the sacred patrimony of truth," the Church "must ever look to the present, to new conditions and new forms of life . . . which have opened new avenues to the Catholic apostolate."

The Pope emphasized that an important goal of the council is to promote church unity.

He said he felt "considerable sorrow to see that the greater part of the human race" is not yet Catholic, and he added that the Catholic Church, through the council, "desires to show herself to be the loving mother of all, benign, patient, full of mercy and goodness towards the children separated from her."

Frequently in the past, he said, the Church condemned errors of belief "with the greatest severity."

Today, however, the Church prefers to use "the medicine of mercy rather than that of severity," in the conviction that "she meets the needs of the present day by demonstrating the validity of her teaching rather than by condemnations."

"The Catholic Church," in the words of the Pope, "considers it her duty to work actively" for the unity of "the entire Christian family."

"Most Fervent Prayer"

In a plain reference to the tribulations of the Church behind the Iron Curtain, the Pope declared he felt "most lively sorrow over the fact that many bishops, so dear to us, are noticeable here today by their absence because they are imprisoned for their faithfulness to Christ or impeded by other restraints. The thought of them impels us to raise most fervent prayer to God."

The opening of the council took place in an atmosphere made scintillating by sumptuous fabrics and by the lights reflected from surfaces of gold, marble and precious gems.

Outside, the day started forbiddingly, for rain poured steadily out of dark skies. Despite the discomfort, however, several hundred persons had assembled in St. Peter's Square by 6:30.

The press and various others assigned places within were admitted around 7:30.

Rain Ceases

Rain continued during the vesting of the clergy in the Vatican palace, but, as if with a perfect sense of timing, it ceased and the sun emerged in time to permit the procession of cardinals, patriarchs, archbishops,

bishops and other high churchmen to move through the square.

Had the rainfall kept up, persons outside the basilica would have had scant opportunity to witness the line of march in all its splendor, for the procession would simply have crossed the porch of the church.

After the sun came out, the square quickly filled with a public eager to see the brilliant spectacle.

The Pope, before walking downstairs to mount his portable throne, prayed in front of the Blessed Sacrament in the Pauline Chapel.

Palatine Guards

The procession was headed by thirteen Palatine guards, in blue uniforms, and by the massed clergy of Rome in choir vestments.

Among other groups that preceded the council fathers were the Sistine Chapel choir; Roman noblemen of the papal court, in medieval dress; bearers of the papal cross, papal tiaras, and the thurbile (for incense), and numerous other persons having special functions of service to the Pope or to other churchmen.

The council fathers formed a striking picture in their tall, glistening white mitres and their copes—white, ankle-length mantles. Upon the snowy surface of their robes glittered gold embroideries of designs in resonant greens, reds or other colors.

The basic attire was uniform, but the nationality of the wearers varied widely, with all races represented.

Papal Entourage

The mark included, at intervals, members of the Swiss Guards in their famous uniforms, predominantly blue and orange.

Finally came the papal entourage, with the Pope on his throne, wrapped in an enormous gold-embroidered white mantle and wearing the so-called Precious Tiara, which sparkled with rare stones.

A white silk canopy was carried over him, seeming to imprison the rays of the sun, and on each side were bearers of large plumed fans, which were not there primarily for ornament but which have an ancient ritual significance.

The crowds cheered and applauded as the Pontiff moved past making his gesture of blessing repeatedly toward each side.

Heads Bared and Bowed

Within the basilica he descended and walked to the council altar which had been set up in the 600-foot nave.

Meanwhile the council fathers had taken their places on each side of the nave, where they awaited the Pope with heads bared and bowed.

At the altar was Eugene Cardinal Tisserant, dean of the College of Cardinals, ready to celebrate the Mass of the Holy Spirit. Kneeling, without his mitre, the Pope intoned the hymn, "Veni Creator Spiritus." After the first verse he proceeded to his throne at the papal altar while the choir continued the hymn.

Descending, he went to the altar again to recite the confession with the Cardinal Dean, who then continued the mass alone.

At the end of mass, the Pope gave his blessing to the council fathers.

The whole ceremony was watched closely by a line of non-Catholic observers seated in honor places near the Pope. These represented the Anglican, Presbyterian and Lutheran denominations, the Evangelical Church of Germany, the World Convention of the Churches of Christ, the World Committee of the Society of Friends, the International Council of Congregationalists, the World Council of Methodists, the World Council of Churches, the Coptic Church of Egypt, the Jacobite Church and the Ethiopian and Armenian churches, as well as the Orthodox Church outside Russia.

Across from them was a gallery for the officials sent by nations from all over the earth as special missions to the council. This group was made vivid by different kinds of special dress, including long black mantles, red tunics, sashes and medals and a splendid white-embroidered robe that swathed an official from one of the African countries.

Variety of Attire

Among figures to be seen elsewhere in the basilica were chamberlains of the Capes and Sword in their elegant black dress of centuries past, white lace at their wrists and white ruffles around their necks. The attire of many assisting clergy added symphonic variety to the palette. Some were clad in red, others in purple and still others were arrayed in embroidered gold.

With the mass completed and the opening ceremonies of the council session finished, the Pope made a complete change of attire, assisted by the papal sacrist and others.

After removing from him the mitre, cope and other garments, the Cardinal Deacon vested the Pope as for mass and placed around his shoulders the pallium, a circular band of white wool taken from two lambs blessed in the Church of St. Agnes on her feast day and presented to the Pope on the Feast of Sts. Peter and Paul.

Kiss Pope's Hand

Next the council made obeisance to the Pontiff. All the cardinals and patriarchs kissed his hand. Two archbishops and two bishops, representing the entire company of their rank, kissed his knees, and two abbots and two generals of orders kissed his foot, acting on behalf of their respective groups.

The Pope had a smile and a word for every cardinal. His greeting for Francis Cardinal Spellman was especially cordial, and he gave an affectionate squeeze to the shoulder of Laurean Cardinal Rugambwa, the only African cardinal.

When this ceremony had been completed, the Pope knelt and recited the solemn Profession of Faith, as required at any general assembly of the church.

Oath of Response

Archbishop Percile Felici, secretary general of the council, and the man responsible for all the arrangements, arose and read the Oath of Response—"I promise and swear May God and God's Holy Gospel help me." This was repeated by every council father, kneeling.

In the ceremonies that followed, the Pope recited and intoned prayers for the beginning of the council.

He then rose and, holding the papal cross in his left hand instead of his bishop's crozier, he blessed the assembly three times.

40-Minute Address

One of the most picturesque elements of the day occurred at that point, when high dignitaries of the Oriental rite, bearded, wearing exotic crowns and splendid robes, chanted the Supplication.

The Pope then made his address, speaking for 40 minutes on the council and its aims, after which he imparted solemn benediction.

Archbishop Felici announced the time of the next council session, 10 o'clock Saturday morning, and assistants removed the Pope's ceremonial vestments.

The Pontiff said a last prayer, mounted his portable throne and was borne out as the fathers applauded. The great basilica began to empty at once and those who had entered in the morning downpour emerged to find a clear sun.

18

The Death of God

When a small group of theologians in 1965 proclaimed God dead in modern Judeo-Christian thought, it set off a firestorm of protests, debates, articles and questions about the role of a personal God in a modern society and curiosity about theologians who could pronounce God dead but still consider themselves Christian. The theologians' views were first published October 17, 1965, in the *New York Times*. Scholars say it was Edward Fiske's *New York Times* piece that started the public controversy. Fiske, the paper's religion reporter, had noticed references to "Death of God" in the Spring 1965 issue of the *Christian Scholar* and elsewhere.

Time magazine ran its own story October 22, 1965, a story researcher Frederick D. Buchstein called "a horrified, pious point of view. It was superficial, hasty, poorly researched and mocking." Buchstein, who later analyzed Death of God coverage in a Spring 1972 issue of *Journalism Quarterly*, pronounced a second *Time* story published six months later less hostile. The April *Time* article, reprinted here, was a cover story that asked in blazing red text, "Is God Dead?" The cover was the first time in the news magazine's history that editors chose to use words alone on the cover.

The radical theologians leading the "God Is Dead" discussions argued that God is not part of modern experience for most people and that references to God are meaningless. The four men who were dubbed the "God is Dead" theologians had two primary understandings, according to Buchstein:

> First, the God who had been the center of faith and theological reflection for the Judeo-Christian tradition is now seen to be nonexistent, unreal and an illusion. . . . Second, Christianity or Judaism must henceforth understand itself and the world without God.

As one of the theologians who proclaimed "God Is Dead," William Hamilton told Buchstein the controversy "made God-talk accessible to cocktail parties." But it also put an uncomfortable spotlight on some of the theologians who before that had toiled in obscurity. By 1969, the controversy had waned, but not before many religion writers across the country wrote reaction stories or other localized versions of the debate. One example of these is former *Detroit Free Press* religion reporter Hiley Ward's "Here's a Third Side in Dead-God Dispute," story from January 10, 1966. That article reported a speech by another prominent liberal theologian, Harvey Cox, author of *The Secular City* and the 1984 book *Religion in the Secular City*. Cox said politics had replaced theology as a way to understand the world.

"There are three ways of regarding God," Cox, a Harvard Divinity School professor, told Ward. "Affirm tenaciously like the fundamentalists that God exists, or accept him as no longer relevant, as the Death-of-God people do, or do some rethinking about God."

Toward a Hidden God

Time, April 8, 1966

Is God dead? It is a question that tantalizes both believers, who perhaps secretly fear that he is, and atheists, who possibly suspect that the answer is no.

Is God dead? The three words represent a summons to reflect on the meaning of existence. No longer is the question the taunting jest of skeptics for whom unbelief is the test of wisdom and for whom Nietzsche is the prophet who gave the right answer a century ago. Even within Christianity, now confidently renewing itself in spirit as well as form, a small band of radical theologians has seriously argued that the churches must accept the fact of God's death, and get along without him.

How does the issue differ from the age-old assertion that God does not and never did exist? Nietzsche's thesis was that striving, self-centered man had killed God, and that settled that. The current death-of-God group* believes that God is indeed absolutely dead, but proposes to carry on and write a theology without theos, without God. Less radical Christian thinkers hold that at the very least God in the image of man, God sitting in heaven, is dead, and—in the central task of religion today—they seek to imagine and define a God who can touch men's emotions and engage men's minds.

If nothing else, the Christian atheists are waking the churches to the brutal reality that the basic premise of faith—the existence of a personal

God, who created the world and sustains it with his love—is now subject to profound attack. "What is in question is God himself," warns German Theologian Heinz Zahrnt, "and the churches are fighting a hard defensive battle, fighting for every inch." "The basic theological problem today," says one thinker who has helped define it, Langdon Gilkey of the University of Chicago Divinity School, "is the reality of God."

A Time of No Religion

Some Christians, of course, have long held that Nietzsche was not just a voice crying in the wilderness. Even before Nietzsche, Sören Kierkegaard warned that "the day when Christianity and the world become friends, Christianity is done away with." During World War II, the anti-Nazi Lutheran martyr Dietrich Bonhoeffer wrote prophetically to a friend from his Berlin prison cell: "We are proceeding toward a time of no religion at all."

For many, that time has arrived. Nearly one of every two men on earth lives in thralldom to a brand of totalitarianism that condemns religion as the opiate of the masses—which has stirred some to heroic defense of their faith but has also driven millions from any sense of God's existence. Millions more in Africa, Asia and South America seem destined to be born without an expectation of being summoned to the knowledge of the one God.

Princeton Theologian Paul Ramsey observes that "ours is the first attempt in recorded history to build a culture upon the premise that God is dead." In the traditional citadels of Christendom, grey Gothic cathedrals stand empty, mute witnesses to a rejected faith. From the scrofulous hobos of Samuel Becket to Antonioni's tired-blooded aristocrat, the anti-heroes of modern art endlessly suggest that waiting for God is futile since life is without meaning.

For some, this thought is a source of existential anguish: the Jew who lost his faith in a providential God at Auschwitz, the Simone de Beauvoir who writes, "It was easier for me to think of world without a creator than of a creator loaded with all the contradictions of the world." But for others, the God issue—including whether or not he is dead—has been put aside as irrelevant. "Personally, I've never been confronted with the question of God," says one such politely indifferent atheist, Dr. Claude Levi-Strauss, professor of social anthropology at the College de France. "I find it's perfectly possible to spend my life knowing that we will never explain the universe." Jesuit Theologian John Courtney Murray points to another variety of unbelief: the atheism of distraction, people who are just "too damn busy" to worry about God at all.

Johannine Spirit

Yet, along with the new atheism has come a new reformation. The open-window spirit of John XXIII and Vatican II have revitalized the Roman Catholic Church. Less spectacularly but not less decisively, Protestantism has been stirred by a flurry of experimentation in liturgy, church structure, ministry. In this new Christianity, the watchword is witness: Protestant faith now means not intellectual acceptance of an ancient confession, but open commitment—perhaps best symbolized in the U.S. by the civil rights movement to eradicating the evil and inequality that beset the world.

The institutional strength of the churches is nowhere more apparent than in the U.S., a country where public faith in God seems to be as secure as it was in medieval France. According to a survey by Pollster Lou Harris last year, 97% of the American people say they believe in God. Although clergymen agree that the postwar religious revival is over, a big majority of believers continue to display their faith by joining churches. In 1964, reports the National Council of Churches, denominational allegiance rose about 2%, compared with a population gain of less than 1.5%. More than 120 million Americans now claim a religious affiliation; and a recent Gallop survey indicated that 44% of them report that they attend church services weekly.

For uncounted millions, faith remains as rock solid as Gibraltar. Evangelist Billy Graham is one of them. "I know that God exists because of my personal experience," he says. "I know that I know him. I've talked with him and walked with him. He cares about me and acts in my everyday life." Still another is Roman Catholic Playwright William Alfred, whose off-Broadway hit, "Hogan's Goat," melodramatically plots a turn-of-the century Irish immigrant's struggle to achieve the American dream. "People who tell me there is no God," he says, "are like a six-year-old boy saying that there is no such thing as passionate love—they just haven't experienced it."

Practical Atheists

Plenty of clergymen, nonetheless, have qualms about the quality and character of contemporary belief. Lutheran Church Historian Martin Marty argues that all too many pews are filled on Sunday with practical atheists—disguised nonbelievers who behave during the rest of the week as if God did not exist. Jesuit Murray qualifies his conviction that the U.S. is basically a God-fearing nation by adding: "The great American proposition is 'religion is good for the kids, though I'm not religious myself.'" Pollster Harris hears him out: of the 97% who said they believed in God, only 27% declared themselves deeply religious.

Christianity and Judaism have always had more than their share of men of little faith or none. "The fool says in his heart, 'there is no God.'" wrote the Psalmist, implying that there were plenty of such fools to be found in ancient Judea. But it is not faintness of spirit that the churches worry about now: it is doubt and bewilderment assailing committed believers.

Particularly among the young, there is an acute feeling that the churches on Sunday are preaching the existence of a God who is nowhere visible in their daily lives. "I love God," cries one anguished teenager, "but I hate the church." Theologian Gilkey says that "belief is the area in the modern Protestant church where one finds blankness, silence, people not knowing what to say or merely repeating what their preachers say." Part of the Christian mood today, suggests Christian Atheist William Hamilton, is that faith has become not a possession but a hope.

Anonymous Christianity

In search of meaning, believers have desperately turned to psychiatry, Zen or drugs. Thousands of others have quietly abandoned all but token allegiance to the churches, surrendering themselves to a life of "anonymous Christianity" dedicated to civil rights or the Peace Corps. Speaking for a generation of young Roman Catholics, for whom the dogmas of the church have lost much of their power, Philosopher Michael Novak of Stanford writes: "I do not understand God, nor the way in which he works. If, occasionally, I raise my heart in prayer, it is to no God I can see, or hear, or feel. It is to a God in as cold and obscure a polar night as any non-believer has known."

Even clergymen seem to be uncertain. "I'm confused as to what God is," says no less a person than Francis B. Sayre, the Episcopal dean of Washington's National Cathedral, "but so is the rest of America." Says Marty's colleague at the Chicago Divinity School, the Rev. Nathan Scott, who is also rector of St. Paul's Episcopal Church in Hyde Park: "I look out at the faces of my people, and I'm not sure what meaning these words, gestures and rituals have for them."

Hydrogen and Carbon

To those who do formulate a God, he seems to be everything from a celestial gas to a kind of invisible honorary president "out there" in space, well beyond range of the astronauts. A young Washington scientist suggests that "God, if anything, is hydrogen and carbon. Then again, he might be thermonuclear fission, since that's what makes life on this planet possible." To a streetwalker in Tel Aviv, "God will get me out of this filth one day. He is a God of mercy, dressed all in white and sitting on a golden throne." A Dutch charwoman says: "God is a ghost floating in space." Screenwriter Edward Anhalt *(Becket)* says that "God is an infantile fantasy, which was necessary when men did not understand what lightning was. God is a cop-out." A Greek janitor thinks that God is "like a fiery flame, so white that it can blind you." "God is all that I cannot understand," says a Roman seminarian. A Boston scientist describes God as "the totality of harmony in the universe." Playwright Alfred muses: "It is the voice which says. 'It's not good enough'—that's what God is."

Even though they know better, plenty of Christians find it hard to do away with ideas of God as a white-bearded father figure. William Mc-Cleary of Philadelphia, a Roman Catholic civil servant, sees God "a lot like he was explained to us as children. As an older man, who is just and who can get angry at us. I know this isn't the true picture, but it's the only one I've got."

Invisible Supermen

Why has God become so hard to believe in, so easy to dismiss as a nonbeing? The search for an answer begins in the complex—and still unfinished—history of man's effort to comprehend the idea that he might have a personal creator.

No one knows when the idea of a single god became part of mankind's spiritual heritage. It does seem certain that the earliest humans were religious. Believing the cosmos to be governed by some divine power, they worshiped every manifestation of it: trees, animals, earth and sky. To the more sophisticated societies of the ancient world, cosmological mystery was proof that there were many gods. Ancient Babylonia, for example, worshiped at least 700 deities. Yet even those who ranked highest in the divine hierarchies were hardly more than invisible supermen. The Zeus of ancient Greece, although supreme on Olympus, was himself subject to the whims of fate—and besides that was so afflicted by fits of lust that he was as much the butt of dirty jokes as an object of worship.

Much closer to the deity of modern monotheism was the Egyptian sun
god Aten, which the Pharaoh Amenophis IV forced on his polytheistic
people as "the only god, beside whom there is no other." But the
Pharaoh's heresy died out after his death, and the message to the world
that there was but one true God came from Egypt's tiny neighbor, Israel.
It was not a sudden revelation. Some scholars believe that Yahweh was
originally a tribal deity—a god whom the Hebrews worshiped and considered superior to the pagan gods adored by other nations. It is even
questionable to some whether Moses understood Yahweh to be
mankind's only God, the supreme lord of all creation. Even after the
emergence of Israel's faith, there is plenty of Biblical evidence that the
Hebrews were tempted to abandon it: the prophets constantly excoriate
the chosen people for whoring after strange gods.

The God of Israel was so utterly beyond human comprehension that
devout Jews neither uttered nor wrote his sacred name.** At the same
time, Judaism has a unique sense of God's personal presence. Scripture
records that he walked in the Garden of Eden with Adam, spoke familiarly on Mount Sinai with Moses, expressed an almost human anger and
joy. Christianity added an even more mystifying dimension to the belief
that the infinitely distant was infinitely near: the doctrine that God came
down to earth in the person of a Jewish carpenter named Jesus, who died
at Jerusalem around 26 A.D.

It was not an easy faith to define or defend, and the early church,
struggling to rid itself of heresy, turned to an intellectual weapon already
forged and near at hand: the metaphysical language of Greece. The alliance of Biblical faith and Hellenic reason culminated in the Middle
Ages. Although they acknowledged that God was ultimately unknow-
able, the medieval scholastics devoted page after learned page of their
summas to discussions of the divine attributes—his omnipotence, im-
mutability, perfection, eternity. Although infinitely above men, God was
seen as the apex of a great pyramid of being that extended downward to
the tiniest stone, the ultimate ruler of an ordered cosmos cooperatively
governed by Christian church and Christian state.

Undermining Faith

Christians are sometimes inclined to look back nostalgically at the
medieval world as the great age of faith. In his book, "The Death of
God," Gabriel Vahanian of Syracuse University suggests that actually it
was the beginning of the divine demise. Christianity, by imposing its
faith on the art, politics and even economics of a culture. unconsciously

made God part of that culture—and when the world changed, belief in this God was undermined. Now "God has disappeared because of the image of him that the church used for many, many ages," says Dominican Theologian Edward Schillebeeckx.

At its worst, the image that the church gave of God was that of a wonder worker who explained the world's mysteries and seemed to have somewhat more interest in punishing men than rewarding them. Life was a vale of tears, said the church; men were urged to shun the pleasure of life if they would serve God, and to avoid any false step or suffer everlasting punishment in hell. It did little to establish the credibility of this "God" that medieval theologians categorized his qualities as confidently as they spelled out different kinds of sin, and that churchmen spoke about him as if they had just finished having lunch with him.

The Secular Rebellion

The rebellion against this God of faith is best summed up by the word secularization. In "The Secular City," Harvey Cox of the Harvard Divinity School defines the term as "the loosing, of the world from religious and quasi-religious understanding of itself, the dispelling of all closed world views, the breaking of all supernatural myths and sacred symbols." Slowly but surely, it dawned on men that they did not need God to explain, govern or justify certain areas of life.

The development of capitalism, for example, freed economics from church control and made it subject only to marketplace supply and demand. Political theorists of the Enlightenment proved that law and government were not institutions handed down from on high, but things that man had created themselves. The 18th century deists argued that man as a rational animal was capable of developing an ethical system that made as much sense as one based on revelation. Casting a cold eye on the complacency of Christianity before such evils as slavery, poverty and the factory system, such 19th century atheists as Karl Marx and Pierre Joseph Proudhon declared that the churches and their God would have to go if ever man was to be free to shape and improve his destiny.

But the most important agent in the secularizing process was science. The Copernican revolution was a shattering blow to faith in a Bible that assumed the sun went round the earth and could be stopped in its tracks by divine intervention, as Joshua claimed. And while many of the pioneers of modern science—Newton and Descartes, for example—were devout men, they assiduously explained much of nature that previously seemed godly mysteries. Others saw no need for such reverential lip service. When he was asked by Napoleon why there was no mention of God in his new book about the stars, the French astronomer Laplace coolly answered: "I had no need of the hypothesis." Neither did Charles Darwin, in uncovering the evidence of evolution.

Prestige of Science

Faith in God survived scientific attack only when the churches came to realize that the religious language of the Bible is what Theologian Krister Stendahl calls "poetry plus, rather than science minus." Nowadays not even fundamentalists are upset by the latest cosmological theories of astronomers. Quasars, everyone agrees, neither prove nor disprove divine Creation: by pushing back the boundaries of knowledge 8 billion light years without finding a definite answer, they do, in a way, admit its possibility. Nonetheless, science still presents a challenge to faith—in a new and perhaps more dangerous way.

Anglican Theologian David Jenkins points out that the prestige of science is so great that its standards have seeped into other areas of life: in effect, knowledge has become that which can be known by scientific study—and what cannot be known that way somehow seems uninteresting, unreal. In previous ages, the man of ideas, the priest or philosopher was regarded as the font of wisdom. Now, says Jenkins, "the sage is more likely to be an authority in scientific methods of observing phenomena, who bases what he says on a corpus of knowledge built up by observation and experiment and constantly verified by further processes of practice and observation." The prestige of science has been helped along by the analytic tradition of philosophy, which tends to limit "meaningful" ideas and statements to those that can be verified. It is no wonder, then, that even devout believers are empirical in outlook, and find themselves more at home with visible facts than unseen abstractions.

Socialization has immunized man against the wonder and mystery of existence, argues Oxford Theologian Ian Ramsey. "We are now sheltered from all the great crises of life. Birth is a kind of discontinuity between the prenatal and postnatal clinics, while death just takes somebody out of the community, possibly to the tune of prerecorded hymns at the funeral parlor." John Courtney Murry suggests that man has lost touch with the transcendent dimension in the transition from a rural agricultural society to an urbanized, technological world. The effect has been to veil man

from what he calls natural symbols—the seasonal pattern of growth—
that in the past reminded men of their own finiteness. The question is,
says Murry, "whether or not a contemporary industrial civilization can
construct symbols that can help us understand God."

Teach-In for God

Secularization, science, urbanization—all have made it comparatively
easy for the modern man to ask where God is, and hard for the man of
faith to give a convincing answer, even to himself. It is precisely to this
problem—how do men talk of God in the context of a culture that rejects
the transcendent, the beyond?—that theologians today are turning. In
part, this reflects popular demand and pastoral need. "God is the question that interests laymen the most," says David Edwards, editor of the
Anglican SCM Press. Last month the University of Colorado sponsored
a teach-in on God, featuring William Hamilton and Dr. George Forell of
the University of Iowa's School of Religion; more than 1,700 people
showed up for the seven-hour session—a greater turnout than for a recent similar talkfest on Viet Nam. At the University of California at
Santa Barbara, students and faculty jammed two lecture halls to hear
Harvey Cox talk on the "Death of God and the Future of Theology."

"If you want to have a well-attended lecture," says Rabbi Abraham
Heschel, a visiting professor at Manhattan's Union Seminary, "discuss
God and faith." Ministers have found that currently there is no easier
way to boost Sunday attendance than to post "Is God Dead?" as the
topic of their next sermon. The new theological approach to the problem
of God is not that of the ages when solid faith could be assumed. No serious theologian today would attempt to describe the qualities of God as
the medieval scholastic did with such assurance. Gone, too, is any attempt to prove God by reason alone.*** For one thing, every proof seems
to have a plausible refutation: for another, only a committed Thomist is
likely to be spiritually moved by the realization that there is a self-exis-
tent Prime Mover. "Faith in God is more than an intellectual belief," says
Dr. John Macquarrie of Union Theological Seminary. "It is a total attitude of the self."

Four Options

What unites the various contemporary approaches to the problem of
God is the conviction that the primary question has become not what

God is, but how men are justified in using the word. There is no unanimity about how to solve this problem, although theologians seem to have four main options: stop talking about God for awhile, stick to what the Bible says, formulate a new image and concept of God using contemporary thought categories, or simply point the way to areas of human experience that indicate the presence of something beyond man in life.

It is not only the Christian Atheists who think it pointless to talk about God. Some contemporary ministers and theologians, who have no doubts that he is alive, suggest that the church should stop using the word for awhile, since it is freighted with unfortunate meanings. They take their clue from Bonhoeffer, whose prison-cell attempt to work out a "nonreligious interpretation of Biblical concepts" focused on Jesus as "the man for others." By talking almost exclusively about Christ, the argument goes, the church would be preaching a spiritual hero whom even non-believers can admire. Yale's Protestant Chaplain William Sloane Coffin reports that "a girl said to me the other day, 'I don't know whether I'll ever believe in God, but Jesus is my kind of guy.'"

In a sense, no Christian doctrine of God is possible without Jesus, since the suffering redeemer of Calvary is the only certain glimpse of the divine that churches have. But a Christ-centered theology that skirts the question of God raises more questions than it answers. Does it not run the risk of slipping into a variety of ethical humanism? And if Jesus is not clearly related in some way to God, why is he a better focus of faith than Buddha, Socrates or even Albert Camus? Rather than accept this alternative, a majority of Christians would presumably prefer to stay with the traditional language of revelation at any cost. And it is not merely conservative evangelists who believe that the words and ideas of Scripture have lost neither relevance nor meaning. Such a modern novelist as John Updike begins his poem "Seven Stanzas at Easter":

> Make no mistake: if He rose at all
>   it was as His body;
> if the cells' dissolution did not reverse,
>   the molecules reknit, the amino
>   acids rekindle,
> the Church will fall.

The century's greatest Protestant theologian, Karl Barth of Switzerland, has consistently warned his fellow church men that God is a "wholly other" being, whom man can only know by God's self-revelation in the person of Christ, as witnessed by Scripture. Any search for God that starts with human experience, Barth warns, is a vain quest that will discover only an idol, not the true God at all.

Holy Being

The word of God, naked and unadorned, may be fine for the true believer, but some theologians argue that Biblical terminology has ceased to be part of the world's vocabulary, and is in danger of becoming a special jargon as incomprehensible to some as the equations of physicists. To bridge this communications gap, they have tried to reinterpret the concept of God into contemporary philosophical terms. Union Seminary's John Macquarrie, for example, proposes a description of God based on Martin Heidegger's existential philosophy, which is primarily concerned with explaining the nature of "being" as such. To Heidegger, "being" is an incomparable, transcendental mystery, something that confers existence on individual, particular beings. Macquarrie calls Heidegger's mystery "Holy Being," since it represents what Christians have traditionally considered God.

Other philosophical theologians, such as Schubert Ogden of Southern Methodist University and John Cobb of the Southern California School of Theology, have been working out a theism based on the process thinking of Alfred North Whitehead. In their view, God is changing with the universe. Instead of thinking of God as the immutable Prime Mover of the universe, argues Ogden, it makes more sense to describe him as "the ultimate effect" and as "the eminently relative One, whose openness to change contingently on the actions of others is literally boundless." In brief, the world is creating God as much as he is creating it.

Perhaps the most enthusiastic propagandists for a new image of God are the Tweedledum and Tweedledee of Anglican theology, Bishop Robinson of Woolwich, England, and Bishop James A. Pike of California. Both endorse the late Paul Tillich's concept of God as "the ground of being." Pike, who thinks that the church should have fewer but better dogmas, also suggests that the church should abandon the Trinity, on the ground that it really seems to be preaching three Gods instead of one. Christianity, in his view, should stop attributing specific actions to persons of the Trinity—creation to the Father, redemption to the Son, inspiration to the Holy Spirit—and just say that they were all the work of God.

Discernment Situations

The contemporary world appears so biased against metaphysics that any attempt to find philosophical equivalents for God may well be doomed to failure. "God," says Jerry Handspicker of the World Council of Churches, "has suffered from too many attempts to define the indefinable." Leaving unanswered the question of what to say God is, some theologians are instead concentrating on an exploration of the ultimate and unconditional in modern life. Their basic point is that while modern men have rejected God as a solution to life, they cannot evade a questioning anxiety about its meaning. The apparent eclipse of God is merely a sign that the world is experiencing what Jesuit Theologian Karl Rahner calls "the anonymous presence" of God, whose word comes to man not on tablets of stone but in the inner murmuring of the heart.

Following Tillich, Langdon Gilkey argues that the area of life dealing with the ultimate and with mystery points the way toward God. "When we ask, 'Why am I?' 'What should I become and be?' 'What is the meaning of my life?'—then we are exploring or encountering that region of experience where language about the ultimate becomes useful and intelligible." That is not to say that God is necessarily found in the depths of anxiety. "Rather we are in the region of our experience where God may be known, and so where the meaningful usage of this word can be found." To Ian Ramsey of Oxford, this area of ultimate concern offers what he calls "discernment situations"—events that can be the occasion for insight, for awareness of something beyond man. It is during these insight situations, Ramsey says, that the universe "comes alive, declares some transcendence, and to which we respond by ourselves coming alive and finding another dimension."

A discernment situation could be falling in love, suffering cancer, reading a book. But it need not be a private experience. The Rev. Stephen Rose, editor of Chicago's *Renewal* magazine, argues that "whenever the prophetic word breaks in, either as judgment or as premise, that's when the historical God acts." One such situation, he suggests, was Watts—an outburst of violence that served to chide men for lack of brotherhood. Harvard's Harvey Cox sees God's hand in history, but in a different way. The one area where empirical man is open to transcendence, he argues, is the future: man can be defined as the creature who hopes, who has taken responsibility for the world. Cox proposes a new theology based on the premise that God is the source and ground of this hope—a God "ahead" of man in history rather than "out there" in space.

German Theologian Gerhard Ebeling of Tubingen University finds an arrow pointing the way to God in the problem of language. A word, he suggests, is merely a means of conveying information; it is also a symbol of man's power over nature and of his basic impotence; one man cannot speak except to another, and language itself possesses a power that eludes his mastery of it. God, he proposes, is the source of the mystery hidden in language, or, as he obscurely puts it, "the basic situation of man as word-situation."

"The Kingdom Within You"

For those with a faith that can move mountains, all this tentative groping for God in human experience may seem unnecessary. The man-centered approach to God runs against Barth's warning that a "God" found in human depths may be an imagined idol—or a neurosis that could be dissolved on the psychiatrist's couch. Rudolf Bultmann answers that these human situations of anxiety and discernment represent "transformations of God," and are the only way that secular man is likely to experience any sense of the eternal and unconditional.

This theological approach is not without scriptural roots. A God who writes straight with crooked lines in human history is highly Biblical in outlook. The quest for God in the depths of experience echoes Jesus' words to his Apostles, "The kingdom of God is within you." And the idea of God's anonymous presence suggests Matthew's account of the Last Judgment, when Jesus will separate the nations, telling those on his right: "I was hungry and you gave me food, I was thirsty and you gave me drink." But when? they ask. "And the King will answer them, 'Truly, I say to you, as you did it to one of the least of these my brethren, you did it to me.'"

The theological conviction that God is acting anonymously in human history is not likely to turn many atheists toward him. Secular man may be anxious, but he is also convinced that anxiety can be explained away. As always, faith is something of an irrational leap in the dark, a gift of God. And unlike in earlier centuries, there is no way today for churches to threaten or compel men to face that leap; after Dachau's mass sadism and Hiroshima's instant death, there are all too many real possibilities of hell on Earth.

The new approaches to the problem of God, then, will have their greatest impact within the church community. They may help shore up the faith of many believers and, possibly, weaken that of others. They may also lead to a more realistic, and somewhat more abstract, conception of God. "God will be seen as the order in which life takes on meaning, as being, as the source of creativity," suggests Langdon Gilkey. "The old-fashioned personal God who merely judges, gives grace and speaks to us in prayer, is, after all, a pretty feeble God." Gilkey does not deny the omnipotence of God, nor undervalue personal language about God as a means of prayer and worship. But he argues that Christianity must go on escaping from its too-strictly anthropomorphic past, and still needs to learn that talk of God is largely symbolic.

No More Infallibilities

The new quest for God, which respects no church boundaries, should also contribute to ecumenism. "These changes make many of the old disputes seem pointless, or at least secondary," says Jesuit Theologian Avery Dulles. The churches, moreover, will also have to accept the empiricism of the modern outlook and become more secular themselves, recognizing that God is not the property of the church, and is acting in history as he wills, in encounters for which man is forever unprepared.

To some, this suggests that the church might well need to take a position of reverent agnosticism regarding some doctrines that it had previously proclaimed with excessive conviction. Many of the theologians attempting to work out a new doctrine of God admit that they are uncertain as to the impact of their ultimate findings on their Christian truths; but they agree that such God-related issues as personal salvation in the afterlife and immortality will need considerable re-study. But Christian history allows the possibility of development in doctrine, and even an admission of ignorance in the face of the divine mystery is part of tradition. St. Thomas Aquinas declared that "we cannot know what God is, but rather what he is not."

Gabriel Vahanian suggests that there may well be no true faith without a measure of doubt, and thus contemporary Christian worry about God could be a necessary and healthy antidote to centuries in which faith was too confident and sure. Perhaps today, the Christian can do no better than echo the prayer of the worried father who pleaded with Christ to heal his spirit-possessed son: "I believe; help my unbelief."

---

* Principally Thomas J. J. Altizer of Emory University, William Hamilton of Colgate Rochester Divinity School, and Paul Van Buren of Temple University. Satirizing the basic premise of their new non-theology, the Methodist student magazine *Motive* recently ran an obituary of God in newspaper style:

"ATLANTA, Ga., Nov. 9—God, creator of the universe, principal deity of the world's Jews, ultimate reality of Christians, and most eminent of all divinities, died late yesterday during major surgery undertaken to correct a massive diminishing influence.

"Reaction from the world's great and from the man in the street was uniformly incredulous . . . From Independence, Mo., former President Harry S. Truman, who received the news in his Kansas City barbershop, said 'I'm always sorry to hear somebody is dead. It's a damn shame.'"

** Almost impossible to translate, the name Yahweh means roughly "I am who I am" or "He causes to be."

*** Probably the most famous proofs for God's existence are the five ways of St. Thomas Aquinas, all drawn from the nature of the universe, that he sets out in his "Summa Theologiae." Aquinas' first proof, for example, is that certain things in the world are seen to be in a state of motion or change. But some thing cannot be changed or moved except by another, and yet there cannot be an infinite series of movers. Therefore, there must be a first, or prime mover that is not moved or changed by anything else—and this is God.

19

All God's Children

The "God is Dead" controversy was born and played out in the halls of academia. But elsewhere during the 1960s, people were looking both for new ways to talk about God and faith and for new ways to live their beliefs.

Civil rights. The Vietnam War. Women's liberation. Political upheaval in Latin America. The general mood of the 1960s created a climate in which all varieties of views became heard. In the ensuing social upheaval, religious people and groups were at the forefront. Their efforts toward peace and justice helped the society welcome a greater religious pluralism that would become one of the major characteristics of U.S. religious life in the late 20th century.

Much has been written about the church's role in the civil rights movement and pictures of marching clergy—blacks and whites, arm-in-arm—have become a clichéd image of the era. Although clergy were prominent in the civil rights struggles, the story often was not perceived as a religion story by newspapers. The threat of violent conflict sometimes led newspapers to send police or general assignment reporters to cover civil rights protests. On other occasions, civil rights became a court story, an education story or even a political beat story. The death of Martin Luther King Jr. in 1968 ranked only fifth in a "Top 10 Religion Stories" poll by members of the Religion Newswriters Association. It trailed behind the Pope's encyclical on birth control, the World Council of Churches assembly, clergy dissent against the Vietnam War and the marriage and resignations of Roman Catholic priests.

A radical response to civil rights protests was the Black Power movement, which also sometimes became a religion story. Within the Black Power movement, some African-Americans sought not just equality but financial repayment for past inequities. For other African-Americans, liberation meant rejecting a fair-skinned Christ. The Black Power movement found further religious voice by incorporating elements of Islam to create the Black Muslim movement.

Civil rights movements spread from the African-American community to other disenfranchised groups. In the United States rights movements sprang up among women, gays and the physically challenged. But throughout the 1960s, the United States was not the only place undergoing radical political or cultural shifts.

In Central and South America, Marxism and Democracy struggled in a tug-of-war, with impoverished civilians often the casualties. Peruvian Roman Catholic priest Gustavo Gutierrez prodded his own faith and that of other Christians by insisting the church should follow Jesus's lead and liberate the oppressed, particularly the poor. In 1968 he coined the phrase "a theology of liberation" and authored a seminal book by that name.

A gathering of Latin American bishops in 1968 interpreted Liberation Theology not only as showing preferential concern for the poor but also as a strategy for defending human rights and an impetus for revolution. In the 1960s through early 1980s, some priests and nuns working in Nicaragua, El Salvador and Guatemala, particularly, espoused Liberation Theology, even when such support was dangerous.

Critics, including Pope John Paul II, say Liberation Theology employs Marxist analysis to incite class struggle and socialism. In a shift away from Liberation Theology, Latin American bishops at 1972 and 1992 gatherings urged more emphasis on spiritual work and less on social activism.

But even as Catholic support for it waned, Liberation Theology received new impetus from other groups in the 1990s. African-Americans adapted Liberation Theology to espouse race consciousness, with women creating their own version, called "Womanist" Theology.

While Liberation Theology was associated with political and economic revolution, antiwar activists in the United States made peace their campaign theme. Their methods, however, were sometimes viewed as revolutionary. And so clergy—Maryknoll priests Daniel and Phillip Berrigan were among the best known—were arrested along with lay protesters and sometimes charged with trespassing at U.S. weapons facilities and military bases.

Many, many clergy and some denominations made pronouncements against the Vietnam War or in support of conscientious objectors. But it would take another decade or so before some of the largest Christian groups would come out strongly in favor of nuclear disarmament. The nation's largest Protestant group, the Southern Baptists, adopted an antinuclear weapons resolution in 1977, which Helen Parmley covered in a February 1, 1977, story found in the *Dallas Morning News*. The U.S. Catholic bishops adopted a pastoral letter condemning nuclear weapons in 1985.

Of course in the absence of any extended, high-casualty war, and in an era of economic boom and prosperity, peace and justice efforts in the United States found it tough to garner attention—media or otherwise—by the mid-1980s. However, the notion of peace and justice became internalized, with new mixtures of spirituality that promoted inner peace, harmony and self respect.

This chapter has four varied examples reflecting efforts at peace and justice in the 1960s and beyond. In his 1969 "How to Read a Manifesto" piece, *Detroit Free Press* religion reporter Hiley Ward explains African-American demands that white churches pay $500 million in reparation for past inequalities.

By the 1990s, the Metropolitan Community Church would have congregations nationwide ministering especially to gays and lesbians, but in the late 1960s, the gay rights movements was in its infancy. *Los Angeles Times* reporter John Dart's 1969 story reprinted here is one of the first stories about that church.

More than a theoretical story, Liberation Theology was really the story of clergy risking their lives as they ministered among the poor in Latin America. Jeanne Pugh of the *St. Petersburg Times* found one such man in a 1986 visit to Nicaragua as part of a "Witness for Peace" entourage. In a sidebar reprinted here, Pugh profiles Father Jaime as the human face of Liberation Theology. A more recent story on liberation theology can be found in the March 16, 1996, issue of the *San Antonio Express-News*.

Richard Dujardin's 1985 story from the *Providence Journal-Bulletin* about passage of the Roman Catholic bishops' statement condemning nuclear arms is a prime example of deadline coverage of official institutional actions. Writing about carefully worded religious pronouncements is a typical duty for religion reporters. The previous day Dujardin covered last-minute wording changes that gave the document added force.

How to Read Manifesto

Hiley Ward, *The Detroit Free Press,* June 28, 1969

There is more than one way to read the Black Manifesto and the controversial speech by James Forman which introduced the Manifesto to the National Black Economic Development Conference convening in Detroit in April.

There are at least three ways to read the Manifesto and its introduction.

1. There is the literal approach, which takes the language with its accrued emotive quality quite literally. It is this category of readers—and by far the biggest group—which finds the Manifesto seditious, treasonous, and Marxist because of its condemnation of an ideal system of capitalism in this country and its call to power and revolution.

In this category of literalists, perhaps, is the FBI, which is proceeding in Detroit and elsewhere to collect information for possible criminal use against the drafters of the Manifesto, if an FBI caller to my desk is correct. In this category are many churches, such as the Jefferson Avenue Presbyterian Church, which last Sunday, in a vote rejecting the Manifesto and its demands for $500 million from the churches, said that "the language of the Manifesto all through is racial, seditious, treasonable, calling for overthrow of the government by rebellion in the streets."

In this category also are leading churchmen, including the Rt. Rev. Richard Emrich, Episcopal bishop of Michigan, who wrote, "I happen to believe that James Forman means precisely what he says."

2. There is the figurative approach, used by those who, beyond reading the document, look at Forman and listen to him personally, and find a certain charismatic quality in him. Those who feel the Manifesto requires a figurative interpretation regard Forman as a sort of modern-day Amos or Jeremiah, going about in angry tones striking consciences into re-evaluation of commitment to black projects.

An example in this category possibly is a New York white Episcopal rector who invited Forman as speaker, and picturing Forman as a prophet, saw Forman come down to the pulpit with an African cane to the tune of "Hallelujah" anthem by the choir and exit with "Mine Eyes Have Seen the Glory."

3. There is also a realist approach to the Black Manifesto. Realism is a term that perhaps best applies to the black revolution today, and is a term that some blacks like but do not use too much. Detroit black militant Albert Cleage thinks "realism" is one way to describe black aspirations.

Realism risks misunderstanding also, but it also provides a vehicle to discovering what the Manifesto is really saying. Realism may not be entirely alien from the literal and figurative approach. Jesus used all three forms of speech: When Jesus said "Go and buy a donkey" for his ride into Jerusalem, he could be taken literally; when he spoke in parables and riddles, he could be taken figuratively; when he said "I have come not to bring peace but a sword," he could be taken realistically.

Consider when Forman says, "Prepare yourselves to seize state power . . . Do not hedge, for time is short and all around the world the forces of liberation are directing their attacks against the United States." Would those who insist on taking that literally, think of taking Jesus absolutely literally when he talked about bringing the sword?

Jesus brought separation and bloody conflict as a result of his policies; death, as well as resurrection, was his legacy. There was a little bit of the literal and figurative and realistic—all in his remarks.

WHEN YOU READ a document realistically, you ask "what does it say," not "what are its most incendiary words," nor "what dream does its imagery foretell?" A realistic reading considers the whole context—past oppression, present difficulties, and the syntax of sentences of the paragraph.

Applying such a total approach to the Manifesto, attention can be given to two factors generally overlooked in it: 1) sequential language, and 2) the context of contemporary meaning of words.

Forman delves heavily in the language of sequence. The language of sequence means certain things happen before the next step, and the next, each conditioned by previous events. Consider this from the introduction: "Time is short and we do not have much time and it is time we stop mincing words. Caution is fine, but no oppressed people ever gained their liberation until they were ready to fight, to use whatever means necessary, including the use of force and power of the gun to bring down the colonizer." (In another context, this could be an excellent rationale for the U.S. involvement in Asia.)

The emphasis is on the provocation initiated by others; in this case, by the whites. And more directly, the Manifesto says, "We know deep within our hearts that we must be prepared to use force to get our demands. We are not saying that this is the road we want to take."

This can be taken literally or figuratively but it must also be taken realistically. The armed revolution doesn't start tomorrow. It may start, if . . . And the decision is up to the whites, according to the Manifesto, which holds little hope in what the authors regard as a thoroughly, profoundly racist country. As Forman said in his statement to New York Mayor John Linsay, "We are pursuing our demands for reparations in peace," but: "We will kill those who kill us." There is a sequence.

SECONDLY THE CONTEXT of contemporary language poses a challenge both to literalists and to those who draw up position documents. For instance, to denounce capitalism vehemently in the present age and to urge areas of government ownership or control and government overthrow does not make one a Marxist or a Communist. Marx himself drew heavily from the Christian philosopher George Friedrich Hegel for his dialectic of history and Marx in excerpt could be taken for Soren Kierkegaard, a theologian of his times, or for some modern critics of the church.

Pope Paul himself has denounced capitalism as a viable way to meet the needs of today's masses. In "Populorum Progressio" ("On the Development of Peoples"), he said in March, 1967, "It is unfortunate that on these new conditions of society a system has been constructed which considers profit as the key motive for economic progress, competition as the supreme law of economics, and private ownership of the means of production as an absolute right that has no limits and carries no corresponding social obligation."

The Pope was criticized for attacking a pure form of capitalism that no longer exists. The U.S. has a form of socialistic capitalism. Msgr. George Higgins, director of the division of Urban Life, U.S. Catholic Conference, has pointed this out. And Economist John Kenneth Galbraith notes that the U.S. government represents 25 percent of the buying power in the United States—close to the percentage of government purchasing in Communist Poland.

Capitalism is not the same today that Marx criticized, and perhaps both the NBEDC and its critics could be advised, as the Pope was advised, to address themselves to current terms and current meanings. The use of the word "manifesto" does not make one a Communist or Marxist because Marx and Engels used it. In 1966, the Lutheran Church in America issued a document of social concern and called it "The Manifesto."

A Church for Homosexuals

John Dart, *The Los Angeles Times,* December 8, 1969

While music played in the background, parishioners took their seats and passed hymn books down the rows, a layman started the worship service by reading from the 37th Psalm.

". . . Cease from anger, and forsake wrath: fret not thyself in any wise to do evil. For evildoers shall be cut off . . ."

"The meek shall inherit the earth . . ."

The service that followed was not too much different from many Protestant services.

But the psalm's prophecy that "the meek shall inherit the earth" undoubtedly has special meaning for this unusual congregation.

The churchgoers that filled the 385-seat Encore Theater on a recent Sunday morning were nearly all males, most of them young.

The church in Hollywood is believed to be the first one in the country to have a homosexual pastor, a predominantly homosexual congregation and to identify itself unabashedly as a church for homosexuals.

Formed a little more than a year ago, the Metropolitan Community Church has grown to more than 255 members and a prominent role in the increasingly outspoken homosexual community in Los Angeles.

The pastor is 29-year-old Troy Perry, who was minister of fundamentalist churches in Florida and Santa Ana before he faced up to what homosexuals sometimes call their "sexual orientation."

Some young women attend the services. Perry estimates that the membership is 70 percent male homosexuals, 15 percent female homosexuals, or lesbians, and 15 percent heterosexuals, some of whom are relatives of members and "some who just like our kind of service."

Although most of the members are not ashamed of their homosexuality, many fear public disclosure—sometimes because it could cause them to be discharged from their jobs.

At several points during the service Pastor Perry gently ribs members for their skittishness and secrecy. Complaining that deacons of the church were having trouble contacting parishioners, the young pastor drew laughs from the pews when he added: "This time, give us your real name and address."

Assistant Minister

After the psalm reading and a hymn, an assistant minister briefly addressed the congregation. "We hope we are a friendly church," he said. Like ministers in churches around the country that Sunday morning, he urged the parishioners to "make it a point to speak to other people here today."

Another hymn, a scripture reading, then another assistant minister asked if there were any special prayer requests. Many hands went up, but only one was acknowledged. "Brother Jack . . . is facing surgery and would like our prayers," said a man in the front row.

But another worshiper, unacknowledged, weeping and with shaking voice, began thanking God for the growth of the church, for a growing public understanding of homosexuals and the assurance he felt that Jesus loved him, too. The impromptu, emotional testimony was not unlike the kind that can be heard in some Bible Belt churches.

Bounces From Seat

After the prayers were said, Pastor Perry bounced from his seat near the temporary altar, took three swift steps to the pulpit, and said loudly in enthusiastic Southern evangelist style:

"If you love the Lord this morning, say, 'Amen!'"

"Amen!" came the deep-throated response from the rows of theater seats.

His Southern upbringing and previous association with the Church of God (Cleveland, Tenn.) is reflected in his pulpit style.

For the Sunday services, however, Perry wears a priest's cassock and vestments. "Catholics and men from the liturgical churches like Lutheran and Episcopal can relate better to someone who looks a little like a priest," he explained.

A calmer style of ministry comes from Metropolitan Community Church's two part-time clergymen, one a former United Church of Christ pastor in the Midwest and the other an ex-Presbyterian minister and missionary. Both prefer to keep their names out of print because they work full time outside the church.

Characteristics of a liberal, activist church are assumed when it discusses "straight" society's discrimination against the "silent minority" of homosexuals.

Urging his churchgoers to attend a rally that afternoon to protest the state law banning private homosexual acts between consenting adults, Perry reiterated: "The church does not stand for adults having sexual affairs with minors, in public or forcing themselves on others." (Applause from the pews.)

Perry is president of the Western Homophile Conference ("homophile" literally means anyone sympathetic to homosexuals though the term is often used as a euphemism for homosexual), chairman of the Los Angeles Committee for Homosexual Law Reform and a board member of the Council on Religion and the Homosexual.

Later Council

The latter council, formed in several major cities in the 1960s, includes many heterosexual clergy from mainline denominations.

Criticism of church appeals for more compassionate views of homosexuals was made recently by a leading conservative churchman, Dr. Carl F.H. Henry of Eastern Baptist Theological Seminary. Some sympathizers seem to be more compassionate than Jesus "toward moral evils," said Dr. Henry.

"In the name of Christian love we hear louder and louder pleas for a new attitude toward divorce and remarriage, toward adultery, toward premarital intercourse and toward homosexuality."

Contributor to "The Gay World and Theology," a book to be published by the Presbyterian-run Westminster Press next spring, Dr. Henry said the Christian community is not called "to dignify homosexuality as a way of life equivalent to heterosexuality."

A minister of a Hollywood church said he was once asked by a homosexual if his friends could come to the church, and the minister replied that anyone is welcome to come to his church. Asked if the group could meet there as a homosexual group, the minister said no.

The same clergyman, while somewhat sympathetic to the homosexuals' plight, said he believes that young men can be and are led into a life of homosexuality by homosexuals looking for new lovers.

Pastor Perry and a number of other outspoken homosexuals, however, believe that psychology and their own experiences indicate a person's sexual orientation is largely determined in his early years of life. Then, they say, it's only a matter of time before the "coming out" of the homosexual, if that's the orientation.

Though he had his first homosexual experience at age 9, Perry said he dated girls in his teens, married at age 19, and later had a child.

"My wife had some knowledge of my homosexuality and she wanted us to stay together anyway," said Perry, "but I felt I was living a lie as far as my church's doctrine was concerned."

Perry said his ministry was successful at Santa Ana. The church grew rapidly in membership in the year he was there. But the denomination, which condemned movie-going and jewelry, also excommunicated any minister who indulged in homosexual acts.

His district leader didn't know how to respond when Perry told him about his feelings, the young pastor said. "Laymen who had confessed their homosexual feelings to him were convinced it was the devil, and if you pray hard enough God would remove it," he said.

Started Church

He was soon excommunicated from the church. After working at various jobs and serving a stint in the Army, he started the homosexual church, meeting in various locations around Los Angeles until a motion picture theater in Hollywood was donated for use on Sunday mornings.

Of biblical strictures against homosexuality, Perry feels the interpretations of the past have been wrong or too literal.

"In Leviticus it says if a man lies with a man, both should be stoned," he said. "But in the same book in the Bible it says it's wrong for a woman to wear a scarlet dress or for a person to eat shrimp."

The Apostle Paul in I Corinthians, 6th chapter, lists the effeminate or homosexuals (depending on the translation) among those who will not inherit the kingdom of God. "The Greek word can mean several things, but if you're going to be that literal you could find the wearing of long hair by men and wearing of gold and pearls by women condemned in the New Testament," he said.

Sodom, from which the term sodomy was derived, was destroyed, according to the Bible, "not for its homosexuality but because they couldn't find 20 righteous men in the city," said Perry.

Making a distinction between sexual lust and sexual love, Perry said Paul wrote in Romans that God gave up some men to dishonorable passions because they worshipped animals and men rather than God. As for the passage about "men giving up their natural relations with women," Perry countered: "How could the homosexuals give up something they never had?"

To say Metropolitan Community Church is one church that has no arguments over sex, and what is appropriate for a church, would be wrong. The current MCC bulletin contains ads from "a private club for groovy guys," a bar and an erotic homosexuals publishing house, but the church bulletin's editors concede there is ongoing discussion of whether it is proper or not for a church publication.

The church has a variety of activities and services besides the worship services. They include:

- Prayer meetings and Bible classes.
- An "Alcoholics Together" group.
- A class for the deaf. (Ten deaf persons attended the recent Sunday's service with an assistant minister interpreting what was said.)

- Marriage ceremonies, though they are not legally binding. ("Couples have to be together six months before I'll marry them.")
- A "ladies auxiliary," designed partly to counsel wives, mothers or sisters of homosexuals.
- A telephone hotline and counseling service for homosexuals.

"The biggest practical need we serve is that of understanding and giving the homosexual a sense of belonging," Perry said.

"Most churches in America don't openly invite homosexuals as homosexuals to come and worship God," he said.

"They feel, if anything, they have to change the person and convert him from his homosexuality to make him a fit member for their church—and that's just impossible," he declared.

Faith and the Revolution Are Intertwined for Padre Jaime

Jeanne Pugh, *St. Petersburg Times*, January 18, 1986

BOCANA DE PAIWAS—The people call him Padre Jaime (HI-may). He is their parish priest and, throughout this mostly rural area in central Nicaragua, he is acquiring a reputation akin to sainthood. He is also one of the area's leading defenders of the Sandinista revolution.

"I hope you will take back to the United States the message that the Nicaraguans have a right to the Process," he said, using the word employed by the Sandinistas to describe the revolution. "They have a right to participation in their own future. The Christian message that is coming out of Nicaragua can be a great help to the people of the United States."

Jaime's real name is Jim Feltz. Tall, gaunt and graying, this 48-year-old Marianist priest from Milwaukee worked seven years in Colombia and Peru and three years with Mexican immigrants in Chicago before coming to Nicaragua. In 1981, he accepted an invitation from another former Milwaukeean, Rt. Rev. Salvatore Schaeffer, now the bishop of the Bluefields Diocese of Nicaragua, to take over the Cristo Rey (Christ the King) Parish in Paiwas. His church in the village of Bocana de Paiwas serves a scattered, rural population of several thousand Catholics and a chain of 36 outpost chapels.

FOR FELTZ and most of his flock, the Christian faith and the revolution are intertwined. They see the revolution as a manifestation of Christ's kingdom on Earth.

Before the "Triumph"—that day in July 1979 when dictator Anastasio Somoza fled the country in the wake of the Sandinista-led uprising— Paiwas had no school, no electricity and no medical services. Now, most of its citizens can read and write. Most of its houses are served by electricity—even if that means just a single light bulb dangling from the rafters of a one-room, thatch-roofed, mud-floored cottage. And the town's medical center, built in 1982, has a full-time doctor and two nurses on duty.

What all this means, according to Carmen Mendieta, one of Feltz' parishioners, is that "God is not in the sky anymore; he is right here on the ground with us."

But, because the church is the strongest unifying factor in the area, Feltz' friends continually worry about his safety as he travels throughout the parish to conduct surveys and minister to its many other needs.

"One gets the feeling that Jim's days are numbered," said Paul Dix, 50, a professional photographer from the United States who has signed on as a long-term volunteer for the U.S.-based Witness for Peace, the group that sponsored our delegation of visitors to Paiwas. "The contras want to get rid of him but they don't know how. He's very pro-Process. Politically, however, it would be unwise to kill a priest, especially an American one."

FELTZ AND Dix had just returned from a 10-day trek through the country side on one of Feltz's regular tours of the parish—a journey that, because of the lack of roads, had to be accomplished by foot, mule, horseback and dugout canoe.

They reported three encounters with the contras, including one that Dix said he feared might be their last. It happened one night, at about 9, just after Feltz had finished leading a prayer service.

"The people were still in the chapel singing," Dix said. "Jim was back in the room behind the chapel where he always stays overnight on these trips. I was out in the yard when, suddenly, I felt someone nearby and looked up. I was surrounded by kids in contra uniforms holding big guns. I picked out five or six in the pale moonlight, but I'm sure there were more. They acted very hyper, very scared—I felt they were very dangerous.

"They ordered me into the back room with Jim and they went through our gear. I figured they were going to steal it. Then they found Jim's

Sony radio. The leader said it was a Soviet-made radio and that I must be a Cuban adviser. Hell, I don't even speak fluent Spanish. The leader said he had orders to do something to us—but he was so hyped up he acted as though he couldn't remember what the orders were.

"Jim took out his letter from the bishop of Bluefields—the one he carries all the time to show who he is and why he goes where he goes. He gave it to the leader, but the leader passed it back. It was obvious he couldn't read—so Jim read it to him.

"Jim finally convinced him that we were neither Russian nor Cuban, and they left. But the next morning we found out they had taken three people (from the nearby settlement) and only one has come back. There's no way of knowing the fate of the others."

Dix said he believes the attempt of the contras to connect him and Feltz with the Soviets or the Cubans could be part of a stepped up effort on the part of the contras to find evidence of Soviet-Cuban participation in Sandinista operations—probably to satisfy U.S. supporters of the contras.

THAT INCIDENT occurred just a few days before Monday, Dec. 2, when a Soviet-made helicopter operated by the Sandinistas was shot down in the same area by contras. Two days later, the U.S. State Department reported that the helicopter was piloted by a Cuban—information, a U.S. spokesman said, that was gleaned from monitoring the helicopter's radio messages and determining that the pilot and co-pilot had Cuban accents.

However, a day earlier, members of the Witness for Peace delegation had talked to a Sandinista Army lieutenant just back from the battle zone. He said that the helicopter carried four Sandinista officers and 10 civilians, women and children being evacuated.

The official Sandinista version, which came out on Dec. 5, was that all aboard the helicopter were Sandinista military personnel. The names of 14 soldiers said to have been killed in the crash were listed in Managua newspapers.

THE CONTRAS, Feltz said, are doing every thing they can to halt the progress brought to Paiwas by the revolution. In the last four years, they have killed 93 civilians in the parish, most of them people involved in the Process—schoolteachers, health workers, members of the new Sandinista-sponsored cooperative farms and businesses, local and district officials.

Measles, which had almost been eradicated by a Sandinista vaccination program, has returned, afflicting 75 children in the past year. The

school in Bocana de Paiwas, swelled by the influx of refugee children,
now operates on double sessions during the March-December school
year. Adult education classes in outlying settlements have had to be
abandoned. About 50 ambushes, carried out by contras on the road between Paiwas and Rio Blanco, have cut down on deliveries of food,
medicine and other much-needed supplies.

Such supplies are crucial, Feltz said, now that the town's population
has been nearly quadrupled by the influx of campesinos, farm families
forced off their land by terrorist attacks. They are housed in flimsy shelters supplied by the government—a leveled mud or concrete floor, four
corner posts and a corrugated tin roof. The refugees use whatever they
can find for side walls—bamboo or sugar cane poles, scrap lumber or
gunny sacks.

Every family can relate tales of murder, torture or kidnapping at the
hands of the contras. Fathers, sons, brothers, mothers, daughters and sisters have been taken from their homes. Those who return tell of beatings,
rape and indoctrination.

FELTZ SAID the worst single incident occurred in May 1984 when
500 contra troops came into the area and killed 35 campesinos in a day.
That operation, Feltz recalled, also included a "political rap session in
the church where the people were told that the Sandinistas don't believe
in God and are persecuting the church."

Feltz scoffs at such a suggestion. The only serious confrontation he's
heard about between the church and the Sandinistas occurred a year ago
when 10 priests, all foreigners, were asked to leave the country because
the government said they were working against the revolution. And,
three years ago, he said, one Nicaraguan priest was at odds with the Sandinistas because he wouldn't let people who had joined the local militia
attend services at his church. All the authorities did was ask the bishop
in Matagalpa "to control this guy who was working with the counter-rev-
olutionaries," Feltz said.

Feltz dismissed the recent crackdown on the Roman Catholic hierarchy in Managua—where publication of a periodical called "Iglesia"
(Church) has been forbidden—as a necessary restraint on activity detri-
mental to the revolution. The Catholic hierarchy, he said, had arrogantly
announced that the new magazine would publish material opposing the
government, particularly its military draft. (Protestant ministers who
have recently been brought in for questioning by the Nicaraguan government authorities are also accused of preaching against the draft).

"In the United States, during the Vietnam War, people who dodged the draft or counseled others to do it were also considered criminals," Feltz reminded his listener.

SANDINISTA officials and the military are not only welcome in Feltz's church, they are active participants in the life of the parish, he said.

One of these is Anselmo Talena, 26, coordinator of the junta (elected town council), a position equivalent to that of mayor. Talena is the only member of the junta who has joined the Sandinista political party—but he is also a Delegate of the Word, a lay person trained by the church to assist the priest.

"The government never interferes with the practice of religion," he told the American visitors during a visit to his office in the village hall. "No one has ever suggested that I leave the church."

MEANWHILE, back at the small concrete block parish house next to Cristo Rey Church, Feltz was getting ready for another trip into the countryside. This time he was going alone. He slipped his knapsack over his bony shoulders, climbed onto his donkey and headed up the road.

"He really doesn't look well," one of our group observed, as we watched his slumped figure disappear over the crest of the hill.

"He thinks he has malaria," one of our Witness for Peace guides said, "but I'm sure he figures the contras will get him before malaria does."

Bishops Call Arms Race "A Curse on Mankind," Vote 238–9 for Letter

Richard C. Dujardin, *Providence Journal Bulletin,* May 4, 1983

CHICAGO—The United States' Roman Catholic bishops voted 238 to 9 yesterday to adopt a pastoral letter on nuclear war that challenges many of the elements of the nation's defense and weapons strategies.

Approval of the document, in a secret ballot, followed two days' debate in which the bishops several times adopted even stronger language than was proposed by the five-member ad hoc war and peace committee headed by Cardinal Joseph Bernardin.

The heavily-nuanced statement, entitled "The Challenge of Peace: God's Promise and Our Response," calls the nuclear arms race a "curse on mankind" which must be opposed.

But it does not rule out every conceivable use of nuclear weapons, even though it registers "profound skepticism" about whether any use of nuclear weapons can ever be morally justified.

The ambiguity of the document was emphasized during yesterday's debate when the bishops, at the urging of San Francisco Archbishop John R. Quinn, voted to adopt stronger language saying that "there must be no misunderstanding of our opposition on moral grounds to any use of nuclear weapons."

But they later retreated from that position toward a statement of skepticism after Bernardin argued that some ambiguity was needed if they were going to retain their moral acceptance of deterrence in however conditional a form.

One major concern of many of the bishops was the moral authority of the document.

AT A MEETING between American and European bishops last January, the head of the Vatican's Congregation for the Faith, Cardinal Joseph Ratzinger, reportedly told the Americans that they had to make clear moral distinctions between universal teachings and principles binding on all Catholics and those specific applications where there might be room for disagreement.

Thus, according to those guidelines, the bishops could outlaw direct attacks on cities since the Church's "Just War" teachings prohibit the killing of innocent civilians. However, they could not teach Catholics that nuclear first strikes and limited nuclear war are inherent evils.

Still, they voiced profound skepticism that the use of nuclear weapons could ever be limited, and thus placed the burden of proof on those who would employ such weapons that this would not lead to wider immoral conflict.

IN A NEWS conference after the historic vote, Cardinal Bernardin said the document brings to bear centuries of Catholic tradition on the critical issues facing society today, but declined to describe the pastoral letter as a major watershed in the life of the Catholic Church.

"I would prefer to leave that judgment for the people of the future to decide," he said. "I'm not sure if it is all that earth-shattering."

However, Archbishop John R. Roach, president of the National Conference of Catholic Bishops, said there was little doubt in his mind that with the wide-ranging discussion that has resulted from the bishops' pastoral letter, "the place of the Church has become very clear" as an institution that can be expected to enter into the public debate.

The bishops broke into applause yesterday when they heard that they had approved the document by so lopsided a margin.

IN THE END there were only a few holdouts, among them Archbishop Philip Hannan of New Orleans, a World War paratrooper. He insisted that if President Harry S. Truman had been guided by the bishops' advice and had not dropped the atomic bomb on Japan, as many as a million more American fighting men would have lost their lives.

Bishop Austin Vaughn, an auxiliary bishop of New York, also said he was casting a vote against the letter, insisting that it had not led to a clear addressing of all the theological issues and because "there is no clear idea on the binding force of what is being taught."

Some of that confusion was also reflected at a news conference where the bishops openly disagreed over the first use of nuclear weapons.

Bishop Patrick V. Ahern, another New York auxiliary bishop, said he believed that the use of nuclear weapons would be justified if the Soviet Union were invading Europe and the United States and its allies could wipe out the threat with "very limited, highly selective" nuclear strikes on the Soviet invaders.

But Archbishop Thomas Kelly of Louisville said he did not know of any case where nuclear weapons could be used.

Archbishop Oscar H. Lipscomb of Mobile, Ala., said that in his judgment there are some elements of Catholic teaching that are so universal—such as the prohibition against the taking of innocent lives—that anyone who advocated nuclear retaliation against enemy cities may no longer be considered a Catholic.

20

The Electronic Church

Religion has been part of radio and television broadcasts even from their experimental stages. When Canadian scientist Reginald Aubrey Fessenden transmitted the first ever wireless voice broadcast in 1906, it was a Christmas Eve service intended for ships off the coast of Massachusetts. In 1920, when KDKA in Pittsburgh, Pennsylvania, became the first regular radio station, one of its earliest broadcasts was an Episcopal church service. The audience responded so favorably that the service became part of the station's regular weekly lineup.

In part because wireless technology was cheap, religious groups were among those obtaining federal licenses to broadcast on the new medium. About 10 percent of the 600 stations operating in 1925 were licensed to religious organizations, most of these evangelical Protestant ones. But new government requirements of standardized equipment and staffing for regular hours cut the number of religious stations in half by 1933. One of the stations that survived was WMBI, operated by the Moody Bible Institute. According to Dennis N. Voskuil's discussion of the rise of religious broadcasting in Quentin J. Schultze's *American Evangelicals and the Mass Media:*

> [WMBI] quickly became the flagship of fundamentalist stations in the Midwest and beginning in 1930 was receiving as many as twenty thousand letters annually. It also became a national center for religious radio productions. In 1942, WMBI released transcribed programs to 187 different radio stations, thus demonstrating that there was a broad market for full-time religious programming in the United States.

Federal regulators in the 1920s viewed stations licensed to religious groups as propaganda channels. But commercial stations, with meager production crews and a federal mandate to provide public service broadcasting, relied on religious groups to provide broadcast content. As competition grew and more stations demanded money to air religious content, evangelicals, particularly, began to learn how to produce programs that could both attract audiences and earn their keep financially. By the late 1920s and early 1930s, some religious broadcasters were paying for airtime on major, high-power stations. Early influential broadcasters included Walter Maier of "The Lutheran Hour" and Charles E. Fuller's "The Old-Fashioned Revival Hour." By 1941, Fuller's "Revival Hour" and a second broadcast were heard over a thousand stations at an annual cost of $1.5 million.

In 1944, members of the National Association of Evangelicals formed a group to combat growing difficulties by evangelicals with gaining access to commercial network radio broadcasts. The result was the formation of the National Religious Broadcasters group, which became an important lobby for the right to purchase commercial airtime and to help what had been perceived as favoritism by national radio networks toward mainline Protestant groups.

Many of the successful religious radio broadcasters moved naturally from radio to television. The first religious television broadcast—Easter Sunday church services from both Protestant and Catholic churches—occurred in 1940. In 1950, Billy Graham presented his first "Hour of Decision" telecast. It was in the 1950s that some of the "giants" of religious broadcasting got their start, including Oral Roberts, who televised his healing crusades beginning in 1954.

Meanwhile, further changes by the FCC that reduced stations' requirement to offer free religious programming hurt radio and television programming by mainline Protestant groups, which were favored by commercial stations but could not afford to buy the airtime. The resulting competition for limited commercial airtime drove up prices and increased the need for effective pitches for money. According to Voskuil, just over half of all religious television was paid for in 1959. That jumped to more than 90 percent in 1977.

It took several decades for what became known as "televangelism" to attract large audiences and major dollars. By the time the secular media were covering the televangelists, it was an industry bringing in millions for its ministries. One of the earliest reports about the business side of televangelism is Jim Montgomery's front page piece in the *Wall Street Journal,* reprinted here.

It would be two years after Montgomery's story before Jerry Falwell and the Moral Majority were household names. But the popularity of the shows was documented in a survey by the *Richmond Times-Dispatch.* This story is a prime example of the use of survey data and the meshing of journalistic and sociological technique. The story carries additional weight because the newspaper is in the home state of two of the largest and most politically active televangelists: Jerry Falwell and Pat Robertson.

Evangelicals were not the only ones on television in the latter half of the 20th century, of course. Roman Catholic masses were a staple of Sunday morning programming and the mainline Protestant churches made earnest, if largely unsuccessful, efforts to harness the power of the airwaves. But without avid pleas for funds, most had limited audiences and airing.

Community cable access channels became a haven for itinerant preachers, private philosophers, atheists and all others willing to set up a camera and vent their views. Also in the late 1980s and early 1990s, public television stations aired occasional "celebrity" specials with religious themes. Broadcast veteran Bill Moyers was perhaps the best known among the hosts for these shows, with his series about the biblical stories in Genesis.

By the late 1990s, it was clear that money was a key stumbling block to getting religion in the broadcast media. To help, the Indiana-based Lilly Endowment, Inc. gave at least $7 million over several years to public station WNET in New York, which produced more than 40 half-hour weekly newsmagazine segments of the "Religion and Ethics Newsweekly."

Meanwhile, evangelicals still dominate any religious presence on television, despite difficulties in the mid-1980s. Between 1985 and 1987, Jim and Tammy Bakker, Jimmy Swaggart and Oral Roberts, along with lesser-known religious broadcasters, all faced scandals and declines in their ministries. In 1987, the *Charlotte Observer* ran more than 600 stories on Bakker's PTL Club. Some of them earned the paper a Pulitzer Prize in 1988.

The kind of detailed, months-long investigation that helped the *Observer* win the Pulitzer was also carried out in Tulsa, Oklahoma, at the now defunct *Tulsa Tribune*. There, in Oral Roberts's backyard, a team of reporters led by Mary Hargrove investigated Roberts for nearly a year, conducting more than 300 interviews and combing countless records. The resulting weeklong series won accolades and awards for its depth and the difficulty of covering a subject that had so many economic ties in Tulsa. Reprinted in this chapter is just one of the stories.

Despite the scandals of the 1980s, the abundance of cable channels helped assure there was still a healthy audience for television ministers in the 1990s. A September 3, 1998, *Washington Post* story said televangelists Robert Tilton and Peter Popoff were experiencing new popularity on the Black Entertainment Television Network, after both were investigated for fraud and unethical fund-raising in the 1980s. Also in the 1990s, many of the aging, charismatic leaders of the ministries—Jerry Falwell, Pat Robertson, even Billy Graham—were looking for successors to continue their ministries. *Houston Chronicle* Religion Editor Cecile S. Holmes wrote a thorough profile of Billy Graham's son Franklin, heir to Graham's ministry, published November 18, 1995.

The stories in this chapter focus on religious programming that began as outgrowths of prominent ministries that are easily found on a wide assortment of channels and times. Much harder to detect is any sort of regular religion coverage on network television news or mainstream radio. However, during the 1990s National Public Radio, with support from grants, appointed a reporter to the religion beat while ABC News became the first, and only, national network to assign a reporter to the beat.

Religious Broadcasting Becomes Big Business, Spreading Across U.S.

Jim Montgomery, *The Wall Street Journal*, May 19, 1978

LYNCHBURG, Va.—It's a typical Sunday morning at Thomas-Road Baptist Church here. Pastor Jerry Falwell is preaching to a full house of 3,200 parishioners—and to four television cameras. In the control room overhead, a dozen technicians scanning 14 screens select the succession of images that will become an "Old-Time Gospel Hour" videotape to be broadcast in a few weeks on 327 stations.

Now it's a typical Monday morning in the counting house—a former department store converted by "The Old-Time Gospel Hour" into an administration building. About 60 women are sorting through the day's mail: 18 sacks, 10,000 or so envelopes. More than half the envelopes contain many checks for $500, $100, $10. The average is $23.

As these scenes suggest, religious broadcasting is big business. The Electric Church, as it is sometimes called, is a booming industry, generating thousands of jobs and an annual cash flow of hundreds of millions dollars. By one estimate religious radio stations in the U.S. number 1,200 and increase at a rate of one a week; the TV-station count is 25 and increasing by one a month.

"We're Going to Get Stronger"

"This has to be understood as a new force" in religion and society, says Martin E. Marty, a Lutheran minister and University of Chicago professor, who considers the Electric Church a mixed blessing at best. William T. Bray, a promoter of the new force, promises that "we're going, to get stronger and stronger."

National Religious Broadcasters Inc., a trade association based in Morristown, N.J., figures that the number of religious radio stations has about doubled since 1972. In a couple of more years, it says, the TV total could double and there is likely to be a substantial increase in satellite and cable distribution of programs.

Accordingly, membership in the trade group is soaring. A decade ago it was 104. Now it is 850—mostly religion-oriented stations and program producers—and they account for 70% of religious air time. They claim audiences averaging 115 million people a week on radio and another 14 million a week on TV.

For many commercial broadcasting stations, these programs are something of a financial bonanza, although they don't generally end up in prime time. Benjamin L. Armstrong, a Presbyterian minister and executive director of the trade group, estimates that purchases of radio and TV time for religious broadcasts have grown roughly fivefold in the past five years to "about $500 million a year."

Born-Again Christians

Who's paying the bill?

"Born-again Christians are the main source of funding, the overwhelming source of support," says Mr. Bray, an Independent Assemblies of God minister in Wheaton, Ill., who works as a marketing and fund raising consultant to evangelical organizations.

Explains the broadcasters' Mr. Armstrong: "As part of the Electric Church concept, the listener is conditioned to give and by giving becomes part of the Electric Church."

This phenomenon is distressing to observers such as Everett C. Parker of New York, a minister and director of the United Church of Christ's office on communications. While most of the paid broadcasting is to spread the doctrines of Christian fundamentalists and evangelicals, he complains, "a lot of the money in their mail comes out of the pulpits of liberal churches." He says this happens because liberal churches "tell you the path isn't clear or easy," but their members "want simple answers" and that's what the fundamentalist broadcasters seem to provide.

A New Church

One important result, according to Prof. Marty, is that the big broadcast ministries are financially, "in effect, becoming a new church." Noting, for instance, that the national headquarters of most major established denominations each receive $20 million to $30 million a year from local congregations, he adds, "Any self-respecting evangelist can do better than that on TV."

Certainly several of them do. Although there are hundreds of local, regional and national broadcast preachers, the field is dominated by eight superstars who raise more than a quarter of a billion dollars a year for their diverse religious enterprises. Besides Jerry Falwell, these are the superstars:

— Oral Roberts of Tulsa, Okla., whose ministry takes in "approximately $60 million" a year and is growing at an annual rate of 25% to 30%. At a yearly cost that he says approaches $8 million, he appears in a weekly half-hour telecast of sermon and song on about 350 stations as well as four annual Prime-time variety specials on about 550 stations.

— Herbert W. and Garner Ted Armstrong of Pasadena, Calif., a father and son team whose Worldwide Church of God takes in "in excess of $75 million" annually, a top official says, "about $65 million" of it in the U.S. A half-hour daily radio monologue by the son runs on more than 60 stations, but his half-hour weekly TV program is being terminated this month. Plans call for a return to television in the fall of 1979 with a new program format and a sharply increased TV budget of $10 million to $12 million a year compared with the recent level of about $3 million.

— Pat Robertson of Virginia Beach, Va., whose Christian Broadcasting Network and related enterprises employ more than 800 people and expect to raise more than $30 million this year. Mr. Robertson is host of the main attraction, a daily 90 minute talk and variety show called "The 700 Club." It is taped and syndicated to about 130 radio stations, 130 TV stations and 3,500 cable systems.

— Jim Bakker of Charlotte, N.C., a Robertson protégé who parted company to form his own PTL Television Network. It has about 450 employees and an estimated gross exceeding $25 million a year. He is host of its two-hour daily talk-variety show broadcast at a cost of $7.4 million last year on 191 television stations and 3,000-odd cable systems. The program is called "The PTL Club." The initials stand for "People That Love" or "Praise the Lord." Mr. Bakker (pronounced "Baker") and his followers aren't amused by a Charlotte radio station's weekly parody that features an avaricious evangelist named Brother Bill Taker as host of "The Pass the Loot Club."

— Billy Graham Evangelistic Association of Minneapolis. Revenue for 1976, the latest year reported, was $27.8 million, excluding a related and controversial education fund. Broadcast expenses were $8.8 million in the U.S. and about $1 million abroad. In 1977, TV spending alone increased $2.3 million.

— Rex Humbard of Akron. His Cathedral of Tomorrow has 300 employees and a 1974 budget of $18 million, up from $14.4 million last year. A one hour weekly service featuring the evangelist's 14 member family and a small orchestra is shown on 237 television stations in the U.S. and another 341 in other countries.

— Robert Schuller of Garden Grove, Calif. His "Hour of Power" is telecast on about 130 stations at a cost for air time of close to $3 million a year. Its operating budget increased to $11 million this year from $10 million last year.

Charm, Talent and Drive

Each of these high-powered preachers projects a skillful blend of worldly and everlasting well-being. But none of them is doing it more successfully these days than Jerry Falwell.

His "Old-Time Gospel Hour" is probably the fastest-growing of any of the big-time religious shows. One reason is the 44-year-old Mr. Falwell himself, a man of charm, talent, drive and ambition. But his ministry's rapid growth is also a tribute to modern marketing and management methods. He is a forceful administrator with a flair for organization and delegation of authority and with a keen understanding of income statements and balance sheets. What separates him from many of his evangelical contemporaries is a strong belief in full financial disclosure.

Pastor Falwell founded his church and started broadcasting 22 years ago. His operations remained fairly modest until 1971, when revenue finally reached $1 million a year. By 1975 it had soared to $1 million a month. "Next year," he says confidently, "it will have to be about $1 million a week."

And, Mr. Falwell says, he is sure that "the Lord will provide" because he and his more than 700 employees—nearly all of them reborn Christians—plan to give him a lot of help. Among other things. he says that "we plan to add a couple of hundred more radio stations" to the 450 that already broadcast his half-hour daily sermons. And the impact of the television programs will be heightened, he says, because on one-fourth of the 327 TV stations, they will be broadcast at a better time. That will put "The Old Time Gospel Hour" in prime time on about 115 TV stations, up from 35 today.

Phone and Mail Response

The broadcasts are carefully produced to generate heavy telephone and mail response. Every week, viewers see a crowded church and attractive young singers. Every week they hear "Brother Jerry" preach against sin, promise salvation and offer free "Jesus First" lapel pins to all who call a toll-free number in Utah: "But keep it short, 'cause . . . we pay for it."

One result, he says, is that his ministry is "the largest 800 user in the nation," receiving "about 15,000 calls a week" on the toll-free number. Of two million Jesus-First pins purchased at 3 cents each, about 1 million have been mailed out. And "The Old Time Gospel Hour" mailing list, growing at the rate of 15,000 names a week, totals more than one million names.

Mr. Falwell says that nearly 80 percent of the $22.2 million in revenue collected in the year ended last June 30 came from 762,000 individual contributions. So many arrive in the 40,000 pieces of mail received each week that envelopes are color-coded for efficient sorting—cream for $10 monthly pledges, gray for a $100 building contribution and rust for a $500 building gift; each of the last two is rewarded with a laser-engraved brick bearing the donor's name.

$13.5 Million for Radio and TV

Now that revenue of about $32.5 million seems assured for the fiscal year ending next month, budgeting is just about completed toward next year's goal of $46.3 million. Nearly $13.5 million is earmarked for radio and television expenses. Payroll will total $8.2 million, including $38,000 for the chief executive officer—Mr. Falwell—who also is provided by the church with an $80,250 parsonage and all the electricity it needs. Other budget items include $3 million of gift offers; $1.9 million for printing; $1.5 million for contract services, such as professional fund-raising consultants; and $1.25 million for postage.

Like many other broadcast ministries, "The Old-Time Gospel Hour" takes in far more money than necessary to stay on the air. The surplus—a nonprofit enterprise's equivalent of profit—is typically used as investment capital.

Oral Roberts is building a medical center in Tulsa. The Armstrongs are financing related educational, missionary and publishing activities. Mr. Schuller is building a $14 million church. Messrs. Falwell, Robertson and Bakker are building colleges and universities. The schools are designed to train more evangelists as well as to instruct them and born-again laymen in sophisticated broadcasting techniques so that future generations of preachers will be able to cover the globe.

Fighting Irish vs. Fighting Baptists

Again, Jerry Falwell's expansion plans and hopes appear the grandest of all. Years ago he was a good enough baseball player to make the St. Louis Cardinals' tryout camp; now, a chancellor of his church's Liberty Baptist College, he is recruiting athletes with the idea of building the school's teams up to championship caliber.

Some day, he says, Liberty Baptist College's football team will beat Notre Dame's. Further, his timetable shows projected 1987-88 revenue of $2 billion for his ministry.

Some observers of religious broadcasting are unimpressed by such goals or the preaching stars who set them. To Prof. Marty, for instance, "These entrepreneurs are comparable to one-issue politicians. They are healers or positive thinkers or what have you. . . . They produce clienteles instead of congregations." But he concedes that their success shows that "what had looked like an ancillary function of the churches has become a self-perpetuating" force.

Paul M. Stevens of Houston, president of the Southern Baptist Convention radio and television commission, takes an even dimmer view of preachers who buy broadcast time to spread the Word. "We don't have any of these tricks," he says of the 39 radio and five television programs—including "The Baptist Hour"—that he produces every week for broadcast in free public-service time by stations. Production costs are subsidized by the Southern Baptist Convention.

Mr. Stevens says: "I have just a little bit of a problem with the idea of trying to get into a man's heart and pocketbook at the same time. The massaging of someone's spiritual convictions simply for the purpose of pleasing him denigrates religion."

Richmonders Watching Religious Shows at 2½ Times National Rate

Thomas R. Morris and Ed Briggs, *Richmond Times-Dispatch,* March 22, 1982

When the television evangelists talk, many, many Richmonders listen. People in the Richmond area are watching religious shows on television at about 2½ times the national rate, a Times-Dispatch poll shows.

The poll of 397 area residents shows that 24 percent of them said they watched a religious program in the past week. The Arbitron rating service, on the other hand, says only 10 percent of Americans do that. But the survey also suggests that the viewers aren't watching instead of going to church.

Critics of the electronic church say they fear the viewers are substituting a seat in front of a TV set for a seat in front of a pulpit, but that's apparently not the case here.

Overall, 44 percent said they attended church in the week before, but among those who watched a religious show on TV during the week, the figure rose to 53 percent.

An intermediate group of TV watchers—those who watched a religious program in the past year but not in the past week—was also above average in recent church attendance: 49 percent of them went to church. But only one of three non-watchers—those who haven't watched a religious show within the past year—went to church in the past week.

The recent watchers also are more likely to be a member of a church or synagogue. Overall, people in the Richmond area belong to churches at about the same rate as Americans do, but the recent watchers belong in disproportionate numbers. Of those willing to say whether they belong to a church or synagogue, 82 percent of the recent watchers are members, but only 66 percent of the non-watchers are.

Moreover, about three of four who watched one of the programs in the past week said they believe the programs have served to increase their involvement in their local church and its activities in the past three years. Only 9 percent said the programs decreased their church involvement; this minority would constitute those for whom the electronic preacher is substituting for the local pastor.

The findings suggest that in the Richmond area, the electronic church seems to fill only part of the appetite for religious activity rather than being an end in itself.

That appetite is strong. Those who watched religious shows in the past week are much more inclined to hold deeply felt religious views and to consider religion a vital part of their lives. A feeling emerges from the study that they are not just watching a TV show because the set is on, as they might tend to watch an adventure story. They are, instead, seeking out a religious program and watching it because they're inclined to think it's important.

Roughly two of three of the recent watchers took the most orthodox stance on a set of questions devised by two sociologists to test the depth of Christian religious beliefs. But only about three out of eight of those who haven't watched a religious show in the past year have the same level of Christian orthodoxy.

Dr. Charles Y. Glock, a retired professor at the University of California at Berkeley, and Dr. Rodney Stark of the University of Washington at Seattle defined the most orthodox as those who unquestioningly believe in the existence of God, the divinity of Jesus, the occurrence of biblical miracles free of natural causes and the existence of the devil.

Negative Answers

At the other end of the scale, the Times-Dispatch poll found that one of four non-watchers but only one of 12 recent watchers said no to all four questions.

The piety and orthodoxy of those who watch the electronic church also is seen in other ways. They're more likely to believe that baptism is absolutely necessary for salvation, that Jesus walked on water and that Jesus was born of a virgin.

Correspondingly, the subject of religion is indisputably much more important to those who watch religious shows on TV than to those who don't. Overall, about half the people in the Richmond area said they rate religion as very important. But three of four who watched a religious show in the past week said so, compared with only three of eight who haven't watched in the past year.

The regular watchers also are more likely to say that certain religious beliefs are needed to ensure entry to heaven: 85 percent of the regular watchers, compared with 68 percent of the non-watchers, said believing that Jesus is the savior is absolutely necessary for salvation, for example. And about half the watchers, compared with only a third of the others, say that regular participation in the sacraments is absolutely necessary.

Only a few television evangelists, like Rex Humbard, attempt to deliver sacraments, like Communion, via the airwaves, so this again underlines the participation of the TV faithful in their local churches.

But many TV evangelists press the need for money to produce programs for the expensive medium of television. The survey found that the regular viewers are more attuned to the importance of donations: 68 percent of the viewers, but 54 percent of the others, said they view tithing as necessary for salvation.

Cause and Effect

Whether the television evangelists generate orthodoxy among their audiences or whether they are simply attracting those who already have theologically conservative attitudes—the question of whether they are teaching new views or reinforcing old views—appears to be a chicken-or-egg question.

But the viewers are not much more inclined to see themselves as necessarily holding theologically conservative attitudes. Overall, one of four in the Richmond area considers himself a fundamentalist, and only one of three of the regular viewers does.

Moreover, only one out of 12 in the survey both considers himself a fundamentalist and has watched a religious show on TV in the past week.

A possible explanation of why relatively few of the self-described fundamentalists watch the TV shows regularly is that they might not have time. Their churches keep them busy several nights a week and on weekends, suggests the Rev. Calvin Eaves of Clover Hill Baptist Church in Chesterfield County.

Mr. Eaves, a self-described fundamentalist and the vice president of the Virginia chapter of Moral Majority, says that in his own life, for example, "I rub shoulders with a lot of these guys, but I don't have time to watch" televised religious shows.

The survey also found that college graduates were only slightly less inclined to call themselves fundamentalists than were area residents generally, but the college graduates were much less likely to have watched a religious program in the past week. About 17 percent of the college graduates, compared with 30 percent of those who didn't complete high school, said they watched one of the programs in the past week.

As a result, college graduates made up only 22 percent of the Richmonders watching one of those programs in the past week.

About a third of the local audience were Southern Baptists. Additionally, three of eight Southern Baptists chose to watch the television programs, compared with only two of eight area residents as a whole. Most of the regular watchers are women, and 70 percent of the electronic church's audience is white.

The local audience also appears to be younger than the national audience found by Arbitron.

Arbitron estimates that two-thirds to three-quarters of the national audience is older than 50, and the Times-Dispatch poll suggests that's twice as high as in Richmond. The newspaper poll found that 36 percent of the local audience is over 50, with roughly an equal number in the 30-49 bracket.

Perhaps that's because of the local influence of the Virginia Beach-based Christian Broadcasting Network. CBN in the past year has added a slate of programs to its daily schedule that is designed to reach out to a younger crowd—a morning talk show and an afternoon Christian soap opera.

Method of Polling Is Detailed

Information for the accompanying story was developed through a poll of 397 Richmond area residents who were selected at random and reached by telephone at their homes between Feb. 10 and 23.

The interviews were ended the day before Ash Wednesday, the first day of Lent; previous studies have shown that church attendance and piety increase during Lent.

Statisticians say that if this poll were repeated with the same size sample, 95 times of each 100 the findings would project the way Richmond area residents as a whole feel about these issues within 5 percentage points either way.

This "sample error" means, for example, that since the poll found that 52 percent of the sample said religion is very important to them, it could be projected that between 47 percent and 57 percent of all Richmond area residents would say so, too. The poll was conducted by the research department of Media General Inc., the parent firm of The Times-Dispatch.

The poll's results were analyzed and written by two Times-Dispatch staff writers. They were helped in analyzing the data by Dr. Jeffrey K. Hadden, chairman of the sociology department at the University of Virginia and an expert in the sociology of religion, and by John B. Mauro, Media General's director of research.

Roberts Faces New Challenges on the Televangelist Front

Mary Hargrove, Grant Williams and Pam Infield, *The Tulsa Tribune*, Special Reprint of February 3-12, 1986

Oral Roberts, a pioneer in television evangelism, has lost more than half of his viewing audience in the past eight years, dropping from first to third in national ratings among preachers.

Fifty-five percent fewer households watched Roberts' weekly "Expect a Miracle" program in November 1985 than in November 1977, according to the New York-based Arbitron Ratings Co.

The 30-minute Sunday program was viewed by 2.5 million households eight years ago but dropped to about 1.1 million last year.

Roberts' national telecast—which topped all others in 1977—now falls behind the weekly "Jimmy Swaggart Show" and Robert Schuller's "Hour of Power."

Roberts drops to fourth behind Pat Robertson's daily "700 Club," Swaggart and Schuller in a survey prepared last year by the A.C. Nielsen Co.

The Nielsen report measures more cable TV households and shows larger ratings for some daily programs.

Swaggart, an old-fashioned Bible-thumping preacher from Louisiana, strides across his auditorium stage hammering out a fire-and-brimstone message flush with anti-Communist conservatism. An estimated 2.2 million households follow his weekly performance that often delves into political issues.

The silver-haired, black-robed Schuller preaches an upbeat gospel of "Possibility Thinking" from his $20 million Crystal Cathedral in Garden Grove, Calif.

Schuller, flanked by two American flags and towering green plants, reaches a television audience of more than 1.9 million households. Near the cathedral, hundreds of followers watch him on a huge TV screen from their cars at a drive-in.

ROBERTS, THE conservative elder statesman of the electronic pulpit, looks the camera in the eye and preaches his sermon of abundant life, his outstretched right hand punctuating his message that God wants you to prosper.

Forty percent of U.S. households tune in televangelists at least once a month, Nielsen reports.

Increased competition among TV evangelists is a big reason for Roberts' rating plunge, experts contend.

When Roberts was No. 1 throughout the 1960s and 1970s, he vied in the ratings with only a few major religious programs.

By 1977 Arbitron measured ratings of 62 national religious programs; in 1985 the number had climbed to 90. Hundreds of other clergy preach on local stations.

Jeffrey Hadden, sociologist at the University of Virginia, and William Martin, sociologist at Houston's Rice University, have spent years becoming experts on TV evangelists through research and writing articles for national magazines.

"You've got, roughly speaking, the same audience being spread among a larger number of programs," said Hadden.

Roberts' steady appeals for money also cost him viewers, said Martin.

The first time Roberts directly asked for money on his television show was in 1979.

An "all-out beg-a-thon" is how Martin described Roberts' pleas for cash to build his City of Faith Hospital.

"All he did was just beg for that thing week after week after week. I know people got tired of that."

LAST FEBRUARY, as a drum rolled and a curtain lifted, Roberts unveiled plans for a $14 million Healing Center which he said "God has commanded me to build."

Roberts' ministry says the Healing Center will treat visitors to "A Journey Through the Bible," a three-hour tour through "three-dimensional exhibit rooms" depicting dramatic biblical incidents including "scenes of creation" and the Garden of Eden.

The center also will include a biographical presentation of "Oral's childhood, sickness, healing, the call of God and other milestone events."

The price of a contribution for the center—"$48 per square foot/$480 per 10 square feet"—appeared in yellow letters underlined in purple at the bottom of the TV screen.

"Pick up your phone" Roberts urged viewers, "and say, 'Put it on my American Express card or my Visa card or my MasterCard,' and say, 'Oral, I'm with you.'"

In August, Roberts warned his audience that the devil struck Oral Roberts University with a financial crisis that might close the school.

"Partner, remember $77 as a seed of faith to Oral Roberts University this week will make a difference . . . in your life," he said.

Many viewers are "disgusted" to hear blatant money appeals continually, said Hadden, author of the book, "Prime Time Preachers."

"It's such a dominant theme in religious broadcasting," he added. An evangelist "who goes on a binge of begging is likely to have people flip the dial. And once they've flipped it, they might find something else they like better in that time slot."

IN THE EARLY 1950s, Roberts, Billy Graham and Rex Humbard saw the potential of television for saving souls and created what Hadden calls "the electronic church."

Roberts carted lights, film, cameras and crews into packed revival tents throughout the 1960s, bringing scenes of mystical healing into American living rooms for the first time.

From 1969 to 1975 Roberts went Hollywood with a series of slickly produced prime-time specials starring Christian and secular entertainers ranging from Pat Boone to Jimmy Durante.

He also launched a new weekly program produced on the Oral Roberts University campus, "Something Good Is Going to Happen to You," with entertainment provided by his university singers.

Roberts abandoned prime time in 1981 after hosting three evening specials featuring talks with the "Fudge Family" Christian puppets.

He emphasized his Sunday morning show, now called "Expect a Miracle" after incarnations as "Oral Roberts and the Miracle of Seed-Faith" and "Oral Roberts and You."

Roberts learned early the methods of fund raising.

"People will give for bricks and mortar while they don't get excited about paying for air time," Hadden said.

With this knowledge, Roberts built a university and medical complex, and Hadden said the principle since has been used by almost every successful TV evangelist.

JIM AND TAMMY Bakker raised millions of dollars from their "PTL Club" audience to build Heritage USA, a 1,200-acre religiously oriented hotel and entertainment retreat near Charlotte, N.C.

Humbard—whose only building project in 33 years of television appearances was the Cathedral of Tomorrow in Akron, Ohio—last year dropped his weekly show in favor of occasional prime-time specials because of sagging Sunday morning ratings.

"In 22 years on television, I never asked for money on TV," said Humbard. "Today, I pleaded and begged to keep [his ministry], and that's a shame.

"People will not give a dollar to win a soul or bring a person to a saving knowledge of Jesus Christ. They give their dollars to build great cathedrals, projects and schools," said Humbard in a documentary produced last year by Post-Newsweek Productions.

The future success of the Roberts TV show is in question as his ratings slip without indication that the necessary large numbers of younger people are tuning in, experts say.

About 63 percent of Roberts' viewers are more than 50 years old compared with Swaggart's 52 percent and Schuller's 68 percent.

Aging evangelists must be "savvy and start trying to build a younger audience," said Hadden.

A former employee of Roberts' ministry said the evangelist may be a victim of his own success.

"In a way, Oral was too successful," said the ex-staffer.

"He showed other people what a TV ministry can do."

21

God and the Ballot Box

Although it had only been 15 years since the "Catholic" question of John F. Kennedy's election was raised, political writers in the mid-1970s, enthusiastic after the media's prime-time role in revealing the sins of Watergate and hungry for more investigative reporting, rarely brought religion into their coverage.

That began to change, but slowly. When Jimmy Carter talked about being a "born again" Southern Baptist, political reporters at the time were naive about the nuances of religious language and their coverage of Carter's religious views showed it. Religion reporters, however, saw a trend of revivalism and recognized the increasing marriage of politics and, specifically, evangelical faith.

Helen Parmley, a long-time religion reporter at the *Dallas Morning News,* noted the trend in one of the earliest pieces about the new alliance between religion and politics. The 1976 story included here also detailed a brewing revival of evangelical beliefs. Parmley continued to break stories about politics and religion, including her coverage of the historic National Affairs Briefing in August 1980. That gathering, which included Jerry Falwell, Pat Robertson and then-candidate Ronald Reagan, was perhaps the first large-scale pairing of the Republican agenda with the evangelical Christian platform: opposition to abortion, opposition to gay and women's rights, and support for prayer in schools. Parmley's coverage is reprinted here as well.

Also in the 1980s, two clergy would run for president—the Rev. Jesse Jackson made attempts for the Democratic nod in both 1984 and 1988, and televangelist Pat Robertson vied for the Republican spot in 1988. Although both men lost their bids, Robertson's political organization devised systematic methods of involving evangelicals in party politics from the ground and grassroots up that laid the groundwork for today's Christian Coalition.

Award-winning *Los Angeles Times* religion writer Russell Chandler's profile of Jackson included here shows how the intertwining of faith and politics found in Jackson's campaign was typical of many in the African-

317

American community, where civil rights protests of the 1950s and 1960s inevitably fused political and religious convictions.

The Jackson and Robertson candidacies, along with the highly publicized televangelist scandals of the mid-1980s, helped bring new attention to the religion beat. Trade publications began to herald a new day in religion reporting. One thing that wasn't touted, however, was the spiritual left. After 1980, there has been little discussion of a liberal, Protestant political agenda. Thus, Gayle White's piece, "What Ever Happened to God's Left Wing?" from the *Atlanta Journal-Constitution* included in this chapter, poses an apt question. Finally, as a reminder that not everyone who votes is of Judeo-Christian heritage, Ira Rifkin at *Religion News Service* explores the Muslim view of the 1996 election between Bill Clinton and Robert Dole in this chapter's final story.

Many other excellent pieces on politics and religion exist in addition to the few stories reprinted here. Coverage of Pat Robertson's campaign can be found in a March 4, 1988, story by John Dart in the *Los Angeles Times*. In the late 1990s Christian family psychologist and radio mogul James Dobson was an important defender of "family values"—the Evangelical code word for an antiabortion, anti-gay rights, pro stay-at-home moms platform. Dobson was the cover story of the May 4, 1998, issue of *U.S. News and World Report*. Ralph Reed, the former Christian Coalition leader, is profiled in the May 15, 1995, issue of *Time*.

A Revivalist Breeze Blows Across the Country

Helen Parmley, *The Dallas Morning News*, September 19, 1976

THE DEMOCRATS had just chosen Jimmy Carter as their presidential nominee and the hundreds of delegates, weary from sitting and listening to speeches, were milling around New York's Madison Square Garden, laughing and talking in a celebrative din.

Slowly, deliberately, Martin Luther King, Sr., affectionately known as "Daddy King," moved toward the podium and called for silence.

When the vast hall was relatively quite, the fiery Baptist preacher lifted his arm and with a trembling voice said, "I have se-e-e-en heaven."

"Surely," he assured the now hushed audience, "SURELY, the Lord sent Jimmy Carter to come out and bring America back where she belongs."

When the zealous preacher finished his prayers, delegates were weeping and the television camera zoomed in on candidate Carter just as his lips mouthed the word, "Amen."

Those who took part in this history-making scenario must have been somewhat taken aback when a month later a Presbyterian minister stood at the podium of the Republican Convention in Kansas City and prayed, "Come into this convention, God, and guide us in our decisions."

IF ONE IS TO BELIEVE such prayers are directly answered, one must assume that God did indeed pop into Missouri's Kemper Auditorium and lay hands on Gerald Ford.

Professional politicos who cut their teeth on the adage that religion and politics don't mix were sent reeling as both candidates began to lace their campaign rhetoric with such ecclesiastical language as "I pray," "God bless you all" and "with God's help."

They sat back to nervously await a sneering backlash that never came. Instead, they were met with an almost universal acceptance of the candidates' openness about their religious faith that sent the strategists back to the drawing board to reassess the mood of the voting public.

What they found was an evangelical community and a fundamentalist religion that has emerged in this country unlike any other time in recent history.

Billy Graham, the most eloquent speaker for the contemporary evangelical-fundamentalist movement, estimates at least 40 million Christians subscribe to this theology.

"About half the country—about 60 percent—is squares," futurologist Herman Kahn told Newsweek magazine.

Kahn, director of the Hudson Institute, a "public-policy think tank" in New York, added, "That's the first good thing about America. Squares make great taxpayers. They make great soldiers and great citizens. They believe in religion . . . They know you've got to earn a living . . .

"The squares are taking over America, and God bless them."

IT WAS CARTER'S ENTRY into the national political limelight that brought the issue of religion in politics to the surface of public awareness. In pre-convention talks and interviews about budgets and foreign policy, it is not unusual to hear the former Georgia governor use such "code words" of fundamentalism as "born again Christian" and "Jesus Christ is my personal Lord and Savior."

When his frankness was accepted with no public protest or ridicule, voters were reminded that President Ford also had a late-blooming, life-changing "born again" religious conversion a few years ago after be-friending Michigan-based evangelist Billy Zeoli, and that he is a member in good standing of one of several prayer groups of evangelical con-gressmen that meet in the early morning hours on Capitol Hill in Wash-ington, D.C.

These facts were widely publicized when Ford took office two years ago, but the issue was dropped when few seemed to notice or care. With a fresh reminder of the cynicism that surrounded Richard Nixon's White House church services, Ford, who is considered by those around him to be as sincere in his evangelical faith as Carter, had chosen to keep his beliefs at a subdued level.

But since Jimmy Carter and the Democrats took sawdust Christianity to Madison Square Garden, religion has become an overriding issue in the campaign. It has not been confined to any geographical area or any level of office, and it includes all faiths.

A revivalistic breeze is blowing across the country that is reflected in every walk of life, and it is based in a groundswell of fundamentalism within and outside organized religion.

Journalist Tom Wolfe wrote in the August issue of "New York" maga-zine: "In this decade, we are seeing the upward roll (and not yet the crest) of the third great religious wave in American history."

For 10 years, headlines were made by hundreds of thousands of American youths running about the country disillusioned by the failure of the technological age and material wealth to bring them peace and a feeling of worth. They indulged in riots, open sex and drugs, rejecting all authority to live by their own rules.

Traditional standards of social behavior seemed to vanish in a divisive era that pitted old against young, black against white, doves against hawks and establishment against the masses.

The country was in no mood for evangelical "born again" Christians who accept the Bible as literally true and believe the only way to save the world is through a personal salvation—save the man, save the world.

But, the dissenters are back, and trends in society are taking on new forms. The so-called "gaps" created by the rebelliousness of the '60s are narrowing because of it. Older generations are more readily accepting lifestyles marked by styles of dress, sexual diversities and use of milder drugs. Studies show a declining interest in hard drugs and a renewed concern for traditional values among the young.

The conservatives and fundamentalists, the "silent majority" of the

'60s, are coming out of their closets en masse and are being joined by increasing numbers of younger people in search of a power greater than themselves.

IN THE PAST FEW years many Americans have been on an identity search in such movements as encounter sessions, Scientology, Zen, Yoga, Transactional Analysis and the Hare Krishna, Maharaj Ji and Sun Myung Moon sects and Jesus People movements.

In the '60s and early '70s, attempts were made by mainline religious denominations to "modernize" Christianity to compete with those movements. They organized beatnik coffeehouses, put a turtleneck sweater on the preacher, brought guitars into worship services and organized civil rights marches.

These efforts proved to be no more than an embarrassment to most young people, and a source of frustration to older ones.

In the last couple of years, however, it has been the hippies themselves who started attracting young people to Christianity when they began to transfer their inner need for ecstatic spiritualism from drugs and radical sects to fundamentalist evangelical "holy-rolling" Christianity.

Young people across the nation are deeply involved in the contemporary charismatic movement which has moved into prestigious divinity schools and the "most mainline" of denominations.

Wolfe declares, "What the urban young people want from religion is a little 'Hallelujah!' and talking in tongues! Praise God!"

"Ten years ago," Wolfe said, "if anyone of wealth, power or renown had publicly 'announced for Christ,' people would have looked at him as if his nose had been eaten away by weevils.

"Today, it happens regularly."

Harold Hughes resigned from the U.S. Senate to become an evangelist. Jim Irwin resigned from the astronaut program to organize an evangelistic outreach. Singers Pat Boone and Anita Bryant announced for Jesus. Charles Colson announced for Jesus.

Singer-actress Carol Lawrence, gourmet Graham Kerr, actors Dean Jones and Mickey Rooney, beauty pageant contestants, prominent sports figures and even black militant Eldridge Cleaver have added their names to the born-again roll call.

And, of course, Carter and Ford.

THE FAST-RISING new fundamentalism is unlike the old time religion that conjures up stereotypes of uneducated rednecks from the Deep South.

Political scientist Steve Hendricks of the University of Texas, Austin, in *Psychology Today* said, "We are seeing a tremendous change in the composition of fundamentalist churches. They are becoming massively middle class."

Hendricks analyzed statistics from the research centers at the universities of Michigan and Chicago and found that young people raised with fundamentalist beliefs are not leaving the church, but are attracting those raised in other denominations.

He found that many highly technically trained persons who formerly turned to more liberal brands of denominationalism, are now in fundamentalist churches.

"These are people," he said, "who are supposed to be winners in society. But due to economic reversals in aerospace and automobile industries, and to social changes, they turned out to be alienated, insecure, frightened and looking for a certain belief system."

Also among the "square majority" are former protesters of the '60s who cut their hair, changed their clothes, got jobs and fled to the suburbs. They bought their dream home, boat and recreational van and settled down to middle-class isolationism.

They make house payments, pay taxes, go to PTA meetings and don't want their children bused to school. They demand their Sunday School teachers "go back to teaching the Bible" and join efforts to put "real Christians" in political office and give the country "back to God."

They found a "personal belief system" in fundamentalist churches that emphasizes "last days" and personal salvation.

Dr. Kenneth Pepper, psychologist director of the Pastoral Counseling and Education Center in Dallas, explained, "People have a yearning to get in touch with the spiritual, and there are indications there is a power within us that is not available through logic.

"We have lost our sense of authority, and people are looking for values. We can't stand to be free. When people have won their freedom, they begin a search for legalistic answers, a set of rules. They put themselves in bondage to those rules, and then the call for freedom goes out once more.

"There is a tendency to get permissiveness and freedom mixed up. The freest concert pianist is the most disciplined."

The psychologist said, "I believe we are in the eve of a Great Awakening. Dr. (Elizabeth) Kubler-Ross put a new perspective on life when she reported people who experience something at the point of death and came back to tell us about it.

"IT MAKES DEATH a more viable option, and people are going to do things differently than in the last decade."

After a decade that included radical dissent, war, racial tension, Watergate and related scandals and sex scandals in government, the word being resounded in every corner of the country is morality. And morality, almost invariably, is intrinsically linked with religion and things transcendent.

The nation's religious climate suggests that the Carter-Ford stance of evangelical theology is not only widely shared, but is also spreading more rapidly than all other perspectives.

The fastest growing denominations are fundamentalist. But, evangelical and fundamentalist Christianity is a state of mind, and it is seen in growing numbers within churches not normally considered fundamentalist. This is punctuated by the candidates themselves. Carter is Southern Baptist, and Ford is Episcopalian.

The contemporary evangelical movement is rooted in classic fundamentalism, but while it has retained some of its inherent biblical and moral theology, it has generally adopted a more tolerant spirit toward religion and the world than was held by its hellfire-and-brimstone judgmental predecessors.

A frequent misnomer about the movement, however, is what U.S. Sen. Mark Hatfield calls "a confusion of labels" which leads people to think that to be an evangelical Christian in the world, one has to be identified as a political conservative.

Hatfield is a Southern Baptist and an evangelical Christian. He is also a political progressive who was among the first to oppose the Vietnam War and an outspoken critic of the Nixon administration, stands which cost him dearly among his evangelical colleagues.

Similarly, some voters are already questioning Carter's born-again fundamentalism in light of some of his political stands. But the difference in this pre-election campaign and those in the past is that people are acquainted enough with religion to ask it.

Without speculating on how Carter or Ford feel about the emergence of religion into the campaign, or whether it unfolded accidentally or intentionally, it is striking at the very heart of where America is today.

This campaign might mark the first in history when voters will be asking not only what the candidates can do for the country, but also, as the old gospel hymn suggests, deciding "Who is on the Lord's Side?"

Clout from the Religious Right: Vote

Helen Parmley, *The Dallas Morning News,* August 17, 1980

A NATIONAL ARMY of Christian soldiers is being recruited and trained by right wing, fundamentalist preachers to wage a holy war on Washington, purging all politicians who do not measure up to their standards of "moral" leadership on targeted issues.

Their battle cry is Christianity against godless humanism.

"We don't need a minority of secular humanists running our country," said Dr. Jerry Falwell, a fundamentalist pastor from Lynchburg, Va., who is a leader of the religious New Right. "No one person is going to turn this country around. It takes lots of people in small towns and big cities to make this country a democratic republic for the moral majority, the heart of America.

"This country was founded on Biblical precepts. We must bring America back to God."

The first real test of strength of the emerging 20th century Christian crusaders since both major political parties met and nominated their candidates will be a National Affairs Briefing Thursday and Friday at Dallas' Reunion Arena. That they have snared GOP presidential candidate Ronald Reagan as featured speaker is an indication of the clout this new religious right wields. Its leaders expect 20,000 to attend the 2-day session.

The goal of these political missionaries is to educate their army to elect a Congress that is strongly pro-defense, anti-communist, anti-abortion, anti-ERA, anti-homosexual, pro-family, pro-school prayer, and pro-Bible.

"The country is in a real moral tailspin," said Falwell. "Ours is an effort to bring it back to moral sanity."

FALWELL WAS best known for his television ministry, "Old Time Gospel Hour," until last year when he founded Moral Majority, the largest religious political action group in the nation. Soon after, another action group, called Christian Voice, was founded in California, followed by Religion Roundtable, organized by Ed McAteer, a Baptist layman from Memphis, Tenn.

Rounding out the coalition are kingpins of Christian television, Pat Robertson, founder and president of Christian Broadcasting Network and its popular talk-show, "The 700 Club," and James Robison, whose popular syndicated Hurst-based television ministry is deeply involved in politicizing moral issues.

At first, politicians viewed these rumblings from the religious right as a burp from the Bible Belt.

But when memberships of the lobbies swelled to hundreds of thousands, the politicians took another look. Combined weekly audiences of the so-called "electric church" have soared to 130 million a week, and donations from viewers and listeners now exceed $1 billion annually. Political hopefuls saw a potential for a formidable voting bloc of an estimated 50 to 80 million conservative evangelicals, and they began to reassess the implications of a coalition with that kind of elective power.

"They [evangelicals] could have a hell of a lot of impact," said Republican pollster Robert Teeter. "They have an incredible network and incredible ability to raise money. Their vote is pretty big and their ability to deliver is pretty great."

SUCH ASSESSMENTS have drawn the attention of political factions in high places. Reagan accepted an invitation to be the featured speaker at the National Affairs Briefing. Jimmy Carter, who is in trouble with the conservative Christian bloc that helped elect him in 1976, declined. But last week, Carter called religious leaders to two White House meetings to discuss strategy for confronting the threat to his re-election raised by the evangelical coalition.

The briefing is sponsored by Religion Roundtable, hosted by Robison, and among the speakers are Falwell and Robertson. Political speakers include Republicans John Connally, Philip Crane, and Sen. Jesse Helms of North Carolina and Alabama Governor Fob James, a Democrat.

The stated purpose of the gathering is to provide "the Christian community with information on moral, military, domestic and international issues," and the outcome will be closely watched by partisans from all bands of the political spectrum.

It has been more than a year since the flag-waving, Bible-toting preachers of the airwaves aggressively turned their attention from the sawdust trail of spiritual revivals to igniting a political awakening.

From their pulpits and microphones, and in their newsletters and magazines, they urge their millions of followers to learn about issues and candidates and then vote. They distribute "Vote" bumper stickers and lapel pins and urge Christian registration drives.

New words have been added to their born-again rhetoric. Falwell, who notched his pulpit with sermons about sin and salvation, now preaches, "Get them saved, baptized and registered. If there is a person in this room who is not registered, repent of it. It is a sin."

If anyone had told Falwell 15 years ago that he would be involved up to his "Jesus First" lapel pin in political action, he would have told them to repent and give up their wicked ways.

A NOMINAL CHURCHGOER during his childhood, Falwell was a young man when he had a born-again experience and decided to get an education and enter the ministry. In 1956, he founded Thomas Road Baptist Church in Lynchburg with a congregation of 35 families. Today, at 46, he presides over the membership that has grown to 17,000. His weekly television ministry, "Old Time Gospel Hour," with an annual budget of $57 million, is carried by 373 stations to an audience of more than 25 million.

Falwell recoils at the suggestion he is a counterpart to the liberal churchmen involved in the civil rights and anti-war movements in the sixties.

"Twenty years ago, I preached against political involvement," he said. "But in 1963, Madalyn Murray O'Hair stirred most of us to think we may have a problem on our hands. During the Vietnam War, the conservative side of the evangelical church was willing to trust our government. No one ever accused us of being rebellious to the government. We are patriotic and are loyal to the government. The National Council of Churches represented the rebellious liberal side."

In recent decades, Falwell says, "we have gotten away from the moral, family-oriented country which was started in the Judeo-Christian tradition." He claims issues that once were considered moral issues have been integrated into the political process.

"Thirty years ago, abortion was not a political issue," he said. "The Supreme Court had not ruled abortion on demand is legal. Homosexuality was not a national problem. It was not even discussed. Pornography and drugs were non-existent 30 years ago.

"Almost every moral issue has become very political, and the trend toward immorality in this country was so subtle, it was the late '70s before our people realized what had happened."

WHEN THE ISSUES moved into the political arena, so did the preachers.

Instead of charting Sunday School attendance, they are tracking voting records of congressmen and senators and are issuing "report cards" to their vast armies of Christian crusaders.

The Christian Voice tally reports how the lawmakers vote on 14 "key moral issues" so its network of 37,000 pastors and 190,000 members may judge stands the legislators take on "Christian" principles.

From this report, Christian Voice, as well as the other New Right political groups, compile a "hit list" of legislators with conflicting views whom they target for defeat in the November elections.

High on that list are local congressmen Jim Mattox (D-Dallas) and Jim Wright (D-Fort Worth). Each has cast enough so-called anti-family, pro-humanist votes that Mattox rated only 38 "correct" votes out of 100 and Wright scored a motley 11.

The coalition plans to lift up the opponents of these two legislators by helping them with their campaigns and funding. Voter registration drives through local churches is a major emphasis of the coalition.

The Christian Right already has scored some successes. In Alaska, Moral Majority won 13 of 19 delegate positions for the Republican National Convention. In Gainesville, Fla., Moral Majority won a third of the positions on the county Democratic executive committee. A heavy turnout by evangelicals is thought to be the reason Sen. George McGovern's opponent in the South Dakota primary gained 37 percent of the vote even though McGovern spent 10 times more money in that election.

"We are confident we will be able to put together a good organization in the Dallas-Fort Worth area," said Gary Jarmin, director of Christian Voice, from his headquarters in Washington, D.C.

Mattox looks on his critics as "the same old ultra-right politics."

"It is amazing with what clarity they can see the will of God," said Mattox, "not only for their own lives, but for the lives of everyone in the nation.

"This nation was founded on the concept of religious liberty, allowing people of different viewpoints to be part of our government. Two Christians can stand side by side, both trying to follow the teachings of the Bible, and come up with different viewpoints. That's called the priesthood of the believer.

"The Bible says, 'judge not . . .' but they are judging who is a good Christian. They are judging politicians in the name of Christ for their own purposes."

QUESTIONING THE ISSUES used by Christian Voice to rate the lawmakers, Mattox said, "I voted to establish a department of education. What has that to do with Christianity? There were Christians on both sides of the issue. I happened to disagree with the administration on the issue of China and Taiwan, but what does that issue have to do with Christianity?"

Wright agreed with the issues Mattox raised, and questioning the criteria used for the ratings, added, "If you voted for a department of education, you voted an un-Christian vote. How they can defend that, I don't know. If you voted for ERA, that went against you as an un-Christian. I voted for these things. I thought they were right.

"I would be terribly arrogant to say someone who voted on the other side of me is un-Christian . . . To try to invest the Almighty with one's own petty prejudices, either Democrat or Republican, is to commit blasphemy. God transcends partisan politics.

"I'm not going to question the sincerity of these people, but surely most Americans and most Texans are smart enough that they aren't going to let someone confuse righteousness with right wing politics."

The New Right insists it is non-partisan, but there is no question that the Republican party has offered the greatest response to their call. Leaders of the Republican National Committee conceded they do not go along with everything the new right stands for, but they see the movement as a potentially potent political force and feel, as the minority party, they need all the help they can get.

Reagan consulted with the evangelical generals of the movement during the Republican National Convention. While those ministers who do not have a non-tax deductible political organization avoid an outright endorsement, it is apparent Reagan is the choice of the coalition.

They even excuse his early "sin" of divorce. Jarmin, whose organization will have a "Christians For Reagan" booth at the National Affairs Briefing, said, "We can't hold over his head everything that ever happened in his life. His deep relationship with Christianity came years after the divorce, and he was able to go on and live a better life. We can't question where someone has been, but how they stand now and where they are going.

"Carter came out in favor of homosexual rights, a major bread-and-butter issue. He is pro-ERA and against the school prayer amendment. These are issues that concern us now."

AMONG OTHER CRITICS of the evangelical political thrust is Congressman Paul Simon (D-Ill.). Simon scored a "0" on the Christian Voice report card and replied, "The nearest base for a rating that I can recall is in Matthew 25, the judgment scene, where Christ lists the questions we will be asked: Did you help the hungry? Did you give water to the thirsty? Did you provide clothes to those who need them? Did you take care of the sick? Did you show concern for those in prison?"

The leaders of the new Christian Right are not the uneducated, hell-fire and brimstone breed that often were associated with the radical ultra-right religious factions of the past. Neither have they surrounded themselves with opulent steel and glass monuments as some of their cohorts have done.

They are sophisticated, well-groomed, often well-read on current affairs and determined. They believe they are answering a driving mandate from God to help turn the country around, and they are attacking the challenge with the zealous, evangelistic fervor of the fundamentalist preachers they are.

They have amassed a multi-million dollar war chest, opened lobby offices in Washington and combined the Bible with the media to mobilize an impressive army of workers to rise up and be counted—at the ballot box.

For Jackson, Religion and Politics Mix into Formidable Campaign Force

Russell Chandler, *Los Angeles Times*, February 9, 1984

During a recent televised debate among the Democratic presidential candidates, a woman in the audience prefaced a question to Jesse Jackson by noting that many people feared voting for John F. Kennedy in 1960 because he would become the nation's first Roman Catholic President.

Would people fear voting for Jackson because he would become the first President to be a minister, she asked.

What followed was uproarious laughter from the audience and other candidates, who expected the question to be about white voters' fears because Jackson is black.

Formidable Force

But, like the woman in the audience, Jackson took the question seriously. A minister has as much right—"and even a moral obligation"—to lead as anyone else, he said.

The exchange was another piece of evidence that Jackson's identity as a black politician is strongly linked to his identity as an ordained minister, and that his candidacy—including the root of his seemingly simplistic sloganeering—is a reflection of his theology.

Although Jackson, 42, generally has been given little chance to become the first clergyman to occupy the White House, his religion-
charged campaign has proven to be a formidable, headline-grabbing
force in the 1984 presidential race.

His campaign proposals—as yet undefined major increases in social
spending, reductions in the military budget, opening new dialogues
with the Soviet Union and Third World nations—are not much different in many respects from those proposed by the other Democratic
contenders.

But he is the only candidate to wrap them in morality and to present
them literally as articles of faith. He is the only presidential contender
who can turn a political stump speech into a hand-clapping revival meeting, and a voter-registration campaign into a crusade where "converts"
are marched down the center aisle to register on the spot. And he is the
only one to openly profess a sense of divine destiny, a belief that he has
been called as a prophet to challenge nations and churches alike.

Critics say Jackson is on an ego trip, that the preponderance of ministers in his campaign organization has caused friction, and that his constant "God talk" is only a rhetorical device to capture the allegiance of
uneducated blacks who identify with a simple, almost magical, faith.

"It's sort of like a plastic Jesus campaign. Anything goes until the
whistle blows," Darryl Cox, a political consultant and Jackson supporter,
said in San Francisco.

A recent editorial in the *United Methodist Reporter,* the weekly newspaper serving United Methodists, questioned why there has not been
greater scrutiny of Jackson's "use of religious imagery and institutions
for political ends."

"We remain steadfast in our belief that it is not only appropriate, but
desirable, that religion and politics be mixed," the editorial said. But it
added: "It is not appropriate or desirable that they should be merged.
Both our political and religious institutions benefit when the insights of
these two arenas interact. Both are endangered when either a direct or
subtle effort is made to imply divine preference for a particular candidate
for political office."

Jackson has tried to allay fears that he would trammel church-state
separation or act as a religious demagogue—or demigod—in the White
House. And he denies that God has directly revealed that he will be the
next U.S. President.

But he hints that a star is overhead.

Biblical Analogies

Using biblical analogies of the Bethlehem Star heralding Jesus' birth and King Herod's futile attempts to put the child to death, Jackson intones:

"When the stars in their courses are with you, when the Star shines, Herod cannot build a stairway tall enough to unscrew it . . . When it's the fullness of man's timing and God's timing, unusual things happen. And unusual things are happening now."

Jackson didn't play down the adulation of the crowd the other night at the Atlanta Civic Center when Minnie Wimbish introduced him, declaring that he needed no introduction "because he has already been introduced by the Father and the Son." A moment later, the audience erupted into wild cheers when, paraphrasing a passage from the biblical book of the prophet Isaiah, she added:

"Unto us a child is born, unto us a son is given; and we shall call his name Jesse . . . Run, Jesse, run!"

On stage after stage he is introduced by black religious leaders as a "prophet for our time," "the man God has chosen for this hour." Jackson himself often affirms that he is, indeed, a prophet led by "a divine plan."

Moral Majority leader Jerry Falwell, who is also a Baptist minister, said he believes Jackson "is a sincere Christian and I don't think he's dangerous." But he added that "I believe Jesse has compromised his positions to be acceptable to the liberal segment of the electorate and to be compatible to the Democratic platform," particularly on the issue of abortion.

During the national debate among the Democratic candidates, Jackson agreed that the right to an abortion should be a woman's individual choice. But he added a qualification, which he couched in moral terms. "One must bear the consequences of that choice," he said, "and . . . put much more emphasis on sex education on the 'day before' and not be reacting on 'the day after.'"

"Bear the Consequences"

His political positions are drawn from activist, mainline liberalism, overlaid with the supercharged attitude of one who believes in a God who always vindicates the righteous.

"I'm driven by the most simple political agenda: feed the hungry, clothe the naked, liberate the captives . . . study war no more," Jackson said in an interview. "If faith is great enough then the weak will lead the strong. Red Seas will open up [a reference to the Bible story of the Israelites fleeing from Egyptian oppression], and lions will lose their appetites in your presence [a reference to Daniel in the Old Testament story of the lions' den]."

He contends that his successful mission to Syria to negotiate the release of Navy Lt. Robert Goodman offers proof that "an eye for an eye and a tooth for a tooth is an archaic form of justice that will leave you blind and disfigured," but following Jesus' admonition to treat an enemy with unexpected love and respect may lead to a break in an apparently hopeless deadlock.

"Calling to Social Justice"

The church has always played a major role in Jackson's life, but it wasn't until he reached college that he decided to become a minister. He was earning a bachelor's degree in sociology and economics at North Carolina A&T, when one Sunday, Jackson reflected, his "calling to social justice" crystallized at a student civil rights demonstration in Greensboro, N.C., when some 700 students were "locked into a retirement home" by police.

"The state troopers were there with their shotguns; the [attack] dogs were there," Jackson recalled. "Tears came uncontrollably. I felt under conviction, obligated to serve . . . to change those conditions."

The Rev. A. Knighton Stanley, then campus pastor at North Carolina A&T, advised Jackson that the ministry, in the style of the Revs. Martin Luther King Jr. and Adam Clayton Powell, offered "the broadest field" for social change.

Jackson enrolled at Chicago Theological Seminary, a United Church of Christ school, on a Rockefeller Foundation scholarship.

Jackson was ordained a minister of the National Baptist Convention, U.S.A., Inc. on June 30, 1968. With almost 7 million members, it is the nation's largest black denomination. Although he preaches often, Jackson has never headed a congregation. For the past five years, he has been co-pastor of Fellowship Missionary Baptist Church on Chicago's South Side. But his role is more "minister at large" than a staff relationship to the congregation.

His subsequent activism in the civil rights movement has helped cement his firm base of support among black religious leaders. Bishop H. H. Brookins of Los Angeles, presiding bishop of the African Methodist Episcopal Conference of Southern California, said Jackson "has brought cutting truths to the [Democratic] campaign that everyone is feeling but nobody is voicing . . . He is using prophetic and Pentecostal style to lift up . . . issues that come right out of the Bible—the heart of the Christian message and the heart of its ethic."

Target of Criticism

"When you find me a Jew who is not for Israel, I'll find you a Negro who is not for Jesse," declared the Rev. E.V. Hill, pastor of Mt. Zion Missionary Baptist Church in Los Angeles and former chairman of Black Clergy for Reagan.

Jackson also has support from many Muslim, Unitarian, Methodist, Baptist and Presbyterian leaders. But it is the Jewish endorsement that he lacks—and broods over.

Jackson has been accused of anti-Semitism and sharply criticized by Jews Against Jackson, an arm of the Jewish Defense League. Jackson insists that he has been misunderstood.

Declaring that "distance from the rabbis . . . and my Jewish friends" had been "one of the great agonies of my life," Jackson said that he supports Judaism—"a great religious flower out of which Christianity sprung"—but that Zionism is a recent "political movement based on race." Zionist leaders have "not been open to the challenges of prophecy as they should be," Jackson said. "He added, however, that he believes Israel should exist "as a democratic state, with security, with internationally recognized boundaries."

What Ever Happened to God's Left Wing?

Gayle White, *Atlanta Journal-Constitution,* October 30, 1994

It's hard to name winners in the Vietnam War, but the Religious Left may have been one of them. Bible-toting, anti-war protesters took the gospel of protest into the public arena, helping to shape the era.

Then religion turned right and the Moral Majority and the Christian Coalition replaced liberal voices.

Now despite this conservative tide there are a few faint stirrings from the spiritual left again. Earlier this year, a group of religious leaders formed the Interfaith Alliance. Although the organization claims to be moderate, rather than liberal (avoiding the L-word), it clearly intends to counter the Religious Right in the marketplace of ideas.

"The Alliance was formed to say that the moderate people need to stand up and be counted," said Presbyterian executive Herber Valentine, its president. "This is no time to be wishy-washy."

Even the People for the American Way, the anti-conservative organization founded by television producer Norman Lear, which long shied away from any form of religious expression in politics, has recently encouraged liberal religious leaders to speak out.

"In the end, it is virtually impossible not to mix religion and politics to some degree," says a new 25-page booklet distributed by the organization. "After all, the same values that shape political beliefs shape religious beliefs."

Seymour P. Lachman, a professor at City University of New York, says the Clinton presidency may be changing the atmosphere.

"For the first time we have a Democratic president who is not afraid to use religious hot-buttons to get the message across he wants," Lachman said. "Bill Clinton pushes some of the same religious buttons as his fellow Baptists Pat Robertson and Jerry Falwell—but he comes out with a different message."

Clinton's comfort with religious themes has been demonstrated many times—from speaking about a "new convenant" during his campaign, to closing an address at the Israel-Jordan peace signing Wednesday with a quotation from the Beatitudes.

Last year, a book called "The Culture of Disbelief" by Yale law professor Stephen Carter decried the absence of liberal religious witness in the political process. The book gained national attention. Carter spurred moderates, liberals and the remnants of the radical left to reconsider the role of religion.

This current flicker of revival pales beside the strength of the left before its decline.

In the '60s and early '70s, preachers and theologians sounded off against the war, confronting the comfortable idea that the interests of God and the United States of America are always one and the same.

Hillary Rodham Clinton first heard the U.S. role in Vietnam challenged by a Methodist theologian. Partly because of her feelings about the war, she changed from a Goldwater Republican to a McGovern Democrat, she told Newsweek magazine.

The activism of the clergy—from Martin Luther King Jr. to Philip Berrigan—gave the anti-war viewpoint a sense of moral authority, and gave a stature to liberal religious views that has not been paralleled since.

Liberals were the image of courageous, radical Christianity. Protestant, Catholic and Jewish clergy and laity had boarded buses for Freedom Rides, sat beside black Christians in segregated lunch counters, and marched on Washington.

The clerical collar became "as much a part of the imagery of the civil rights protest as the bearded students in sandals," wrote sociologist Jeffrey Hadden of the University of Virginia in his 1969 book, "A Gathering Storm in the Churches."

In the last fifteen years, however, political liberals have largely ignored religion as a framework for their views; religious liberals seemed to fade into community ministries and small protest movements and away from the public eye.

Ralph Reed, executive director of the Christian Coalition, acknowledges that his organization's opponents with the "L" label, the Liberals, seldom claim the scriptural mandate for their stands that his own group does.

"There's no doubt now that the institutional left views invocations of moral beliefs and religious principles with a certain degree of wariness and suspicion," he said, "which is rather ironic given their embrace of those values and that rhetoric in the '50s and '60s."

Clergy Voices Discomfort

The heyday of late 20th-century Christian liberalism arose out of a period of incredible synthesis between religion and culture.

James Hudnut-Beumler, dean of the faculty at Decatur's Columbia Theological Seminary, chronicles the period in "Looking for God in the Suburbs."

In the '50s, Norman Vincent Peale's "The Power of Positive Thinking" was on the bestseller list for three years. Congress added "under God" to the Pledge of Allegiance to the U.S. flag and made "In God We Trust" the national motto. "Dial-a-prayer" came to the telephone and *The Ten Commandments* to the movie screen.

Then a few scholars, church members and clergy began to voice discomfort at such complacency. They began to think of Jesus and the prophets as anti-establishment and to view the American dream through that lens, says Hudnut-Beumler.

In the conflict between the church's role as comforter and challenger, the challengers became vocal, visible and largely successful. Jim Crow was disarmed in the legal system. The war ended. Women achieved significant gains in the workplace and in government.

Even conservatives began to accept integration and gender equality. The positions that galvanized the left became mainstream opinion.

But no left-wing nirvana followed—and disillusion came with victory.

Among the old liberal guard, some retired, some went on to writing and teaching. And some became known as clamoring conservatives. No new left rose in their place.

"Something of the steam got lost in there," said Wade Clark Roof, professor of religion and society at the University of California at Santa Barbara.

The denominations that fostered the Religious Left lost members— not through a massive exodus, but from a slow leak through death and defection, not replenished through recruitment or reproduction.

Meanwhile, evangelical groups grew rapidly and conservative Christians came together in formidable national organizations behind clear-cut positions on issues from abortion to school vouchers.

This, too, may be changing.

Within the last two or three years, much of the decline of the so-called mainline as well as the growth of the more conservative groups has leveled off. Major denominations gained or lost less than 1 percent, according to the 1994 "Yearbook of American & Canadian Churches."

At the national level, some liberal Christian leadership has experienced a shift in its view of the church's role from pronouncing to educating, said William McKinney, professor of religion and society at Hartford Seminary. "They see their role as really to stimulate conversation."

At the local level, many people work hard for social causes with hands-on care instead of political fervor, several observers said.

"On issues of poverty . . . there's a lot more activism," said David C. Leege of Notre Dame. "But the Religious Left went into community action kind of stuff. Food banks, care for the homeless. There's a lot more activism, but it's moved out of demonstration kinds of things into personal benevolence."

"There is more there than we know about," said Leon Howell, who edited the now-defunct *Christianity and Crisis.* "Certainly it is more fragmented and doesn't appear as much."

While some voices on the Left are calling for a greater role for religion in politics, some voices on the Right are beginning to cry out for a de-politicalization of religion. In a new book, Michael Horton, founder of Christians United for Reformation, charges that the church has strayed from its true mission by tying itself too tightly and too predictably to specific political positions.

In "Beyond Culture Wars," he writes: "One wonders today what would be more dangerous in some evangelical gatherings: disagreeing with someone over the doctrine of the Incarnation or disagreeing with Rush Limbaugh."

The ultimate solutions to society's greatest ills won't come from either side alone, Jim Wallis, editor of *Sojourners* magazine, predicts in "The Soul of Politics," because the personal morality of the right and the social compassion of the left are needed.

"What has so divided and polarized these virtues, which are all at the center of our great moral and religious traditions?" Wallace asks.

There are signs of hope for real conversation, in civil tones, between the two armies of Christian soldiers with a common enemy called evil.

The Religious Left won its most public battles, then, it seems, the public deserted.

Why? A dozen books about Christianity in the late 20th century and an equal number of interviews with scholars of sociology, religion and politics offered these reasons:

1. **No depth:** Even in their heyday, religious liberals may never have had a number of supporters equal to their influence. "They were often a leadership without much following," said Martin Marty, church history professor at the University of Chicago.

2. **The nature of liberals:** The very inclusivity advocated by liberals resulted in a lack of cohesiveness. "People on the Religious Left tended to be so inclusive of diversity, so understanding of people of other faiths, that their own internal logic didn't demand that you be a member of their group," said James Hudnut-Beumler, dean of the faculty at Columbia Theological Seminary in Decatur. Also religious liberals are issue-oriented rather than power-oriented, explained Thomas McCullough, associated professor of religion at Duke University.

3. **Lack of organization:** The movement failed to organize from the grass roots. "One criticism is that liberals are able to articulate their passion but often do not organize around that passion in ways that effectively create the kind of transformation they're wanting," said Luther Smith, associate professor at Emory University's Candler School of Theology.

Also the correlation between theological liberalism and political liberalism is low. "People don't live the culture war or divide themselves up along those lines," said William McKinney, professor at Hartford Seminary.

4. **Disillusion and burnout:** Many religious liberals became disillusioned with a lack of systematic change. "I suppose there was a kind of utopianism about what would be accomplished by the civil rights movement and the women's movement," said Leon Howell, editor of the now-defunct liberal religious journal *Christianity and Crisis*. David C. Leege of Notre Dame University agreed: "We had several decades of social reform. I think people's energy is spent."

5. **Not in my church:** Many positions, such as homosexual causes, that are popular among some liberals today are largely rejected within their own religious denominations. "I think there are persons who get so tired of the battles within churches . . . that they would rather give their loyalty to secular organization that's working on behalf of those issues," said Smith of Emory.

6. **Black, white disaffection:** Black separatist and black power movements have created suspicion on both sides of the liberal white-black church alliance that worked so effectively for civil rights. "Black consciousness movements seem to place some barriers between blacks and otherwise empathetic whites," Leege said.

7. **Change is difficult.** The law of inertia works against liberals because change takes more energy than maintaining the status quo. "The Right always has the attraction of tradition behind it," said Hudnut-Beumler.

8. **Lack of spirit:** Some liberals of the '60s weren't motivated by religion but adopted the structure of the church as a convenient base of operation.

9. **No leader:** Liberal Christians have no one of the stature of Jerry Falwell or Pat Robertson and, by nature, resist a voice that claims to speak for the entire movement.

10. **Climate of fear:** Because they fear attacks from the right, many are mute. "Some of the people in positions of official church leadership in mainline Protestant denominations who, in the past, have tended to represent strong liberal positions have become more cautious," said Alan Geyer, professor of political ethics at Wesley Theological Seminary in Washington.

For Muslim Voters in Presidential Race, Party Lines Are Nothing Sacred

Ira Rifkin, *Religion News Service,* May 14, 1996

WASHINGTON—Ask Earl El-Amin about his choice for president and he's quick to say that party labels have little to do with his selection process.

"I'm not a Democrat or a Republican. I'm a Muslim. That means if the candidate is aligned with my religious beliefs, I vote for them," said El-Amin, a Baltimore resident who works on juvenile justice issues for Maryland Gov. Parris Glendening, a Democrat.

Because his Muslim religious beliefs cut across party lines and the liberal-conservative divide, El-Amin said choosing a candidate can be tough. This year's presidential campaign is no exception.

El-Amin's situation typifies the political predicament of most American Muslims, members of a fast-growing faith that is struggling for mainstream acceptance and a place on the national political stage. Muslim concerns are so varied that neither of the two leading candidates—President Bill Clinton and Senate Majority Leader Bob Dole—is a clear favorite among Muslim voters.

"There is absolutely no such thing as a monolithic Muslim voting bloc," said Salam Al-Marayati, director of the Muslim Public Affairs Council in Los Angeles.

"With the Jewish community, there's a consensus of agreement on the need to support Israel. Muslims may have an emotional feeling about Bosnia or Palestine because Muslims are involved, but there's no real consensus. The community's just too diverse," he said.

About 40 percent of the nation's estimated 3 to 6 million Muslims are African-Americans. Most of the rest are relatively recent immigrants and their descendants. One-quarter of the Muslim population is of South Asian descent—mostly Indian and Pakistani—and about 12 percent traces it roots to Arab nations. The remainder are Iranians, black Africans, Afghans, Indonesians, Malaysians, Turks, Albanians and others.

This myriad of ethnic, racial and cultural backgrounds is reflected in the broad range of Muslim political viewpoints.

"Muslims can be compared to Catholics," said Sulayman Nyang, a professor of African studies at Washington's Howard University and a close observer of the American Muslim scene. "They are as different as Mexican-American Catholics in Southern California are from Polish and Italian Catholics in Chicago or Philadelphia."

Muslims from the Middle East, for example, follow closely what Clinton and Dole have to say about the conflict between Israel and the Palestinians—and are generally disappointed by both men, who they say show favoritism for Israel in a play for American Jewish votes.

But for South Asian Muslims, the more important foreign policy issue is Kashmir, the Muslim state that Hindu India and Muslim Pakistan have fought over repeatedly. On this issue, said Nyang, the Republicans' Cold War tilt toward Pakistan still plays well among Pakistani-born American Muslims. Conversely, Muslims from India view the Republicans with suspicion for the same reason.

African-American Muslims, on the other hand, tend to focus on domestic issues, particularly those that impact inner-city communities.

"My heart goes out to Muslims in Lebanon, but that's not the main issue for me," said Melvin Bilal, an African-American Muslim who in 1986 lost a bid to become lieutenant governor of Maryland running as a Republican. "We're from here."

The Muslim community is also far from unified on domestic issues.

African-American Muslims tend to support increased aid to public schools, for example. While Muslims religious schools have begun to spread across the nation, most African-American Muslims still send their children to public schools.

That position puts them in conflict with those suburban, white-collar South Asian immigrants who want Washington to approve a school voucher plan that would help them pay their kids' private school tuition.

However, two common threads to some degree bind American Muslims together politically.

The first is their deep conservatism on matters of personal morality, a reflection of Islam's traditional teachings on such issues. Muslims general oppose abortion and homosexual rights and support positions that they feel will strengthen families.

"Middle-class Muslims in particular see themselves as defenders of morality," said Nyang.

The second is a desire to see Islam accepted as a major American faith. Islam, often called the fastest-growing religion in America, is expected soon to surpass Judaism as the nation's largest non-Christian faith.

Still, said Al-Marayati of the Muslim Public Affairs Council, "all this talk about how fast we're growing hasn't translated into political influence yet. Muslim political development in the United States is still embryonic. We're still the new kid on the block."

Pollster George Gallup Jr. said the scant attention that's been paid to Muslim voting patterns is evidence that they have yet to be taken seriously by the political establishment.

No one, he said, has ever statistically separated out the community's voting history. "Muslims are still lumped into a very large group known as 'other,'" he said.

Muslim social conservatism works in favor of Republican candidate Dole because Muslims perceive his party to have a corner on family-values issues.

"Muslims want to be associated with people who take a moral stand," said Bilal, who runs a temporary employment agency in the Washington suburb of Landover, Md. "That puts them on the same wavelength as the center of the Republican party."

Working against Dole, however, is the feeling of some Muslims that the GOP is taking too harsh an approach to cutting back welfare and other public-assistance programs. While Islam teaches self-reliance, it also stresses compassion and social justice.

"Muslims are Republicans on family values," said Nyang, "but Democrats on social welfare."

Muslims—particularly the nearly 60 percent who are members of immigrant communities—are also put off by Republican efforts to sharply reduce immigration.

In addition, many Muslims are concerned by the influence they feel conservative Christians have over Dole and the Republican party. Muslims fear that conservative Christians regard them as non-believers whose growing numbers represent a threat.

"We're not sure how they feel about us," said Imam Abdulmalik Mohammed, national spokesman for the Ministry of W. Deen Mohammed, by far the largest movement within the African-American Muslim community, claiming more than 2 million followers. "There is a concern they want to impose their beliefs on others."

Imam W. Deen Mohammed—the son of Nation of Islam pioneer Elijah Muhammed—supported Republican President George Bush in the 1992 campaign. This year he favors Democrat Clinton, according to Abdulmalik Mohammed.

One reason for that is Clinton's attempts to reach out to American Muslims to a degree unmatched by any previous president.

In February, the White House hosted its first-ever reception to mark the Muslim feast of Eid al-Fitr, which signals the end of the holy month of Ramadan. First lady Hillary Rodham Clinton called the Eid celebration "an American event."

Her words spoke directly to the Muslim community's desire for full acceptance. Even Republican Bilal said he was impressed by the Eid reception.

"Regardless of whether you agree with Clinton or not, you have to admit he's given Muslims more respect than they have ever received from a president," said Khaled Saffuri, deputy director of the American Muslim Council, a leading pro-Islamic lobbying group in Washington.

Still, Clinton has plenty of negatives for Muslims, said Saffuri, an acknowledged Clinton supporter.

Clinton has not appointed a Muslim to his administration and "still doesn't include mosques along with churches and synagogues" in his pronouncements, said Saffuri.

Clinton also is perceived by Muslims to be too liberal on abortion and other moral issues and opposes organized school prayers—another position favored by many Muslims.

But the issues over which Muslims find the greatest fault with Clinton are in the area of foreign policy—particularly what they regard as his overwhelming bias toward Israel in its struggle with the Arab, and overwhelmingly Muslim, world.

"President Clinton is beyond the pale on this one for Muslims," said Yvonne Haddad, a University of Massachusetts professor of Islamic and Middle East history. "A great many Muslims believe the American government is anti-Muslim."

However, Dole also holds no great attraction for Muslims on this issue. Last year, the Kansas Republican pushed legislation to move the American embassy in Israel from Tel Aviv to Jerusalem. Muslims looked upon the bill—which was approved—as a bid by Dole for Jewish political support that undercut Palestinian and Muslim claims to Jerusalem.

"When Dole spoke up on Jerusalem, he threw people for a loop," said Haddad.

For Al-Marayati, the Jerusalem issue is proof positive that neither of the 1996 presidential candidates is a strong supporter of Muslim interests. Yet, Al-Marayati—who will be a Clinton delegate from California at this summer's Democratic party nominating convention—is far from discouraged.

That's why the emphasis during this presidential election year for Al-Marayati's organization, as well as other politically oriented Islamic groups, will be voter registration and education.

"The American lesson is you have to earn your way into the political process. You can't expect change overnight," he said.

PART 4

Coping with Diversity, Connecting to Readers

Ira Rifkin's story about Muslim voters in chapter 21 is just one sign of a greater religious pluralism in the country. With eastern faiths being imported from Asia and finding celebrity support from rock musicians and other pop culture icons in the 1960s, the religious landscape changed. Even in the American heartland, Buddhist centers were springing up. Islam grew so fast that, by the 21st century, Muslims are expected to surpass the number of Jews in the United States.

The former liberal powerhouse churches of the 1950s, in particular, watched membership literally die off, without rejuvenation from new members. In response, those churches sought ways to transform themselves to avoid becoming observers to their own demise. In some cases, the transformation included mergers or agreements to share communion or clergy. However, many people searched for spirituality outside the churches, in places they had never looked before.

With this diversity of faiths came a collision of values. To conservative Christians, the legalization of abortion, gay rights and changing family structures meant the nation was suffering from a lack of faith that would destroy it. Medicine, genetic engineering and other technology put new and serious questions of morals and ethics on the table. The lack of clear answers to those questions seemed, to many, to signal further spiritual decline.

In response to a changing culture, religious conservatives turned to the political arena and to the courts to protect and defend what they saw as their inherent right to practice their religion however they saw fit. Religious conservatives also believed it was their duty to make America that shining Christian city on a hill it was meant to be.

Of course, not everyone subscribed to the religious right's views. Even within religious groups, opposing sides have battled over many of the same issues that have proved divisive among religions. The question of gay rights, for example, separates conservative Christians from more lib-eral mainline Protestants. But the question of gay rights and the ordination of homosexuals has also occupied the national agendas of nearly every mainline Protestant group at one time or another in the past decade. And there is no sign the battles will soon end. Richard Cimino and Don Lattin write in their 1998 book, *Shopping for Faith: American Religion in the New Millennium:*

> Conflicts arising over moral issues will continue to spark divisive debates within American religion and society, although there are signs that the people in the pews are growing tired of polarization over hot-button issues like abor-tion, euthanasia, feminism, and gay rights.

During the 1980s and 1990s, increasing religious diversity, heavily nu-anced ideological battles and complex legal wrangling have made cover-ing an already complicated beat even more challenging. They have also made news executives more aware of the importance of having a special-ist on the religion beat. The Religion Newswriters Association, a 50-year-old trade association for secular journalists who cover religion, saw active membership increase 40 percent between 1996 and 1998.

At the same time, newspapers sought ways to find and keep new read-ers as circulations leveled and even dropped. Armed with market research showing that religion was of special concern to women—a key demo-graphic group newspapers sought to lure—some newspapers created "megasections" with four and six pages weekly packed with stories about religion.

But these megasections carried broader content than their precursors, including stories about values, ethics and spirituality. Staff artists de-lighted readers with elaborate and fanciful graphics to illustrate the elu-sive. Weekly information graphics about religious books, houses of wor-ship or the volunteer of the week, for example, all helped give readers more religion news each week than they used to get in a month or more. Once again, as in the 1950s, testimonials at journalism conferences touted the religion beat as "hot." Finally, religion reporting, it seemed, had come into its own.

History, however, suggests this renewed interest might not last. But at least one cultural observer believes the fascination with religion is more than a fad. Commentator Michael Novak, in a May 24, 1998, column for the *New York Times,* predicted the 21st century would be "the most reli-gious century in 500 years." New democracies asking basic questions of how people should live in peace and freedom is one reason. Another reason:

> For some five centuries, a leading secular elite has held that moral questions can be resolved on the plane of reason alone. Some still believe that. But it has become ever more apparent that such a belief is only a belief, a faith, a kind of religion of its own.

If indeed this modern day "age of reason" has been tempered by a mandate that matters of the soul will remain front and center in the national debates is hard to know. What is certain, however, is that whatever stories do emerge about religion in the next decade, they will have a legacy of stories from the 20th century that point to increasing depth and excellence.

Stories in this section illustrate religion reporting in the 1980s and 1990s—modern religion reporting in all its depth and complexity. Chapter 22 presents three stories of the many that address hot-button issues in the clash of religious cultures. Chapter 23 highlights legal tussles between religions and between religion and a government bound by the First Amendment to preserve the separation of church and state. Stories about the many religions that by the 1990s helped make the United States among the most religiously diverse nations in the world are included in chapter 24. Organized religion, however, does not always have all the answers sought by spiritual seekers. Chapter 25 documents new religious forms that help make up the "cafeteria style" faith of the 1990s. Money, a curse or a blessing for most faiths, is the subject of chapter 26. Examples of theological and ethical interpretations covered by some of the best religion reporters are found in chapter 27. The final chapter points to the future with stories about U.S. religiosity and apocalyptic expectations in the new millennium.

22

Culture Wars and Hot-Button Issues

The youth culture of the 1960s, women's and gay rights movements and the 1973 decision to legalize abortion became the fuses for the sociopolitical feuds that would become dubbed the "Culture Wars" by sociologist James Davison Hunter in a book by that name. Although these wars are fought in the political and cultural battlefields, their casualties are the nation's core institutions, including the family, education and politics. At the heart of the battles: values and beliefs that are inspired, guided and mandated by religious thought.

Many hot-button issues are not represented here because of space. But a well-done *Washington Post* piece by Laurie Goodstein about the removal of elementary school Halloween parties can be found in the October 31, 1994, *Washington Post*. Mark Pinsky's July 16, 1995, story in the *Orlando Sentinel* details the absence of religion in Disney movies, although it was Disney's policies toward employees in same-sex relationships that led the Southern Baptists to later boycott Disney.

The Pensacola Journal won awards for its series by reporter Alice Crann about homosexuality and the church, which ran May 10–16, 1997. Euthanasia, meanwhile, is a troubling topic to many. *Los Angeles Times* Religion reporter Russell Chandler's March 9, 1975, story details the issue years before Dr. Jack Kevorkian made physician-assisted suicide a household term.

This chapter does include a story about the anti-abortion movement and its reaction to the murder of an abortion clinic worker by an anti-abortionist. The story, written by Laurie Goodstein when she worked for the *Washington Post,* notes the tensions within the movement itself as it struggled with limited wins in the courts some 25 years after abortion was legalized. For coverage of Pope John Paul II's pastoral letter condemning abortion, see Ann Rodgers-Melnick's March 30, 1995, story in the *Pittsburgh Post-Gazette* and *Newsweek*'s April 10, 1995, cover story.

As scientists continue to unlock the codes of creation, researchers continue to push the ability for humans to become creators themselves. With cloning now a reality, ethicists debate its proper use in medicine and science. Sandi Dolbee of the *San Diego Union-Tribune* writes a reaction piece about religious leaders' views of Dolly, the first reported fully cloned animal. The story also is a good example of a reaction story, a common story type for religion reporters.

Anyone covering the religion beat in the past decade has likely written at least one story about tensions over acceptance of homosexuality and whether or not homosexuals can be clergy. Cecile S. Holmes's profile of a gay Episcopal clergyman includes a synopsis of views from other religious groups and unites tender personal details with points of institutional policy into one easy read.

Life and Death Choices: Anti-Abortion Faction Tries to Justify Homicide

Laurie Goodstein, *The Washington Post,* August 13, 1994

The only doctor who still admits to performing abortions in Mississippi wore an Army combat helmet and bulletproof vest as federal marshals drove him past a row of protesters to his clinic in Gulfport this week.

Two weeks ago, 128 miles away, a Florida physician and his civilian escort were shot to death in a pickup truck outside a Pensacola abortion clinic. Many anti-abortion leaders have condemned the bloodshed and denounced Paul Hill, arrested minutes after the shooting, as a lone, sick extremist.

But there is a sizable faction among the anti-abortion movement's activists—the "rescuers" who use civil disobedience to disrupt clinic business—who have applauded Hill as a righteous defender of babies. Most leaders of this week's Mississippi protests still stand by the petition that 32 of them signed last year at Hill's request declaring that murdering abortion providers is "justifiable homicide." They call their new campaign "No Place to Hide."

They have spent the last 18 months, since the first assassination of a doctor outside a Pensacola abortion clinic, forging ethical and theological justifications for killing in the name of saving babies.

Promoters of this doctrine include fundamentalist Christian preachers, lay leaders of anti-abortion "ministries" and several Catholic priests, one of whom was suspended by his archbishop. They cite the Bible, the

Holocaust, the fight top to end slavery and the theory of "just war."

"Any force that is justifiable to protect born children is also justifiable to protect unborn children," said Cathy Ramey, associate director of Advocates for Life Ministries in Portland, Ore., one of the few women among the 32 signers of Hill's petition. "It's dishonest for somebody to say that they care about unborn children and then in the same breath condemn Paul Hill for having shot the abortionist."

Donald Spitz, spokesman for Operation Rescue Chesapeake, said, "If there was a sniper in the school yard sniping off children one by one and the only way you could stop him was by stopping that sniper . . . you would stop that sniper."

This position has become a subject of heated debate among anti-abortion activists in meetings, churches and newsletters. And now the debate has split the ranks of the activists in Operation Rescue, which until recently could mobilize thousands to risk arrest for blockading clinics.

A new group called the American Coalition of Life Activists (ACLA), with members in nine states, is mounting the "No Place to Hide" protests. Organizers say their goal is to expose doctors performing abortions until neighbors, relatives and other patients pressure the physicians to quit.

They not only refuse to condemn but speak warmly of Hill—who faces two counts of murder and was indicted yesterday by a Tallahassee grand jury for allegedly violating the new federal clinic-protection law— as well as two other activists who have been convicted in previous shootings. Yet they have asked every demonstrator participating in this past week's protest against Mississippi physician Joseph Booker to sign a "nonviolence" pledge in language that is itself something of an incitement.

It begins, "I will not engage in, plan or recruit for any acts of violence toward the child killer . . ."

Believers in "justifiable homicide" cite moral absolutes and "truth" to explain their position. If the fetus is a child, just not yet born, then doctors who perform abortions are "serial child killers," they say, in a theme repeated in interviews with a dozen activists around the country. Killing a doctor who performs abortions thus becomes an act of defense.

The approach varies, but the logic does not. Michael Bray, a Bowie, Md., pastor, who served four years for bombing clinics in the Washington area and has just written a book called "A Time to Kill," said, "There is no prohibition in the Bible against killing." The ancient Hebrew world translated as "kill" in the Sixth Commandment—"Thou shalt not kill"— does not refer to self-defense, Bray argues.

Says the Rev. David Trosch, the suspended Catholic priest in Mobile, Ala.: "It took World War II to stop the slaughter of millions of innocent people."

All of these activists say they would not themselves kill a doctor. They say they are either too important to the cause, too committed to their families or too smart to publicly proclaim their intentions. Before the recent murders in Pensacola, Paul Hill assured several friends that he would not himself resort to violence either.

The increasing visibility of this more militant anti-abortion faction is both painful and infuriating to the leaders of mainstream groups that have relied on organizing and lobbying since Roe v. Wade legalized abortion 21 years ago. The national Right to Life Committee, with 3,000 local chapters, prohibits its staff and board members from even picketing or blockading clinics because such actions could be illegal.

Mainstream anti-abortion leaders have denounced shooting doctors in equally absolute terms. "The shooting itself bears too much resemblance to abortion," said the Rev. Frank Pavone, founder of Priests United for Life. "It is violence . . . and it buys into the same mentality that death can be a solution. And that's precisely what we reject."

Cardinal John J. O'Connor, a staunch abortion opponent, wrote in his column in *Catholic New York* last week, "If anyone has an urge to kill an abortionist, let him kill me, instead. That's about as clearly as I can renounce such madness."

But some mainstream anti-abortion leaders privately voice fears that they have arrived at a philosophical quandary: If they agree that fetuses are children, why isn't it right to resort to the most desperate measures— even violence—to save them?

Instead, they argue strategy: that killing one doctor will not stop others, and that violence alienates potential supporters and provokes a government repression. They talk of the need to reach the women who choose abortion. But they admit that such reasoning fails to convince extremists prone to think in absolutes.

"There's been some frustration on our part, because I think our side has not come up with a clear, concise response," said Frederica Mathewes-Green, director of communications for the National Women's Coalition for Life. "All our explanations for why this is wrong are that people have reached an explosive level of frustration."

On the other side, prominent abortion rights leaders have accused anti-abortion leaders of bearing some responsibility for the bloodshed. "The inflammatory rhetoric . . . and concepts such as 'murder' and 'baby killer' create the conditions for extremist individuals to feel justified in taking violent actions," said Kate Michelman, president of the National Abortion and Reproductive Rights Action League.

Cardinal O'Connor retorted that this is like saying author Harriet Beecher Stowe caused the Civil War. O'Connor wrote that just as Abraham Lincoln credited Stowe's "Uncle Tom's Cabin" for calling attention to the injustice of slavery, "One day this great country of ours, and perhaps even a president, will thank pro-life leaders for raising the consciousness of so many about treating unborn human babies as non-persons."

Insiders describe an anti-abortion movement in disarray, with five branches that sometimes cooperate but often fail to work together: the "politicals" who work on electoral strategies; the "culturals" who teach about the value of life; the "crisis-pregnancy workers" who minister to women; the "religious" who hold prayer vigils; and the "rescuers" who rely on civil disobedience to disrupt clinic business.

Leaders in the political and cultural branches say that those now endorsing deadly force originated in the "rescuers" faction, first mobilized when Randall Terry began his highly visible Operation Rescue campaigns in the 1980s. Among Terry's slogans: "If abortion is killing, act like it is."

Terry has left Operation Rescue and now travels the speakers' circuit railing against homosexuals and President Clinton. The Rev. Flip Benham, the new director of what is now called Operation Rescue National, announced at a Chicago summit meeting of anti-abortion activists in April that anyone who believes in deadly force could not participate in his group's activities. The move prompted the creation of the more militant ACLA.

Proponents of "justifiable homicide" defy characterization by class, profession or educational background. But all describe themselves as Christians committed to a literal interpretation of the Bible.

Spitz dabbled in Eastern religions in San Francisco's Haight Ashbury district before becoming a born-again street preacher in New York's Times Square. Bray, a Baptist seminary graduate, began as a youth minister who tried to wrest young people from cults. Trosch was a small businessman, never married, who at 46 entered the priesthood.

What they share is a desperate frustration with legal tactics and a biting disdain for their more moderate colleagues in the cause.

"There is no pro-life movement," said Spitz. "The pro-life movement is getting its butt kicked . . . They can't even go out and picket in front of an abortion mill because it's a federal penalty . . . If they want to do that for 20 more years and have 50 million more dead babies, that's all they're going to get."

Cloning of Dolly Poses Challenge to Local Religious, Ethics Leaders

Sandi Dolbee, *San Diego Union-Tribune*, February 27, 1997

The lamb, it seems, is leading the shepherds.

In the North San Diego County city of Encinitas, a rabbi is planning to devote his sermon to her. The head of the county wide ecumenical council is suggesting a forum to discuss her. And a professor at a local seminary is updating his syllabus to include her.

Her name is Dolly. She is a sturdy white ewe named after country-western singer Dolly Parton and created not by a mom and dad sheep, but by scientists in Scotland.

Dolly, as the science journal *Nature* will detail in Thursday's edition, was cloned. And her introduction to the world a few days ago has launched a brave new push for religion to catch up to a futuristic technology hurtling past at warp speed.

"Those of us who are out there in the theological, ethical and philosophical worlds ought to make sure we have a place at the table," said Robert Wagener, a United Methodist minister and president of the Center for Medical Ethics and Mediation in San Diego. "If we don't do it, who will?"

The Rev. Glenn Allison, executive director of the Ecumenical Council of San Diego County, agrees. With this region's bounty of biotechnology, Allison says San Diego would be an ideal site for a public forum on the cloning issue.

"I think it ought to be discussed," Allison said. "In my mind, it does raise some very critical issues about where we're headed in all the uses of technology."

Rabbi David Frank, of North Coast's Temple Solel, plans to make this "new reality" his sermon topic tomorrow night, the start of the Jewish Sabbath.

Frank Warns Against Snap Judgments

"I think that trying, at this point, to give easy answers is the wrong thing to do," he cautioned. "If anything, this discovery highlights the need for us to give a lot of ethical and religious thought to the moral dilemmas we are going to be facing down the line."

Glen Scorgie, professor of theology and ethics at Bethel Theological Seminary-West, offers much the same caution.

Scorgie said students at the Protestant seminary, near San Diego State University, are talking about the morality of this breakthrough and many are chalking it up as another apocalyptic example of how humans are going too far.

But Scorgie's message to students, when he teaches about Dolly, will be to urge them to think through the subject carefully. Science and cloning are here to stay, he said.

A Matter of Time

For him, the challenge is to consider ways to control them. He hopes his students, the future pastors, will someday challenge their congregations to do likewise.

"The genius of Protestant Christianity has always been an informed laity . . . the laity must get a lot more informed and a lot more capable of critical thinking about the integration of their faith with the issues of the day," Scorgie said.

It is not just the cloning of a lamb that has captured the attention of these religious leaders. Despite scientific assurances to the contrary, many are convinced that it is only a matter of time before yet another story breaks onto the front pages—the cloning of a human being.

And Creation Is Sacred Turf

"I'm sure it's playing God," said Allison, who is also an Episcopal priest. "I don't have any doubt in my mind. Not only is it playing God, but it advances us one more step further in the many things we have done that somehow lead us to believe that we're the ultimate in creation. I think we're created beings and not the Creator, and in my mind that is where we are stepping beyond the roles."

Of course it's playing God, "but we always play God," said the Rev. Rob Calderhead, pastor of Hope United Methodist Church in Rancho Bernardo, Calif.

Calderhead said God and humans are partners.

"What bothers me," he added, "is people playing God without understanding that they're playing God."

A Line Not Crossed?

So, for some people of faith, the distinction may come in the execution. Science can be good—and bad.

The Rev. Doug Webster, pastor of First Presbyterian Church in downtown San Diego, puts it this way: "Sometimes, the line between playing God and serving humanity can be in the heart and in the motive."

Like many other ministers, Webster supports expanding knowledge "until it gets to the point where human values are challenged." And like many other ministers, Webster says that cloning humans is a line he would not cross.

But Rabbi Lisa Goldstein, executive director of San Diego's Hillel program for Jewish college students, wonders whether cloning humans is really much different from artificial insemination.

"It's not so much the technology itself but the ways that it's used that is moral or immoral," Goldstein said.

Yet from his office at Most Precious Blood Roman Catholic Church in Chula Vista, Calif., the Rev. Frank Wagner takes a dim view of the religious community's ability so far to influence technology.

"Tragically," Wagner said with a sigh, "I foresee another runaway locomotive. That's what concerns me more than anything else."

A Vatican official warned yesterday against human cloning, saying it would violate human dignity, the dignity of marriage and the principle of human equality.

Even animal cloning should be performed only under strict guidelines that maintain respect for the various species, Bishop Elio Sgreccia, the Vatican's leading expert on medical ethics, said in a written statement.

The questions abound: What role does God play in this? Would a cloned human have a soul? How does the meaning of life change because of this new ability? Would cloning lead to eugenics and social engineering?

Of course, voices of different faiths may come up with different answers. And complicating, or perhaps enriching, the conversation is the emerging pluralism of San Diego County—and the nation.

While Muslims, Jews and Christians may debate the concept of playing God, for example, that's not exactly the language that Hindus and Buddhists would use.

"We believe in a oneness with divinity rather than a separation, and for us playing God isn't a consideration," said Hindu Swami Atmarupananda of San Diego's Vedanta Society. "Hurting other beings—that's a consideration."

For him, whether cloning is good or bad probably would depend on whether it was being used for good or bad purposes.

In Buddhism, "There is no God; we are the creators of our experience," said Gen Kelsang Tubpa of the Vajrarupini Buddhist Center in Mission Hills.

Internal Peace

To Tubpa, a Buddhist nun, cloning "is just another example of man's belief that by manipulating the external environment he will create happiness for himself and freedom from suffering."

The Buddhist view, however, is that happiness does not come from external manipulation, but from internal peace.

Still, Dolly the lamb may be just the nudge needed for these shepherds to step into this biotechnological stampede.

"I don't think we should wait until our first human is cloned to get people in an interfaith community together to talk about these issues and say, 'Now what do we do?'" said Wagener, the minister and bioethicist.

He and others lobby for communication that comes both from the top of religious leadership and from the rank-and-file members in the pews.

But they warn that it will take more than rhetoric—it will also take knowledge.

"My biggest concern is: It needs to be a well-educated, intelligent, rational voice that can speak from our faith," said Calderhead of Rancho Bernardo. ". . . If we don't speak in a well-educated voice as to what's going on, we come off as Bozos and people ignore us and I think that's happened too often in the past."

Some clergy, meanwhile, admit that they haven't given Dolly much thought this week.

"I've got more important things to think about," said the Rev. Patricia Bush of St. Elizabeth's Episcopal Church in Linda Vista. "It seems so removed from things I have to deal with every day."

Ditto with the Rev. C. Dennis Williams, who spent part of Tuesday presiding over a funeral for a member of his Bethel African Methodist Episcopal Church in Logan Heights.

Said Williams, "I think it's a lot of money ill spent."

A Complicated Calling: Homosexuals Seeking Place and Peace in Clergy

Cecile S. Holmes, *Houston Chronicle,* November 12, 1995

Divorced, a former U.S. Navy lieutenant and gay, the Rev. Glynn C. Harper was in his late 30s when he finally answered a call to the priest-hood.

As an Episcopal priest celebrated the Eucharist, Harper felt a deep sense of homecoming and a certain knowledge that Jesus was present in the bread and wine.

"I think I actually heard the Gospel for the first time," Harper said. "I heard that salvation comes from grace, not the good works we do, which gave me the freedom to try to find out who I was as a whole person. I could not claim who I was—a child of God—until I claimed myself as a homosexual."

Harper, now 60 and associate rector of St. Peter's Episcopal Church in Pasadena, is celibate in a denomination which officially disapproves of homosexual practice. The issue so divides the church that retired Iowa Bishop Walter C. Righter—accused by fellow prelates of heresy because of his positive outlook and action on ordaining gays as priests—goes on trial before a church tribunal in January in Chicago.

Because Harper is gay, obstacles, prejudice, misconceptions and pain littered his path to ordination, starting before he entered seminary in the 1970s.

His local Episcopal diocese—the Houston-based Diocese of Texas—would not send him as a sponsored candidate, the traditional path to the priesthood.

After seminary, he could not find a church job.

Even after getting his first church post, paid work as a clergyman was hard to find.

A Pasadena native, Harper wanted to be a minister in high school, but took a different course after getting an appointment to the U.S. Naval

Academy at Annapolis. He married in 1958 right after graduation, but was divorced in 1963.

Harper struggled with depression, a drinking problem and his sexual orientation. He returned to Pasadena, working at different jobs and seeking meaning in a rough-and-tumble gay culture.

"It was beer-hall, meat-rack kind of world, no redeeming social value at all," he said.

But still he worshiped in an Episcopal Church.

His call to ministry was renewed. He did not forsake it even when the diocese would not sponsor him. He attended Episcopal Seminary of the Southwest in Austin on his own. He received honor grades, was elected student body vice president and found that his maturity proved a stabilizing influence for younger seminarians.

Difficult Path to Priesthood

With no sponsoring diocese, Harper had little hope of ordination until a tiny California diocese agreed to accept him as a candidate. He served three years, and was ordained a deacon and then a priest.

He finally left because he could not make ends meet on his $630-a-month salary. He returned to Houston. After initial difficulties because of his sexual orientation, he obtained paid work as a priest at St. Stephen's Episcopal Church after serving three years without pay and supporting himself with a technical writing job.

In May 1994, he was hired at St. Peter's as associate rector. The rector, the Rev. Ben Skyles, knew that Harper was gay and told the church's governing board. No one on the vestry objected.

He has gradually won acceptance in the 500-member congregation. Both Anglo and Hispanic parishioners praise his dedication and commitment to ministry. While some members have reservations about Harper because of his sexual orientation, they declined to talk about them for publication.

Harper says some believers view him as more accessible because he has struggled. "People think I'm less judgmental because I have a perceived flaw," he said. "It's sort of the myth of the wounded healer."

He loves being a priest and feels at home at St. Peter's.

"Once you get to a point where you know you're a child of God, there is a legitimacy to who you are that transcends who society values," he said. "You stop being afraid."

For him, celibacy is not "an unbearable condition" given "the joy of being a priest." But he would not impose that condition on "every homo-sexual called to the priesthood."

Harper decided to talk about his ministry and his sexual orientation because his conversion experience and his ministry have changed his un-derstanding of life's purpose. He said the church loses when its gay clergy fear being honest.

Bishop Claude Payne of the Episcopal Diocese of Texas backed Harper's decision to be interviewed.

"I supported his decision . . . because he is a wholesome example to the church," Payne said. "It is appropriate and quite fitting that this be acknowledged."

The bishop said Harper's celibacy is in keeping with church tradition on this issue.

"There have been and always will be homosexuals in the church who exercise ministry outside and within the priesthood," Payne said. "The expectation is that they lead a celibate life. It is no different than what the church expects from any single person."

Unusual Candor

Harper is unusual in his willingness to talk and in his openness with his congregation.

Many gay clergy cannot afford such candor. Some say they married to hide their sexual identity. In Houston, even successful ones are reluctant to discuss their sexual orientation or how the church has treated them. Sexual issues so plague today's church, they say, that the level of homophobia is up in the church despite growing acceptance of gays in secular life.

The message from the church is simple, gay clergy say: It doesn't matter if sexual identity results from nature or nurture. If you're gay, keep it to yourself. If you're sexually involved, don't reveal it.

Forcing gays to keep their sexual orientation secret subverts the gospel and provokes two main responses from gay clergy, said Mel White of Dallas, one of the most prominent evangelicals to disclose in recent years that he is gay.

"There are two kinds of internal responses," said White, a former ghost writer for Billy Graham and Jerry Falwell. "If you really feel con-fident that it is OK to be gay and Christian, then there's a period of time when you can say, 'I want to minister. Because these folks are so misin-formed, I'm not going to get into being gay.' There are some who can do that without feeling guilty or feeling terrorized.

"For the other group, it tears you up 100 percent of the time because ministry at its heart is simply being honest for folk," said White, who now works as a justice minister for the national Metropolitan Community Church. "It kills you not to be honest. It locks you off from sharing your life. If you can't be proud of your life, your relationships, it is the most destructive, polarizing, upsetting thing in the world."

In Houston, 25 to 30 gay clergy attend Crossroads, a monthly support group designed to help them deal with the conflicts of their life and ministry.

A former Southern Baptist clergyman, who requested anonymity, helped organize the group. He lost his church position after revealing he was gay in a counseling session with a young man struggling with homosexual feelings. "It was very confusing. I didn't get angry with God. I got angry with the people," he said. "It was a good learning and maturing process for me."

He works in another profession today and ministers as a volunteer at a local gay church.

A younger gay clergyman works at a Houston church known for ministry to gays and to gay and straight people with AIDS. At age 35, he is in a committed, faithful relationship with another man. The minister, who also requested anonymity, said he frequently counsels homosexuals who are priests or ministers.

"They are in Southern Baptist, Methodist, Roman Catholic, Lutheran, Episcopal, Presbyterian churches," he said. "They'll come in and talk about the fact that they have to hide. Every gay person is created in the image of God just like every handicapped person, every racially ethnic person, every woman, every man. Not to recognize that is not to be able to see God.

"You're taught in the Christian faith to let that light shine, to be truthful, to be honest," he said. To completely do that, gay clergy find they must be open about their sexual orientation, he said.

Divisive Issue

More divisive than ordaining women priests, and more controversial than the charismatic renewal, homosexuality evokes righteous indignation among many Christians. They believe any acceptance of homosexual practice—not to mention gay clergy—means sanctioning sin.

Only a handful of churches—including the Unitarian Universalist Association and the United Church of Christ—ordain openly gay clergy.

The Vatican repeatedly has spoken out against homosexuality among its priests, who must be male and take vows of celibacy.

The United Methodist Church has repeatedly refused to alter church policy against ordaining "self-avowed, practicing" homosexuals because "the practice of homosexuality is incompatible with Christian teaching." At its 1992 national meeting, the denomination voted to retain that wording in a church document known as its Social Principles statement, but to also support civil rights for gays.

The decision came after Methodists voted against the recommendation of a churchwide study committee that the phrase be eliminated. The committee urged the phrase be deleted because of "the lack of a common mind" in the church on the issue of ordaining gays. The 1992 vote marked the third consecutive Methodist General Conference where ordaining gays was discussed. The next meeting is in 1996.

The Episcopal Church's General Convention in 1979 adopted a resolution which affirmed the ordination of "qualified persons of either heterosexual or homosexual orientation whose behavior the Church considers wholesome." But the resolution also said "it is not appropriate for this Church to ordain a practicing homosexual."

The denomination remains sharply divided over how to interpret the resolution. Some bishops have ordained practicing homosexuals, insisting the resolution is not church law. Their colleagues have been infuriated, charging them with deliberately violating agreed-upon standards.

Widely Split Opinion

While church after church conducts denomination-wide studies of sexuality, the tensions mount between those believers who would treat being gay like being white or having brown eyes and others who would defrock gay and lesbian clerics.

Even an openly gay or lesbian minister accepted by his or her congregation risks losing his pulpit in an unsupportive denomination. For example, the Rev. Jane Adams Spahr, a lesbian and now an evangelist for a California gay organization, was called in fall 1991 as co-pastor of Rochester, N.Y.'s Downtown United Presbyterian Church. But regional and national officials overruled the Rochester church and ordered the job offer set aside.

Evangelicals who preach a conservative but compassionate theology want to preserve the Bible's teaching. They believe the Bible says sexual intimacy "only properly occurs within the bounds of a relationship that is heterosexual, lifelong, faithful and confirmed by marriage," said

Richard Mouw, an ethicist and president of Fuller Theological Seminary in Pasadena, Calif.

But evangelicals must forsake arrogance, Mouw said. "We've often had a kind of arrogant tone, a self-righteousness that doesn't signal to the world what is certainly true, and that is that we are all sinners who struggle with our sexuality."

Many Christians who condemn gays cite Old and New Testament passages to defend their position.

"We have to be very careful about the Old Testament passages," Mouw said. "We need to look at the ways in which the New Testament reaffirms certain things in the Old Testament as still relevant today." He urges the church to practice compassion, support gays who choose celibacy and strengthen its ministries to gays in general, developing programs as comprehensive as those offered in the gay community itself.

Another leading theologian and ethicist urges the church to re-examine some facets of its position on gays in ministry. "When the church either condemns their orientation as such or insists upon celibacy, the church is saying that their sexuality—which these individuals know is an essential part of themselves—is somehow deficient or depraved," said the Rev. James B. Nelson, a married heterosexual and the respected author of books on Christianity and sexuality.

Too often the church seems to be "saying that it places a priority on harmony more than it does on justice," said Nelson, professor emeritus of Christian ethics at United Theological Seminaries of the Twin Cities in Minnesota.

A Place to Call Home

In a landscape of human sexual tension, the Houston Metropolitan Community Church of the Resurrection is a place where people heal wounds and build bridges. Many gay Christians end up there after years of masking their sexual orientation in other denominations.

The local church is one of 250 congregations in an international gay denomination founded in 1967 by the Rev. Troy Perry. It has about 400 members, most of them gay, and a weekly attendance of 600 to 700.

As the congregation sang "How Great Thou Art" one Sunday morning, a tall black man held a little black girl's hand. Nearby a white woman braced a pregnant Hispanic woman's back. A youthful Asian man lowered his hymnal so a gray-haired white woman could read the words.

All that happened in the balcony.

Down front a white gay excommunicated Jesuit in blue corduroy shared the platform with a black lesbian in white vestments. When he preached to the overflow crowd of several hundred, the Rev. John Mc-Neill called them to seek wholeness, not fragmentation.

"Maturity for a gay person must include coming out of the closet just as spiritual maturity must include coming out of the closet with God and trusting that we are loved," McNeill, a well-known author and gay theologian, said in his sermon. "My own church has excluded me from the pulpit and I'm not allowed to speak in any of them."

The church reacts with fear and hostility to gay people, he said. But "nowhere in Scripture is there condemnation of a loving relationship between two gay men or two lesbian women."

Individual Struggles

While the debate over ordaining homosexuals continues to polarize denominations, individual gay clergy struggle to reconcile their sexual orientation with their calling.

A former Assembly of God pastor and Christian school teacher told his wife and sons last year that he is gay. Now divorced, he is struggling to rebuild his faith and his self-image and is active in a Houston mainline church that ministers to gays and is open to gay ministers.

He is certain he made the right choice to tell his family the truth.

Attending Bible school, marrying and immersing himself in the church did not bring him the peace he sought, he said. "I thought, 'This is a way to deal with my sexual identity. Surely if I seek God, that will help.' I chose to be straight. I lived in a straight fashion. I did everything I could to be straight. . . . I was never with a man sexually in my whole marriage. Never in my whole marriage. I was enamored and had fantasies. But I was true, faithful and upright."

To this former pastor, being able to keep his marriage vows was a victory. He does not believe being gay or having homosexual relations is sinful. He sees sexuality as a sacred trust, to be used in a monogamous, faithful relationship.

Today he is celibate at age 48. He is romantically attracted to a clergyman, but says the relationship will remain a friendship because the other minister is married.

"My strength is that I handled it right, all through life. There is a negative side to that, but it was right for me," he said. "The question I still have is, 'What is the best way and the most powerful and effective way to translate who I am into what I'm called to?'"

23

Church and State

When the founding fathers adopted the First Amendment in 1791, they disagreed among themselves about just how "separate" the establishment clause intended religion and government to be. They agreed, however, that the First Amendment was a protection only from the federal government and that states and local entities were not affected. But that understanding became untenable with passage of the Fourteenth Amendment, which ultimately had the effect of protecting all citizens from actions by state and local governments that would interfere with freedoms promised by the Bill of Rights—including freedom of religion. But in spite of constitutional guarantees, clashes between a highly religious citizenry and a government mandated to keep religion and state affairs distinct are practically inevitable.

Like most Americans, the courts originally assumed the United States was essentially a Christian nation. But in recent years, courts have come to recognize increased religious pluralism in America through decisions that protect the rights of all religious people, along with those who choose not to have a faith. In their efforts to prevent establishing a particular faith through favoritism while still protecting basic rights to practice religion, provided the practice doesn't interfere with other freedoms or harm public safety, they now tend to adopt Thomas Jefferson's notion of a "wall of separation" between church and state.

However, courts, like the American public, still differ as to how high that wall should be. Many church-state decisions are won or lost with close votes. And those on the losing side often feel that their basic right to religious freedom has been abridged. Thus, the very personal nature of any legal battle and the closeness of court decisions provides drama that begs for news coverage, making church-state disputes a prime topic for religion writers in the 1980s and 1990s.

Church-state struggles have been at the heart of several articles in previous chapters: clashes between Mormons and the government over their church's sanction of plural marriage (chapter 9), attempts by creationists to squelch the teaching of evolution in public-funded schools (chapter 14), and the quest of Jehovah's Witnesses for exemption from requirements to salute the flag (chapter 15).

Included in this chapter are other church-state issues, from school prayer to faith healing. Even before Pat Robertson's Republican primary loss in the 1988 election, his political organization, along with others, had learned the courts were the overseers of religious freedoms as Robertson and his followers defined them. David Waters's story from the *Commercial Appeal* in Memphis is a review of the groups battling for and against the religious right's agenda in the courts. The story includes the issue of school prayer—one of the most litigated and debated of church-state issues, along with other free exercise cases.

Also in this chapter, the rights of parents to practice their faith and the rights of the government to protect children clash in a story from the *Columbus Dispatch*. For the most part, Christian Scientists, Jehovah's Witnesses and others who have faith-based views on healing and medical care are left to practice their faith freely. But when a child's life is in danger or the child dies, then the government has, at times, stepped in. In this 1987 story, prosecutors pursued the case after several children in Indiana and Ohio died of treatable illnesses.

The issue of when the government protects children from religious views and when children have religious rights of their own is muddy at best. The rights of coaches and teachers can conflict with the rights of students. The interplay between culture and church-state issues is clear in Mark O'Keefe's piece from the Portland *Oregonian* about sports teams that play—and pray—together. It shows how the ideal of the separation of church and state has been enculturated into even nongovernment groups like the National Collegiate Athletic Association.

Readers searching for additional stories can check out Jeanne Pugh's story of legal wrangling over public school textbook language in the March 21, 1987, religion section of the *St. Petersburg Times*; John Dart's "Indian Religions Finally Gain U.S. Protection Under Act" in the February 18, 1979, issue of the *Los Angeles Times,* which gives a thorough review of Native American religious rights up to that point; and David Waters's story in the December 5, 1993, *Commercial Appeal,* which provides an in-depth look at one of dozens of school prayer cases.

Religious Right Using Arm of Law to Push Its Agenda

David Waters, *The Commercial Appeal,* January 3, 1994

The new Christian soldiers carry legal pads and march to court.

When parents in a California town thought public schools were teaching their children witchcraft, they didn't call the school board. They called Donald Wildmon's American Family Association (AFA) Law Center.

When a minister in New York tried to rent a school building after hours to show a film on family values, he didn't call his congressman. He called Pat Robertson's American Center for Law and Justice (ACLJ).

Robertson's attorneys took their case to the U.S. Supreme Court and won. Wildmon's attorneys lost their argument in federal district court, but they have appealed.

Those cases are two of the more prominent examples of the nation's budding religious rights movement, an activist strategy modeled after the court-anchored civil rights struggles of the 1950s and 1960s.

Religious leaders like Robertson and Wildmon moved from the pulpit to the political arena in the 1980s to advance their social agendas. Now they're changing their strategy and taking their agendas to court.

Some critics accuse the movement's lawyers of opportunism, saying tactics are superficial and geared to grab headlines and raise money. Yet they say the new religious rights activists are having an impact.

In the past two years, Robertson and Wildmon have hired a cadre of attorneys to arrest and reverse what they view as the slow but steady erosion of religious liberties caused by wave after wave of court rulings from the U.S. Supreme Court on down.

"Religious and civil rights have been under attack in this country for so long by groups like the ACLU that people aren't sure what they can or can't do when it comes to school prayer or religious expression in the public arena," said Keith Fournier, executive director of Robertson's ACLJ, formed and named specifically to counter the American Civil Liberties Union (ACLU).

Scott Thomas, general counsel for the AFA's Law Center in Tupelo, said the only way to stop the judicial pendulum and start it going back the other direction is to fight lawyer with lawyer.

"In their zeal to protect individual First Amendment rights of free speech and religion," Thomas said, "the courts over the past 30 years have gone beyond protection to restraint.

"We got to this point one court case at a time. To get back to where we need to be is going to take time and can only be accomplished one court case at a time."

Religious rights attorneys are looking for their Brown vs. Board of Education, the 1954 Supreme Court case that ended the "separate but equal" approach to schools and triggered desegregation and the modern civil rights movement.

They think they might have it. Last month the Supreme Court agreed to decide whether the creation of a special public school district to accommodate disabled Hasidic children violates the constitutional separation of church and state.

By taking the New York case, the court agreed to reconsider its controversial 1971 decision that established a test for determining when the church has crossed state boundaries.

"It may be a watershed," said Larry Crain, an attorney for the Rutherford Institute in Arlington, Va., another organization that fights for its agenda in court.

"This case could have implications for school prayer, public support of private schools and all sorts of religious liberty issues."

The 1971 Lemon vs. Kurtzman ruling drew contemporary church-state boundaries. The court ruled that any government action regarding religion must have a secular purpose; its primary effect must neither advance nor inhibit religion; and it must not foster "excessive entanglement" with religion.

Lemon drew the lines, but the battle began in 1962 when the Supreme Court banned prayers and Bible readings as regular devotional exercises in public schools.

"It is no part of the business of government to compose official prayers for any group of the American people to recite," Justice Hugo Black said for the majority.

Separationists like Black say church and state must remain clearly apart. They believe that with 1,200 religious bodies in the country, there's no way to safely integrate all of them into secular society, so it's best not to allow any.

But accommodationists say there should be a line, not a wall between church and state. They argue that an overly protective court has infringed on the religious liberties of believers.

Their champion is Justice Antonin Scalia, who in the late 1980s applauded the entry of religious activists into the judicial arena.

"Political activism by the religiously motivated is part of our heritage," Scalia said in 1987.

Last year, a federal appeals court used one of Scalia's recent dissents as a road map to rule in favor of graduation prayers in Jones vs. Clear Creek. When the U.S. Supreme Court declined last summer to review that ruling, religious rights activists saw the beginnings of a tiny crack in the church/state wall.

Last summer, Tennessee legislators relied on the Jones ruling to enact a law that permits public school students to propose and lead nonsectarian, nonproselytizing prayers on public school grounds during noncompulsory student gatherings.

The Rutherford Institute helped a Sumner County principal sue the ACLU, claiming the ACLU harassed him to prevent him from allowing his students to read a graduation prayer. Rutherford's attorneys have asked the court to use the case to rule on Tennessee's new law. The case is hung up in pretrial motions.

Last month, a high school principal in Jackson, Miss., relied on his understanding of the Jones ruling to allow his students to read a prayer over the school's intercom. At first, he was fired, but later was suspended for a year.

Attorneys for Wildmon and Robertson have stepped into the fray; AFA attorneys are representing principal Bishop Knox. They also are talking to several students who were suspended for supporting Knox. ACLJ attorneys negotiated on the students' behalf with the Jackson school system.

AFA's Thomas said this is the kind of courtroom trench warfare that must be waged if the religious rights movement is to succeed.

But some critics say the efforts are superficial.

Hedy Weinberg, director of the Tennessee ACLU, said her organization was targeted by Rutherford simply to make fund-raising headlines, not to make case law.

"The Tennessee law hadn't even been passed when this principal filed his lawsuit," she said. "There's only so much funding available out there, and now Rutherford is having to compete for it with Robertson and Wildmon."

Critics accuse the movement's lawyers of opportunism in the Mississippi principal's case as well.

"They are very careful, the ACLJ especially, not to take cases to court they know they can't win," said Robert Boston, assistant director of Americans United for Church and State Separation.

Lynn Watkins, director of Mississippi's ACLU, said Robertson is encouraging legal novices to test and sometimes break clearly defined laws regarding church and state.

"They're looking for someone to push the envelope for them, then they'll sweep in and take the glory," she said.

But AFA's Thomas said the Mississippi case proves that religious rights activists are in it for the long haul.

"We took that case not only because we wanted to defend Mr. Knox's religious rights, but also because we wanted to defend everyone's rights," he said. "We don't always win, but we always fight."

Wildmon's AFA Law Center is smaller but older than the ACLJ. Wildmon started his law group in 1990; Robertson started his the following year. Wildmon has four lawyers on his staff, Robertson a dozen.

Despite the attention both have garnered, the Rutherford Institute is acknowledged as the father of the movement. Formed in 1982 by John Whitehead, an attorney who wanted to provide free legal representation for defendants in religious rights cases, it has more than 50 attorneys today working on cases from coast to coast.

Litigation is just one of the strategies Robertson and Wildmon use. Litigation is all Rutherford does.

Crain, an attorney for the institute's Nashville office, said there are plenty of cases out there for everyone. But he is concerned about the movement's expansion for other reasons.

Crain also is worried about the headlines generated by groups like the ACLJ. "I am concerned that people will perhaps receive false hopes that these cases are easily won," he said.

Still, ACLU's Weinberg said, the new religious rights activists are having an impact, particularly with her organization.

"They're not only aggressive but clever, so we've had to get more aggressive and more clever," Weinberg said. "They're raising an incredible amount of money, so they're teaching us a lesson about the importance of grass-roots organizing."

Sect Members Go on Trial in Baby's Death

Debra L. Mason, *The Columbus Dispatch,* January 21, 1986

CELINA, Ohio—It wasn't Kimberly D. Miller's parents who summoned the doctor last April 3 after she had been ill several days with vomiting and diarrhea.

It was the funeral home, because Kimberly was dead. The doctor was Donald Fox, the Mercer County coroner.

The 23-month-old girl's parents, Steven and Diane Miller, belong to Faith Assembly, a fundamentalist Christian sect that believes only prayer, and not medical care, can heal.

THE MILLERS go on trial today on child endangering charges because they did not seek medical care for Kimberly. The child died of pneumonia and bronchitis—illnesses that are normally treatable—the coroner's report said.

The trial, in this farming community 125 miles northwest of Columbus, highlights a growing national debate on whether members of faith-healing sects can be forced to provide medical care for their children. The issue also is expected to be debated in this session of the Ohio General Assembly.

Kimberly was the third Mercer County child in five years to die of a treatable disease because medical treatment was withheld for religious reasons.

The Miller case represents the first time anyone has been prosecuted in this county for withholding medical treatment on religious grounds and only the second such prosecution in Ohio.

THE COUPLE waived a jury, so the trial will be heard by Mercer County Common Pleas Judge Dean James. It is expected to last two days.

The parents, both 27, attend services at David Miller's Celina home, which serves as a place of worship for Faith Assembly members. David Miller is Steven's father and grandfather of the dead child.

Among biblical passages the group invokes is James 5:14-15, which says, "Is there any among you sick? Let him call for the elders of the church, and let them pray over him, anointing him with oil in the name of the Lord, and the prayer of faith will save the sick man, and the Lord will raise him up; and if he has committed sins, he will be forgiven."

UNDER OHIO law, if a sick child is treated "by spiritual means through prayer alone, in accordance with the tenets of a recognized religious body," the parents or guardians can't be convicted of a criminal offense, as long as they prove their membership in such a religious group.

Defense attorney Garrett Gall, appointed by the court, said he expects the couple's affiliation with the religious group to provide them with the defense they need.

"I think it is a right for them, and testimony for them that will be presented at the trial will show that they are entitled to it," Gall said. He and his clients declined to discuss the case further.

Forty-seven states have religious exemptions to juvenile or criminal codes. But publicity about high numbers of deaths in some faith healing groups has recently led to more frequent prosecution of parents or guardians.

IN INDIANA, where Faith Assembly is based, six couples have been tried after their children died of normally treatable illnesses. All those cases have been won by the prosecutors, said Rita Swan, president of CHILD Inc.

"I think Faith Assembly has gotten so notorious there that you could convict them of anything," Swan said in a telephone interview from her home in Bronson, Iowa. CHILD stands for Children's Healthcare Is a Legal Duty, and Swan works to get religious exemptions repealed in state laws.

She was to arrive in Celina today to attend the Miller trial as an observer. She will visit Columbus later this week to lobby lawmakers to do away with religious exemptions for parents.

The only other Ohio case in which parents faced criminal charges because they did not seek medical help for their child ended in the parents' acquittal on a manslaughter charge.

In the 1984 Coshocton County trial of Larry and Roberta Miskimens, Common Pleas Judge Richard Evans said the spiritual exemption was unconstitutional, but he found the couple not guilty anyway.

THE COUPLE belonged to an offshoot of Faith Assembly, and their 13-month-old son, Seth, died of pneumonia Aug. 1, 1983, without ever seeing a physician.

But because the constitutionality issue was never appealed, it does not apply outside Coshocton County.

Mercer County Prosecutor Daniel Myers said he decided to seek an indictment in the Miller case because Kimberly was the third Celina child to die after medical treatment was withheld.

The first child to die was Christina Miller, 12-year-old daughter of David Miller, who led the Faith Assembly affiliate in Celina. Christina was also the younger sister of Steven Miller, Kimberly's father.

Christina's death was what alerted Mercer County officials to Faith Assembly's beliefs.

"Had there not been any deaths, I probably wouldn't have known what these people were doing," Myers said. "They're not like Hare Krishnas; they don't go door to door to get you to contribute or join the church."

THE CORONER'S report said Christina died on Christmas Eve 1981 of heart problems that usually are not fatal when treated.

The child was smaller than average, and her lips and fingers were always blue. Her classmates taunted her and called her "Bluelips." The coroner's report said her heart did not pump enough oxygen through her blood.

Because of the religious exemptions in state law, Myers said, he did not file charges against Christina's parents.

The second case involved 8-month-old Meredith Adele Hinton. Her parents, Kent and Dawn Hinton, called the coroner July 10, 1984, to have Meredith pronounced dead.

The sheriff's report said Mrs. Hinton was feeding Meredith cereal in her baby seat when the baby suddenly stopped breathing. Mrs. Hinton told sheriff's deputies the baby in recent days had been vomiting and had diarrhea from cutting teeth.

A CORONER'S REPORT listed Meredith's cause of death as pneumonia and excessive vomiting, among other things. Again, because of the religious exemption, Myers did not prosecute.

Kimberly Miller's death—the third in Mercer County—convinced Myers that he should prosecute the parents despite the religious exemption, he said. The child endangering charges against Steven and Diane Miller are a felony and carry a maximum penalty of 18 months in prison and a $2,500 fine.

"You've got a 23-month-old baby who's dead," Myers said. "As far as I'm concerned, her death could have been prevented through proper medical treatment."

Myers says winning may be difficult.

"If in fact they are acquitted," Myers said, "then the only way to effectively save children in that same situation as Kimberly is to change the legislation."

Mercer County Sheriff Joseph Gilmore agrees. "It's difficult to prosecute something when the exemption is so unreasonable. It's worded so that almost anything could be exempted," he said.

STATE REP. Paul H. Jones, D-Ravenna, last Friday introduced legislation that would revoke the religious exemption to criminal law. Jones had introduced a similar version of the law during the last legislative session, but Rep. Francine Panehal, D-Cleveland, who was chairman of the House Children and Youth Committee, killed the bill after lengthy hearings in 1985.

After pressure in part due to Kimberly Miller's death, Panehal revived a version of the bill in November, too late to pass before the end of the legislative session. The bill was also changed so much that Jones, its original sponsor, and some organizations withdrew their support.

Swan, of CHILD Inc., is not coy about blaming the General Assembly for Kimberly's death.

"They had full warning," Swan said. "I really feel that the blood of this child is on their hands."

Swan's son, Matthew, died of bacterial meningitis in 1977 after Swan took him to a Christian Science prayer healer (called a practitioner) and was discouraged from seeking medical help until it was too late. She then quit the church.

Swan said that in 1974 the U.S. Department of Health, Education and Welfare required states to pass spiritual exemptions to either juvenile or criminal codes if they wanted to continue receiving certain federal money. The exemptions were urged by high-ranking Christian Scientists, she said.

IT WASN'T until 1982 that prosecutors again began seeking charges against parents or guardians whose children suffered harm because of their parents' religious beliefs, Swan said.

Then in 1983, the federal government removed the exemption requirement. That same year Oklahoma became the first state to remove the faith healing exemption from its criminal codes.

Last month, the American Medical Association joined what appears to be growing opposition to spiritual healing exemptions. Its board adopted a resolution supporting repeal of religious exemptions from child abuse laws.

The board said that "laws enacted to protect and provide for the medical needs of children should be fashioned so as to protect the constitutional rights of both parents and children."

SWAN, JONES and others trying to repeal the religious exemption can expect a fight from William R. Evans of the Christian Science Committee on Publication in Ohio. He is the chief Ohio lobbyist for the group, which encourages healing by prayer.

Evans said that Christian Scientists, unlike Faith Assembly, do not prohibit the faithful from seeking a physician. But he said Christian Scientist practitioners should not have to fear being charged with a crime if something goes wrong.

The Bible Is Their Playbook

Mark O'Keefe, *The Oregonian,* November 19, 1995

Kneeling at midfield of Parker Stadium in Corvallis, running back Cam Reynolds of Oregon State grasps the hand of California linebacker Marlon McWilson.

Coaches look on approvingly as the two players and a dozen others bow their heads moments after the October game.

"Lord," prays Reynolds, "I just thank you for the friendly competition today. I just thank you that everything we did today was for your glory."

The increasingly familiar scene, replayed after public high school and college games across the country, is more than just a ritual in a nation that worships sports. It's a sign that the playing field has become a mission field, with evangelical coaches acting as ministers of the Gospel.

Religion always has been a part of sports, but never like this. The success of praying teams such as Nebraska and UCLA—the college football and basketball champions—plus the explosion of The Promise Keepers, a sports-minded Christian men's movement, has made 1995 the year of the athletic amen.

It's not by accident. With the college football season ending for some Saturday and basketball just beginning, hundreds of coaches in college and thousands in high school are carrying out an organized crusade with the help of more than 100 evangelical sports ministries.

The Bible is their playbook. A macho Jesus is their inspiration.

Prayer on the playing field appears popular, with relatively few complaining or suing. But groups that advocate a high wall of separation between church and state say coaches on the state payroll must keep their religion to themselves.

"There is a constitutional problem with coaches promoting religious activities," says Naomi Gitting, attorney for the Virginia-based National School Boards Association. "Students perceive them to be somebody connected with the school and as someone with authority. I don't think any school can get away with them actually leading prayers or anything even close to that."

Coaches and their lawyers disagree.

They say they have a First Amendment right to express their beliefs, that prayer and Bible studies are usually optional, and that religion brings team unity and sorely needed values.

Some go so far as to suggest a born-again team is a better team.

"The idea is to play hard. Jesus Christ was the most intense man on the face of the Earth. He went to the cross. His guts were spilled," says assistant football coach Ron Brown of Nebraska.

"It's a ministry. It's worship. It's an altar right out there on the football field. You're worshipping God every play. You're saying, 'Thank you, God.' A Christian player says, 'This one's for you, Lord.'"

Brown says he and other Nebraska coaches routinely pray with players, lead post-practice Bible studies and arrange for vans to take athletes to evangelical services.

The Cornhuskers' weekly scouting report includes a motivational Scripture verse from head coach Tom Osborne, who gathers his staff every morning for prayer.

THE EXECUTIVE director of the American Football Coaches Association, Grant Teaff, calls this God's plan to reach America through college sports.

Teaff is the former chairman of the Fellowship of Christian Athletes, the largest of the sports ministries, which also includes groups such as Athletes in Action, Champions for Christ and, in the Portland area, Beyond Victory.

"There are 670 head football coaches in America," says Teaff. "My word, there are probably 450 or more who are very solid, Christian men. Easily."

"It's the golden opportunity that there is more to be taught than winning the football game or getting a pro contract," he says.

Other sports also have caught the fire.

Meet Ritchie McKay, the Apostle Paul of college basketball and the new coach at Portland State, which is resurrecting the sport after a 14-year absence. Last year, while an assistant coach at the University of

Washington, McKay started a national group called "Coaches for Christ." It had 50 members.

Hired in August, McKay is bracing for criticism once people discover his passion for evangelism.

After school administrators received complaints in 1993, Portland State forbid its football players from saying the Lord's Prayer at midfield at the end of games. That didn't stop the football players—they're praying again—and it's not going to prevent McKay from communicating his beliefs.

On the bulletin board behind the coach's desk are the five biblical concepts he plans to build his program on: "humility—know who you are," "passion—do not be lukewarm," "unity—do not divide our house," "servanthood—make teammates better" and "thankfulness—learn from each circumstance."

While he says he will recruit non-Christians, McKay hopes to convert them once they join his team.

"I want to spread the good news," he says. "I want to make disciples of Christ. I've also been able to share with players. With the Holy Spirit's leading, they have been impacted as well. So I definitely think coaching is a ministry opportunity."

McKay and other coaches have been inspired by the Promise Keepers, the evangelical men's movement that has filled football stadiums across the country. Its founder is Bill McCartney, the former head football coach at the University of Colorado.

At the core of the movement is an interpretation of the Bible that emphasizes "the Great Commission," in which Christ tells his followers to "make disciples" by teaching them "everything I have commanded you."

McCartney says: "It's a whole new way to live and die. It's a whole new way to compete."

But is it legal?

The First Amendment addressing religion and free speech has been one of the most hotly debated parts of the Constitution. To clear up the matter, some conservative groups are pushing the Republican Congress to back a religious equality amendment, introduced last week in the House. It would give students, teachers and coaches greater freedom to pray and proselytize in the public schools.

Even without a constitutional amendment, some argue that coaches have a right to create a spiritual climate on their teams.

It is constitutional "as long as there is no compulsion or coercion to join in the prayer," says Dean Whitford, an attorney for the Virginia-based Rutherford Institute, a conservative organization that defends the advancement of religion in the public square.

Earlier this year, the Rutherford Institute and the Rev. Jerry Falwell of Liberty University double-teamed the National Collegiate Athletic Association in legally appealing its ban of post-touchdown prayers in the end zone. The ban was lifted.

But that was only a small victory.

Recent court rulings indicate state-supported schools can be one lawsuit away from trouble when teachers, and by implication coaches, endorse a particular religion. While judges generally permit prayer if it is student-led and student-initiated, they forbid school officials from orchestrating anything.

One of the few cases involving coaches occurred in 1994 in Duncanville, Texas, where the girls basketball team traditionally knelt at midcourt to say the Lord's Prayer. After a player and her family complained, a federal judge ruled the players could pray on their own, but the coaches must not participate.

At Oregon City High School, where the girls basketball team was ranked No. 1 in the nation by *USA Today* last season, coach Brad Smith says he often leads prayers before games.

Smith, who attends Oregon City Evangelical Church, as do his assistant coach and two of the team's starters, says he also incorporates biblical principles in his coaching.

Take, for example, his rule against swearing.

"But if a kid did swear, it's not like I would punish them by not playing them, or say, 'Hey, you're a sinner.'. . . I'd just say, 'I'm not going to swear at you, so you don't swear at me.'"

He recoils at the suggestion that he would favor a Christian athlete.

"If you can shoot the jump shot and knock it down, you're going to play, whether you share my religious beliefs or not," says Smith.

PUBLIC OPINION polls show most Americans favor school prayer. Coaches contend athletes and their parents also appreciate a spiritual approach.

A few have complained. At Sam Barlow High in Gresham, boys tennis coach Ron Suelzle was called into the vice principal's office last spring and told to stop proselytizing after a parent protested.

"I am a minister of the Gospel" says Suelzle. "I also coach. My faith is all-pervasive in my life. I have a real struggle in what I can say and not say."

The most alarming struggle, says Arthur Berger, spokesman for the New York-based American Jewish Committee, is for students. They shouldn't have to worry about the religious beliefs of a coach. Pressure, even if subtle, can be intense.

"It bothers us if anyone, Jewish or not, weren't part of that belief," says Berger. "You're not talking about a denominational team run by the church. You're talking about a public team. The character should be secular and nonreligious."

It's not that way at UCLA.

After winning the NCAA championship in April, nearly the entire team dropped to its knees, in full view of the national TV audience.

"Father, we've gone with you all year," said assistant coach Lorenzo Romar. "We've played for you, and you have been first."

When the scene was replayed on a giant screen at a Promise Keepers rally in Los Angeles last May, more than 72,000 men rose to their feet in emotional applause. Romar emerged to give a spiritual explanation for UCLA's success.

Romar says UCLA has received a few complaints, but for every negative comment, there have been 100 positive ones.

AT NEBRASKA, the theme is similar: Christians are winners, in football and in life.

When players eat lunch at the university's Hewitt Center, a Fellowship of Christian Athletes representative is available for optional Bible study. Before postseason bowl games, a Fellowship of Christian Athletes prayer breakfast is mandatory. The postgame prayers are so popular they sometimes resemble an on-field tent revival.

For the fans, it's as if there is a Great Cornhusker in the sky, smiling on coach Tom Osborne.

"Tommy's integrity, character and ability to win games has put him on a platform where we can go anywhere in the state and proclaim the good news of Jesus Christ," says assistant coach Brown. "The people come in the name of football. We go in the name of the Lord Jesus Christ."

At Gill Coliseum in Corvallis on Oct. 28, the spiritual lure was basketball. The "Winning on the Court" event was sponsored by Northwest Hills Baptist Church, Oregon State basketball coach Eddie Paynes and his assistant, Michael Holton.

"We spoke about our basketball lives and our spiritual lives," says Holton. "They're intertwined now."

The two insist they don't require the same from their players.

"I've seen a lot of heathens that are good players," says Payne. "but they've done what they have to do to stay in good graces. I'm going to fight hard to not be judgmental on those things."

THE FOOTBALL stadium lights are dimmed after Oregon State's 13-12 loss to California last month, and the judgment is still on the scoreboard. The loss ensures a 25th straight losing season for the Beavers.

Still, athletic director Dutch Baughman has faith. He stands in the end zone in front of more than 100 teen-agers gathered for the Fellowship of Christian Athletes "Oregon witness day."

He tells the kids how he found God while serving in Vietnam and how they should find their own salvation. He turns to coach Jerry Pettibone, who has just emerged from the losing locker room.

"The blessing here is that this man has such a strong, courageous relationship with Jesus Christ," says Baughman. "He knows we'll come through this despite the doubters and the skeptics looking at Oregon State."

Surrounded by fellow believers in the nearly empty stadium, Pettibone seems buoyed by the support.

A teen-ager asks the coach to sign his football jersey. Pettibone does, writing "Jeremiah 29:11."

Pettibone has the verse memorized: "For I know the plans I have for you, declares the Lord. Plans to prosper you and not to harm you, plans to give you hope and a future."

"I'm clinging on to that," says Pettibone, "for myself and for this season. I know God does have a plan for us here at Oregon State, and it's for prosperity, not disaster."

24

Pluralism Takes Hold

As a nation formed largely of immigrants, the United States necessarily had some religious pluralism from the start. But the diversity was limited. Whether they were Quaker, Puritan or Congregationalist, there was still more that united the beliefs of colonists and founding citizens than divided them. And despite the antiestablishment clauses of the Constitution, most states had established religions. Some even had laws restricting the rights of Jews, other non-Christians and atheists to hold elected office.

However, the Great Awakenings led to the creation of some religious groups that fell outside the norm of typical Christianity—Spiritualists, the Mormons, Christian Scientists, Seventh-day Adventists and Jehovah's Witnesses, among others. And waves of immigration, especially in the late 1800s, brought increasing numbers of Roman Catholics and Jews to the country.

In the next 100 years, other forces, including new immigration patterns that brought more new citizens from Asia and Africa, contributed to increasing the ethnic and religious diversity in the United States. By the 1990s, every major world faith had more than just a token presence in the United States.

While the number of followers of non-Christian groups remains small, those groups have commanded significantly more attention from religion reporters in recent years. Expanded religion sections offer the space needed to present complex stories about a faith most people don't know anything about.

Even with greater religious diversity, however, the combined number of non-Christian adherents in the United States is less than 10 percent, with Islam considered by most sources as the fastest growing. *Providence Journal* religion writer Richard Dujardin's Sunday magazine piece about the struggle of practicing Islam in a non-Islamic nation gives readers a real feel for the typical day of a strict practicing Muslim. The story also makes clear the degrees of orthodoxy that separate some Muslims, much like the differences in orthodoxy that exist among Christians or Jews.

Of the Eastern religions, Buddhism—in all its varied forms—has been perhaps the most successful in becoming adopted in the United States, with the meditational practices of Zen Buddhism, particularly, becoming incorporated into the religious routines of Christians, New Agers and others. Although it only experienced great growth in the late 20th century, Buddhism has been in the United States for 150 years, mostly on the West Coast where Asian immigrants toiled. This chapter reprints a story by *San Francisco Chronicle* religion reporter Don Lattin, who looks at Buddhism in his corner of California.

Most of the growth in Hinduism in this country has occurred in recent decades, following increased immigration from India. But the creative religious mix of the 1960s also led to Hindu offshoots such as the International Society for Krishna Consciousness (Hare Krishnas) and the Transcendental Meditation movement. This chapter includes Ira Rifkin's story for *Religion News Service* chronicling Hinduism's growth on these shores.

Paganists, Druids and Wiccans received renewed attention in the late 1990s, perhaps as part of the fetish for all things Irish or Celtic among Americans. But the Internet's ability to link all corners of the world as part of one huge global chat meant former solitary practitioners of some faiths—such as Pagans—were able to find communities of believers. The *News & Observer*'s religion reporter Yonat Shimon linked both these trends in her story about Raleigh-area "Techno Pagans," who use the computer for ritual and community.

Keeping the Faith

Richard C. Dujardin, *The Providence Sunday Journal,* August 19, 1990

> Bear then, with patience, all that they say, and celebrate the praises
> of thy Lord, before the rising of the sun and before (its) setting.
> —The Koran

It is 3 a.m., a warm starlit night, when Skeikhu Abu Abdullah breaks from his slumber. He has been asleep only a few hours, but now his internal alarm clock tells him it is time to rise.

With a quite prayer, the slender, wiry man places his feet upon the floor. His wife, Aisha Abu Abdullah, stirs, but then turns back to sleep. She knows that when it is time Sheikh will be calling her, as he does every morning, with the ancient chant that has been used by muezzins for more than a thousand years to bring Muslims to prayer.

"In the name of Allah, the Beneficent, the merciful . . ."

Outside, a bar of light is just beginning to break through the blackness on the horizon. Birds begin to chirp. Sitting on the porch of their modest frame house in rural Rhode Island, Abdullah contemplates the fullness of the moment.

He has not always been a Muslim. But reaching back to when he was a child, in Brooklyn, he can remember certain people who were Muslim believers: "There used to be guys in the neighborhood that were Muslims, and they used to sit down in the park and they'd have to hide their Koran, because it wasn't allowed. If they were praying, the police would come and interrupt their prayer and literally chase them out of the park."

In the pre-dawn light, Abdullah says that he can feel a connection now with those men. They had to struggle to live their faith. The Muslims call it the jihad: the holy struggle. Some people think that jihad refers to warring against the infidels—cutting off heads as a favor to God. But the Koran forbids aggression. The real jihad, Abdullah says, is the one that people must wage with themselves, against the demons within.

It's by putting aside one's own will, Abdullah says, that people find "the Straight Path" that brings them to the "face of God." He says that for him the Koran has provided the understanding that the only way he will find true freedom is by submitting himself to the will of Allah: the omnipotent and everlasting.

The eastern horizon has grown a little brighter. Abudullah knows that it is time to wake his wife.

"Allahu akbar . . . Allahu akbar . . . Ashadu an la ilaha illa-llah. . . . Hayya 'ala-salah . . . Hayya ' ala-k-falah . . ." (The words in Arabic are "Allah is great . . . Allah is great . . . I bear witness that there is no god apart from Allah . . . Come to prayer. . . . Come to salvation.")

Hearing her husband's words, Aisha Abu Abdullah jumps from her bed and thumps barefoot to the bathroom sink to perform wudhu: the ritual washing of the face, arms, and feet required of every believer, to assure cleanliness at prayer.

A few minutes later she is coming down the stairs, covered by a long cotton gown and a cloth kimar, which hides her hair. She and Sheikh unroll one of the embroidered prayer mats that they keep in their prayer room, which also holds lots of book-filled boxes and a personal computer. It may not be the ideal spot for prayer, but at least the room has no statues, pictures, or animals, all of which are proscribed from places where Muslims pray. (Yasminah, their 10-year-old daughter, does have a hamster, as part of a science project, but she keeps it in another room.)

Of all the moments of the day, the hour between 4 and 5 a.m. is Aisha's favorite. It gives her time, she says, to meditate and to feel the peaceful presence of God.

She takes her place behind Sheikh, and the two begin the recitation of the first prayer of the day – Fajr – confident that their action will be pleasing in Allah's eyes.

Reciting the prayers in Arabic isn't always easy for a pair of native New Yorkers. But, like so many non-Arab Muslims before them, Sheikh and Aisha have mastered the words.

As the words roll from their lips, they bow, stand, kneel on the prayer mat, and bring their noses, foreheads, and palms to the floor—following the set movement established by the Prophet Muhammad 1,400 years ago.

A FEW MILES AWAY, in a former funeral home on Cranston Street, in Providence, some 15 men assemble for Fajr prayer. Many of the men are black—native Rhode Islanders who have tasted the waters of both Christianity and Islam and decided that Islam's are the sweeter. But here, too, are men who have followed Islam all their life—natives of Syria, Jordon, Iraq, Malaysia, Nigeria, and Pakistan, who have been made brothers by a common faith.

It is past 4:30 a.m. Imam Abdul Hameed, spiritual leader of the Islamic Center of Rhode Island—Masjid Al-Karim—turns east toward Mecca and starts the chant-like prayer.

Tradition has it that in the year 610 Muhammad first encountered the archangel Gabriel in a cave outside his birthplace, Mecca, in what is now Saudi Arabia. It was not a chance meeting, for the angel had a message for the onetime shepherd and camel driver: he had been selected to be God's final apostle and prophet—to complete the revelations that God had given to Jews and Christians through Abraham and Jesus. It was here, Muslims believe, that Muhammad learned that he—not the Holy Spirit—was the one who Jesus had predicted would come after him to guide his followers. In this way, the story goes, over a period of 23 years, Muhammad received the Koran: Allah's testimony to humanity as to what men and women must do to avoid eternal damnation.

Twelve years after he first reported receiving the divine messages, Muhammad and his followers were forced by persecution to retreat from Mecca to Medina; eight years later, the refugees returned to drive their opponents out of Mecca and to take over the sanctuary of Ka'ba, thought to have been built by Abraham 4,000 years ago. That shrine has now become the focal point for a religion with some 900 million adherents—close in size to Roman Catholicism and, after Christianity (which claims some 1.7 billion adherents), the second-largest religion in the world.

Although Islam is spiritually and psychologically rooted in Arab soil, the vast majority of Muslims today do not live in the Arab world. The country with the most Muslims—at 180 million—is Indonesia, and tens of millions of Muslims live in Pakistan, Malaysia, and the Soviet Union.

In the United States, Islam has over the last 25 years made tremendous strides, growing from fewer than 1 million followers in 1965 to close to 3.5 million today. The growth is attributed to the combination of increased immigration from the Near East, Far East, and Africa; conversion, especially among black Americans; and a higher birth rate than among other religious groups. Demographers believe that if the rate of immigration continues, by the year 2000 the Muslim population in the United Stated could reach 6 million, edging out Judaism as the nation's largest non-Christian religion. Right now, say the experts, there are more Muslims in America than Episcopalians or members of the United Church of Christ.

Yet, for all that, there is worry among some of those in Rhode Island's 700-member Muslim Community. Although growth here has been strong—up by nearly 30 percent in the past five years (for the same reasons as the nationwide increase)—some fear that the future of the religion in Rhode Island is in jeopardy unless an Islamic school is established for young Muslims.

Presented here are the perspectives of two couples—one born in America, the other born on the other side of the world, but both trying to live and raise their children in a faith and a culture that are often at odds.

TO MOHAMMAD KHADIM, 43, formerly of Pakistan, and his wife, Salma Khadim, 37, of Kenya but of Pakistani descent, it is not all that difficult to lead an Islamic life in Rhode Island—once you've learned the ropes.

Mohammad Khadim says that when, four years ago, he applied for his job as a chemist in the research division of Hoechst-Celancese, in Coventry, he made sure to advise the company that he would have to take an hour on Friday afternoons to go to the local mosque, the Islamic Center of Rhode Island, for sabbath prayers. On other days of the week, he can pray in a conference room: "If I don't have a prayer rug, I can always use computer paper—I have no problem at all."

But Khadim remembers that his feelings were mixed 19 years ago, when he went to Canada to study and, for the first time, found himself in a culture in which Muslims were not the overwhelming majority. His biggest problem was figuring out how he was going to eat, for the dietary laws of Islam, like those of Judaism, require that animals be slaughtered in a special way, with the name of God recited over them. The laws also, as in Judaism, prohibit the eating of pork.

These days, Khadim has the eating problem solved. Whenever his wife tells him they're low on meat, he goes to the Antonelli Poultry Co., on DePasquale Avenue, in Providence, and asks the butcher to allow him to pray over and slaughter a few chickens. Or he'll go to a farmer in Westport, Massachusetts, who allows him to pray over and slaughter three goats or, if the freezer is really low, a cow.

The Khadims' three children—Usmaa, 11; Hamzah, 10; and Haashir, 5—frequently come along to watch. "It is very bloody," says Mohammad Khadim, "but I believe it is good for them to see. Last time, Hamzah wanted to do it, but I told him he is still too young."

By now, the children know the ins and outs of the Islamic diet. They know that when they go to a fast-food restaurant, hamburgers are strictly off-limits—because the animals have not been slaughtered in the approved manner—but that fish-burgers and French fries are okay, as long as the restaurant uses vegetable shortening, rather than animal fat, which is forbidden.

The children also know that there are five major requirements imposed on every adult Muslim: the daily recitation of the creed ("There is no God but Allah, and Mohammad is his messenger"); praying at the five prescribed times each day; giving alms, fasting during Ramadan, the ninth month of the lunar calendar; and making the pilgrimage (hajj) to Mecca at least once in one's life.

Since none of the Khadim children has turned 12, they are as yet exempt from the requirements. Still, Usmaa and her two brothers were all gung ho when their parents invited them to join in the month-long fast of Ramadan last spring.

"We got up very early, before dawn, and had a big breakfast; then we said our prayers," says Usmaa. For the rest of the day, until the sun went down, they were not allowed to eat. Usmaa was quite happy with what she achieved: she managed to fast for 8 of the 28 days. Her brother Hamzah fasted for 6.

(Like other Muslim children, Usmaa and her brothers look forward to the festival of Eid, at the end of Ramadan—a time of candy and presents. Muslims do not celebrate Christmas, because although they believe in Jesus's virgin birth, they do not believe he died on the cross, and so do not consider him divine.)

But it is not enough for the children to be filled with religious laws, says their father, for them to love and keep their faith. They must also, he says, be helped to understand why Muslims do what they do, and to see the beauty of Islam.

One of the first stories that Muslim children hear is how the Koran came to be. Though the details can differ, the children are told that Muhammad, a deep and sensitive man, went to think in a cave one day, when he saw a great light. The light turned out to be the archangel Gabriel, who had come to bring instructions from God on how people on earth should live. Muhammad listened to the words, memorized them, and later recited them to scribes, who wrote them down.

Because of the way the Koran came down, Muslims regard it not so much as a book as a living, breathing reality: God's voice speaking to the world. Many believe that those who listen to the sounds of its Arabic words—even without understanding them—cannot help receiving a blessing from God.

For that reason, Usmaa Khadim, who is entering the seventh grade at Coventry Junior High, has already read the Koran aloud from beginning to end, even though she has not yet learned enough Arabic to comprehend what she has read. (She is more familiar, of course, with English and with her parents' Pakistani tongue, Urdu.)

As with many couples belonging to the Islamic Center, Salma and Mohammad Khadim say that they often wonder whether they are giving their children enough of an understanding of their faith to allow them to hang on to it when they encounter peer pressure here in America.

Reflecting on the question in their spacious split-level house, the couple say that it is almost impossible to predict what one's children will do with the temptations that will come their way. "We try our best," says Mohammad Khadim. "We are teaching them, we hope, by our example, and the example of those at the mosque. We are teaching them how to pray, and to know that being a good Muslim is better than being a good American. That is all we can do."

The Khadims say that they also limit their children's television believing that much on the airways goes counter to the obedience and chastity that Islam values.

Many of the Muslim parents in Rhode Island worry, not just about such aspects of the culture as television and movies, but also about what will happen when their children go away to college, where there [are] more opportunities for straying from Islam. Among other things, both drinking and unchaperoned dating are forbidden in the code of the Koran.

Many of the parents feel that their children would be better able to withstand social pressures if, from grade 1 through 12, they could attend Islamic schools, which would ground them in the values of the religion. Mohammad Khadim says that there are 49 such schools in the country "but I do not see one being opened here soon. We are still too small in Rhode Island."

Not all the Muslim parents worry about what will happen to their children when they enter college. Naeem M. Siddigi, a Cumberland physician, says he's sure that his two sons, Faraaz, 19, and Omar, 17, are going to turn out fine, even though Faraaz has been dating and Omar has had to skip some of the Ramadan fasting, to keep up his strength as a member of the rowing team at Moses Brown School.

"The more important issue for us is not the dating, or the food, but being a good person, believing in one God, in charity, doing the prayers when you can," says Siddigi, who came to the United States from Pakistan in 1958. "We are in an American culture and we are not going to create another culture here. You cannot be prejudiced about the culture you are living in."

Mohammad Khadim agrees that people should not worry so much. His own experience, he says—first as a student in Canada and now as a scientist in the United States—shows that a Muslim can keep the faith outside the Islamic culture.

Salma Khadim says she thinks living in the United States does require certain adjustments. Back in Kenya and Pakistan, for example, she would not have gone without a veil; here, she does not wear one, because she says people would find it startling. But she does wear her long, silky Pakistani outfit. "People like it and ask me where I got it."

The Khadims recognize that many Americans frown upon such female dress codes as the veil, as well as the Muslim teaching that the husband is the head of the household. But they say that the Koran's dictating that a woman's body be covered in the presence of a man is a way of protecting women from assaults on their person and dignity. The

Khadims say that most Pakistani Muslim women arriving in the United States conclude that they are better off than the American women, who think that they are liberated.

In fact, say the Khadims, Muslim women enjoy a distinct advantage over non-Muslim women, because of the Koran's stipulation that a husband give his wife a dowry—in the amount specified by the wife—which becomes hers to spend as she likes, while her husband must support her. The Khadims can't remember the amount of the dowry Mohammad gave Salma ("maybe it was a hundred dollars"), but they once attended a wedding in which the dowry was $100,000.

They say in Pakistan, where the Islamic code is followed strictly, the parents arrange their child's marriage, although the young man or woman may refuse the designated partner.

That's the way the Khadims were wed, and they like it that way. Salma, who was living in Kenya, met Mohammad's parents on a trip to Pakistan; the parents liked her so much that they decided she would be the perfect daughter-in-law. They wrote to Mohammad, who was then in Canada, proposing the match; he agreed, without even seeing the young woman. Married by proxy, when Mohammad and Salma met they were already husband and wife.

Salma Khadim says she sees it as a workable system, and hopes her children will agree to having their parents arrange their marriages: "I think parents are more wise."

CONSIDER NOW Sheikh Abu Abdullah. He is the imam, or spiritual leader, of the Community of Al Masjid Shari'ah Allah (The House Where God's Law Is Practiced), a Muslim group that, unlike the Islamic Center on Cranston Street, has its meetings in members' homes.

During the last three years, Abdullah has developed a reputation as possibly Rhode Island's most outspoken Muslim. When a group of clergy came out against Governor DiPrete's proposed death penalty for drug dealers, Abdullah sprang to the governor's defense, even suggesting that executions be held at the Brown stadium. "A death penalty that is not seen is not a deterrent," he declared unswervingly.

Last January, Abdullah was the first Muslim to go to the State House to join in an ecumenical Day of Prayer for Peace. When organizers of the anti-abortion organization Operation Rescue staged a meeting inside the Cathedral of SS. Peter & Paul, Abdullah was there (sweating, because "I'm not used to being around so many statues"), announcing that Muslims, too, oppose abortion.

When the Ayatollah Khomeini offered a $1-million reward for the murder of writer Salman Rushdie, Abdullah was the first local Muslim to declare on television that he thought Khomeini was wrong—an announcement that he says engendered a nighttime visit to his house by supporters of the Ayatollah, hinting that Abdullah's life could be in "serious" jeopardy.

But for all his public presence—including also a school anti-drug program run by members of his Muslim group, a Saturday-morning cable-television program dealing with the issues of Islam, membership on the mayor's Council on Narcotics and on the Visiting Nurse Association's board of directors—Sheikh Abdullah commands what is now only a tiny congregation of Muslims: his wife, his daughter, and four others.

Why that's so, Abdullah says, is not really hard to explain. At Al Masjid Shari'ah Allah, the people are told that there can be no cheating on the Koran and, says Abdullah, "some of these families could not take this. So they went back on their own, where they could 'live free,' as they call it, without saying their prayers or doing what Allah says we all have to do."

The membership loss has created a personal dilemma for Abdullah. In the system laid down in the Koran, wives are expected to stay at home, while the husbands are out earning a living. If the husband cannot earn a living because he is working as an imam, support should come from the congregation. But with his congregation almost vanished, Abdullah's wife must make the money to pay the family's bills.

"It has created a strain," says Aisha Abu Abdullah, 34. "We almost separated because of it. We all know that the wife shouldn't have to work outside the home."

Sheikh Abdullah, 56, acknowledges that their life these last couple of years has been hard. Because of the threat he felt from the Khomeini sympathizers, Abdullah decided about 10 months ago that he had to move his family from their home, on Jenkins Street, in a racially mixed neighborhood on Providence's East Side.

Then, a few months ago, the Abdullahs had their telephone service cut, because of $600 in unpaid bills—most for calls to Saudi Arabia to try to get money to establish a Muslim day school. Sheikh and Aisha maintain hope that the money will come through, but in the meantime Aisha gets in touch with the rest of the world through a public telephone.

For all the inconvenience of leaving their home, the Abdullahs say that they are getting in tune with their new surroundings. Yasminah (who still attends school in Providence, at the Community Preparatory School, where she's a top pupil) enjoys the spacious yard and the chance to ride her bicycle. And her father finds it a good place in which to converse with followers, such as Imir Ibraham Abdus-Sabur, the former imam of the Islamic Center of Rhode Island, and Mujahid Abdullah, a Brown University senior from Alabama who came to Islam out of the Southern Baptist Church.

Not that the Abdullahs don't miss Jenkins Street. Sheikh Abdullah recalls the time he spotted drug dealers in the neighborhood and politely asked them to leave his block; they complied:

"They did what I asked because I had their respect. They could see me out there trying to help their little brothers and sisters and mothers. They could see I was a Muslim—a protector of the weak and a fighter against evils. And Allah always protects those who stand on his testimony."

Aisha Abu Abdullah describes what she sees as her husband's ability to speak the language of the people: "If Sheikh would see a bum on the street, he'd say, 'Hi, how ya doing?' He'd talk to him the same way he'd talk to the president of the United States. People could sense that."

She says that she's a stickler for the rules of her religion. In an interview with a reporter, she makes sure to keep her distance, sitting in the kitchen while the reporter asks his questions from an adjacent porch. She also makes sure that all the hair on her head is covered.

But she says that she is no longer so strict in her dress as when she first converted to Islam, 15 years ago. She showed up at her job, at Arthur Anderson & Co., a large Manhattan accounting firm, wearing an outfit that covered everything but her eyes: "There was a real uproar—people couldn't take it, the younger women especially," she says, laughing. "They couldn't understand why a woman would want to cover her body. I finally resigned. . . . I said, let them live in peace."

Here in Rhode Island, in her succeeding jobs as officer manager of Sojourner House (the shelter for battered women), as coordinator of the general-equivalency-diploma program at the Mount Hope Neighborhood Association, and now as a secretary at the Urban Collaborative (a job-training program), the former Army Reservist no longer wears the veil. But she still wears her long, flowing outfit and the kimar head covering.

"I just wouldn't feel right without it," says Aisha Abu Abdullah. "I've always been a modest person."

Vincent Brown, chairman of the Mount Hope Association, says that while working at his agency she turned in an impressive performance: "She was an extremely intelligent woman. She could have been the executive director if she wanted it."

Brown notes that her husband, Sheikh, always made sure to pick her up after work, because he didn't want her going home alone.

Citing the Koran, Sheikh Abdullah also goes to great lengths to protect his wife's modesty. He has erected a wall of sheets next to his house to hide his wife and daughter from the eyes of strangers when the Abdullahs use their small swimming pool.

He says he wishes his neighbors would do the same, so that he wouldn't have to see his female neighbors in their bathing suits. All he wants, he says, is a little consideration: "Sometimes we say a Muslim is always in prison, because we're always surrounded by things that go against what we believe. Like here, for example. They're infringing on my rights, because I'm not supposed to look at naked women."

Since their move out of Providence, the Abdullahs have become frequent visitors to the Super Stop & Shop, in Warwick, where they scrutinize all the ingredient listings to make sure that they aren't buying forbidden foods. A former Roman Catholic (she attended parochial school), Aisha Abu Abdullah says she smiles when people mistake her for a nun, as they sometimes do at the supermarket. (At other times people ask her what country she's from. "They say I speak English so well—it makes me feel so strange. I tell them, 'That's because I'm an American.'")

Aisha Abu Abdullah says she is astonished by the number of Muslim women who disregard the Koran's code of dress. She recalls a recent visit to her place of work by a Moroccan woman who teaches French at Brown; although the woman identified herself as a Muslin, she wore, says Aisha Abu Abdullah, "American" clothes:

"I do not see how people can say they are Muslims when they do not act like Muslims. But I do not wish to judge. Only Allah can see what is in people's hearts."

Unlike the black Americans who in the 1960s and early '70s were drawn to Islam by the black-power ideology of Elijah Muhammad, the Abdullahs say that his Nation of Islam was not a factor in their becoming Muslims.

Aisha, a descendant of a North Carolina plantation slave, grew up in Bedford Stuyvesant, New York, where her mother was a community activist. She says that although Elijah Muhammad's Black Muslim move-

ment was strong in their neighborhood, the young woman never accepted it: "Any religion that preaches hatred for another group of people
does not seem correct to me."

Sheikh Abdullah says that he always thought Elijah Muhammad's
teachings rather strange, because they contradicted the vision of brotherhood and love that comes through the Koran and the example of
Muhammad.

Sheikh Abudullah says that it is especially necessary to preach Islam
now, because he sees the country heading into a moral tailspin. He's
convinced that if America committed itself to Islamic principles there
would be no extramarital relations, divorce, or drug abuse.

Take teenage pregnancy, he says. Rhode Island could eliminate it
overnight if unmarried couples caught in the act of fornication were
"dealt with" according to Islamic law: strapped to two posts in a public
place, such as McCoy Stadium, and given 100 lashes.

But he realizes that's not likely to be. In his view, not even the Islamic
community appears willing to apply Islam's penalties to its own who
have gone astray.

Often, Sheikh Abdullah says, Muslim groups send a chaplain to the
state prison, where the person ministers to the convicts. "I don't mind a
chaplain serving a man who stole and then became a Muslim," says Abdullah. "But Muslims who commit a crime should not be serviced; they
should be dealt with according to Islamic law."

For a Muslim who commits a crime, that could mean either good
news or bad. On the one hand, Islamic law is protective of the rights of
the accused, normally requiring four witnesses or a confession from the
defendant. On the other hand, the prescribed penalties can be harsh; a
person found guilty of stealing more than the equivalent of $120 can
have a hand cut off.

The trouble today, Abdullah says, is that too many people are trying
to bend the rules, accepting some aspects of Islam while ignoring others.
But, he says, "Islam is not a cafeteria where you pick and choose what
you want."

ON A RECENT Monday afternoon on Cranston Street, the sun
shines brightly as Marium Adio, eyes peering from her black veil,
emerges from the Islamic Center of Rhode Island, her four children in
tow.

Inside, 20 other of the young people attending the summer school
have finished the day's lessons, including a class in basic Arabic. Among

them is Azizeh, 15, a student at Providence's Lincoln School, who asks
that her last name not be used.

No, she says, she doesn't have any trouble with the Muslim ban on
unchaperoned dating. Azizeh says that when she first when to Lincoln,
"I told my friends dating is something I do not do. I have good friends—
they haven't put a lot of pressure on me."

It is young people such as Azizeh who will help determine whether
the faith of Islam will be stronger or weaker in the next generation.

Waleed A. Muhammad, 44, a student photographer and father of six
who has stopped by the Center, speaks of the frustrations that parents
sometimes feel.

"It's not easy. It's a struggle. It's a lifetime work.

"You try to teach them certain values. You can bring them up to a certain point—but then it's up to them. You have to let them go."

Buddhism Takes Root as Mainstream Religion

Don Lattin, *San Francisco Chronicle,* October 5, 1992

Buddhism has come of age in the Golden State.

Nearly 150 years after it was first carried to San Francisco on the
backs of Chinese laborers, Buddhism is no longer hidden in the back al-
leys of immigrant ghettos nor claimed as the exclusive domain of an
avant-garde Zen counterculture.

In both Northern and Southern California, Buddhist priests hold key
positions on interfaith agencies with Christian clergy and Jewish rabbis.
Buddhist chaplains minister in veterans' hospitals, prisons and military
bases.

As Buddhism becomes an accepted part of the California religious
landscape, a new form of this ancient faith is taking root.

Forged in a melting pot of immigrant devotion and Western meditation, it is a unique blend of Buddhism—where the laity meditate like
monks, where women run temples and where Old World rivalries vanish
like passing clouds.

At the Wat Buddhanusorn temple in Fremont, a Thai Buddhist shrine
under construction amid the new subdivisions and shopping centers of
southern Alameda County, the sounds of hammers pounding and saws
buzzing punctuated a recent working session of the Buddhist Council of
Northern California.

Representatives from the 22 Buddhist groups that make up this ecumenical council—Japanese, Tibetan, American, Thai, Korean, Vietnamese—discussed such issues as the portrayal of Buddhism in public schools, problems new temples face getting construction permits, and plans for a big Enlightenment Day celebration December 20 in Hayward.

They began their meeting by gathering in a temporary temple to chant and meditate together before a golden statue of Buddha.

"Only in California can all these Buddhist groups come together like this," said Ken Tanaka, a professor at the Institute of Buddhist Studies, the first seminary outside the Judeo-Christian tradition to join the Graduate Theological Union consortium in Berkeley. "It has never happened in all the history of Buddhism."

Long Tradition

That history began six centuries before Christ, when a warrior-prince named Siddhartha Gautama was born in the foothills of the Himalaya mountains. According to Buddhist lore, Siddhartha had everything he wanted, yet still felt empty. One day, he left his palace and saw the real world of suffering, sickness and death. Prince Siddhartha, the man who would become Buddha, began searching for a way to end suffering.

After meditating in a forest retreat, Buddha realized that the cause of suffering was desire—the obsessive craving of our hearts and minds. For the rest of his life, Buddha preached the "Middle Way" between self-indulgence and self-denial. His teaching became known as Buddhism.

It caught on, spreading to India, China, Japan and Southeast Asia to become one the world's major religions.

Buddhism's influence on the California spiritual scene runs deeper than construction of new temples and appointment of priests.

Its teachings about self-understanding, the oneness of the universe and the interconnectedness of all beings contributed much to the human potential and "New Age" movements. It has profoundly influenced the practice of psychotherapy and helped inspire an almost-mystical crusade for greater ecological awareness.

Philosophical Approach

It is also changing the way some Christians and Jews think about God.

"Theologically, the Christian seminaries are challenged by the Buddhist philosophical approach," said the Rev. LaVerne Sasaki, pastor of the 94-year-old Buddhist Church of America congregation in San Francisco, one of a dozen such Japanese American temples in the Bay Area.

At Hsi Lai ("Coming West") Temple in suburban Los Angeles, a vast 16-acre Chinese shrine that opened in Hacienda Heights in 1988 and is the nation's largest Buddhist temple, the Rev. Hui Chih said Americans have many misconceptions about Buddhism.

"Buddhism is more than just sitting cross-legged or bowing before the Buddha," he said. "It's about changing your whole being, and the way you treat other people."

Chih sat in the back corner of Buddha Hall, the centerpiece of a $25 million project paid for by donations from Hong Kong and Taiwanese devotees, and designed to be the U.S. headquarters of the Taiwan-based "humanistic Buddhism" movement of Master Hsing Yun.

Like other ambitious Buddhist shrines recently erected around the state—such as the 117-acre City of Ten Thousand Buddhas near Talmage or the Odiyan Tibetan temple north of Jenner—the ornate pagodas of Hsi Lai rise incongruously from the surrounding landscape, a Chinese landmark amid the Taco Bells and tract houses of the San Gabriel Valley.

"This is a hybrid of a Buddhist temple and modern community center," said Chih, looking on as a young Chinese American family entered the hall and showed their young son how to hold a stick of incense before one of three Buddha statues towering above him.

"Buddhism is intertwined with Chinese culture very deeply, like Christianity in America," said Chih. "These visitors may not be Buddhist in the religious sense, and only come here to pay respect to their ancestors, or for good luck, but we try to educate them about what Buddhism really means."

Chih, 38, was born in Hong Kong and educated in a Baptist missionary school there. When he was 19, he moved to the United States to study engineering at Cal State Long Beach and the University of Southern California, going on to get his MBA at Pepperdine University.

After college, Chih landed a high-paying job as a computer engineer with Citibank and was on the financial fast-track.

"At a certain point in life, you see there is more to life than money," said Chih, explaining his decision to become a Buddhist monk. "Why are we here? I had my home, my car and pretty much all I wanted, but didn't have fulfillment."

World Fellowship Meeting

The most auspicious event in Hsi Lai Temple's short history occurred just after its opening, in November 1988, when the World Fellowship of

Buddhists convened there—the first time that organization has ever met outside Asia.

Their decision to meet at Hsi Lai Temple underscored the rising influence of Buddhist America. According to one estimate, there are between 2 million and 3 million practicing Buddhists living in the United States—numbers roughly equal to the membership of the Episcopal Church.

The gathering at Hsi Lai Temple was also a chance for leaders of the faith's numerous Asian sects to get a first-hand look at Buddhism, California-style, and many were shocked at what they saw.

Women were running the show.

While they have since moved onto other projects, such as building a temple in Australia, two women, Abbess Hsin Kuang and the Rev. I Han, oversaw the construction of America's largest Buddhist temple.

"In Asia, women are not seen as equal," said the Rev. Havanpola Ratanasara, president of the Buddhist Sangha Council of Southern California and executive chairman of the American Buddhist Congress.

Ratanasara, a native of Sri Lanka, has ruffled a few feathers back home by ordaining women priests at his Southern California temple.

"They don't like the idea much in Sri Lanka," he said during an interview in his downtown Los Angeles office. "It's a difference of cultures, not religion, but it is slowly changing in Asia."

Ratanasara, 73, shares a cluttered office with the Rev. Karuna Dharma, 52, a Caucasian, American-born woman priest and director of the International Buddhist Meditation Center in Los Angeles.

Dharma, raised as a Baptist, came to Los Angeles from Indiana in 1957, when her husband went to work for an aerospace firm. A public school teacher for 18 years, Dharma discovered Buddhism in 1968 when she attended a course at UCLA taught by a Vietnamese Zen monk named Thich Thein-An.

It was the height of the '60s counterculture, and like thousands of young Californians, Dharma embraced Zen as an alternative to mainstream American religion.

Her meditation practice, however, was suddenly interrupted in the summer of 1975 when Saigon fell and waves of Vietnamese refugees began showing up at Thein-An's temple. Like it or not, the "dharma bums" of downtown Los Angeles began practicing Buddhism Asian-style.

"I guess you could call it cross-fertilization," she recalled. "You'd go into the Zendo and see these Americans meditating very sternly, and in would come these old Vietnamese ladies chattering and doing prostrations and offering incense. Each would look at the other, saying, 'What are they doing?'"

There are really two Buddhisms in California—one for people of Asian ancestry and another for mostly Caucasian converts from the Judeo-Christian faith.

Nowhere is this more apparent than in Berkeley, on the 1900 block of Russell Street.

At the Berkeley Zen Center, founded 25 years ago by the late Japanese Zen master Shunryu Suzuki Roshi, about 50 Buddhist converts—many of them veterans of the spiritual counterculture of the 1960s and '70s—file into the rustic elegance of a traditional Japanese meditation hall hidden behind several older Berkeley homes. In the stillness and shadows of an early Saturday morning, they sit in robes atop round black cushions, backs straight, facing a white wall.

Three doors down the street, at Mongkonrattanaram Temple, about 200 Thai immigrants and guests crowd into the back yard for a noontime feast of Thai food and boisterous conversation. Above the din, in an upstairs flat converted into a makeshift temple, a Thai family presents a plastic laundry basket filled with bottles of Calistoga fruit juice, rolls of paper towels and other household supplies. As one man tapes $30 in $5 and $10 bills to a flag on a Buddha altar, two monks lead the family in chanting the Buddhist sutras.

"This is a center for the well-being of the people," said Phramahasumon Sukswadi, president of the 1,250-member temple. "When the Thai people are unhappy, they come to the monks."

Down in the backyard, Anchalee Kurutach, a young Thai woman who came here four years ago to attend college, explains the temple's attraction.

"It's a place where people can come and feel they are Thai. Some of the older people come to pray in the shrine or light candles, but no one really meditates. I don't feel like I have to study Buddhism. It's part of my culture."

The Rev. Alan Senauke, a musician and Zen priest who lives down the street, sits at the table with Anchalee and ponders the differences between the two Buddhisms of California. Raised on Long Island, Senauke lost touch with his Jewish faith shortly after his bar mitzvah, came out to the Bay Area in 1968 and started sitting at the just-opened Berkeley Zen Center.

"For the Thais, Buddhism is about cultural survival—a way to preserve their traditional values," said Senauke, who is also the national co-ordinator of an anti-war group, the Buddhist Peace Fellowship.

"For us, this is not the air we breathe. It's a choice," he said. "Many of the people who come to us for Zen practice have some problems, some need to work on themselves, to inspire themselves, to learn how to deal with their suffering."

At the San Francisco Zen Center, founded 30 years ago by Suzuki Roshi, Buddhist converts who now run the organization wrestle with the question of how much of their founder's Japanese ritual they need to preserve. One of the nation's best-known Buddhist institutions, the Zen Center runs a city meditation hall, scenic Green Gulch Farm near Marin County's Muir Beach and Tassajara Zen Mountain Center, a monastery and retreat center in rugged mountains east of Big Sur.

"We're trying very hard to find an American Buddhism, without throwing away the Buddhism we already have," said the Rev. Michael Wenger, president of the Zen Center. "It's not accidentally that the Zen Center is in San Francisco. We have our own tradition, going back to the Beat scene and the 'dharma bums' in the 1950s, and are also open to the Asian stream."

Rick Fields, author of "How the Swans Came to the Lake: A Narrative History of Buddhism in America," said the split between immigrant Buddhists and American converts runs deeper than ethnic differences.

"Many young Americans who were attracted to Buddhism were reacting to what they perceived as hollow religiosity and piety in the Judeo-Christian religions," he said.

Misunderstandings

Jack Kornfield, a psychologist and Buddhist teacher who studied in Thailand, said many European-American Buddhists misunderstand the devotional aspects of Asian Buddhism.

"Buddhism in Asia is like Christianity here," he said. "There are lots of temples, like we have lots of churches. People go once a week, light incense, pray and hope for better conduct next week and good fortune in the future. It's like going to church here."

Both Fields and Kornfield predict that the devotional aspects of Buddhism will become more important as the American converts mature in their faith, and begin pondering the religious education of their children.

At the same time, Asian Buddhist leaders are learning from the rigorous meditation practice of many American converts.

"This is how Buddhism revivifies itself. In Bangkok, which is like the L.A. of Southeast Asia, there is growing interest in meditation among the middle class," said Kornfield, who teaches at Spirit Rock Meditation Center in Marin County.

Hinduism Community Large and Growing in U.S.

Ira Rifkin, *Religion News Service,* August 2, 1995

CHICAGO—By early afternoon, the thermometer was pushing 100 and the asphalt surface of the Soldier Field parking lot was blistering to the touch. At one edge of the lot, four large, open-sided tents sat clustered and baking in the bright sunlight.

In the largest of the tents, a football field-size affair holding some 3,000 chanting Hindu worshipers, it was even hotter.

Inside the tent, acrid, black smoke that spiraled upward from hundreds of small ritual fires fed by clarified butter and Indian spices settled over the crowd. The smoke obscured the 10 orange-robed Hindu priests seated onstage at the front playing instruments, chanting mantras and instructing participants in the intricacies of the ancient ritual.

Yet despite the horrendous heat, virtually no one left the tent—save a few mothers with crying children. Instead, they sat cross-legged on mats for the 90 minutes the fires burned.

For the devotees, the smoke and heat were a spiritually purifying experience, appropriate for their worship of the sun goddess Gayatri, who represents the source of all earthly life.

The location was equally appropriate. Hinduism was formally introduced to America in Chicago by Indian religious leader Swami Vivkenanda at the 1893 Parliament of the World's Religions. Last weekend (July 28-30), it was evident just how much the 5,000-year-old teachings of Hinduism—the world's oldest major religion—have become a part of the changing American religious scene.

"The history of Hinduism in America is still being written," said Diana Eck, a Harvard University professor of comparative religion and Indian studies. "It's much too early to say how it will affect this country and how it will ultimately be affected by this society.

"But clearly it's here to stay and will continue to grow."

Eck and others put the U.S. Hindu population at about 1.2 million—a tiny fraction of the 800 million Hindus worldwide. The vast majority of American Hindus are Indian immigrants who began arriving in great numbers after 1965, when immigration laws were loosened. Today, their greatest concentrations are around Los Angeles, New York City-northern New Jersey, Houston, Washington, D.C., and Chicago (where about 60,000 live).

Others are people of Indian descent whose ancestors left the Asian subcontinent generations ago. *Hinduism Today,* an international Hindu monthly newspaper based in Kauai, Hawaii, recently noted the presence of more than 200,000 Hindus from the South American nation of Guyana living in New York City.

"In many families it has been several generations since a member set foot on Indian soil yet the music, the dance, the foods—but most especially the religion—are an integrated part of their lives," said the paper.

A small number of non-Indian Americans have also fully adopted Hindu religious practices, such as the 12,000 "initiates" who belong to the International Society of Krishna Consciousness—more popularly known as the Hare Krishnas.

However, many more Americans—estimates run into the millions—have incorporated such elements of Hinduism as meditation and yoga into their lives as a spiritual supplement, or just to help relieve stress. Almost all see themselves as still being Christians or Jews—although others might consider them New Agers—and wouldn't dream of calling themselves Hindus, said Eck.

Not that this matters to Hindus. Stripped of its Indian cultural trappings—which are considerable—Hinduism presents itself as a statement of universal understanding about the nature of reality open to as many interpretations as there are people. Its boundaries are ill-defined and broad enough to encompass a dazzling array of philosophies and practices.

Hindu scripture—a set of writings known as the Vedas, or "knowledge" in the ancient Sanskrit language—says there are 33 million divinities and Hindus are free to regard one or any combination of them in a literal sense. But these deities can also be thought of as mere symbols of the many ways in which one all-pervasive supreme entity, or creative energy, manifests itself in the physical world.

"Hinduism is not so much one religion as it is a collection of 10,000 related religions that intermingle," said Palaniswami, an American-born non-Indian who 30 years ago became a Hindu monk. Today he is editor of *Hinduism Today*.

"Hinduism has no outer limit, no picket fence. You can be an atheist, believe in a personal God, or that everything in this world is an illusion, and still be a good Hindu because the Hindu heart loves the all-embracing approach. There is a trust that each soul knows what it needs in this lifetime and creates that for itself."

Hinduism's permeability allows 53-year-old Prithvi Raj Singh to include a Christian cross among the images of Hindu deities on his home altar in Diamond Bar, Calif.

"According to our definition, anyone who is doing something good is like an incarnation of God. Jesus is also that for me, but I am not a Christian," he said.

It also enables Janice Cady of the Kansas City suburb of Olathe, Kan., to feel comfortable at last weekend's Soldier Field Hindu festival. Cady and a friend were among the handful of non-Indians at the three-day event — which at its height Sunday morning had about 7,000 in attendance, according to organizers.

Cady, who grew up in the Reorganized Church of Jesus Christ of Latter Day Saints, a Mormon offshoot, said she "still believes in Christ" but is drawn to Hinduism's ornate and emotional style of ritual worship, in addition to its absence of dogma.

"I like that they say there isn't just one way," she said.

In India, myriad Hindu sects based on regional loyalties to particular deities and practices hold sway. Hindus have brought that aspect of the faith with them to the United States.

The majority of those at Soldier Field, for example, were associated with the Cayatri Pariwar sect popular in the west Indian state of Gujarat. They came from as far away as Montreal and California for the Ashwamedh Yagya fire ceremony, a ritual once reserved for kings. Gayatri Pariwar, which claims followers in 86 nations, is but one of a host of Hindu groups now established here.

"I don't see much difference between the way Hinduism is practiced in the United States and the way it is practiced in India," said Singh, who is president of Southern California's Federation of Hindu Associations. "People remain loyal to their regional deities and practices and group themselves accordingly wherever they are."

That is not to say that life in America has not impacted the practice of Hinduism. One change is the importance placed here on weekend temple worship.

In India, Hinduism is largely home-based, with the practice of meditation, the recitation of mantras (word combinations believed capable of evoking the presence of specific deities), and even miniature fire rituals taking place before a small altar on which images of favored divinities are placed. Moreover, temples and public shrines are everywhere in Hindu India, allowing individuals to worship at any time.

Here, home worship is still the backbone of Hindu practice, but the nation's 827 Hindu temples have also taken on a cultural role unknown in India and distinctly apart from their religious significance.

To accommodate the American work week, Sunday has become a favored day for temple attendance, but not just for worship. Classes in Indian culture, language, dancing and cooking are also held in an effort to counter what many Hindus fear will be an inevitable diminishing attachment to Indian beliefs and customs among those born into America's religious and ethnic melting pot.

"A lot of people who were not very religiously involved in India go to temples in the U.S. because they're worried about their children," said Lise McKean, an anthropologist who has studied Gayatri Pariwar in India and who is the managing editor of the University of Chicago's journal *Public Culture*.

"Their concern is common to most immigrant groups."

That concern was evident at Soldier Field, where several parents asked Pranav Pandya, Gayatri Pariwar's international director, how they could keep their children connected to their Indian roots.

"Our children know nothing of the rituals and are losing our values," one mother said.

In response, Pandya spoke of plans to build as many as 100 Indian cultural centers around the United States. But in a separate interview, he emphasized another approach that his and other Hindu groups in America are also taking in an attempt to transcend generational and cultural bounds.

Pandya, a 45-year-old medical doctor, said Hinduism needs to emphasize its "scientific basis." Hindu mantras and rituals, he said, are proven powerful instruments for uplifting individual consciousness and promoting world peace.

Not only will this "liberal Hinduism" appeal to westernized Indians, he said, it will also appeal to non-Indian westerners.

Included in his description of scientific Hinduism was an end to the guru tradition. Traditional Hinduism holds that studying with gurus—enlightened spiritual masters—is essential to spiritual growth.

"The time has come to get rid of hero worship," said Pandya, who is billed as Gayatri Pariwar's spokesman, not its guru.

Yet the next day, following completion of the afternoon fire ceremony, Pandya, wearing orange robes as a reminder of the sun goddess Gayatri, sat on a couch draped with red material as the faithful filed by to pay homage.

First they bowed before a chair on which sat the flower-covered sandals of the sect's dead gurus—Sriram Sharma Acharaya and his wife, Mata Bhagwati Devi Sharma—who were also Pandya's in-laws. Then they bowed before him and touched his feet, a common Indian sign of respect.

Putting aside his talk of Hinduism's need to modernize, Pandya played the role expected of him by both sari-clad grandmothers with tattooed hands and forearms and by young men with beepers on their belts.

Hinduism's encounter with America may someday reshape the ancient faith, as Pandya suggests. But it's clear that beliefs and practices thousands of years old will not soon disappear from the American Hindu scene.

Computerized Faith

Techno-Pagans Thrive in Triangle, Worshipping at the Altar of the Keyboard

Yonat Shimron, *The News & Observer,* Raleigh, N.C., September 6, 1996

From their keyboards, hundreds of people across the Triangle are forging a new religion that merges the ancient with the high tech. For them, the computer is more than tool.

It is an altar.

They use it to send out energy. To perform magic. To cast spells.

They call themselves Techno-Pagans. And every week, thousands of them log on to America Online's daily Pagan chatrooms and surf the World Wide Web's numerous Pagan pages. They exchange information, meet one another, pray and perform online rituals.

Paganism, or Neo Paganism, is generally understood to be a polytheistic nature religion that celebrates the gods and goddesses of Greek, Roman, Norse, Celtic, Egyptian and Sumerian traditions. But Techno-Pagans pray in ways as varied and distinct as the many gods they worship.

Although modern day Paganism has been around since the 1950s—100,000 to 150,000 adherents live in the United States—its spread has been greatly bolstered by the computer, particularly in the Triangle, where computer analysts, programmers and technicians abound.

"For a computer addict like I am, the Interent and the World Wide Web are an easier place to find people," says Jenna Parons, 23, a software developer for Ventana Communications in Durham who goes by the name Tigerheart. "I can sit right here and find five different Pagan groups without going out."

Out of the Closet

For many of the older Pagans, this is whole new world.

In the 1950s and 1960s, when interest in Paganism resurfaced, finding good literature was a challenge. Finding fellow nature worshipers was even harder.

Brydie Palmore, 66, of Hillsborough, remembers a lonely exploration into the faith that she says has guided her ever since childhood—a faith in The Goddess, the feminine spirit that is Mother Nature.

When Palmore left the Presbyterian church 30 years ago, she didn't know where to turn for information about Paganism and dared not ask just anyone. It took years before she pieced together an understanding from rare books and chance encounters.

"My exploration was solitary," Palmore said. "I didn't know how to find anybody else."

Many Pagans still find it difficult to talk about witches and spells in polite company. And usually it takes years before Pagans are ready to embrace the faith publicly.

Enter the computer.

"I doubt I would have become thoroughly Pagan if I wasn't on the Internet talking to others and finding out this was a valuable faith," said Greg Woodbury, a computer systems administrator at Duke University, who goes by the name Wolfe. "I had a community of people who said, 'We're here, we're supportive. Why don't you come out of the closet?' And I did."

But Pagans don't find only friends on the Internet. Conservative Christian critics who see Pagans as evil or as satanists sometimes "flame" Pagans in newsgroups such as alt.pagan.

Still, across the Triangle, a dozen autonomous Pagan groups practice the faith in their own way. They can be found at Unitarian Universalist fellowships, in student groups at the University of North Carolina and N.C. State University and in a variety of small covens usually of no more than 10 people.

Pagans celebrate by creating rituals that correspond to the orbit of the sun, the waxing and waning of the moon and seasonal changes. At harvest time, they may share the bounty of the fields or the gifts of wisdom they have acquired, in the fall, when the fields are fallow, they may enact a drama about death.

But beyond the core groups that meet in person, thousands of larger communities, including private mailing lists and public forums, exist on the Internet.

A New Cyber Faith

America Online offers daily chat rooms for new Pagans, teen Pagans and Wiccans—Pagans who practice witchcraft.

Pagan jewelry, trinkets and herbs are sold online. Virtual reality software designed for Pagans has been introduced.

"What you have here is the expression of a new religious phenomenon," said Thomas Tweed, a professor of religion at the University of North Carolina in Chapel Hill.

Tweed notes that use of the computer, and specifically the Internet, is not only a Pagan phenomenon. There are thousands of religious sites on the World Wide Web, but Pagans have adopted it as a metaphor for the way their religion has evolved.

Instead of the hierarchies of most denominational structures, Pagans have embraced the freedom, and chaos, of the Interent.

"Some religions use a structure shaped like a pyramid with God on top and human beings and animals on the bottom," said Selena Fox, executive director of Circle Sanctuary, a Pagan resource center in Mount Horeb, Wis. "We work with circles, spirals and webs. We see ourselves as part of a great web of life that connects us not only with each other but with the Divine."

And Pagans are among the leaders in using the computer for ritual.

Rituals are typically conducted on Internet Relay Chat, or chatrooms, that allow participants to type out electronic messages, creating an ongoing conversation. Pagan computer rituals typically begin by casting a circle among a fixed group of participants. Someone in Raleigh, for example, will call on the spirit of the South, which represents fire. A person living in California will call on the spirit of the West, representing water.

After the four directions have been called, an invocation may be typed to summon forth a particular god or goddess, say Dionysus, the god of wine.

Then the group will begin the ritual, whose subject is agreed on in advance. It may be a ritual devoted to sending out energy to help a participant recover from an illness.

It may be a ritual in which the group celebrates its ancestors by typing poetry or essays to help them reconnect with their forebears.

Pagans consider computer rituals serious business. They will shut off the TV, disconnect the telephone and make sure the kids are asleep or safely preoccupied. Before the ritual begins, many Pagans light a candle and burn incense in the space they have created beside the computer screen.

Margo Adler, the author of "Drawing Down the Moon," the seminal introduction to Paganism, says computer rituals can be a potent form of worship.

"My assumptions before going into it were that it wouldn't really work, and later we would have an intellectual discussion," Adler said. "But the depth of the participation was exciting. Some very personal stuff came forward. It was emotional. I felt I was in a very strong community."

Last year, after the Oklahoma City bombing, Lynn Pawelka, a secretary and computer problem-solver at NCSU, participated in a healing ritual as part of a women's-only electronic mailing list called Aphrodite, after the goddess of love and beauty.

The ritual, she said, was more powerful than many of those she attended physically.

"Our intention was to offer psychic support to the people who were involved in the bombing and to those who were killed," Pawelka said. "We wanted to extend support to those spirits that were ripped out of bodies so traumatically,"

Earth Mother Meets Computer Techie

Using the computer for ritual is only a natural extension of a tool many Pagans use daily.

As Adler noted in her book, technical or computer-related fields make up the largest occupational group among Pagans.

To a casual observer, the connection between the scientifically educated computer techie and the eco-friendly, season-centered earth religion is jarring. What would a science geek want with a goddess worshiper?

A lot, as it turns out.

Techno-Pagans share many traits. Chief among them is an inclination to challenge authority.

When Lance Brown was a boy, he used to ask his parish priest difficult questions like, "If Jesus is the only way, why are there so many religions?" He wasn't satisfied with the answers he received, and as a teenager, he turned to computers for answers.

"There's a kind of open-mindedness and eagerness to learn new things that draws people to computers," said Brown, 29, a Pagan and computer programmer for Info Systems and Networking in the Research Triangle park.

The same qualities draw people to Paganism, Brown says.

Others, like Firestorm Hyde, nee Debora Weaver, came to Paganism through science and fantasy fiction. From an early age, Hyde preferred stories that explored visionary tales of war and peace, good and evil, life and death.

"In science fiction and science fantasy, you set aside preconceived notions of what society needs," Hyde said. "The authors tended to give you the flexibility to question where you were and to help you explore different philosophies without judgment."

When Hyde discovered Paganism, she found a religion that challenged followers to construct their own path and respected the traditions of those who chose the road less traveled.

Many Techno-Pagans tend to be shy, solitary people. For them, the computer is a way to reconnect with nature, society and the divine without relinquishing their desire for privacy, said Diana Rice, high priestess of a group called The Lunatic Fringe in Saxapahaw, a community in Alamance County.

Techno-Pagans say computer specialists can be attuned to the mystical, even while applying logic in climate-controlled environments.

"Computers may use zeros and ones," said Laura Keen, a Raleigh resident who goes by the name Moon Dance and whose new venture is a magazine called *The Web*. "We use gods and goddesses, but it's just another form of energy—another form of magic."

Indeed, if there's one philosophical principle that unites Pagans it's the notion of pantheism. Pagans believe the Divine spirit can be found in the air, in water, in rocks and in human beings, too. All things are imbued with a life force. Even the computer.

"The creative aspect of making technology do what you want it to do is overlooked by a lot of folks," Woodbury said. "It's not very different from being Merlin."

Still, many Techno-Pagans point out it's not the computer they celebrate so much as its ability to create energy among a group of people.

"It's easier to go to the computer than to track people down," Pawelka said. "The Internet is a godsend."

The Pagan World View

Although Pagans have been around since the dawn of civilization, modern-day Pagans—sometimes called Neo Pagans—are breathing new life into the nature faith of long ago.

Pagans are people who believe that the stories and myths surrounding the deities of our pre-Christian tradition still hold pearls of wisdom. The word Pagan comes from the Latin "pagus," which means "locality," but in the Christian era it has come to mean "country dweller" or "heathen."

A diverse and eclectic group, Neo Pagans draw inspirations not only from the Greek and Roman pantheon, but from Celtic, Egyptian, Nordic and Native American traditions.

In the Pagan world view, male and female gods complement one another and present a more complete understanding of the Divine—one they believe has been lost since Christians appropriated the image of a male God.

To some extent, the re-emergence of Paganism comes from a feminist critique of an exclusively masculine God.

Many modern Pagans say they want to honor the powers of magic and myth by bringing back to life such maligned figures as the shaman, the priestess or the witch.

They're not interested in black magic, animal sacrifice, sexual degeneracy or Satanism. Rather, they believe the human mind has untapped powers that can help heal and effect positive change.

One of the first principles in modern-day Paganism is the saying: "If it harms no one, do what you will."

Thousands of different Pagan groups exist around the world. No two traditions are quite alike. Pagans are fiercely independent. They do, however, share basic characteristics.

In putting flesh on the bones of their ancient, pre-Judeo-Christian faith, Pagans have fashioned a yearly cycle they call the eight-spoked wheel. The holidays correspond to the sun's orbit, the waxing and waning of the moon and the seasonal changes.

Most Pagans share a deep environmental concern for the planet that comes from their belief in pantheism—the idea that the Divine is present in nature and in each one of us. They believe it is unwise to upset nature's balance, exploit its resources or destroy its beauty.

Pagans, most of all, seek to bring a sense of the sacred down to earth. They don't believe in a remote or transcendent God, and they reject the distinction between the sacred and the secular. Pagans see sparks of divinity everywhere: in the trees, in other creatures and in humanity.

"We're all part of the Divine," said Nancy Carroll, a member of the Unitarian Universalist Fellowship in Raleigh. "It's in people and nature."

25

Spiritual Journeys

Perhaps one of the biggest stories of the late 20th century is the transformation from a religious culture in which children stayed in the faith of their parents to a culture in which people sought unique, and sometimes creative, answers to matters of faith. Many of the most important recent trends can be pegged to this wandering, including the decline of mainline churches and the rise in Eastern faiths.

As part of their quest, consumers went outside the walls of religious institutions and into the mainstream culture. In the late 1990s book publishers, for example, reported sales increasing as much as 40 percent for books that had spiritual content. Popular culture reflected the pervasive theme of spirituality as television shows starred angels and priests; popular movies followed the childhood of Tibetan Buddhism's Dalai Lama or the afterlife of lovers. Whole industries catered to these spiritual seekers with an array of religious and quasi-religious merchandise, books and tapes.

In a sense, American faith in the 1990s in part reflected the individualism that had been a hallmark of American culture from the country's founding. Researcher George Barna in his 1996 book *The Index of Leading Spiritual Indicators* described American religion in the last decade of the century as "a personalized, customized form of faith views which meet personal needs, minimize rules and absolutes, and which bear little resemblance to the pure form of any of the world's major religions." Wade Clark Roof's 1994 book, *A Generation of Seekers: The Spiritual Journeys of the Baby Boom Generation,* also documented the change.

In recognizing the shift, some newspapers changed the names of religion sections to reflect the broader religion coverage. Thus, "Faith and Values," "Beliefs" and "Religion and Spirituality" became popular headings for what many papers in the 1950s once called the "Church News."

Many stories noting the spiritual transformation have appeared in the past decade. But the so-called New Age movement and its subsequent popularization in the literature, music and personal development industries was an early indicator of the searching many people started in the wake of the 1960s. The New Age movement, which emerged in the 1980s, wove together mysticism, Eastern spiritual traditions and fragments from Christianity and paganism in a unique blend.

One of the earliest and most thorough treatments of New Age views is Russell Chandler's 1981 story written for the *Los Angeles Times* and reprinted here. This story also documents the survivalist tendencies of these non-traditional groups.

"In Search of the Sacred," one of *Newsweek*'s popular religion cover stories, describes the eclecticism of Americans' spiritual journey and the uniqueness of that search for each person. The story explains how concerns about mortality by aging baby boomers and the approaching year 2000 are resulting in creative and unpredictable answers to spiritual questions.

"New Age" Religionists Head for the Hills

Russell Chandler, *The Los Angeles Times,* October 18, 1981

A Santa Barbara-based religious community that fuses Judeo-Christian and American Indian beliefs and operates a large natural-food business sells its 3,600-acre ranch and buys 740 square miles in the hinterlands of Nevada—one of the largest single ranches in the nation.

A metaphysical religious group headquartered on a country estate in the Malibu hills buys 12,000 acres of prime property adjoining Yellowstone National Park—"an Inner Retreat out of harm's way" designed to become a self-sufficient community.

The transaction follows by only a few weeks the purchase of 100 square miles of remote agricultural land in central Oregon by a guru from India. He has announced plans to build an entire city—"a community to provoke God . . . isolated from the outside world."

And a militant, fundamentalist Christian organization based in rural Illinois offers memberships in a kind of survival franchise—country outposts throughout the "mid-America survival area" stocked with food and weapons where members are assured of lodging and protection.

"Like it or not, it will be the survival of the fittest," the promotional brochure warns.

In increasing numbers, religious groups—most of them non-traditional—are abandoning their urban bases, forsaking the large cities and heading for the hills and sylvan countrysides where life is less harried, if not less complex.

The name of their game is survival.

"We are teaching survival in Jesus Christ," says evangelist Susan Alamo, who, with her husband, Tony, left their Southern California "Jesus People" ranch for Alma, Ark., in the belief that California is "too violent and dangerous" nowadays and that "cities are unsafe."

And though owning retreat grounds in peaceful places is not new for either established religions or the so-called "New Age" religious groups, the reasons for the spreading exodus dovetail with the general survivalist trend of the times.

A foreboding spirit broods over the survivalist band, stoked by economic doomsday prophets and purveyors of coming hard times.

There is fear that the end of civilization is coming. Soon.

Doomsday groups teach that chaos, revolt in the inner cities, nuclear attack and a Communist invasion may follow; and that mass hysteria will leave the unprepared battling one another for food, water and shelter. Some believe that the return of Jesus Christ and the final bloody battle of Armageddon are imminent.

"There are a lot of radio programs and churches that teach the Lord's going to return as King of Kings and Lord of Lords," declares John Robert Stevens, head of the Walk, a worldwide fundamentalist movement headquartered on a farm in Washington, Iowa.

"But right now, what we're concerned about is we'd like to see the Stars and Stripes still flying when the Kingdom of God comes."

And Victor Paul Wierwille, founder of the Way, a fire-and-brimstone organization based on a farm near New Knoxville, Ohio, adds a rationale for militancy:

"If a non-believer, an enemy, or anybody else comes in and burns your house down, you have a right to fight to take back what was given you in the first place. If you have to kick a few butts, well, you have to do it. Christians aren't a bunch of lollipops."

There are other reasons, too, that some religious groups are withdrawing to more secure and less accessible quarters.

Some face financial difficulties, which, when coupled with legal hassles and tarnished public relations, cause them to seek asylum farther from media scrutiny and the reach of the law.

There is disillusionment, not only with the perceived lack of progress of establishment society, but, in some cases, with the original goals of the religious groups themselves.

Hence, a desire to make a new beginning, to try again to create the utopian community envisioned by the founders—but this time in a "safe place" unfettered by the restrictions of contaminated cities and the skepticism of a chary public.

And there is persecution. Always faced by new religions—harassment dogged the westward footsteps of the Mormons in the last century—persecution is a legacy of being an unknown, different, and therefore suspect, group; of having goals and life styles thought to be at odds with mainline religion and a threat to mainline morals.

Today's withdrawal groups vary from low-key societies that offer courses in meditation and nonviolent survival techniques to tightly ruled encampments that bristle with automatic weapons, stockpiles of food and zealous instructors who teach warfare tactics to khaki-clad militants carrying Bibles and rifles.

The Christian-Patriots Defense League, an outgrowth of the Christian Conservative Churches of America, teaches survival at the "personal, family, community and national level," according to founder-leader John R. Harrell of Flora, Ill.

The league's annual Freedom Festival and Citizens Emergency Defense Systems Conference features a smorgasbord of survival-related courses, including "Special Weapons and Tactics," "Knife Fighting," "Guard Dog Training," "Subsisting on Wild Plants" and "Women's Responsibility to God and Country."

The league's estimated 25,000 members tend to agree with Harrell's belief that the United States will have "a full-scale revolution" with "blood and guts strewn all over this country" within several years.

They aim to be ready. And fire.

Meanwhile, Harrell's other organization, Outposts of America, is offering "time-share" memberships in rural "safe retreats" strategically scattered throughout Middle America.

"For a few dollars per year you can have full access and use of these valuable lands and facilities on a year-round basis," promises a flyer. "Membership certificates . . . lodging and quartering rights are awaiting your arrival. We will help you pass through government roadblocks if proof of a residential living area is needed."

The Way International, the biblical research and teaching ministry based in New Knoxville, Ohio, has a training program for its full-time ministers called the Way Corps. Members were encouraged to take weapons training at the Kansas National Guard unit in Emporia, Kan., where the Way has an unaccredited college.

Way officials said the arms training was actually a hunters' safety course.

But Kansas critic Allen Denton told *U.S. News & World Report,* "You don't need to know how to hit a bull's-eye from three different positions—prone, sitting and standing" for that.

Several religious groups, including the Brotherhood of the Sun in Santa Barbara and the Krishna Consciousness Society, have in the past admitted having large caches of guns and ammunition.

But, after confrontation with law enforcement officials and the spotlight of media attention, both groups have apparently disposed of the stockpiles and now de-emphasize firepower.

Some New Age groups preach the virtues of storing dehydrated foods, tools and medical supplies as well as hard assets such as gold, silver, precious gems and art objects.

The Church Universal and Triumphant, which last month bought the 12,000-acre retreat bordering Yellowstone National Park in Montana, has dealt in—and sold to its members—precious metals and survival equipment.

The church, led by Elizabeth Clare Prophet, envisions a self-sufficient community at its Montana spread (much as the followers of Indian Guru Bhagwan Shree Rajneesh are building a "city of God" in central Oregon).

Church Universal leaders are screening prospective members who have agricultural and survival skills and who desire to live (at their own expense) at "Inner Retreat."

Roy Masters, radio pop psychologist and survival buff, also is promoting primitive-society skills in the belief that knowledge acquired in traditional schools is inadequate for survival in coming hard times.

A 378-acre ranch near Grants Pass, Ore., owned by Masters' Foundation for Human Understanding, functions as a kind of low-key survival school. Young people "burned out from stress in the big cities" go there for from three to six months to "get their heads together" and learn how to tend livestock, raise vegetables, keep bees, butcher meat, mix cement and hang dry wall, among other skills.

In exchange for $2,500 and the experience, the students donate their labor to keep the ranch running.

"Skills will be like oil one day," Masters predicts.

Masters insists that he isn't building a commune or a personality cult, but he claims that he has influenced about 1,500 families to move from urban areas, particularly Southern California, to the Grants Pass area, considered a survivalist haven. There, most have settled into their own retreat properties and small business enterprises in association with other Masters admirers.

Masters' approach typifies the bond between new age religionists and survivalists.

For decades, the 2.8 million-member U.S. Mormon Church has taught its families to stow away at least a year's supply of food and water. But now the preparedness ethic has spread to other conservative religious bodies.

Preparedness books and supplies are advertised in the religious press, and survival theology is debated in leading evangelical magazines. For example, if during a famine a Christian householder's ample food supply is threatened by a takeover from others, should he share the provisions or shoot the outsiders? The answer may depend on how a survivalist interprets God's will.

Although no one knows the number of survivalists in the general population, some dealers in survival goods estimate that from 2 million to 5 million Americans are regular or sporadic customers.

The belief that the United States is careening madly along a four-lane interstate to moral and civil collapse is hawked by economic gurus like Howard Ruff (a Mormon), whose best-selling book, "How to Prosper in the Coming Bad Times" has sold more than 3.5 million copies. His monthly 170,000-circulation investment newsletter—"The Ruff Times"—aptly describes how many survivalists view the future.

An approving review of Ruff's book in the magazine of Yogi Bhajan's Sikh community based in West Los Angeles concludes that it should "be almost a Bible for everyone in our 3HO Family."

Ruff has been a consultant to several religious groups whose end-times vision squares with his financial advice.

And Masters, who urges his followers to meditate and buy rural retreats, was a close friend of the late Mel Tappan, a leading survivalist whose $125-a-year "Personal Survival Letter" gives hard-line advice on what kind of food and guns to have around when the hungry hordes descend.

Though many religious groups with large rural holdings specialize in agriculture, it is not uncommon for their members to staff a variety of business enterprises.

Steve Gaskin's Farm, a 1,750-acre commune in Summertown, Tenn., for example, has spun a web of cottage industries that include solar-powered CB radios, rock records, book publishing and an ambulance service. Self-sufficient, the farm supports 1,300 communal dwellers.

Followers of the Korean evangelist, the Rev. Sun Myung Moon, (known as the Moonies) are well known from their ventures into the fishing industry.

The Krishnas, in addition to 10 large U.S. farms, operate a $3-million-a-year publishing business, a chain of vegetarian restaurants, a cookie factory and assorted handcraft industries.

Followers of Yogi Bhajan, leader of the off-beat Sikh Healthy-Happy-Holy Organization (3HO), have set up partnerships and corporations including eight Golden Temple vegetarian restaurants, Sunshine Brass Beds, Shakti Shoes, Sunshine Scented Oils and Golden Temple Health Foods, which makes a candy bar called Wha Guru Chew.

Virtually every society has had its "withdrawal" groups.

Sociologist Ron Enroth of Westmont College in Santa Barbara sees parallels between current New Age religious movements and some that flourished in the United States in the last century.

"In both cases there is a preoccupation with perfection," he said in a telephone interview. "There is a vision also of a commune or community. By that I mean retreat centers . . . and a utopian view."

Enroth also sees similarities between current withdrawal communities and the "negative disdain of the city by the earlier Protestants. The city was seen as evil and the focus of contaminating influences."

Robert Ellwood, professor of religion at USC, noted that Buddhist groups have long had contemplative communities and mountain retreats, and that Roman Catholic and other established religious orders have sponsored monasteries and convents in country settings.

Ellwood noted that the Oneida Community, a settlement of communists in New York in the mid-19th Century, stressed perfectionism and eventually became very successful as a result of its manufactures and industries, particularly silverware.

The Shakers are another withdrawal group that has mellowed with time and enriched U.S. culture.

"The industrious and celibate Shakers, once the victims of appalling cruelty from their neighbors and of attempted legislative vendettas, have contributed such practical inventions as the circular saw and made beautiful furniture," Ellwood said.

Harmony and Amana

Other 19th Century communities that combined an idealized view of rural life with a rejection of the ills of industrialization and the evils of the city were the Harmony Society in Pennsylvania and Indiana, and the Amana Society in Iowa—which still maintains seven villages on the Iowa River. (A subsidiary of the society manufactures the appliances of the same name.)

Ellwood, who has made a special study of tightly knit and unusual religion groups, also sees antecedents from the days of the 1960s Flower Children and their hippie communes in the insular groups currently attracting attention.

"It is definitely a trend, perhaps a replay of Haight-Ashbury," Ellwood said.

He added that the new religious movements founded amid the flowers and spiritual highs of that era are now at a critical stage at which the initial euphoria may have worn thin and there is a transition from the original leadership.

"People living together in an intense religious group develop tensions within the community," he explained. "And outside, a toll has been taken with friends and neighbors. There may be some disillusionment; the charisma is gone, and the first glorious dreams of changing the world haven't materialized as expected."

"Really Nothing New"

Enroth, who has written extensively on New Age religions, thinks some of today's withdrawal groups are "successors to the human potentials movement. They stress self-realization, personal growth and transformation. The goal is to become godlike. That's really nothing new."

Ellwood and Enroth are not unmindful of withdrawal groups that have ended in self-destruction or disaster. The Jonestown mass suicide-murder of 913 followers of the Rev. Jim Jones in Guyana in November, 1978, is, of course, the most shocking example.

"The danger," Ellwood said, "is that, after a group isolates people out of the social mainstream and gives them intensive confirmatory experiences, these adherents become more and more centered on the group's own values. The group's beliefs, its very life and survival, become the followers' main or only drive."

To ensure survival, leaders of such groups may do things ordinarily considered immoral or criminal, Ellwood said.

If religion watchers see parallels between current New Age groups and those of the last century, they also see distinct differences.

"The new religious movements are largely middle- and upper-middle-class" and are relatively affluent and well educated, Enroth said, while earlier communal groups "attracted from the margins of society—the underclass . . . the poor and despised—and ethnic minorities."

Enroth added that Jonestown is an important exception to the current pattern:

"The Peoples Temple of Jim Jones appealed across the board, and, of course, the majority of his followers were blacks."

But, part of the stance that withdrawal groups take toward the "outside world" is predicated on paranoia and an exaggerated "persecution complex," sociologist Enroth said, adding, "Most of the problems rural communes bring on themselves."

Often, the problem is that the more a novel, little-understood group is harassed, the more it retreats from mainstream society.

And the way some New Age groups acquire property when they move into a rural setting only inflames the friction: They set up "dummy" corporations with names that do not reveal the real buyer. When local residents ascertain the purchaser's identity, it is too late to stop the transaction.

More than a week after escrow had closed on the Church Universal and Triumphant's deal for publisher Malcolm Forbes 12,000-acre ranch in Montana, the local newspaper and even county and city officials were still mystified over who bought the land. The buyer was Royal Teton Ltd., a Montana corporation with only a Helena post office box address.

Gloucester, Mass., residents were particularly irked last year when waterfront property there was sold by a Roman Catholic organization to a New Hampshire businessman, who reportedly told Gloucester citizens he had no connection with Moon's Unification Church.

The next day, the *Washington Post* reported, the man sold the property to the Moonies for $1.1 million—$127,000 more than he paid for it.

The perceived deception led to so much harassment that the Moonies encircled the place with an eight-foot-chain-link fence and posted armed guards.

Residents of Pope Valley, a pastoral Shangri-La near Napa, also bridled when the Moonies used a similar tactic to buy a 672-acre family resort for a retreat and seminar facility.

The Moonies have pleaded that because of religious discrimination, they are unable to buy property if they are known as the buyers.

To some groups, persecution is a badge of approval from God—the sign that community members are indeed the "chosen ones."

"Expect persecution, and beware when everyone speaks well of you," their leaders say, quoting Luke 6:26 and other Bible passages, like Matthew 10:34, which says Jesus came not to bring peace, but a sword.

In Search of the Sacred

Barbara Kantrowitz with Patricia King, Debra Rosenberg, Karen Springen, Pat Wingert, Tessa Namuth and T. Trent Gegax, *Newsweek*, November 28, 1994

Rita McClain's spiritual journey began in Iowa, where she grew up in the fundamentalist world of the Pentecostal Church. What she remembers most about that time are tent meetings and an overwhelming feeling of guilt. In her 20s she tried less doctrinaire Protestantism. That, too, proved unsatisfying. By the age of 27, McClain had rejected all organized religion. "I really felt like a pretty wounded Christian," she says. For the next 18 years, she sought inner peace only in nature, through rock climbing in the mountains or hiking in the desert. That seemed enough.

Then, six years ago, in the aftermath of an emotionally draining divorce, McClain's spiritual life blossomed. Just as she had once explored mountains, she began scouting the inner landscape. She started with Unity, a metaphysical church near her Marin County, Calif., home. It was a revelation, light-years away from the "Old Testament kind of thinking I knew very well from my childhood." The next stop was the Native American spiritual practices. Then it was Buddhism at Marin County Spirit Rock Meditation Center, where she has attended a number of retreats, including one that required eight days of silence.

These disparate rituals melded into a personal religion, which McClain, a 50-year-old nurse, celebrates at an ever-changing altar in her home. Right now the altar consists of an angel statue, a small bottle of "sacred water" blessed at a women's vigil, a crystal ball, a pyramid, a small brass image of Buddha sitting on a brass leaf, a votive candle, a Hebrew prayer, a tiny Native American basket from the 1850s and a picture of her "most sacred place," a madrone tree near her home.

Maybe it's a critical mass of baby boomers in the contemplative afternoon of life. Or anxiety over the coming millennium. Or a general dissatisfaction with the materialism of the modern world. For these reasons and more, millions of Americans are embarking on a search for the sacred in their lives. Not all have a journey as extreme as Rita McClain's. Some are returning to the religions of their childhoods, finding new meaning in old rituals. Others look for wisdom outside their own cultures, mixing different traditions in an individualistic stew.

The seekers fit no particular profile. They include Wall Street investment bankers who spend their lunch hours in Bible-study groups, artists rediscovering religious themes, fitness addicts who've traded aerobics classes for meditation and other spiritual exercises. No matter what path they take, the seekers are united by a sincere desire to find answers to profound questions, to understand their place in the cosmos. "Living in a secular world is like living in an astrodome with a roof over the top," says Roy Larson of Northwestern University's new Center for Religion and the News Media. "The temperature is always 70 degrees and the grass is always green. Even in a place that holds 70,000 people, you feel claustrophobic. You need to breathe some fresh air."

Americans have always been a religious people, of course. Even during the past several decades, when it seemed like the prevailing culture was overwhelmingly irreverent and secular, legions of the faithful filled pews every Sunday. But for baby boomers in particular, spirituality was off the radarscope. Instead, as a generation, boomers embraced political activism, careerism, even marathon running, with an almost religious zeal. Now it's suddenly OK, even chic, to use the S words—soul, sacred, spiritual, sin. In a *Newsweek* poll, a majority of Americans (58 percent) say they feel the need to experience spiritual growth. And a third of all adults report having had a mystical or religious experience.

Check out the barometers in the cultural marketplace. Bookstores are lined with spiritual missives. Music stores feature best-selling Gregorian chants. Hollywood salts its scripts with divine references and afterlife experiences. Want to give that special seeker on your winter-solstice list a crystal? Be sure to wrap it in angels gift paper. These are amazing times: Pope John Paul II's new book, "Crossing the Threshold of Hope," tops the best-seller list, beating out Faye Resnick's raunchy tell-all about Nicole Brown Simpson. James Redfield's spiritual novel, "The Celestine Prophecy," is at the top of the fiction list. In the music world, Motown no longer has the monopoly on soul. Since March, Angel Records has sold 2.8 million copies of the CD "Chant" by the Benedictine monks of Santo Domingo de Silos. The Beastie Boys included a Buddhist rap on their last album; gospel rap is competing with the usual misogynistic fare.

Something's going on, and people want to talk about it. Celebrities as different as tennis star Andre Agassi and playwright David Mamet tell interviewers how they've found God in their lives. Kathleen Norris's 1993 book, "Dakota: A Spiritual Geography," is on the paperback best-seller list. She has received 3,000 letters from people wanting to share their spiritual lives—an amazing amount of mail for a book of reflective essays. *Newsweek* publishes a story about Czech President Vaclav Havel's speech on the search for meaning, and readers call for weeks, wanting to describe their own journeys.

Politicians, like Newt Gingrich, have pushed school prayer onto the national agenda. Talk shows, such as "Oprah," have featured spirituality. Physicists debate the spiritual significance of quantum mechanics. Attendance at religious retreats has skyrocketed. The Abbey of Gethsemani, 45 miles south of Louisville, Ky., is booked through the end of April. "For people who are really insistent," says brother Patrick Hart, "we say we'll put you on standby, just like on the airlines."

Courses and lectures with spiritual themes are drawing standing-room-only crowds. Interface, a holistic-education center in Cambridge, Mass., offers 700 courses to 20,000 registrants this year, up from 13,000 just three years ago. This fall, 2,000 people showed up for a conference on body and soul featuring such heavy-hitting speakers as Dr. Dean Ornish, who advocates a diet-cum-spiritual cure for heart disease, and Dr. Bernie Siegel, author of "Love, Medicine and Miracles." "People are really hungry for this," says program planner Anne Arsenault. "They're hungry for meaning in life."

FOR ENTREPRENEURS with a keen sense of the Zeitgeist, this is an obvious opportunity. Deja Vu Tours, based in Berkeley, Calif., specializes in "spiritual adventure" travel. It boasts that its clients have "seen the sun rise at Stonehenge, visited the 'Room of Spirits' at the Dalai Lama's Monastery, participated in rituals led by a shaman at Machu Picchu, sung a greeting to the Kumari, the Living Goddess of Nepal, and received baptism in the Jordan River." Susan Hull Bostwick, who started Deja Vu Tours 13 years ago, says her clients are people who have a sense that they've lived before and want to stand in the scared places of their past.

There are spiritual seekers of all ages, but baby boomers are at the head of the march. Wade Clark Roof, a professor of religion at the University of California, Santa Barbara, says that as the boomers enter their 40s, they must face the inevitable: neither jogging nor liposuction nor all the brown rice in China can keep them young forever. "As our bodies fall apart, as they weaken and sag, it speaks of mortality," says Roof, author of "A Generation of Seekers: The Spiritual Journeys of the Baby Boom Generation." Boomers, says Roof, "are at a point in their lives where they sense the need for spirituality, but they don't know where to get it." Another trigger: parenthood, and the desire to give children a moral and spiritual foundation.

The boomers' search is eclectic, as befits children of a skeptical age. "Each generation is trained to look at spirituality differently," says Rabbi Robert N. Levine, 43, of Congregation Rodeph Sholom in Manhattan. "Our generation participated in civil-rights and Vietnam marches. Now we want to have a dialogue." That dialogue can take place within a traditional denomination. Yvette Perry, 39, a member of Rabbi Levine's congregation, celebrated her adult bat mitzvah earlier this year. Perry says she needed to step off the fast track; her career, running a music-marketing firm, just wasn't enough. Studying with Levine, she says, is "all about dealing with learning and growing and changing . . . You can read something and the rabbi can read it and there are different viewpoints and you get to argue about it. It's a quest for knowledge."

WHILE PERRY IS ABLE TO integrate her spiritual and professional lives, other seekers find their search means a radical new path. In 1989, Mary Helen Nugent was a 33-year-old hospital administrator in Michigan. She had a master's degree, earned a healthy salary and was very career-minded. In her personal life, she says, "I thought what I wanted was marriage, family and all that." But that year, she gradually began questioning all her assumptions about the direction of her life. No single experience brought this on, she says; rather, it was a slow process of self-discovery. "I came to the conclusion," Nugent says, "that a religious life was something I wanted to try and needed to try."

Today Nugent is a nun, living with two other nuns in a single-family home in Dallas, Pa. Her paycheck from Mercy Hospital in Scranton goes directly to the Sisters of Mercy. In return, she gets a small stipend for living expenses. "I'm not running away from anything," she says. "I'm trying to share a life and a faith."

At the other end of the spiritual spectrum are seekers who move beyond conventional boundaries, to a kind of cafeteria religion, a very American theology. In a pluralistic society, "one institution feels a little spiritually claustrophobic," says James W. Jones, a religion professor at Rutgers University and the author of the upcoming book "In the Middle of This Road We Call Our Life: The Courage to Search for Something More." Jones recalls deriding this kind of pick-and-choose religion as frivolous and narcissistic a decade ago. But now he believes that a person who has synthesized different traditions can find a path that "may be as spiritually profound as traditional religions or even more spiritually profound."

At the very least, adopting a cross-cultural spirituality brings an appreciation of very different worlds. As an English major at the University of Wisconsin in the late 1960s, Edward Bednar was on the usual college-career path. But after nearly dying in surgery, he dropped out of school and studied with a Zen master. Meditation helped him "find truth" in the details of everyday life, he says. Eventually, Bednar discovered he could also find truth in a place he had long abandoned, the Roman Catholic Church. He found new inspiration studying the mystics and the saints. Now 50 and living in Brooklyn, N.Y., Bednar teaches meditation to businessmen on Wall Street and goes to mass on Sundays. He also integrates spirituality into his everyday work at the New York Association for New Americans, an organization that resettles 20,000 refugees each year. After meeting the Dalai Lama, the Tibetan spiritual leader, he helped bring 1,000 Tibetan families to this country and is helping them set up new communities here.

Inevitably, there's a high-tech component to this phenomenon, too. On the Internet, devotees can find Bible-study groups, meditation instruction and screens of New Age philosophy. A self-described futurist in Amherst, Mass., who calls herself Doctress Neutopia, has created her own online religion. Anyone with a modem can join her congregation. In Sunnyvale, Calif., Jeff Manning, 37, has produced a CD-ROM version of the tarot—and taken up Siddha Yoga, which he considers the most spiritual tradition he has encountered. As his two young children grow older, Manning is considering "doing an organized-religion tour," exposing them to major denominations the way wealthy parents once took their offspring on a tour of Europe.

As we approach the millennium, some theologians expect an increase in spiritual seeking. The calendar watershed itself inspires anxiety and soul-searching. At the same time, more baby boomers will be approaching dreaded middle age. Spirituality could be just another boomer passion, stuck in the closet next to the rowing machine—or it could be a powerful force for personal growth. "A lot has changed in the last half century," says Charles Nuckolls, an anthropologist at Emory University who studies religion and healing. "We've stripped away what our ancestors saw as essential—the importance of religion and family . . . People feel they want something they've lost, and they don't remember what it is they've lost. But it has left a gaping hole." That, in essence, is the seeker's quest: to fill the hole with a new source of meaning. Why are we here? What is the purpose of our existence? The answers change in each generation, but the questions are eternal.

26

God and Mammon

There is no way to write about religion without also writing about money. Religious groups bring in billions in donations annually—vital money that supports a group's hierarchy and pays for its outreach.

Some of the most celebrated religion stories of the century have been about abuse of money. A 1973 Pulitzer Prize went to the weekly *Sun Newspapers* of Omaha, Nebraska, for stories about the financial mismanagement of donations to Boys Town. In 1988 the *Charlotte Observer*'s series about Jim Bakker's bilking of the Praise the Lord (PTL) ministry also won a Pulitzer Prize.

More recently, the Episcopal Church was astonished to learn its treasurer coolly swindled $2.2 million out from under its nose. At about the same time, John C. Weber, a Roman Catholic accountant, stole $1 million from the Diocese of Wilmington, Delaware.

Some blame the general material culture of the late 20th century for these high-stakes thefts. Others cite human sinfulness itself. And still others note ministers of today who are more likely to exhibit an affluence that was once eschewed, thus leading by silent example that more is better. Other clergy openly boast a theology of prosperity, in which God rewards the faithful with spiritual *and* material wealth.

In his book *God and Mammon,* sociologist Robert Wuthnow reports on a survey of churchgoers, nearly 80 percent of whom said they yearned for more money. But only 16 percent said the church taught them that wanting money is a sin. Wuthnow in part blames the high-dollar scandals affecting some religious groups in the late 20th century on those groups' failure to teach the pitfalls of greed.

Often religion reporters cover money stories only when the avarice of a wayward steward violates the trust of the faithful. Criminal investigations and court cases make records and details public, when such specifics typically would be known only by a religious group's trusted inner circle.

Laurie Goodstein's piece "Thou Shalt Not Lie," which ran in the *Washington Post*'s Sunday magazine, is a riveting account of how one woman embezzled more than $2 million from the Episcopal Church. Although this story reads as a profile and indeed falls into that category of writing, it is also exceptional reporting that keeps the reader's attention, much like a good suspense novel. Judges in the Religion Newswriters Association's John Templeton Reporter of the Year contest in 1996 said the story helped Goodstein net the award's first prize that year.

Scandals, however, are not the only stories about God and money. While at the *Wall Street Journal,* reporter Gustav Niebuhr wrote about declines in church contributions. The bottom-line financial implications of declining mainline Protestant membership is further described in the *Newsweek* story "Dead End for the Mainline?" reproduced in chapter 28.

Every variety of religious entrepreneur exists: plumbers, truckers, lawyers. In most professions you can find individuals merging their faith and vocations in a sometimes lucrative mix. And the merchandise of faith—some call it "Jesus Junk"—is an expanding part of displays at the Christian Booksellers Association's annual meeting.

Christian bookstores were among the earliest businesses catering to the needs of religious groups. But as religion reporter Mark Pinsky of the *Orlando Sentinel* reports in a story reprinted here, the popularity of religious books has led to greater competition from general bookstores and megastores, such as Wal-Mart, putting a pinch on the traditional, family-owned shops.

Thou Shalt Not Lie

Ellen Cooke Lives a Grand Illusion. Then the Walls of Her House of Cards Came Tumbling Down

Laurie Goodstein, *The Washington Post*, June 4, 1995

Ellen Cooke left no doubt that she came from a monied family—a background befitting the chief financial officer for the Episcopal Church's national headquarters in Manhattan.

Friends had heard her "Gone With the Wind" accounts of relatives hiding jewelry in the draperies during the Civil War. Colleagues knew about her chauffeur, her antiques, her weekend flights to Virginia to her farm with the tennis court and deep-water dock. Churchgoers knew that when the New Jersey church her husband pastored lacked a coat rack or a new altar, the Cookes' largess could cover it.

So last month, people who thought they knew her were stunned to learn that the money Cooke had spent so freely was neither hers nor her family's. The hard-working woman whom colleagues thought of as "Mrs. Episcopal Church" had embezzled $2.2 million over five years while serving as the church's treasurer, at the same time she helped to sack nearly 100 staffers because of apparent "budget shortfalls." Prosecutors in the U.S. attorney's office in Newark are investigating. The Internal Revenue Service is on the case, and criminal charges are likely.

The scandal has also wrecked the career of Cooke's husband, until last month the pastor of St. John's Episcopal Church, a prominent McLean parish. The bishop of Virginia announced yesterday that Nicholas Cooke III has resigned from the priesthood.

Church and bank officials have slowly reconstructed exactly how Ellen Cooke duped them. She manipulated trust funds and trust. She exuded absolute confidence and control. She was feared and despised by co-workers who would have jumped at any opportunity to see her fired. But no one who knew Ellen Cooke knew what she had to hide.

Says Vincent Currie Jr., chairman of the church's administration and finance committee, "I'm on a long list of a hundred people who would have said, 'If you said you thought she was stealing, you'd be lying.'"

Just as no one suspected Cooke's financial dealings, few questioned the portrait she drew of herself. But the swindle appears to be Cooke's grandest deception in a lifetime built on illusion.

SHE HAD no family fortune. Ellen Fahey Gerrity was the oldest of six children in a Vienna, Va., household often wanting for money and affection.

She had no degree in economics from Georgetown University; she never went there. She flunked out of George Washington University after only two terms.

She handled hundreds of millions in investments for the church, but she had no background in high finance.

Finally, she had no aristocratic Episcopalian bloodline; her roots were working-class Catholic.

Mrs. Cooke

The 12-story headquarters of the Episcopal Church occupies prime real estate on Manhattan's East Side. Contradicting stereotypes of stuffy Episcopalians, it is an informal place where laypersons call priests by their first names and even the church's leading cleric—Presiding Bishop Edmond L. Browning—is referred to by many as "the PB" or just "Ed."

Ellen Cooke, however, insisted that she be addressed as "Mrs. Cooke" and signed her correspondence "Mrs. Nicholas T. Cooke III." Some co-workers assumed that Cooke, 51, was simply proud of her second husband, an affable priest marked early on as "bishop material."

She dressed primly in flowered Laura Ashley dresses and matching headbands, white stockings and a Dutch-boy bob. She ran the treasurer's office, say co-workers, like Marie Antoinette.

Initially this looked like progress. Before she arrived in 1987, department heads spent without regard for their annual allotments. Cooke made sure they stayed within their budgets. She demanded to see canceled checks or receipts even for expenditures of less than $3.

She won respect for narrowing the gap between the salaries and benefits of the mostly female lay employees and the predominantly male clergy who worked at headquarters. She computerized the accounting procedures.

Meanwhile, Cooke undermined the church's own version of separation of powers. She held not one potent position, but two: She was both executive officer for administration and finance appointed by the presiding bishop, and the treasurer of the church, elected by the General Convention of clergy and lay. Cooke persuaded the church's corporate legal counsel to combine two positions that, traditionally, had kept each other accountable. The church's laws were rewritten to accommodate her.

"It all seemed so reasonable at the time, in the interest of eliminating redundancy and overhead," said Barry Menuez, formerly the senior executive for planning and development and now a church consultant.

In a few, short years, Cooke commanded sole control over nearly every function of church finance. She oversaw the investment of trust funds. She granted and withheld scholarships. She paid the heating bills.

"She probably exercised more control over the church center and beyond that into the national church than any other single person," says Pamela Chinnis, president of the church's elected House of Deputies.

"She controlled everything in this building, including the temperature we worked at," says Nan Cobbey, an editor at *Episcopal Life* magazine.

Program Director Diane Porter recalls being at a meeting of the National Council of Churches where a list of annual contributions to the council from each denomination was circulated. "For the Episcopal Church there was a big fat zero," said Porter. But she knew she had submitted the request for a wire transfer to Cooke six months earlier. Porter says she confronted Cooke and found the request in her briefcase.

Colleagues assumed she was simply overworked. Some hesitated to challenge her because they were dependent on her—after all, Cooke had successfully steered the Episcopal Church through years of downsizing and belt-tightening. The presiding bishop, known to champion lay-women, stood by Cooke when anyone complained, though even that relationship started to unravel at the end.

Still, everyone knew she served the church with total devotion. Many nights she was the last to leave. Sometimes her husband would come in from New Jersey for dinner with her and would wait "like a schoolboy," says Porter, occasionally until after 10.

Her spacious corner office faced Second Avenue. One door opened onto a hallway that led directly to the presiding bishop's office, giving her unparalleled access to the man and his accounts.

Cooke had attained a stature that her co-workers believed suited her origins: She talked of debutante balls, her father's prominence in publishing and her family's inclusion in the Social Register.

But to her family, Ellen Cooke's high perch in the Episcopal Church was a source of marvel.

Life at St. Luke's

John F. Gerrity disciplined his six children "with the techniques he learned from the Marine Corps," says his son Kevin, a journalist in Kansas City. His wife, Evelyn, suffered from grand mal epileptic seizures that sent her to the hospital on occasion. As the oldest of four boys and two girls, Ellen served as substitute mother.

"There was a tension in the air as if something were going to break or things were going to get out of control," Kevin Gerrity says. "We were not blessed with great coping skills. We reacted to pressure in sometimes thunderous ways."

JOHN GERRITY had been a staff writer at *The Washington Post* for about a year when he and four other *Post* newsmen enlisted in the Marines in May 1942 as combat correspondents. He was wounded in action in Guam. At home, his leg riddled with shrapnel and his foot mangled, he sometimes tried to drown the pain in drink. He returned to writing but didn't always have a staff job. For seven years he supported his large family by freelancing, recalls Kevin Gerrity, who says, "I grew up knowing that times were lean and we had to be cautious."

Yet John Gerrity gave his elder daughter a glimpse of high society, squiring her to cocktail parties and dinners that her mother refused to attend out of fear her husband would get sauced, the son says. Ellen "learned the proper way to mingle. She was a fast study," he says.

Ellen graduated from Georgetown Visitation School, a Catholic girls school adjacent to Georgetown University. On her resume she claims a B.S. in economics from Georgetown, but she never enrolled there. She attended George Washington University for two semesters but was put on academic suspension when she earned one B, one D and four F's. School records show she never re-enrolled.

Nevertheless, she managed to climb through the Episcopal Church bureaucracy, beginning with a part-time job in 1969 in the business office of Washington National Cathedral. The same year, the 26-year-old progressed to business manager at the National Cathedral School, and in the early '70s was made assistant treasurer of the Diocese of Massachusetts. She had married the Rev. W. Christopher Koch, an Episcopal priest 16 years her senior, in 1971. After more than a decade, the marriage broke up; she was left with two sons of her own and one from her husband's previous marriage.

She was 41 and still living in the Boston area when she married Nicholas Trout Cooke III, 30, a seminarian from Richmond, in 1985. He had been a practicing attorney with a University of Virginia law degree, but told friends he felt called to the priesthood. When he was made assistant rector at Christ Church in Alexandria, Ellen Cooke took the job of assistant treasurer at the Diocese of Virginia.

Within six months, she was promoted to treasurer of the national church on the recommendations of the bishops of Boston and Virginia. (In both those dioceses, her successors have searched for any clues that she misused funds, and found none.) Nicholas Cooke was made rector of St. Luke's, a landmark church with Tiffany windows in a section of Montclair, N.J., where spring brings the power-tool buzz of gardeners manicuring the lawns of palatial Tudor homes.

After first living in the large rectory adjacent to the church, the Cookes paid $465,000 for the historic Crane Homestead abode of Azariah Crane, son of Montclair's first settler. It was built in 1740 and is only three blocks from the church. It is actually a compound with a four-bedroom main house, a separate three-bedroom cottage in the rear and a two-car garage, all linked by a long lawn planted with tulips and towering trees. With this property and the Virginia farm, the Cookes owed $6,000 in monthly mortgage payments. Yet they spared no expense renovating the Montclair house with a wraparound porch, deluxe kitchen and the finest in wallpaper and tile, according to those who know of their expenditures.

At St. Luke's the Cookes rearranged things to their liking because they could pay for the changes. When the Rev. Cooke wanted to relocate the altar among the pews to signal that the priest is one among the worshipers, he quashed any resistance by paying to build a sliding altar. In honor of a former warden, the Cookes donated an ornamental metal screen that some parishioners resented because it blocked their view of the Tiffany windows.

Yet many parishioners adored the Cookes, and regretted only that they never seemed to set down roots in New Jersey. They frequently spent time at their riverside farm in Ottaman, Va. For years they kept their Virginia license plates—"RITE I" and "RITE 2." They sent the children to private schools, though Montclair's integrated public schools are a point of pride for its residents.

To her siblings, among them a carpenter and a taxi driver, Ellen Cooke appeared the family high achiever. She seemed free of financial worries and emotional demons—one brother wandered the streets for years until he was institutionalized, and two others have wrestled with depression. Ellen's sons were bright, well-adjusted and engaging. Her salary was $125,000, her husband's was $70,000, and Kevin Gerrity figured they could afford to live so well because "along the way she had made some wise investments."

Sudden Riches

No one was more shocked and delighted than the members of St. Luke's Episcopal Church to discover that they suddenly were blessed with the funds to hire two part-time assistant rectors. William Lashbrook, the church's senior warden—the equivalent of chairman of the board—heard the news while standing on the steps of the church one Sunday in March last year. Ellen Cooke ceremoniously handed him a check for $24,000 and a letter from church headquarters saying that St. Luke's had been awarded a grant from the national church for "ministry in changing communities." The letter and the check were signed "Mrs. Nicholas T. Cooke III."

Sure, it was a little surprising, recalls Bruce Stransky, treasurer of St. Luke's. The church had never applied for the grant. And the Rev. Cooke hadn't mentioned it to the church's board of directors.

"At the time he [Lashbrook] thought it was 100 percent legal, and so did I," says Stransky.

They were unaware that in the previous five years while Nicholas Cooke served as rector, a windfall of $66,000 in checks from the national treasurer's office, all bearing Ellen Cooke's signature, was deposited into the Rector's Discretionary Fund controlled by her husband. Most church rectors have such funds to be used for people in need—widows facing eviction, the unemployed who fall sick, the neighborhood homeless.

Now a committee of priests in the Diocese of Newark has been convened by the bishop there to investigate how Cooke used his discretionary fund. He freely wrote checks but did not fill out the stubs. When he left St. Luke's, $500 remained in the account.

Shell Game

When Presiding Bishop Browning fired Ellen Cooke, it was not for embezzlement. The two had clashed repeatedly over the budget in public meetings last year, and several months of mediation sessions for the staff with a trained negotiator didn't reduce the friction. Browning allowed Cooke to resign in December 1994 after eight years of service, leaving the impression it was necessary because her husband had been transferred to St. John's Episcopal Church in McLean.

Before she left, Cooke received and cashed a check for $86,000. She told the human resources director at the church it was for back pay and vacation pay, and that she would provide documentation to authorize it. When a month later she still hadn't, the presiding bishop was informed.

Investigators from the accounting firm Coopers & Lybrand called in by the church discovered that Cooke had concocted an elaborate shell game.

Wealthy Episcopalians have left their church 955 trust funds and securities, all worth about $226 million. Only in retrospect did colleagues think it strange that Cooke knew the account numbers of many of these trusts by heart.

She regularly transferred the interest on some of the funds to the church's operating account at the First American Bank, now First Union, in Washington. The church had not always banked at First American. Cooke moved its accounts there in 1990, after she and other church officials expressed dissatisfaction with the service they received at the church's New York bank.

For Cooke, there was one other advantage: She and her husband maintained their personal accounts there.

From the church's operating account, Cooke would periodically write checks made out to First American Bank to be transferred to another account there. On the surface this too appeared entirely innocent, "since it was a normal and appropriate practice to transfer funds between the various church accounts," as the presiding bishop said in a statement last month.

But most of these checks were deposited into Cooke's personal account.

Other times the deposits had the account number of the presiding bishop's discretionary fund, a unique pocket in the elaborate garment of church assets. Discretionary funds are considered the assets of the presiding bishop and so went unaudited by the church's outside accountants. Cooke then wrote more checks from the discretionary fund and deposited these into her own account.

Through these conduits, Cooke diverted $1.5 million over five years. The presiding bishop himself was unaware Cooke was plundering his account because, he said in his statement, she "prevented others from having access to the presiding bishop's discretionary account ledgers." He refused a request for an interview.

She also wrote about $225,000 in unauthorized checks to third parties—including her sons' private schools and her husband's church. She used her corporate credit card and other corporate accounts for 99 plane trips that she and her husband took to Richmond, running up about $325,000 in personal expenses. In this way she paid for fancy meals, hotel rooms, catering services, flowers and a $16,000 Tiffany necklace. And she wrote herself small checks that eventually added up to $28,000.

To volunteers serving on two committees that were supposed to oversee the national church's finances. Cooke appeared, if anything, overly conscientious.

They would arrive for their meetings and Cooke would provide each member with a six-inch stack of reports, ledgers and figures.

"She drowned us in paper," said Marjorie Christie, a member of the administration and finance committee. In oral reports, Cooke would drone on in impenetrable accounting jargon until the members were too confused or impatient to ask questions.

"Her style made you think, well, I just don't understand," Christie said.

Admits committee Chairman Vincent Currie Jr.: "She didn't have to manipulate the books. There wasn't anybody checking behind her."

The Final Chapter

The Cookes' Montclair house now has a yellow sign in front that says "Historic Home for Sale." It's on the market for $695,000, reduced from $725,000. The Virginia farm is for sale for $850,000.

The church owns the properties now because the Cookes cooperated in turning them over. Church lawyers suspect the Cookes may have assets that they haven't revealed and have hired the corporate sleuths from Kroll Associates to track them down. They are still searching for the Tiffany necklace.

The Cookes decline interviews. Ellen Cooke has spoken only once, through an open letter to the church's executive council, released to the public through her attorneys.

"I am one of a small percentage of the population who by reason of personality are simply unable to stop in the face of enormous pressures and stress," she said. The psychiatrist she began seeing in February "believes that my subsequent actions, blocked from memory during this time, were a cry for help which I fully expected to be discovered and questioned, and which escalated as I tried to escape from a situation which had become intolerable."

She says little more of her psychological state except to mention "the pain, abuse and powerlessness I have felt during the years I worked as a lay woman on a senior level at the church headquarters." This claim provoked outrage from the Episcopal Women's Caucus and many of her coworkers long frustrated by Cooke's inordinate power.

To most she appeared a model mother and professional. A few observed things that appear to them in retrospect like telltale signs: Cooke's frequent absences from work and her feeble excuses; her failing to appear at dinners and social events she said she would attend; her intense need to control.

Her father died of cancer on May 31 at age 81. Ellen and Nicholas Cooke arrived at his bedside hours before he died. In one of his last duties as a pastor, Nicholas Cooke brought prayer books and held a bedside service for the dying man.

The couple are being permitted to live in the rectory at St. John's for part of the summer, but Nicholas Cooke is looking for work in a Richmond law firm or the civil service. Privately, to the senior warden of St. John's, Nicholas Cooke has insisted he didn't know about his wife's embezzlement.

From Episcopalians nationwide, there are calls for the presiding bishop to resign. Barbara Bunten, a former file clerk with no college degree whom Cooke appointed church controller, was fired June 5 and escorted from the building. The treasurer who succeeded Cooke, Donald Burchell, whom Cooke hired from First American Bank, has resigned because of stress. Browning has appointed a chief operating officer to handle day-to-day church administration.

Faced with the hard example of betrayal by a trusted insider, many dioceses and parishes are reviewing their own accounting procedures. In January, the church published a revised 185-page Manual of Business Methods in Church Affairs detailing precise procedures for auditing records and building internal controls. There is a whole chapter on safe stewardship of clergy discretionary funds.

"Dear Friends," says the introductory letter in the manual. "The Church has entrusted us with funds placed in its hands for mission and ministry. This trust is deserving of our nurturing and careful attention to detail, and demanding of our accountability."

The letter is signed "Mrs. Nicholas T. Cooke III."

Churchgoers Are Putting Smaller Portion of Their Incomes into Collection Plates

R. Gustav Niebuhr, *The Wall Street Journal,* July 31, 1992

As the collection plate makes its way through the aisles of U.S. churches, the people in the pews aren't digging as deeply into their pockets as they once did.

Churches across the country are starting to feel the effects of congregations who are increasingly wary about how they spend—and donate—their dollars. The Presbyterian Church (USA) is working to reduce its annual missions budget about 10%. The Episcopal Church has slashed its national staff one-fifth. Catholic dioceses, particularly in the Northeast, have closed the doors of schools.

Now, in a comprehensive study of donations to U.S. Protestant churches, a research group finds that, although individual contributions are rising, the faithful are giving an ever-smaller percentage of their after-tax income to their houses of worship. That cutback is costing religious organizations about $2 billion a year.

The figures point to a "weakening of the church" in U.S. society, says Sylvia Ronsvale, executive vice president of Empty Tomb Inc., the non-profit Christian research organization that conducted the ongoing study, which is being funded by the Lilly Endowment Inc. She adds: "The church as an institution has been commanding a smaller and smaller portion of its members' income."

"Consumerist" Mentality

This trend, say some religious observers, stems in part from disagreements with national church bodies. In the case of Roman Catholics, "much of the decline can be accounted for by changing attitudes on sexuality and authority," says the Rev. Andrew M. Greeley, a research associate at the National Opinion Research Center at the University of Chicago. Some church members, he says, have cited their unhappiness with the 1968 papal encyclical against birth control and with a lack of control by lay people over church spending.

Some researchers and educators also cite a rising "consumerist" mentality in U.S. churches. Like shoppers in a mall or grocery store, younger churchgoers want to see some value for their money, says Elmer L. Towns, vice president of Liberty University in Lynchburg, Va.

Mrs. Ronsvale agrees. "People have changed from stewards into consumers," she says, "and they have brought attitudes to their churches where they are buying specific services—a youth program, a music program."

Churches are also beset by rapidly rising fixed costs, which means that less of the money being dropped in collection plates on weekends is going to governing bodies and to programs outside the church walls. According to the Empty Tomb report, churches' spending on charitable "benevolences"—everything from soup kitchens to missionary work—is shrinking, compared with spending on such in-house items as salaries, building maintenance, utilities and programs for members.

Local church "expenses are up considerably," says Kenneth Inskeep, director of research and planning for the Evangelical Lutheran Church in America. "You take a look at pension costs, they've gone up dramatically; health costs for clergy, they've gone up dramatically; insurance costs, lights, everything."

The report from Empty Tomb, titled "The State of Church Giving Through 1990," is part of a continuing study of the financial records of about 30 Protestant denominations that together represent more than 30 million people. The findings, to be released today, are based on 22 years of records obtained from the National Council of Churches. The council annually collects information from financial officials in a broad array of Protestant denominations.

Some church officials disagree with the study's finding that members—at least in their own denominations—are giving less of their incomes.

"Our research shows that the Presbyterian percentage hasn't decreased for the past 25 years but has remained the same—slightly over 2%" of income, says John M. Coffin, director of stewardship and communication at the Presbyterian Church (USA). "We do have fewer members, which means we do have fewer dollars, but it is a decline in membership and not a decline in income giving."

Similarly, Mr. Inskeep says surveys of Lutherans in the late 1970s and again in 1988 showed giving remaining at about 2.3% of family income.

Appearances Are Deceiving

The decline in giving cited in the Empty Tomb study—from about 3.1% of members' after-tax income in 1968 to 2.6% in 1990—appears modest. However, in 1990, members of the denominations studied gave a total of $12.4 billion to their churches. Had they given at the 1968 rate, that figure would have been almost $2.1 billion higher, Mrs. Ronsvale says.

That trend parallels a pattern among Roman Catholics, as tracked by the National Opinion Research Center. Polling by the center has found that Catholics have been putting less and less in parish collection plates—from about 2.2% of their income 30 years ago to less than 1% currently, according to Father Greeley.

"You could build a lot of new schools, help a lot of old schools, help a lot of missionaries and house a lot of the homeless" with the missing money, Father Greeley says.

J. Thompson Hiller, assistant treasurer of the 2.4 million-member Episcopal Church, says the church hasn't tried to track members' giving as a proportion of their income; but overall donations, he says, have been rising. Still, he says, local parishes are increasingly retaining larger proportions of the money. "So all that is translated to less funding for diocesan and [national] church structures."

Cutting Staff

The findings from Empty Tomb come at a time of increasing financial stress within the top tiers of America's most historic and influential Protestant churches. Earlier this year, Presbyterian officials warned that a decline in donations by member congregations was producing deficits so severe they threatened to wipe out the church's reserves. Since then, the denomination has pledged to reduce its annual $118 million missions budget by about 10% by 1995, a church spokesman says.

Last fall, the Episcopal Church—which has long claimed some of the most generous donors among Christian churches—made the move to reduce its national staff. Since then, the church has also pledged to cut spending on some of its national program 35%.

And this spring, the 5.2 million-member Evangelical Lutheran Church eliminated 15 jobs at its Chicago headquarters, a spokeswoman says.

Traditionally, many clergy, particularly in more conservative denominations, have urged members to tithe, or give a tenth of their incomes, to the church. Indeed, the concept of tithing is as old as Genesis, which tells how Abraham gave a tenth of the spoils of battle to the priest-king Melchilzedek.

But "to a generation that resists any sense of obligation, the tithe is a central symbol they would often choose to ignore," says R. Albert Mohler Jr., editor of the *Christian Index,* a Baptist newspaper published in Atlanta.

Dr. Towns of Liberty University says he tells pastors that churchgoers born since World War II tend not to give in response to appeals to tradition or to guilt. "I think we live in a more materialistic society," he says, adding that younger churchgoers are more likely to choose a church based on what benefits they expect from it, such as family-oriented programs or even "a good handball court."

Among Catholic congregations, adds Father Greeley, "people mind much less giving to the parish than they mind giving money that goes downtown," referring to diocesan headquarters or the Vatican. "They don't trust downtown, whatever 'downtown' might be."

Small Bookstores Struggle in Fight against Goliaths

Mark I. Pinsky, *The Orlando Sentinel,* December 25, 1995

Standing amid stacks of unsold Christian books and boxes of dismantled fixtures, Nancy Logue totaled the cost of a changing marketplace for religious books. Logue's Bible Bookstore was closing its doors after nearly half a century of serving downtown Orlando.

"It's getting more and more difficult to make a living," Logue said, as the store's demise neared last month.

"Although competition is good in a lot of businesses, too much competition in an area is not necessarily profitable," said Logue, whose 6,000-square-foot business was Orlando's oldest continuously operated Christian bookstore.

Industry observers agree that the pressures on locally owned, family-operated Christian bookstores such as Logue's are not unlike those facing all small retailers: population shifts away from downtown areas to the suburbs; the rise of chains, megastores and discounters and glitzy merchandising.

"Closing was a bittersweet time," Logue said. "We liked the store, even though we weren't making a lot of money. It was an enjoyable experience . . . a tool for us to minister to our unsaved neighbors, friends or relatives. That's the goal of the Christian bookstore, to provide material to direct people to Christ."

Although there are no separate figures available for Christian bookstores, adult book sales for all types of independent bookstores have dropped from 58 percent of the market in 1972 to 21.4 percent in 1994. At the same time, chain stores surpassed independents in sales for the first time in 1994, with a 25 percent share, according to the New York-based Book Industry Study Group. Discount and warehouse stores, book clubs and mail-order companies accounted for 44.6 percent.

"Within the next six years, 50 percent of mom-and-pop stores as we know them will not exist," Illinois-based consultant Bob Streight predicts. "During that same period, the sale of Christian products will double."

The demand for religious and inspirational literature has grown enormously in the past decade: Total U.S. sales are estimated at more than $1 billion annually. Crossover titles such as "Angels," "Embraced by the Light," "Course in Miracles," "The Celestine Prophecy" and "Where Angels Walk" regularly appear on best-seller lists. Publishing giant Random House established its own Christian subsidiary, Moorings, in 1994.

This growth has been fueled in part by the surge in evangelical Protestantism, although most Christian retailers say they either carry or will order a wide spectrum of Christian books. Christian fiction, including romances, mysteries and a novel by Pat Robertson are especially popular.

The American Booksellers Association set up its first religion section at this year's convention. *Publishers Weekly,* the bible of the publishing industry, has launched a separate, twice-monthly newsletter on religious books.

Book sales have increased threefold in the past 15 years, according to Bill Anderson, president of the Christian Booksellers Association, another trade group. These books have won readers because they address "real-life issues from a Bible-based standpoint," he said.

The CBA publishes a slick, thick monthly, *Bookstore Journal,* packed with advertising. The religious best-seller lists put out by the ABA and CBA are carried in many newspapers.

But as the size of the retail pie has increased in religious publishing, the number of pie lovers has grown as well, and some big eaters have elbowed their way to the table.

Megastore discounters such as Borders, Bookstar, Crown and Barnes and Noble have intensified competition for the religious market. A Georgia-based company, Disciples, has opened a 25,000-square-foot megastore in Birmingham, Ala., and is planning 20 more stores of similar size. Family Bookstores, Inc. a chain of 175 Christian stores whose outlets average 5,000-6,000 square feet, is also experimenting with megastores. Bypassing retailers entirely, Christian Book Distributors markets to church members through a direct-mail catalog.

"Unfortunately it's going to be increasingly difficult for independents to make it," said Les Dietzman, president of Family Bookstores, which has stores in Altamonte Springs and the Florida Mall.

"Just like in other industries, it's only the biggest and the best that are going to hang in there against the secular stores and the better operators in the business," said Dietzman, whose privately held company was founded by religious publisher Zondervan.

Bookstore chains are not the only threat to independent retailers.

In its stores across the South, Wal-Mart has set up displays featuring "inspirational best-sellers." Warehouse stores such as Costco, Sam's

Club and Price Club have gotten into the Bible business, provoking mixed reaction among independent retailers.

Marie Smith of Best Friends Retreat Christian Book Store in Union Park said warehouse stores are retailing Bibles for less than it costs her 800-square-foot store to buy them.

"Our customers come back because we try to get the very best price we can," Smith said, and that is undercut by the sale-priced Bibles.

But some bookstore owners say warehouses serve a beneficial purpose, whetting the appetite of consumers for Christian books that can be found only in retail stores.

Roger Long, owner of Long's Christian Book & Music Store in Orlando, sees this brighter side to competition from warehouse stores.

"When the person wants more [inspirational reading], they're going to seek out a Christian bookstore," Long said. "In some sense it might help long term. Short term, sure, we lose a few bucks."

Mike Jolly, manager of the Baptist Book Store in Herndon Plaza in Orlando, agrees, saying the warehouses are "creating more awareness in the general market for what's available. It almost works in our favor."

Jolly's 5,000-square-foot store is operated by the 15 million-member Southern Baptist Convention. Four of the nonprofit chain's 63 stores are in Florida.

As a subsidiary of the SBC's publishing arms, the Sunday School Board, the Baptist chain enjoys a competitive edge: Popular Sunday-school lesson materials are retailed in its stores at the same price they are sold wholesale to competing bookstores.

Experts say that some of the difficulty independent retailers find themselves in is their own fault.

"Independent Christian retailers have been somewhat self-serving . . . and have not been aggressive in reaching out to the general market-place," Illinois consultant Streight said. He has helped design more than 400 Christian bookstores, including Long's and a 1,900-square-foot store at Calvary Assembly Church in Winter Park.

In order to survive, store owners will have to adapt to the changed retail environment, with increased selection, night hours, big, safe parking lots and upscale ambience.

"This is what you're going to have to do if you want to survive," Streight lectures clients. "Or else fold and die."

Those independent retailers that have survived have done so by adapting, moving to much larger quarters, diversifying product offerings, adding stores or joining networks to increase buying clout.

Successful Christian independents have set up cappuccino bars and frequent-buyer programs, adding music, videos, apparel and toys to their stocks.

It is no longer uncommon for Christian stores to feature CD listening stations and banks of television monitors playing videos, along with racks of books. Most of all, they emphasize personal service.

Long's Christian Book & Music Store, in business for 30 years, is one of those family-owned independents that have recognized the marketplace's new realty.

"This business was driven by mom-and-pop operations a decade ago," Long said. "Times are more competitive now, and we have been forced to be more aggressive. The people who don't get more aggressive are going to lose out."

So three years ago, Long built his 11,5000-square-foot superstore on Edgewater Drive, doubling his floor space.

He installed many of the features consultants such as Streight recommended, added several of his own, and he has never looked back.

Two months ago, Long took the next step, investing $60,000 in a 30-seat coffee bar called The Gathering Place, offering cappuccino and lattes, croissants and pastries.

"It's one of the best things I've ever done," Long said.

"It adds a whole other dimension of atmosphere that you couldn't find otherwise. People feel at home."

Long says the changes, though costly, have paid off.

"All I know is that my business is going up and up and up," he said, noting that sales on Friday after Thanksgiving set a record.

From her own perspective of 20 years in the Christian book business. Nancy Logue said if she and her husband had decided to stay in the business, they probably would have gone in the same direction as Roger Long.

"I don't know what all the answers are," she said.

"If I did, we might still be running the store. The industry has changed so much. In order to compete, you have to change your idea from what the Christian bookstore used to be.

"The ultimate focus point has got to be ministry," she said.

"That's what started the Christian bookstores, and that's what the owners and managers want to continue to do . . . The real challenge is to provide material that we need, and to also make a decent living. It takes a real juggling act to do that."

27

Insights into Interpretations

Surveys of religion reporting in recent decades have documented what others have been saying anecdotally as well: That news about religion has become longer, more in-depth and better written than before the 1980s. Other studies show many religion reporters have degrees from seminaries or have taken courses in religious studies. And beginning in the 1990s, some of the nation's most prestigious journalism programs began offering master's degree programs or individual courses uniting training in religion and journalism.

One type of religion story that exemplifies the necessity for in-depth, specialized knowledge is the theology story. Often complicated and heavily nuanced, a finely written story about a person's core system of beliefs does more than just enlighten. It can reflect tensions within an institution or emerging faith systems. It can also help explain motivations for actions.

The interpretation of a faith's sacred texts can often be a source of division among the faithful; that is certainly true among Protestants, whose biblical views are key to determining where along a continuum from mainline to fundamentalist a person belongs. One of the persistent stories in recent decades has been the discovery of ancient sacred manuscripts or efforts to reinterpret them. Reprinted in this chapter is a story by John Dart of the *Los Angeles Times*—one of the first written about the Jesus Seminar, a group of scholars attempting to evaluate the true words of Jesus based on biblical texts. More recent treatments of the story include Gustav Niebuhr's December 25, 1994, story about the "New Quest for Historical Jesus" in the *New York Times*.

The second example in this chapter shows how what could have been a mundane assignment—a story for Martin Luther King Jr. Day observances —wound up as an in-depth look at the theology of the slain civil rights leader. Richard Scheinin's story for the *San Jose Mercury News* is an example of a profile that goes beyond the simple details of King's life to illuminate the core beliefs that motivated his leadership in the civil rights struggle.

Perhaps taking their lead from the struggles for racial equality in the

1960s, women began calling for equal rights in pay, job opportunities, education and leadership. The major faiths were not untouched by the feminist revolution. Groups with male-only religious leaders began to authorize and ordain women as clergy, rabbis, cantors, deacons and bishops. The new feminism also required a reappraisal of some faiths' core beliefs, some theologians argued. When people started wondering, "Is God a She?" John Dart wrote one of the first lengthy discussions on the topic for the December 12, 1970, issue of the *Los Angeles Times.* Gayle White's updated version from the *Atlanta Journal-Constitution* appeared May 22, 1994, and includes a succinct history of the movement.

In 1994, mostly mainline Protestant women gathered in Minneapolis to celebrate the femininity in their faith. But some members in the denominations that helped pay for the conference said participants went too far. The controversy that ensued from the now-famous "Re-Imagining" conference is the subject of Ann Rodgers-Melnick's piece from the *Pittsburgh Post-Gazette,* one of more than a dozen stories she wrote after the event. It is an example of how theological differences can infect existing wounds, sometimes leading to schism.

The intertwining of liturgy, song and theology is seen in the carefully crafted story on Kol Nidre that appeared in the *Orange County Register.* Writer Carol McGraw uses a holiday—Yom Kippur—as the background for this look at a melody that represents the essence behind the somber Jewish holiday. Rather than being a dry, cerebral treatment of forgiveness and atonement, McGraw uses description, history and events to weave a compelling story.

The depth and complexity of stories explaining a group or person's theology is matched by the tough ethical deliberations surrounding daily choices of life and death in the medical profession. Former *Associated Press* reporter David Briggs tackled the issue of medical ethics in a four-part series entitled "Do No Harm." One part of that series is reprinted as the final story in this chapter. Not only is it an excellent example of an ethics story but it also reflects the breadth now found in religion reporting.

Bible Scholars Vote: What Did Jesus Say or Not Say?

John Dart, *Los Angeles Times,* November 11, 1985

ST. MEINRAD, Ind.—Thirty Bible scholars passed a ballot box around the table, dropping in colored pegs or beads—red for yes, pink for maybe, gray for probably not and black for no.

They were voting on which sayings in the New Testament's Sermon on the Mount probably go back to Jesus himself and which were put into his mouth by gospel writers or church tradition.

The scholars were to base their votes on what the weight of biblical critical scholarship says and on their own research on the historical Jesus. The group, which includes some of the top American specialists on the New Testament, eventually will consider all of the roughly 500 sayings attributed to Jesus in the New Testament and non-biblical sources, some of which have been discovered and translated in relatively recent years.

"Ignorance of the Uninformed"

If the idea of voting on Jesus' sayings sounds provocative, that is precisely the intent of organizers of the so-called Jesus Seminar, a five-to six-year project just under way. New Testament scholar Robert W. Funk, the principal organizer, said he wants to seize the initiative from television evangelists who, in his view, deal in pious platitudes. He also wants to counteract apocalyptic writers who purport to describe a coming Armageddon—writers, he said, who "have too long played on the fears and ignorance of the uninformed."

Funk wants to acquaint the public with mainstream biblical scholarship and their findings about the most likely teachings of Jesus, even though the results may disturb Christians.

The balloting, conducted at the Roman Catholic Saint Meinrad Archabbey and Seminary here in southern Indiana recently, amounted to bad news for the beatitudes and other sayings:

> • Blackballed with virtually no discussion was one of Christendom's favorite beatitudes, or statements of happiness: "Blessed are the peacemakers, for they shall be called sons of God." Simi-

larly, "the meek who shall inherit the earth" got only six pink-red
votes out of 30 cast.

• Only three of a dozen "blessings" and "woes" in the Gospels of
Matthew and Luke were deemed to have derived from Jesus, and
a fourth ("blessed are you when men hate you . . .") produced an
even split after some debate.

Three Beatitudes Pass

Winning favor were the first three beatitudes as found in the Gospel
of Luke, "Blessed are you poor . . . you that hunger . . . you that weep."

Also, scholars felt the historical Jesus probably did advise followers
to "turn the other cheek" and to give money without promise of its return. The advice on giving was said to be best represented in the Gospel
of Thomas, an apocryphal text discovered 40 years ago.

Funk said it is understandable that the findings and working assumptions in biblical critical studies sound so strange to the average Christian. And he is trying to convince New Testament scholars that they
"have not fulfilled their obligations to report their work to a broader
public."

They "have limited their pronouncements to the classroom or buried
their considered judgments in scientific journals and technical jargon,"
he said. "They have hesitated to broadcast the assured results of histori-
cal-critical scholarship out of fear of public controversy and political
reprisal."

That hesitation also comes from fear of being accused by their academic peers of "popularizing or sensationalizing," according to Marvin
Meyer of Chapman College in Orange, one of the additional 40 seminar
members who keep in touch by mail. "As a result, much of our research
is kept within the guild, in discussions among ourselves."

All four New Testament Gospels—Mark, Matthew, Luke and John—
were written in the last third of the 1st century, about 40 years or more
after Jesus' Crucifixion. Though church tradition says the apostles
Matthew and John wrote those Gospels, mainstream biblical specialists
doubt that any gospel writer knew Jesus during his lifetime.

Differences in Passage

The gospel writers, they say, were dependent on written and oral accounts that had already undergone theological changes reflecting the
needs or expectations of believers. Attempts to peel back those layers

have continued, off and on, for 100 years, but rarely do advances in the field receive wide notice in churches.

To be sure, many churchgoers know that Matthew and Luke differ on the contents of Jesus' Sermon on the Mount. Some also know that most biblical commentators say that those two gospel authors based their accounts on a common source of Jesus' sayings, a collection that scholars label "Q."

But how many church members are also told that, according to scholarly consensus, the author of Luke added four "woes" (to the rich, the satiated, and so forth) as counterpoints to his four "blesseds?" Catholic scholar Joseph Fitzmyer, not a member of the Jesus Seminar, agrees with this view, citing "the heavy incidence of Lukan vocabulary in these verses" in his *Anchor Bible Commentary on Luke.*

In addition, liberal scholarship has maintained for decades that gospel writers had Jesus say and do things that hark back to Old Testament language and deeds. Matthew's beatitude about the meek inheriting the earth echoes Psalms 37:11 and the "blessed pure in heart who shall see God" may have been inspired by Psalms 24:3-4.

Many scholars say Matthew's unique beatitudes are betrayed as his creations by the author's tendency to give sayings a spiritual cast (as in, "blessed are the poor in spirit . . .").

An evangelical Protestant scholar, Robert H. Gundry of Westmont College in Santa Barbara, maintained in a commentary on Matthew a few years ago that Jesus was not the source for all of the beatitudes in Matthew. Gundry's book, which said Matthew's "creativeness" was similar to Jewish commentary techniques of that era, eventually got him kicked out of the Evangelical Theological Society.

Evangelical's Reactions

The Gundry affair has sent up warning flags among evangelical Protestants, however. The Oct. 18 issue of *Christianity Today* quotes a panel of evangelical scholars who backed a limited use of biblical criticism to account for different descriptions of similar events. But the panel stopped short of saying that Bible writers invented events that did not occur.

Editor Kenneth Kantzer seconded the panel, declaring that the biblical authors always tell the truth. "If they say Jesus said something, he really did say it, whether or not we have the exact words he used," Kantzer wrote.

However, in the same issue, New Testament Prof. Robert Thomas of Talbot Theological Seminary in La Mirada disapproved even of the cautious approval of analytical techniques given by the panel. Thomas said historical criticism endangers the premise that the Bible is errorless. "When the critical, subjective element intervenes, doubt about the historical accuracy of Matthew is inevitable," Thomas wrote.

The Jesus Seminar has at least two evangelicals in its ranks—R. Alan Culpepper of Southern Baptist Theological Seminary in Louisville, Ky., and John Lown of the Nazarene-related Point Loma College in San Diego.

The implications for faith and theology were rarely discussed in the weekend sessions here; biblical studies normally leave those matters to pastors and theologians. Nevertheless, the scholars who met here usually became interested in pursuing the historical Jesus because of their links with the church.

"Origins with Jesus"

"I am seeking an understanding of the Jesus tradition, of what must have been done and said to generate such immediate diversity of interpretation," said DePaul University's John Dominic Crossan, an influential voice in the Jesus Seminar. "But I do not really know how to comprehend the tradition without asking also about its origins with Jesus."

Similarly, Karen King of Occidental College, the lone female charter member of the seminar, said she is less interested in the historical Jesus than in how the traditions developed. King said some Jesus Seminar members believe it is impossible to get a full, or even adequate, picture of Jesus.

"Our motives are not to be destructive of faith, nor does anyone think we could be," she cautioned. "But scholars do not want to sacrifice intellectual integrity for a naive approach to the texts."

Yet, if the seminar catches the ear of the church, confidence about what Jesus probably taught could be shaken.

Sayings in which Jesus depicts himself as the suffering Son of Man destined to return in the future are likely to be voted down by the Jesus Seminar. Many of those apocalyptic sayings are increasingly regarded in biblical critical circles as additions to the earliest layers of tradition about Jesus.

Other sayings unlikely to pass muster, based on past scholarship, include the "seven last words" attributed to the dying Jesus on the cross and the calls by Jesus to preach the gospel to all nations. "Jesus did not anticipate a mission to the Gentiles," Funk said.

Likely to Be Blackballed

Even a favorite Jesus verse of ecumenical church leaders—Jesus' prayer that all believers "may all be one"—is likely to be blackballed, Funk said. It occurs in the Gospel of John (17:21), which scholars consider the most theologically creative of the four New Testament Gospels.

Funk admits that scholars, often unaccustomed to defending their conclusions and methods to lay audiences, "are going to look bad when people say we don't believe in the Bible."

But not all people will react negatively, contended seminar member Hal Taussig, pastor of a United Methodist Church in Philadelphia. He said he sees "a new segment that really needs good, objective information about Jesus" and "feels threatened by religious fundamentalism."

Moreover, simple integrity calls for seminary-trained pastors to pass along the findings of biblical critical scholarship to church members, said Taussig, who teaches New Testament in the summer at the School of Theology at Claremont.

Taussig said, however, that denominational leaders "don't see that as a good strategy," and he conceded that churches that do adopt that approach might lose more than they gain in membership and contributions.

For many clergy, disputes over the historical Jesus are fruitless exercises, whereas efforts to apply the tradition about Jesus to people's lives is seen as meaningful.

"Passed the Test of Time"

The Rev. Robert Schuller recently preached at his Crystal Cathedral in Garden Grove on the "Be Happy Attitudes," also the title of his latest book. The upbeat advice from Schuller is based on the Sermon on the Mount, which the television minister says is composed of classic sentences that have "passed the test of time" by transforming depression into positive attitudes.

Nonetheless, the field of biblical studies, like other research disciplines, has undergone a "knowledge explosion" triggered by manuscript discoveries and new methods of critical analysis.

A relatively new source for Jesus' sayings is the narrativeless Gospel of Thomas, part of the Nag Hammadi Library discovered in Egypt in 1945 and translated widely in the 1960s. A straw vote taken here showed that participants unanimously believe that its versions of parables, proverbs and other sayings are independent of and not rewritten from the New Testament Gospels—a major swing from previously divided opinions on Thomas.

The Jesus Seminar hopes to publish a Jesus Bible with the "authentic" sayings printed in red ink, the "inauthentic" in black, and perhaps the gradations of probability in pink and gray ink.

Will anything be left to put into the red? Scholars usually favor those teachings that are attested by more than one source and sayings that are different from the commonplace observations or admonitions in 1st Century Judaism, Greco-Roman culture and the fledgling Christian churches.

A solid consensus exists that Jesus taught about the "kingdom" that his disciples were to enter; thus, many parables told about the nature of the kingdom, and the requirements of discipleship are good candidates, scholars say without hazarding guesses at the percentage likely to be published in red.

The seminar plans to take about five years to consider the nearly 500 items—33 parables, 290 aphorisms, 81 dialogues and 90 stories.

The Reverend: He Was a Preacher

And King's Dream, His Words, His Leadership All Grew Firmly on That Foundation

Richard Scheinin, *San Jose Mercury News,* January 15, 1994

> *In the quiet recesses of my heart, I am fundamentally a clergyman, a Baptist preacher. This is my being and my heritage, for I am also the son of a Baptist preacher, the grandson of a Baptist preacher and the great-grandson of a Baptist preacher.*
> —Martin Luther King, Jr., August 1965

In February 1954, more than a decade before he spoke those words and nearly two years before his emergence as a national leader, the young Martin Luther King Jr. gave a sermon to a large black Baptist congregation in Detroit.

At the time, he was a 25-year-old doctoral candidate in theology, an intellectual immersed in the philosophies of white, liberal Protestant social reformers. But with his palpable presence and powerful voice, young King came on like the son of a Southern black Baptist preacher, holding forth on the majesty of a God he talked to and prayed to and believed to be an active, present force in history, guiding the powerless in their struggles to transform society.

"I'm here to say to you this morning that some things are right and some things are wrong," said King, born 65 years ago today. "Eternally so, absolutely so. It's wrong to hate. . . . It's wrong in America, it's wrong in Germany, it's wrong in Russia, it's wrong in China! It was wrong in 2000 B.C., and it's wrong in 1954 A.D. It always has been wrong, and it always will be wrong! . . . Some things in this universe are absolute. The God of the universe made it so."

The speech, to be published this spring in the second volume of the "Martin Luther King Jr. Papers," provides insight into the spiritual style and faith of a man whose religious roots have at times been obscured in the quarter century since his assassination.

It sometimes seems that only a handful of stock images of King have survived the years: King in the Birmingham jail, or marching for voting rights in Selma, facing the police cattle prods and whips. Our media memory focuses on Washington, D.C., where he speaks about his dreams for black people and the nation in front of a crowd of more than 200,000 at the steps of the Lincoln Memorial. The future Nobel Peace Prize winner wears a crisp suit and tie. He is Doctor King, an icon like Lincoln himself, largely stripped of his notable religious heritage.

"He's portrayed as a secular leader who used religion as a prop or as a tool when it came in handy," says Stewart Burns, an editor of the King Papers and Stanford University historian. "In terms of today, Jesse Jackson might be an extreme example of what I'm getting at here. I see Jackson as someone who uses his ministerial trappings as needed. I don't see him as very spiritual, and I think that's the typical characterization you get of King these days."

But those who really knew King understand that his persona has been distorted over time.

"I don't know anything in Martin's life that he loved more than delivering a sermon Sunday morning from a pulpit," says the Rev. Hosea Williams, a longtime colleague of King's. "Come Monday morning, he would be out in the streets—as Jesus Christ did—putting flesh on the bones of his sermon, making it a reality. That's why people believed in that man so and supported him so. As we used to say in the movement, King, as a minister, talked that talk, but he also walked that walk. When

I used to listen to him speak from the pulpit in all his eloquence and in-
tellectualism, I could sense the impending confrontation in the street."

For more than 20 years, academics have emphasized the centrality of
King's spirituality and religious beliefs in his political leadership. But
they have offered shifting definitions of King's religiosity.

Early biographers emphasized the impact of modern white theologians such as Walter Rauschenbush, the Christian social gospel philosopher whose writings King studied in graduate school. King also studied
the works of Christian realist theologian Reinhold Niebuhr, who argued
that in a world that's rife with social evil, ministers must at times consider forceful action.

After King's death, many academics tended to argue that King's commitment to social justice could be understood only in the context of his
exposure to these thinkers. Certainly, they had their effect on King, who
may have viewed Gandhian non-violence as a tool to solve the dilemma
posed by Niebuhr: how to effectively fight social injustice in ways that
are morally pure.

But in the past few years, an increasing number of academics, many
of them black, have taken to studying King's early sermons and correspondence. A new picture of the civil rights leader has emerged, tracing
his activism directly to the black Baptist church.

This view of King states that a black religious vision of social justice—merely reinforced by Rauschenbush and others—was the lifelong
catalyst for King's political action. Why did it take so long for academics to examine King's roots in the black church? Lewis V. Baldwin, the
Vanderbilt University author of "There is a Balm in Gilead: The Cultural
Roots of Martin Luther King," attributes it to "the inherent racism of
scholarship . . . the longstanding notion in academia, going back to the
1960s, that the black family and church are dysfunctional institutions
that couldn't possibly have produced such a strong man as King."

King is now widely seen as a transmitting force who both reaches
back to the optimistic longings of the black church in slavery days and
sets the stage for the emergence, after King's death, of a contemporary
black theology. That theology places a "radical emphasis on the justice
and transformative aspects of the Christian Gospel," says Dwight Hopkins, professor of religious and ethnic studies at Santa Clara University.

"The whole idea that the black church should leave its sanctuary and engage in massive civil disobedience in the '50s and '60s was revolutionary. The idea that the central message of the Christian gospel was to take to the streets—this was revolutionary, and that's what King brought."

As the second volume of papers is prepared for publication by Stanford University's Martin Luther King Jr. Papers Project, King scholars there and around the country are poring over the long-ignored texts of King's early sermons before black congregations, mostly in the South.

In those texts and in letters written to black ministers, says Vanderbilt's Baldwin, "King emerges as a man nurtured in the black church and the black family. He tended to use the black style of preaching. He would fling his hands and stand on his tiptoes and actually, in some cases, would sing the sermon—it takes on a mournful, singing quality, which he knew deeply inspired people.

"He was deeply rooted in that tradition," says Baldwin, who has listened to tape recordings of early sermons. "The whole idea of the personal relationship with God, of a personal relationship with Jesus Christ—that goes back to the days when slaves spoke of walking with God and talking with God. The sense of Christian optimism, that justice and the righteousness of God will ultimately win out over injustice and evil—this comes out of the slave spirituals of the 18th and 19th centuries. The notion that God will ultimately bring together the disjointed elements of reality into a harmonious whole—this is all part of the black church tradition, going back to slavery days. And of course, King drank deeply from that well."

But to the popular mind, much of this is lost. How ironic that King, whose birthday is celebrated as a national holiday on Monday, should be so yanked out of the religious context that forged him. After all, his role as preacher is what allowed him to originally build a base of support to lead the Montgomery, Ala., bus boycott in 1955 and 1956. Without his religious base there would have been no desegregated bus lines, no voting rights, no social progress—and King knew it.

"One of the interesting things to me about King is the longer you study him, the more you recognize his conviction that the underpinnings of democratic thought are as religious as they are political," says Taylor Branch, author of "Parting the Waters: America in the King Years 1954-63," which won the Pulitzer Prize in 1989.

"We commonly think of democracy as a concept that goes back to secular philosophers. By contrast, King said that the origins of democracy go back to the Hebrew prophets who were the first people to teach that all souls are equal in the eyes of God. That idea—'all souls are equal'—leads to the idea that 'all votes are equal.' And when you put the two of them together, you have an immense chamber of meaning that is both religious and secular, and that's where King operated."

———————

There was nothing unusual about King, a preacher, operating in the political sphere. Nat Turner, leader of the best-known slave uprising in the South, was a Baptist preacher. Black churches were stations on the Underground Railroad.

King's great-grandfather, Willis Williams, was a slave preacher who belonged to a bi-racial church in Georgia before the Civil War. King's grandfather, A.D. Williams, was a Baptist preacher who led a boycott against the *Georgian,* an Atlanta newspaper that published racial epithets. King's mother, Alberta King, was organist and choir director at Atlanta's Ebenezer Baptist Church.

And his father, Martin Luther King Sr., was Ebenezer's preacher. "Daddy King" was a widely admired leader of Atlanta voting-rights drives in the 1930s and '40s who refused to ride segregated elevators and spearheaded a drive to equalize salaries for black and white school teachers.

King Jr. belonged "to the social milieu of the African-American preacher," reiterates Pete Holloran, an editor of the first two volumes of Stanford's King Papers. "Even his jokes were about other preachers. He was incredibly skilled at mimicking preachers. Preachers were role models for his lifestyle and political beliefs—that ministers should not just preach the Gospel, but preach the social gospel."

"His early memories of growing up in the Depression were of people being in bread lines," says Clayborne Carson, director of the King Papers Project at Stanford, which will run to a projected 14 volumes. "And in the midst of that, the church was involved in programs to feed and clothe the needy. As I imagine it, Ebenezer must have been something like what you see today at Glide Memorial Church in San Francisco . . . feeding the homeless. Ministers had to set an example for the people in terms of political awareness and action. And King was part of the new generation that started to link that Baptist tradition to the white theology of the social gospel.

"There was a tension," Carson says, "because going off to predominantly white seminaries, as King did in 1948, kind of separated him. But it also gave King new tools to take the African-American social gospel into the modern age. He was very much extending his father's ministry. . . . What he was suggesting is that the correct role of the church is to always be in tension with society and to always be the corrective to social evil."

King has typically been portrayed as a religious liberal who broke away early from his father's literal reading of the Bible.

In "An Autobiography of Religious Development," a short essay written as a graduate student in 1950, King recalled how he "shocked" his Sunday school class by denying the bodily resurrection of Jesus. He described how "the shackles of fundamentalism were removed from my body" during his undergraduate training at Atlanta's predominantly black Morehouse College. He stated that underlying the "legends and myths" of the Bible were "powerful truths," even as he concluded that "final intellectual certainty about God is impossible."

In the essay, King laments never having had "an abrupt conversion experience," but ends with the simple statement that "religion for me is life."

The conversion may have occurred during the Montgomery bus boycott of 1955-'56, when King was unable to sleep one night. "His life was being threatened," recounts Burns, the Stanford historian who is also author of "A People's Charter: The Pursuit of Rights in America," "and he sat down at the kitchen table and he really felt more and more that he was carrying out God's will. I think he felt absolutely no doubt that he was acting as God's instrument and he knew he was going to be killed. He just felt that his life was not his own anymore, and he was totally dedicated to this cause which he never really wanted to carry forward. . . . To King, God really stood for justice and black people were a chosen people just like the Israelites. Through their liberation, they would be the agents for liberating the rest of humanity."

In his own mind, King was "an evangelical liberal. That's how he described himself" for most of his life, says Baldwin. And his sermons reverberated with some of the same fiery language that infuse the oratory in many evangelical churches.

"He didn't leave out redemption or the blood of the lamb—no, he didn't neglect that," says Santa Clara's Hopkins. "He felt himself—and this is my interpretation, because I don't think he would have ever made such a comparison—in the trajectory of Moses and the Old Testament prophets. 'Thus saith the Lord!' And then there's a passage in the New Testament in the Book of Luke that's relevant to King: 'The spirit of the Lord is upon me, because He has anointed me to preach good news to the poor. . . . to set at liberty those who are oppressed.'

"That passage from Luke is what contemporary black theology is based on," Hopkins says, "but King said it first: 'If the Gospel means anything, it means helping the poor beggar on life's highway.' He said it's all right for preachers to talk about golden slippers and white robes over yonder, but people on this side of the River Jordan need shoes and robes right now. And late in his life, when he went through such a revolutionary change, he said, 'I'm going with the poor and if that means dying, I'm going that way.'"

Heresy Charge Leveled after Women Recast Church Imagery

Ann Rodgers-Melnick, *Pittsburgh Post-Gazette,* March 6, 1994

Our maker Sophia, we are women in your image. With the hot blood of our wombs we give form to new life . . . Sophia, Creator God, let your milk and honey flow.

With that litany at a November conference in Minnesota, 2,200 Protestant and Catholic women ignited a furor that has led to accusations of heresy against some female national staff members of the Presbyterian Church (USA) and the United Methodist Church.

Supporters of the conference—including most who attended—say the accusations are meant to stop women from shaping Christian imagery in ways that white European males have always done.

"Re-Imagining . . . God, Community, The Church" was organized by ecumenical groups in Minnesota to honor the World Council of Churches' Decade of Churches in Solidarity with Women. Many Protestant denominations promoted it and subsidized the attendance of women from 29 nations.

Major protest has erupted only in two denominations with large, organized networks of theological conservatives. Good News, a United Methodist group, and the Presbyterian Layman sent reporters to the conference, then publicized it churchwide through their magazine and newspaper.

The most serious accusations involve prayers to "Sophia" and a workshop that challenged basic teachings about Jesus. *Sophia* is Greek for wisdom. The biblical Book of Proverbs praises wisdom, personified as a woman. The Apostle Paul cited that passage in reference to Christ. Thus, some Christian feminists use "Sophia" as an alternate name for "Jesus."

Critics claim that this has evolved into a denial of Jesus' historic reality and has led to worship of a pagan goddess Sophia.

The Rev. Richard Wolling, whose Beverly Heights United Presbyterian Church has stopped paying its assessment to the headquarters of the Presbyterian Church (USA) to protest the conference, isn't satisfied with any explanation he has heard from headquarters.

"No one has said to my satisfaction that they were identifying Sophia with Jesus Christ, which is what the Scriptures do. I have an uneasy feeling that Sophia is something other than the person of Jesus Christ," Wolling said.

Accusations of heresy have also been directed at a workshop dealing with Jesus' atonement for sin, a central doctrine of the Catholic, Protestant and Orthodox churches. In her workshop, Delores Williams, professor of theology at Union Theological Seminary in New York City, said it was wrong to teach that Jesus died for humanity's sins.

Substitutionary death is offensive because black women have been oppressed by substitution, Williams said. The idea that Jesus was their substitute on the cross justifies black women's forced substitution as "mammies" for white babies and sex surrogates for white men, she said.

"I don't think we need a theory of atonement at all," Williams said. "I think Jesus came for life and to show us something about life and living together and what life was all about. Atonement has to do so much with death. I don't think we need folks hanging on crosses and blood dripping and weird stuff."

Williams noted that her interpretation conflicted with the writing of the Apostle Paul. But because Paul condoned slavery, "black women have . . . historical license for ignoring Paul," she said.

Our sweet Sophia, we are women in your image; With nectar between our thighs we invite a lover . . . with our warm body fluids we remind the world of its pleasures and sensations . . .

As the Rev. Christiane Dutton, associate pastor of Providence United Presbyterian Church in Brighton Heights, uttered those words at the Re-Imagining conference, they struck her as "a little far out."

Then she pictured the battered women she counsels at a shelter and their need to hear that their bodies are precious. She remembers a 19th century evangelist who had instructed women to "cross your legs and close the gate to hell."

She began to say the litany with some conviction.

Three months later, when the Pittsburgh Presbytery demanded a theological investigation of the conference, debate was cut off while Dutton stood waiting to speak.

"I felt invisible, standing on the floor, not being seen. That is what the conference was about: so many invisible women," she said. "The presbytery's discussion was led mostly by men . . . They were not at the conference. It was a beautiful experience and they make it sound like a crime."

Objections to the conference run in proportion to the contributions of each church's bureaucracy.

The Evangelical Lutheran Church in America Women's Commission gave $4,000 to help female seminary students attend and has received a few hostile inquires about it, according to its national office.

The United Methodist Church Women's Division spent $30,500 to send 56 national Women's Division directors, staff members, regional vice presidents and some additional Minnesota Methodists. That has prompted more than 1,000 cards and letters of complaint. The evangelical group Good News has asked the Methodist bishops to investigate and eliminate heresy in the Women's Division.

The largest uproar ensued in the Presbyterian Church (USA), whose Women's Ministry Unit gave $66,000 from undesignated gifts of congregations. The director of the Women's Ministry Unit was on the Re-Imagining steering committee.

More than 100 congregations and presbyteries, including Pittsburgh Presbytery, petitioned church leaders to investigate the conference and the role of some staff members at denominational headquarters in Louisville, Ky., in planning it. The Rev. R. Leslie Holmes, pastor of the

First Presbyterian Church of Pittsburgh, joined nine pastors nationwide in a letter threatening church legal action if heretical staff members were not fired.

In response last month, the denomination's General Assembly Council affirmed basic church doctrine and authorized a review of personnel policies regarding study leave and employee actions that contradict church teachings. The council also sent a rare pastoral letter to every congregation, saying "our unity in Christ does not demand uniformity."

Few critics, if any, say they are satisfied.

We celebrate the sweat that pours from us during our labors . . . our oneness with earth and water.

As Marjorie Cavett, a Bible teacher at Sunset Hills Presbyterian Church in Mt. Lebanon, listened to tapes of the conference, she considered leaving the Presbyterian Church (USA). Instead, she organized a protest. Both her congregation and its women's group put a hold on giving to national headquarters until they receive a satisfactory response.

"This is paganism in its worst form," she said. "A liberal feminist movement [in church headquarters] no longer represents the grass-roots women in the Presbyterian denomination."

No one who joins an ecumenical gathering should expect to agree with everything said there, said Sally Ernst of Bethel Park, immediate past national president of United Methodist Women, who attended Re-Imagining. Her United Methodist convictions "kept me from feeling threatened, even though I did experience some new things," she said.

"I think all the fallout is coming from the issue of whether women have the legitimate right of participation in the church at levels of theology and theological reflection . . . It's a case of orthodoxy against the evolving images of God that we have not all come to know yet or to understand or accept."

But Bishop George Bashore of the United Methodist Conference of Western Pennsylvania believes the conference exceeded the boundaries of legitimate Christian ecumenism, though he is not convinced it was truly heretical.

"I think expression [at the conference] moved from ecumenism to inter-religious and inter-philosophical conversations," he said.

Speculative theology may be legitimately discussed in a workshop but should not be the basis for ecumenical Christian worship, he said. Some women who attended told him that they felt like captives who had been manipulated into worship that troubled their conscience, he said.

But "it is a bit frustrating as a male even to respond to your questions because . . . somebody will just say, 'You see, the ones who are objecting are male,'" he said.

Christiane Dutton's husband, Donald, pastor of Providence United Presbyterian Church and one of 80 men at the conference, knew he was not invoking a pagan goddess. He joined in greeting each speaker with a song of invitation to Sophia.

"We understood it as an invitation to people who had wisdom to share that with us," he said.

Many church leaders say the fault for the controversy lies with the conservative groups Good News and Presbyterian Layman for blowing the conference out of context and proportion.

"I think we have repeatedly seen a kind of over-reacting that comes from the same quarter that, in fact, sort of seems to be seeking to damage the church," said Jean Kennedy, a former moderator of the Pittsburgh Presbytery who is running for moderator of the Presbyterian Church (USA).

"From what I have read about the intentions of this international ecumenical meeting, and what I have heard from those who did participate, no one felt it was worthy of being called heresy . . . Certainly it was on the boundary, and certainly it was intended to be," she said.

But strong objections are coming from people far outside the constituency of the Presbyterian Layman and Good News. The Rev. John Lolla, pastor of Plum Creek Presbyterian Church, is a theological moderate who is active in inter-faith dialogue.

"I think the church has been afraid to use the word pagan or heretical. But I hear more and more clergy beginning to use that type of language to describe ministry," he said. "I think there is a growing consensus among people who have been rank and file church leaders that there is an extreme group that is out to promote its own issues even at the expense of the church. And that group is not concerned about preserving the unity of the church, nor is it necessarily concerned about preserving the identity of the church around the lordship of Christ."

The Rev. Alice Petersen, associate pastor at Beulah Presbyterian Church in Churchill, feels caught in the middle.

"As a biblical feminist, I'm annoyed at the whole thing. I'm annoyed at the radical feminists for overkill and for shooting themselves in the foot. Because when they shoot themselves in the foot, they shoot my foot, too.

"And I'm annoyed at the Layman. While I think there is some cause for concern, I think in the past the Layman's style has been more divisive than reconciling," she said. "I just feel saddened that something like this sidetracks the church from getting on with what we need to be getting on with—the love of Christ to a needy world."

Unchained Melody

The Kol Nidre Sung at High Holy Days Links Modern Jews to Rich Yet Mournful Legacy

Carol McGraw, *Orange County Register,* September 28, 1997

Kol Nidre v'esarei vacha ramei v'konamei v'chinuyei v'kinusei ush'vuot . . .

From out of the past, the prayer has persevered.

The words are Aramaic, a language of ancient Jews.

Never mind that many today cannot translate the words; the melody alone speaks the soulful language of the heart.

The Kol Nidre is chanted but once a year—during the High Holy Days, Judaism's 10 days of repentance and renewal. It is the first music one hears at temple at the beginning of Yom Kippur.

The service itself takes its name from the prayer: Kol Nidre.

It means "all vows."

It is considered by many to be not only the high point of the High Holy Days but also the most profound melody in Jewish liturgy.

Words born out of persecution.

A melody drenched in the pain of forced conversions.

It brings forth tears, soul searching, connection to God.

Beethoven used pieces of it in the sixth movement of his String Quartet No. 14. Tolstoy once called it "a melody that echoes the great martyrdom."

It is actually not a prayer at all, but a legal formula set down in Talmudic style.

Kol Nidre is also a tie that binds Orange County's 70,000 Jews to millions of others around the world.

And it's a chant that lies heavy on the shoulders of many cantors, such as Jonathan Grant of Temple Bat Yahm, who with his rendering can kindle a congregation's heart.

It's also a prayer that this year has a renewed and poignant meaning for Obadiah Hasson, a retired Irvine businessman, and Bonita Nahoun Jaros, a Santa Ana College professor. The two found this summer how the Kol Nidre links them spiritually with their past, present and future.

Twilight hush at Temple Bat Yahm in Newport Beach is broken by the hurried footsteps of late-arriving choir members echoing through darkened halls. They have gathered here like this for weeks, finding second wind after tiring days so that they can practice High Holy Days music.

Starting Wednesday with Rosh Hashana, the Jewish New Year, and concluding 10 days later with Yom Kippur, the Day of Atonement, the High Holy Days are the most important spiritual observance for Jews.

The 10 days are also called teshuvah—the turning—because this is a time to turn inward, to examine which vows one did not keep in the past year, and how to repair wrongs against men and God.

With the observance only days away, the tension hangs over choir practice like a woolen prayer shawl. No one needs reminding that the temple's upcoming services can either soar or fall with the music.

Clumped together near the piano, almost giddy with the pressure, choir members find relief in a bit of clowning around.

Back in his cramped office, Grant, the temple's cantor, or musical leader, paces in front of his bookcase crammed with prayer books and music tomes.

Grant, 38, one of only two fully accredited cantors in the country, was lured back to his spiritual roots 13 years ago by Jewish music. The more he listened, the more Jewish he became, he says, until finally one day he flung away an opera career and went back to New York's Hebrew Union College. There he embarked on a four-year postgraduate program so he could serve as sheliach tziebbur, the community's musical emissary to God.

Grant's hands are outstretched, palms up, agonizing over words to describe the indescribable Kol Nidre.

Singing this song, Grant says, "is a tremendous kevod," a Hebrew word referring to honor but also denoting heaviness. "You have the heavy weight of tradition on your shoulders."

Kol Nidre is generally chanted at the onset of the evening of Yom Kippur, this year Oct. 10. Because it is considered to be a legal action, tradition dictates that the song must be completed before sunset, when the observance officially begins.

Lights are dimmed. Several temple members stand on each side of the cantor, holding copies of the Torah, the Scriptures said to have been dictated to Moses by God after the Exodus from Egypt. This grouping represents the beit din, the ancient religious tribunals empowered to make legal decisions for the community.

There is no dramatic buildup. As the service begins, the Kol Nidre is just there—the first music that the faithful hear as they begin 25 hours of fasting and reflecting on their relationships with one another and with God.

"It's a haunting, wrenching, yearning melody," Grant says. So powerful that it can propel the congregation spiritually inward to face themselves and their maker.

It is sung three times and lasts about 20 minutes. Traditionally, the words are sung in low volume and pitch the first time, then louder and louder. In some congregations, including Grant's the choir also sings. Sometimes the congregation joins in.

The incantation, more than any other, is said to define the Judaic experience not only for the faithful, but also for those who don't regularly attend services. It's one song that "opens the kingdom of our memory to Yom Kippurs past," Grant says.

The melody probably dates back to medieval Rhineland, the words to ancient Babylonia. There are several versions; the most famous has roots in Ashkenazi, or Eastern European, Judaism. In other traditions, the words are whispered and the effect is syllabic rather than melodious.

The earliest record of the Kol Nidre was found in an eighth-century prayer book called the Seder Rav Amran. But some believe it could be much older.

No matter its age, the song is the one in which people expect the most from the cantor, because it is so steeped in tradition. But the music is technically problematic. Coming where it does at the first phase of the service, there is no suspenseful buildup, and the cantor has no time to warm up to it.

Sometimes cantors have trouble controlling their own emotions during the soulful chant. When Grant feels as though he might be overcome, he concentrates on the technical aspects. His breath. The timing.

"This is the one you can't goof up on," he says.

He notes that the melody of the Kol Nidre has been just as emotionally inspiring as the words, or more so.

In fact, the words to the prayer itself have confused Jews and non-Jews alike for centuries, scholars say. Translated from the Aramaic (it also has a single Hebrew phrase), the words to Kol Nidre are:

> All vows, bonds, promises, obligations and oaths wherewith we have
> vowed, sworn and bound ourselves:
> From this Day of Atonement unto the next Day of Atonement, may it
> come unto us for good; lo, all these, we repent us in them. They shall be ab-
> solved, released, annulled, made void, and of none effect.
> They shall not be binding nor shall they have any power.
> Our vows shall not be vows.
> Our bonds shall not be bonds.
> And our oaths shall not be oaths.

The significance has long been debated. Explains one scholar, "The words seem to be a confused confession, paradoxical, even."

Many scholars surmise that in its earliest form, the Kol Nidre may have focused on impulsive religious and political oaths, and eventually evolved into heartfelt contrition, taking on its most mystical, reverential aspect when used as a prayer of forgiveness by those forced to convert to Christianity during the Spanish Inquisition.

One thing everyone seems to agree on is that Kol Nidre does not refer to promises or legal contracts to other people. In Judaic law, trespasses against other people can only be wiped away by agreement with the offended.

But to chant Kol Nidre is to talk directly with God.

In the 19th century, a group of scholarly Reform rabbis eliminated Kol Nidre from the prayer books because for centuries it had been fodder for racial bigots who said that Jews recited it so they never had to keep vows or legal contracts. The rabbis failed in their mission, because the prayer's melody had such strong emotional impact on the faithful that cantors sang it anyway.

"The Kol Nidre brings instant awe to us," says Rabbi Lawrence Goldmark, president of the Board of Rabbis of Southern California and head of Temple Beth Ohr in La Mirada. So strong is the melody, he says, that the evening of Yom Kippur eventually was dubbed the Kol Nidre service.

"That is why Reform Judaism put the Kol Nidre back into the Yom Kippur service. They realized that the essence of religion is not the individual words; it is the spirit, the feeling evoked in the minds and hearts of the people, that make it so meaningful."

Obadiah "Obe" Hasson figures he has heard the Kol Nidre chanted scores of times during his 67 years.

But this year is different. Even talking about the ancient melody leaves his voice throaty with emotion and his heart near bursting.

Hasson, a retired Irvine businessman, grew up in Southern California in an Orthodox household. Over the years, he attended synagogue most often when his kids were young, less regularly since then. Like many Jews, he always tried to make it to the High Holy Days services.

But it wasn't until this summer that Hasson was spiritually overcome by the significance of the prayer and his ancestral connection to Inquisition martyrs.

A down-to-earth person, Hasson says he has had to finally acknowledge to himself that what happened to him on a trip to Spain with fellow members of University Synagogue in Irvine could not be called anything else but a "spiritual experience."

Hasson and his late grandfather both were named after the biblical prophet Obadiah, who lived in the harsh times following the capture and destruction of Jerusalem by the Babylonians. His grandfather spoke Ladino, a mixture of Spanish and Hebrew.

His ancestors had been part of the great exodus of Sephardic Jews fleeing the Spanish Inquisition. The summer trip was the Irvine man's first to the country of his forefathers.

Historically, Jews have been on the Iberian Peninsula long before the Inquisition, arriving after the destruction of Solomon's Temple in the sixth century B.C.

Sephardic civilization peaked in the 13th century, with Jews enjoying prestige and influence. Eventually economic and political imperatives, religious intolerance and racial bigotry in Catholic-dominated Spain provoked the Inquisition, according to Cornell Professor emeritus Benzion Netanyahu in "The Origins of the Inquisition" (Random House, 1995).

During the Inquisition, which began in the late 1400s and lasted about 350 years, Jews and other so-called heretics were persecuted. Many Jews converted to Catholicism to save their lives and their converts who lived as secret Jews were known as Marranos, a derogatory word meaning swine.

Both willing and unwilling converts were dragged before Inquisition courts, where tribunal priests handed down sentences of torture and burning at the stake to those who refused to accept Catholicism.

In all, more than 100,000 Jews were persecuted, unable or unwilling to flee. And in 1492, Ferdinand expelled the Jews from Spain altogether.

Rabbi Arnold Rachlis, who led members of his congregation on the heritage tour to Spain, notes that the Kol Nidre is often referred to as abaryanim, meaning those who cross over. It refers not only to Jews who had to convert, but to the fact that they remained "secret Jews," crossing over fields in the dead of night to worship in secret.

Rachlis sees the Kol Nidre as a ritual drama that can be interpreted in light of that history. "The secret Jews came to the synagogue, where they faced their fellow Jews who were at even greater risk because they did not convert.

"The secret Jews asked forgiveness through the Kol Nidre, and said, 'What else could we have done?'" Rachlis said. "The nonconverted Jews, in turn, do not say, 'Well, you saved your necks. Get out of here.' Instead, they recognized why the others had to do it and asked God to forgive. And then, God does forgive."

Rachlis notes that today, Spain grants automatic citizenship to those who return and can prove they are descendants of those who had to leave. While the Jewish population of Spain was once one of the largest in the world, today the numbers are much smaller, Rachilis says.

Hasson recalls that he and others from the Irvine synagogue had spent the day in Granada at the Alhambra Castle, where Queen Isabella had held court. In 1492, she signed the edict to have the Jews kicked out of the country.

After a day of sightseeing, Hasson and his wife returned to the hotel.

"As I rested in my hotel room, I was suddenly overcome," Hasson says quietly. "It was an extraordinary experience. I can't explain it. I have never felt anything like it in my life. It didn't feel like it was me. I mean, I wasn't guiding these emotions. It was like something deep from my past welling up."

There was anger. At one point, he screamed out loud. Then came sorrow. And cleansing tears.

And, he says, now he can feel the full impact of the Kol Nidre chant, how it must have felt when the secret Jews repeated the words asking God's forgiveness.

Bonita Nahoum Jaros found herself spiritually affected by the University Synagogue trip to Spain—even through she did not go along herself.

She, too, has Sephardic roots. Her grandfather, Alberto Soto, taught her more than 300 Jewish chants and Sephardic folk songs, including the Kol Nidre. But only this summer, after hearing about her synagogue's trip, did she link that song to a small, tarnished key Soto had given her as a child.

An English professor at Santa Ana College, Jaros has a group called Los Tanyaderos that specializes in Sephardic music and is dedicated to preserving endangered cultures.

As a child, she spoke only Ladino. Her family's ancestors had fled during the Inquisition to Salonika in northern Greece, then part of the Ottoman Empire.

The huge Sephardic population was not allowed into the mainstream culture. Her grandfather eventually fled to the United States so he did not have to serve in the Turkish army.

"My grandfather was very well educated; he spoke eight languages, but in New York he had to work as a shirt presser in a garment factory. I think it broke his heart,"Jaros said.

But she says, "He taught me everything—French, the mandolin, literature. Everything I am today, I owe to him."

Recently, Jaros was working on a music project with a professor from Queens College, who asked her to sing "The Key."

The song refers to the keys Sephardic Jews in Spain kept as they fled the Inquisition. Many locked their houses, expecting to be able to return someday.

"I was thunderstruck," Jaros said, "because I realized that I have such a key."

Jaros went home and dug among keepsakes until she found it. Her grandfather had given it to her 25 years ago. "All I remember was that it seemed a very solemn occasion; it was one of the few possessions he brought with him to the United States."

Jaros was not positive that the key dated back to Spain. It could even be from the home in Greece her grandfather had to leave. During the Holocaust, which claimed the lives of 90 percent of Salonika's Jews, many victims carried house keys with them to the death camps.

Within days of hearing the song about the key and finding her own heirloom, she attended synagogue. There Rabbi Rachlis talked about the trip to Spain—and Jewish tourists carrying keys their hopeful ancestors had kept.

Jaros says that now, as Rosh Hashana and Yom Kippur approach, she thinks a lot about the Kol Nidre and how it will link Jews around the world in their spiritual quest.

"The key and the Kol Nidre chant—they bring back all my ancestors, my grandparents, great-aunts and -uncles, my mother who died last year, and all those I didn't know, too. I feel them coming to me at this time. I cannot explain how intensely this feeling is building now. It's like they are showing us the future that they made possible for us."

Do No Harm—Part IV

David Briggs, *Associated Press,* October 27, 1992

New York (AP)—Tracy Smith couldn't face the sign in the doctor's office again: the one informing patients their first test would be a financial one.

So he waited until the strain on his heart became so painful that he had to stay in the car when he took his two young children to the park.

"I was afraid I wouldn't be able to pay for it," he said. Smith, 48, made it to a Seattle hospital in time to be treated for a near-fatal atrial fibrillation. But he still didn't have the insurance or the $50,000 in the bank to pay for the heart transplant he needed.

His only hope was to wait until the new year, when Medicare might approve the funds for the operation. He never made it.

In the world of medicine today, the Tracy Smiths can die for the lack of a $50,000 heart transplant, while thousands of comatose patients with no hope of recovery may be kept alive indefinitely on respirators and ventilators because their insurance will pay for it.

"What we have done is hidden our eyes so the poor get next to nothing, and some of us can get the best medical care," said John Golenski, president of the Bioethics Consultation Group Inc. "In the last 10 years, we have injected the metaphor of the free market into health care services."

This is an injustice, say a broad range of ethicists, physicians, economists and religious leaders.

They advocate rationing health care to limit extraordinary services to the dying and unnecessary tests for the insured, while providing ordinary care to the millions of American left out of the health care system.

"There is no question that rationing is going to be necessary, and morally necessary," said Robert Veatch of the Kennedy Institute of Ethics at Georgetown University.

But many still consider rationing to be un-American, and it is often the core argument used against adopting the universal health care plans of other nations such as Canada or England.

"When we have identifiable lives, you look people in the eye and see somebody dying, we have a generous impulse," said George Annas, professor of health law at Boston University.

Ruth Fischbach, an ethicist at Harvard Medical School, said she believes a nation as wealthy as the United States should be able to provide health care for everyone.

"I would tend to hope that we're not rationing," she said.

In 1950, the United States spent 4.5 percent of its Gross National Product on health care. But that was before the widespread use of ventilators, respirators and transplants and an explosion of costly experimental drug therapies helped send health costs soaring to more than 12 percent of the GNP in 1990.

"We're now at the point where we spend so much and what we get back is so little, we can improve the health of our people by spending more on police, schools, parks, libraries, " said Dr. Thomas Preston, a Seattle cardiologist.

The basic problem is that Americans cannot choose between either a capitalist or socialist approach to health care, according to economist Lester Thurow of the Massachusetts Institute of Technology.

"We say every rich person can buy anything they want, and every middle class person has to get what every rich person can buy," he said.

And the bubble is about to burst, Thurow and others say.

Corporations, which now pay nearly four times the cost of health insurance they did 10 years ago, have steadily pushed back more of the costs to employees, and some small businesses no longer can afford to offer coverage. An estimated 37 million Americans lack any insurance coverage even though at least one family member is employed in most of those families.

"We clearly have a health system that grossly limits access to large segments of our population," said James Gleich, former executive director of the Disability Rights Education and Defense Fund.

For the wealthy, the system still works fine.

In 1989, more than half of the respondents in households with incomes $50,000 and above rated their health as excellent. The percentage of those in excellent health declined steadily with household income, with only 27.6 percent of those with incomes under $14,000 giving high ratings for their personal health.

On the other end of the scale, only 3.7 percent of well-off households rated their health as fair or poor, while one in five people in low-income households said their health was fair or poor.

The infant mortality rate for blacks is twice as high as that for whites, and white males on average live 7.4 more years than black males. Nearly 80 percent of white women received prenatal care in the first trimester, compared to 61 percent of black women.

No group is worse off than children.

A third of the nation's uninsured are children. More than 23 percent of all 2-year-olds did not receive the recommended doses of polio vaccine in 1985. In 1970, 80 percent of preschool children were vaccinated against diphtheria, tetanus and whooping cough; by 1985, only 69 percent received the vaccinations.

A chart in the office of Dr. Ian Gross, director of newborn services at Yale-New Haven Hospital, shows the infant mortality rates in the Hill section of New Haven at 38.8 per thousand—"Third World numbers." Move over a few blocks to the predominantly white, more affluent Westville area and the mortality rate drops to 5.7 per thousand—"Good First World numbers."

But that doesn't mean Gross will withhold care from a severely disabled infant in the hopes that money would be redistributed for preventive care.

The system doesn't work that way.

"It's an open-ended system," Gross said. "All that will happen is $50,000 less will be spent on health care this year."

No one wants to make the tough choices—sentencing some people to die days, months or even years before the time modern medical technology had allotted them so that others may be given the resources to live.

In an October AP poll taken by ICR Survey Research Group of Media, Pa., part of AUS Consultants, 90 percent of Americans surveyed said people who can afford it should have the right to treatments that have a low success rate and that many doctors consider a waste of medical resources.

But if universal health care is to become a reality, even the wealthy must be told no for treatment that offers little chance of survival, said Dr. Stephen Post of Case Western Reserve University.

"No, society is not going to give you that 1 percent chance, that 5 percent chance, or even that 10 percent chance," Post said. "There comes a point that in the name of the common good, from education to rebuilding the infrastructure, we have to put some limits on autonomy."

Unless an ethical consensus develops, many fear the nation will continue down the path of a free-market approach to health care.

In that scenario, Thurow said, expect the rich to purchase 11 times the
health care services available to the poor and likely even more, since
health care is a basic need that individuals are willing to spend a disproportionate amount of income on.

And more Tracy Smiths will die at an early age.

Preston, one of the doctors who treated Smith for free but was helpless to provide the heart transplant that could have enabled his patient to
watch his children grow up, indicts the American health-care system.

"The point is that rationing is much more fair than arbitrary exclusion
of some people, and giving everything to the rest. . . . It's a hell of a lot
more ethical than what's going on," Preston said. "We don't know who's
dying out there. We don't care. That's the worst part."

28

Toward a New Millennium

As religious groups prepared for the year 2000, some patterns for faith that began in the late 20th century were clearly going to continue. But the precise contours of the new century's religious landscape have yet to be decided. Despite strategies that included updating worship, improving leadership savvy and employing marketing strategies, the bleeding of members and dollars from mainline Protestant groups may continue.

By the end of the century every major religion—along with hundreds of nonmajor and fringe groups—now had an electronic presence on the World Wide Web, giving mainline churches even more competition from curious soul searchers. Ecumenical groups that were powerhouses in the 1950s—the National Council of Churches of Christ, U.S.A., and the World Council of Churches—face futures without the political and spiritual force they had when created 50 years ago. Now their budgets are shrinking as supporters, mostly mainline groups, have fewer resources to spend.

The steady growth of American-born groups, such as the Church of Jesus Christ of Latter-day Saints, both domestically and abroad is likely, with predictions of worldwide membership reaching well over 200 million in the next 100 years. Don Lattin traveled some 35,000 miles to document the Mormon's evangelization efforts worldwide for the *San Francisco Chronicle* in 1996. His stories appeared in a special reprint from that paper dated April 8, 1996. For a discussion of the Mormon Church's vast business empire, see *Time* magazine's cover story "Kingdom Come" in the August 4, 1997, issue.

The increasing ethnic pluralism of the United States will play a major impact—as it has already—on the religious makeup of the United States. Given that fact, religious groups are expected to continue healing old divisions that separated denominations by race. Until the 1950s, some newspapers segregated church announcements by "Church News" and "Negro Churches."

Although certainly many congregations and denominations remain racially distinct, the number is diminishing as increasingly affluent

African-Americans move to the suburbs and religious groups compete for their allegiance. Similarly, institutional divisions are being reevaluated as all religious groups cast a critical eye toward racially motivated church burnings.

A personal spirituality, as demonstrated by stories in chapter 25, is expected to continue, driven, as are many trends, by the aging baby boomers. These boomers—the largest segment of the book-buying public—fueled hikes in the sales of religious books that took media watchers in the late 1990s by surprise.

Just as the U.S. religion scene continues to evolve, so too does the religion beat. Stories from the 1980s and 1990s in part reflect the work of a highly educated, specialized group of religion reporters who were given the luxury of space to report the complicated stories of change, transition and spiritual searches that typified trends of that era.

The stories in this chapter represent just four examples that point toward the "what next" of the U.S. religious scene.

A frequent commentator on religious topics for network television, Kenneth Woodward is *Newsweek* magazine's religion expert. In "Dead End for the Mainline?" Woodward shows ways some mainline groups—Lutherans, Methodists, Presbyterians among them—are trying to reverse recent patterns of declining membership.

Most of the nation's Pentecostal denominations were founded at the last turn of the century, with the largest Pentecostal churches maintaining racially separate denominations. A story in this chapter tells of a historic 1994 meeting for African-American and white Pentecostal groups. The future is not fraught without uncertainties, however, and David Waters of the Memphis *Commercial Appeal* tells readers why.

Many uncertainties await the Roman Catholic Church in the next few decades as well. A shortage of priests and nuns, combined with Vatican II reforms that opened up roles for the laity, have redefined how clergy and nonclergy interact. Diane Winston's report for *The Baltimore Sun* on the role of the laity printed here was originally written as part of a series about U.S. Catholicism on the eve of the Baltimore Archdiocese's 200th anniversary.

Finally, *Dallas Morning News* religion reporter Deborah Kovach Caldwell previews the millennium frenzy. Her story describes a few of the apocalyptic groups expected to attract followers in the new century.

Dead End for the Mainline?

Kenneth L. Woodward, *Newsweek,* August 9, 1993

To join it, one would never know that the Community Church of Joy in Glendale, Ariz., is Lutheran—or that Pastor Walter Kallestad had been educated in a traditional Lutheran family, college and seminary. From the Steven Spielberg-like Sunday-school gimmicks to the generic Amy Grant music at worship services, everything is designed to "meet the needs" of his nondenominational baby boomers. "Be quick" is the first commandment. Moving faster than a Wendy's at lunch hour, the Church of Joy needs only five minutes to distribute communion to 1,000 worshipers. Still, Pastor Kallestad insists, "It's a very meaningful moment for our people." Sermons take a bit longer because Terey Summers, Arizona's Actress of the Year, likes to stage skits in the sanctuary instead of having ministers preach from the pulpit. "People today aren't interested in traditional doctrines like justification, sanctification and redemption," the pastor concluded.

Whatever it is, it works. The Church of Joy has over 6,000 members and another 6,000 who participate in the more than 100 recovery and other special-interest programs that keep the church doors turning seven days a week. That's not what Martin Luther may have had in mind when he set out to reform Christianity—but that's the point. There's a new Reformation in American religion, and this time it is not the Church of Rome but Lutheran and other mainline Protestant denominations that are under siege. Like the officers of beleaguered IBM and other seemingly solid American institutions, the leaders of the nation's once robust Protestant establishment face the loss of brand name loyalty.

Aging Flocks

For 25 consecutive years, liberal Protestantism's seven-sister denominations* have watched their collective membership decline. Although the number of Protestants in general is growing—an evangelical church is opening somewhere almost daily—the mainline denominations are not. They now account for just 24 percent of the American population. Their flocks are aging, their budgets shrinking. Morale is low. Many local congregations are rejecting control by denominational leaders and cutting back on funds to support their national programs. From every angle, mainline Protestantism is gripped by crisis: of identity and loyalty, membership and money, leadership and organization, culture and belief.

Across the mainline this summer, there's a mood of embattled introspection. Just last month the bishops on the United Methodist Church's Executive Committee pushed aside their position papers and for three hours simply searched their souls. "What does it mean to be a United Methodist?" they asked each other. "What, if anything, is distinctive about our church?" "Churches without any self-understanding lose members," acknowledges the Rev. Jim Andrews, head of the Presbyterian Church (U.S.A.), which recently eliminated 175 staff positions for lack of sufficient funds from its declining flock. And in a remarkable gesture of defiance, more than 1,000 dissatisfied Episcopalians will pay their way to St. Louis later this month to air ideas for radically decentralizing church authority. If this breakaway pattern persists, observes Methodist Lyle Schaller, a consultant on church development, "denominations will be left with what they do best—administering clerical pension funds."

Mainline Protestants were bred for bigger things. For more than a century, these seven denominations helped define America and its values. Now they are struggling to define themselves in a world where adjectives like "Methodist" or "Presbyterian" no longer mean anything to most Americans. "God is killing mainline Protestantism in America," says Methodist theologian Stanley Hauerwas of Duke Divinity School, "and we goddam well deserve it."

As a way of organizing believers, the religious denomination is essentially an American innovation. In their infancy, the oldest denominations were like extended ethnic families: voluntary confederations of like-minded Scottish Presbyterians or English Congregationalists who looked after their own and competed with each other for converts under the constitutionally mandated separation of church and state. But after the Civil War, the mainline developed—like American business—into large, bureaucratic national corporations. In addition to controlling their own foreign and domestic missions, denominations produced Sunday-school curricula, hymnals and other products that they marketed to local congregations. They also credentialed ministers and ran colleges. By the middle of this century, the corporate denominations were the most prominent feature of American Protestantism. Politicians heeded their leaders, and the circulation of journals like the now defunct *Presbyterian Life* almost matched *Newsweek*'s.

For most of this history, observes D. Newell Williams, a church historian at the Christian Theological Seminary in Indianapolis, "denominational differences were important and the people understood them." Some, like Lutherans, united around inherited confessions of belief. Baptists stressed adult baptism and individual liberty, Congregationalists the life of the local church. Methodists sang the hymns of Charles Wesley and preached the social gospel. Presbyterians were cerebral, self-contained and bent on making civic life conform to God's will. Episcopalians prized the liturgy. And while they all defended the solemnity of the Sabbath—and of marriage—many were loath to see their children marry a Protestant of a different denominational stripe.

What happened? Some leaders see the loss of denominational distinctiveness as an inevitable result of Christian ecumenism. "We have said implicitly and explicitly throughout this century that the difference between denominations are negligible," says John M. Mulder, president of Louisville Presbyterian Theological Seminary. Others blame the triumph of a self-critical liberal theology within the mainline churches. "The denominations no longer offer a distinctive Christian standard for judging statements about God or moral action," says historian Williams, who counts himself a political liberal. "Many people now see no reason to be Christian. The mainline churches are just plain boring, but the Gospel is not boring."

These churches have lost their children. Few baby boomers raised in Presbyterian families, for example, have become adult Presbyterians. Rather than join other denominations, surveys show, fully 48 percent opt out of church going altogether. "There used to be an ecology that nurtured the faith of children through parents, Sunday schools, youth conferences, summer camps and church-related colleges," observes Mulder. But in the last 25 years, the Presbyterians and other mainline denominations have diluted these programs. "We provided our children with a theological rationale for embracing secularism," says the Rev. William Willimon, Methodist dean of the chapel at Duke Divinity School.

The mainline is also suffering from its own urge to merge. Over the last decade, parishioners found themselves belonging to newly formed national denominations that often did not mesh well. Synergy is as hard to come by when three distinct branches of Lutherans are bound together as in any corporate conglomerate. To the people in the pews, the national denominations look increasingly like "regulatory agencies," says Craig Dykstra, vice president for religion at the Lilly Endowment in Indianapolis. For example, denominational program officers tax the congre-

gations for support of political and social movements that the local faithful sometimes do not want or think they can't afford. Moreover, in most
denominations, there is a large gap between the liberal national staff and
its more conservative congregational constituents. One reason the United
Church of Christ moved its headquarters from New York City to Cleveland last year was to blunt the denomination's liberal East Coast image.
But leaders of the denomination have alienated many of their new neighbors by launching a fruitless crusade against Chief Wahoo, the Cleveland
Indians' popular logo, as an offense to Native Americans.

Rather than support denominationally determined national programs,
more and more local congregations are running their own projects for the
homeless and commissioning their own foreign missionaries. "The leadership forgets that the parish church is the front line, where people are
taught and served," says Jon Shuler, the rector of an Episcopal parish in
Knoxville, Tenn., who is organizing next month's protest meeting in St.
Louis. "We are not here to serve the dioceses or the presiding bishop.
What a lot of us on the local level want is an entire rethinking of the
church's constitution."

New Age

In response to such grass-roots demands, church leaders are gradually
granting more freedom to their local congregations. The more optimistic
are talking about reinventing the denomination for a new, post-Protestant
age. But they may already be behind the curve. Television preacher
Robert Schuller recently formed Churches Uniting in Global Mission, a
national coalition of 200 pastors of "the most dynamic and successful"
congregations, like Arizona's Community Church of Joy. The aim of this
determinedly antidenominational network is to lure baby boomers back
to church by welcoming all comers regardless of their beliefs and appealing to their lack of theological convictions.

This, of course, is precisely how American denominations got
started—by belittling the competition. The difference is that the old-line
Lutherans, Calvinists and Anglicans saw themselves as heirs to coherent
traditions they thought worth passing on. Even when competing for converts, they put doctrinal and devotional integrity before success. "To give
the whole store away to match what this year's market says the
unchurched want is to have the people who know least about faith determine most about its expression," warns American church historian Martin E. Marty. The mainline denominations may be dying because they

lost their theological integrity. The only thing worse, perhaps, would be the rise of a new Protestant establishment that succeeds because it never had any.

---

* The Episcopal Church, the Presbyterian Church (U.S.A.), the United Methodist Church, the American Baptist Church, the United Church of Christ, the Christian Church (Disciples of Christ) and the Evangelical Lutheran Church in America.

Pentecostals Black, White Aim to Heal Racial Rift

David Waters, *The Commercial Appeal,* October 16, 1994

They met at a stormy revival on Azusa Street in Los Angeles nearly 90 years ago, blacks and whites alike swept off their feet by the sanctifying gusts of the Holy Spirit.

They called themselves Pentecostals because they believed they were repeating the supernatural experiences of the first Pentecost, as recorded in the Book of Acts of the Apostles. For several years they worshipped together in religious ecstasy.

But the blood of Jesus washed away their sins, not the color of their skin. What began as an interracial religious movement in the century's first decade splintered along racial lines by the end of the second.

Now in the century's last decade, a new spirit is sweeping across American Pentecostalism.

This week, black and white Pentecostal leaders from across the country plan to meet on Main Street in Memphis. They pray that God's reconciling Holy Spirit once again will rain on them and wash away decades of racial separation.

The focus of the meeting is the Pentecostal Fellowship of North American or PFNA, an organization formed in 1948 exclusively for white Pentecostals. The group now numbers 21 predominantly white denominations.

On Tuesday at the Memphis Cook Convention Center, PFNA members will meet one last time. Then the PFNA will be dissolved.

On Wednesday, 100 black and 100 white Pentecostal leaders will meet to establish a new association that includes whites, blacks and charismatics from other traditions.

"It's historic," said Dr. Vinson Synan, Pentecostal historian and dean of the Regent University School of Theology in Virginia.

"It means that all major Pentecostal groups in the United States will be under the same umbrella of fellowship, really for the first time since Azusa Street."

Organizers say the meeting won't reverse the course of history but will repair it by ending a decades-long debate over the history of Pentecostalism.

The meeting also could lead the historically white denominations to become more active in social issues. And it should encourage the development of more racially mixed Pentecostal churches.

The meeting will include members of the nation's most prominent Pentecostal bodies, including the two largest: the predominantly black Church of God in Christ, based in Memphis, and the predominantly white Assemblies of God, based in Springfield, Mo.

But not all Pentecostal groups have been invited. "Oneness" Pentecostals who reject the Trinity never have been part of the fellowship, but they represent a small segment of the movement.

Leaders of all major Pentecostal denominations are participating with one exception. While several leading bishops in the Church of God in Christ have embraced the effort, presiding Bishop L.H. Ford has not.

"Any local bishop is allowed to meet with whomever he likes," Ford said, "but this is not a general church project."

Ford declined to say why he turned down an invitation to the meeting.

COGIC Bishop G.E. Patterson of Memphis and others say they regret Ford's decision, but it won't stop them from proceeding. Patterson said he expects most COGIC bishops to attend or send representatives. Patterson and two fellow bishops on COGIC's general board have been actively involved in the effort.

"We have no reason to be estranged and every reason not to be," Patterson said.

"Until we are willing to throw down these racial divisions and come together as a united body of Christ, we really can't help the world."

Synan said Ford's rejection will slow but not derail the effort.

"This is a significant and historic first step," Synan said, "but the process will continue with or without Bishop Ford."

The PFNA was formed in 1948 "to demonstrate to the world the essential unity of Spirit-baptized believers, fulfilling the prayer of the Lord Jesus 'that they all may be one.'"

Despite the movement's interracial origins, not a single black denomination was invited.

Today, the nation's largest Pentecostal denomination is predominantly black: the 5.5-million member Church of God in Christ. Its exclusion from a group that purports Christian unity has weighed for years on the hearts of many white Pentecostal leaders.

In recent years, the PFNA issued invitations to COGIC and other black Pentecostals. Bishop B.E. Underwood, PFNA chairman, said they were rejected, "understandably so," as tokenism.

"We were asking them to join us," said Underwood, general superintendent of the Pentecostal Holiness Church, based in Oklahoma City. "But we weren't asking to join them."

"It took us a while to realize what was wrong with that. We realized that it might be necessary for us to disband our fellowship and start over for this to work."

In 1992, the PFNA executive committee agreed to initiate reconciliation. A handful of black and white Pentecostal leaders met for the first time at the Dallas airport to begin discussions.

Among the participants was COGIC Bishop Ithiel Clemmons of New York, also a member of the church's general board.

In January 1993, black and white leaders held a multiracial summit in Phoenix. They agreed the time had come to reconcile. "We sensed that God was telling us to pursue the matter seriously," Underwood said.

Last October, COGIC's Patterson was invited to address PFNA's annual meeting. Patterson is a member of the church's general board and one of the nation's most sought-after preachers, but he hadn't been involved in the early discussions.

"I had never heard of PFNA," Patterson said.

He was followed onstage by Dr. Jack Hayford, pastor of The Church on the Way in Van Nuys, Calif., the largest church of Aimee Semple McPherson's Pentecostal branch, the International Church of the Foursquare Gospel.

In a stirring climax to his sermon, Hayford embraced black educator Dr. Oliver J. Haney of Emory University. Hayford apologized for decades of prejudice and misunderstanding that kept the churches apart.

Patterson joined Hayford onstage, and together they called for a healing of the wounds that have separated the groups.

The first meeting to prepare the way was last January at the Adam's Mark Hotel in Memphis.

Rev. J.D. Middlebrooks, pastor of Raleigh Assembly of God, was chosen to represent his denomination. He joined 19 whites and 20 blacks in a daylong discussion that became a transforming experience.

"We prayed together, we cried together," he said. "God was saying something to us. I came out of that meeting transformed and repentant. I realized I had not been open to see. I felt that I personally had not treated any black person badly, but I was repentant for not having done anything to right the past of my church and past of my nation."

Patterson said he was deeply moved and renewed by the meeting: "If we had gotten together years ago, maybe we could have done more to help with the nation's racial reconciliation."

Said Underwood of this week's gathering, which begins Monday evening with a celebration service: "The ultimate intention is to draw the family circle large enough to include all the children of the Pentecostal revival."

Altering an Institution

Faith of Many Is Bolstered as Role of Laity Grows, but Divisions Remain

Diane Winston, *The Baltimore Sun,* November 5, 1989

The Roman Catholic Church that Barbara A. McLean knew as a child offered few opportunities for women. Ladies could wash the altar linen, attend the women's club or enter a convent. For an energetic young girl in a post-World War II Govans parish, such limited options had little allure.

But Dr. McLean, a medical director with the Baltimore County Employees Health Services, discovered in the 1980s what she never imagined in the strait-laced, clergy-led, male-dominated congregations of the 1940s and 1950s: She found men and women sharing the responsibility of leading the church and taking its word to the world.

"When I was a child, I went to church dutifully because I was supposed to, but it never meant as much to me as it does now," Dr. McLean said. "Now, so much of what I do is related not just to the church but to my faith. I am living my faith."

A growing number of the nation's 53.5 million Catholics are living their faith in ways that were unthinkable to earlier generations. Lay people sit on parish councils, directing church governance and finance. They assist at Mass, reading Scripture and distributing Communion. They prepare for "lay ministries," helping out in hospitals, soup kitchens and shelters—as well as bringing religious convictions to bear at home, at work and in the community.

Lay participation has wrought other changes in a church that, 200 years ago, Baltimore Archbishop John Carroll blessed in a new land of pluralism and religious liberty. Today, the U.S. church begins a yearlong bicentennial celebration with a Mass for the National Conference of Catholic Bishops, meeting in Baltimore this week for the first time since 1884.

Since Archbishop Carroll's time, the church has been shaped by democracy, disestablishment and an active, educated laity in ways that even the prescient priest could not predict. Individual conscience competes with church dictum, believers pick and choose dogma, and some Catholics simply ignore papal pronouncements with which they disagree.

"American Catholics have made their peace with the church; they stay in even when they don't agree with it," said Jim Castelli, co-author with George Gallup of "The People's Religion: American Faith in the 1990s." "They may not agree with what the Vatican says about birth control, but they stay, and that attitude drives the Vatican crazy."

Vatican officials and U.S. conservatives want a reassertion of church authority. They say positive advances, such as integrating the church into the culture, need to be tempered by obedience to religious teachings.

But for others, the evolution of American Catholicism heralds a new day: lay leadership in all aspects of church life, equality for women and the emergence of religious alternatives to secular values.

Dr. McLean, whose involvement with the church embodies these trends, participates in parish and diocesan councils, educational and hospital ministries, church retreats and Sunday liturgies.

But she says her first task is applying her faith in the everyday world.

"You can do that taking care of patients, picking up your garbage or giving out traffic tickets," said Dr. McLean during a break at her Towson office. "You don't consciously sit down and talk to a patient thinking how your faith is affecting you, but it's there in the advice you give, your reaction to a problem and how supportive you are."

Dr. McLean's manner, like her words, is direct. The 52-year-old daughter of Scotch-Irish parents, she respected the church but resisted its pull. For more than a decade, she attended services sporadically. When she returned to the fold in 1980, Dr. McLean found an institution transformed by the Second Vatican Council (1962-1965).

"When the Vatican Council was convened by Pope John XXIII, it opened the windows to allow in fresh air, but a lot of things got blown out of place," said Bishop John Ricard of the Baltimore Archdiocese. "We are still into some institutional change. Things will be a little different than they were in the past."

The bishops of the council rejected the conservative spirit that, only 60 years before, reined in experiments with modernism. But this time, authoritarianism gave way to community decision-making and respect for individual conscience.

No longer would Catholics march in lock step conformity to Vatican commands. Instead, the bishops envisioned the church as "the people of God" transforming the world with the gospel.

In the United States, the council's recommendations were seized by a restive laity who, better educated and more affluent than their forbears, wanted a bigger stake in the church. These Catholics, unlike earlier generations, were comfortable being both American and Catholic. The worst of the bigotry unleashed by the nativist and know-nothing movements was past; Americans had recently elected a Catholic, John F. Kennedy, as president.

"People attribute so much change to Vatican II, but there was change happening. Vatican II drew attention to it and sanctified it," said David Leege, a sociologist at the University of Notre Dame in South Bend, Ind. "With greater education, people aren't just going to just pay, pray and obey. They are going to say, 'I don't want to be a spectator; I want to participate.'"

After the Vatican Council—which coincided with the culture-changing tide of the 1960s—participation became a buzzword. Shaping the service and administering the parish were part of a new and, for some laity, liberating process.

Masses, open for revision, throbbed with twanging guitars and rattling maracas. Some flocked to folk or gospel-flavored worship. Others, missing Latin prayers and traditional service, deserted a church they felt had left them behind.

At the same time, clergy sought new ways to serve. Sisters shed their habits, priests took off collars, and both brought the gospel message to the ghetto. The U.S. hierarchy, through the newly formed National Conference of Catholic Bishops, addressed social issues from a religious perspective. Some church members applauded their progressive stands on war and peace, the economy, race relations and women. Others wondered why bishops were meddling in areas far removed from their religious expertise.

Those were vibrant times for the church, but the new roles and changing expectations exacted a toll; some clergy left their orders, and the number of new candidates for the priesthood plummeted.

"Part of what we have experienced, since the Second Vatican Council, is change, and change in religion is very uncomfortable," said Archbishop Daniel E. Pilarcyk of the Cincinnati Archdiocese and vice president of the bishops conference. "A lot of the change after the council was very painful for some people. And some of the changes now, such as the decline in the number of priests and the rise of lay ministry, are painful for some people, too."

The Rev. Robert Leavitt, president of St. Mary's Seminary in Baltimore, thinks the precipitous drop of priestly candidates has leveled off but that the clergy shortage will continue throughout the 21st century.

Father Leavitt says lay people will be called on to staff parishes and service parishioners. But priests will still play the key role, educating lay people about the faith and administering the sacraments.

Still, the development of lay ministries has sparked an implicit challenge to traditional authority: How can the clergy demand obedience from an increasingly self-confident church?

"In the post-Vatican II church, the problem of authority becomes very hard to figure out," Father Leavitt said. "You get people involved and then you ask, 'Who's in charge?'"

"You can't throw out authority, and you can't throw out participation. So the two are in tension with each other, and you just have to work your way through it."

Some Catholics say "working through it" will push the church closer to a Protestant model—an understandable move in a society where mainline Protestant values predominate. Church members will make moral decisions based on individual conscience, women and married men will be ordained as priests, and lay people will shift the church's focus from institutional infighting to saving the world.

"There is an inevitable convergence in religious life because of social pressures," said Dean Hoge, professor of sociology at the Catholic University of America in Washington. "Catholicism is moving in the general direction of Lutheranism and Episcopalianism. Catholics looking at those groups will have a glance at their future."

Eugene Kennedy, a psychologist at Loyola University in Chicago and a longtime commentator on U.S. Catholics, says tomorrow's church will be led by lay believers who place individual devotion above institutional dogma.

"The growth of the laity has already affected the institution," Mr. Kennedy said. "The institution, grand and imposing as it is, no longer commands the obedience of the people. They have great affection for it, but they no longer look to the church to help them live their lives. They look to themselves."

Mr. Kennedy's claims are heretical to many, but underlying his words is a new reality: Lay people are seeking new ways to demonstrate their faith. Some volunteer in soup kitchens, hospices and shelters. Others choose work where they can express their religious commitment:

• Patty Dondanville Berman, a Chicago attorney, hopes her under-standing of ethics and values—shaped by Catholic teachings—infuses her law practice. Ms. Berman thinks Catholics ought to offer ethical alternatives in everyday life rather than focus on the inter-church issues. She attends Mass but is not active in her congregation.

"I think the church could be more effective in developing parish life if it focused more on people's roles in society for the other six days a week," said Ms. Berman, who is treasurer of the National Center for the Laity, a Catholic organization dedicated to encouraging lay witness in the world. "The church should be like a company's headquarters. You come in and get literature and conviction. Then you go out in the world and do what you have to do."

• Enrique Codas left Paraguay in 1967 because his political activities against a repressive regime jeopardized his career. He eventually settled in Columbia, where, as a professor at the University of Maryland's School of Social Work, he hopes his research on Hispanics in the United States will help his people.

Mr. Codas, who has served on national committees advising U.S. bishops on social issues, says the church can—and should—transform the world with liberation-theology, a school of belief that reads the Bible as an ever-relevant history of the human struggle from slavery to freedom.

"For me, as a lay person, it does not make any sense to be deeply involved in church activities if you are not deeply and effectively trying to transform society by your daily activities," Mr. Codas said.

• Colleen G. Parro, a Dallas resident, wonders whether the role of the lay person has been overdeveloped. Mrs. Parro, worried by what she perceives as a subversion of church authority, is critical of lay participation at Mass and in setting church social policy.

Mrs. Parro says her faith has led her to be an active proponent of traditional values. She has spoken out in both Washington and the Vatican on the need for anti-abortion legislation and a strong defense. She also serves on the board of the Cardinal Mindszenty Foundation of Texas, a Catholic anti-Communist organization.

"At some point, American Catholics are going to have to decide whether they want to be members of the Roman Catholic Church or the so-called American church," Mrs. Parro said. "The biggest challenge is to decide whether they wish to reaffirm the fact they are subject to papal authority in everything from the liturgy to the ordination of women."

Everything from the liturgy to the role of women is open for debate in the U.S. church today. The shortage of priests, the influx of minorities and the new affluence of white ethnic Catholics has created a heady stew of success, challenge and change.

Fewer people attend Mass than did 10 years ago but, for many, their commitment to the faith has never been stronger. Conservative Catholics decry the shift away from bedrock values, but Protestant leaders look to Catholicism to provide a renewed moral and spiritual vision for the nation.

This challenge—developing core values in a pluralistic context—also interested Archbishop John Carroll. He thought the competition between churches would strengthen national values. For Catholics today, facing an increasingly secular nation, the struggle remains.

"The greatest challenge I hear is: 'How do we pass on a living faith to a generation growing up in a culture oriented to consumerism and selfishness?'" said Archbishop William H. Keeler of Baltimore. "The range of human issues—bioethics, morality in business dealings, good government, war and peace, racism, sexism—all of these have a profoundly religious dimension."

Archbishop Keeler and other church leaders think lay people have a distinct mission: bringing that religious dimension to the workplace, the marketplace and the home. Pope John Paul II has called for developing a "spirituality of work"; believers such as Dr. McLean are trying to live it.

"We are called to minister, and everyone is beginning to believe it," Dr. McLean said. "The shortage of priests may have started it, but that's not what is sustaining it.

"We now know we have a role in the church by virtue of our baptism. And once you have awakened a sleeping giant, it is hard to put him back down."

New Millennium Filling Minds with Things Fantastic

Deborah Kovach Caldwell, *The Dallas Morning News,* November 19, 1996

The world's odometer is inching toward a millennial milestone. When the calendar finally rolls over to Jan. 1, 2000—an event long anticipated, often feared—it will mean far more than just a humongous New Year's party.

For a lot of people, the year 2000 will herald the biggest spiritual event ever.

"People notice when their odometer turns to triple zero," says Ted Daniels, director of the Millennium Watch Institute in Philadelphia. "It's a milestone. That's exactly what the millennium is. And like any milestone, we take it as a marker of change. It gets people anticipating with longing and dread."

The planning is already under way.

The pope will start a jubilee celebration at St. Peter's Basilica by opening bronze Holy Year Doors, used only every 25 years, at midnight Mass on Christmas Eve 1999. In Colorado, a man who calls himself the Millennium Doctor hopes to lead a five-month caravan through the Middle East. In Virginia, the Millennium Institute is planning three years of sacred celebrations that will bring together world religious leaders. And Campus Crusade for Christ is leading a coalition trying to convert 1 billion people by 2000.

In Dallas, the Roman Catholic diocese plans to build new spires on its cathedral as an emblem of the millennium. A local composer is writing a cantata in honor of the calendar change.

Pastors are preaching about the Battle of Armageddon described in the Book of Revelation. A Plano woman says aliens are trying to warn us that the end is near. And a fellow from Garland is said to be building a fleet of blimps that will airlift him 14 miles above the Earth as it is tossed by a cataclysmic shift on its axis.

Across the nation, deep thinkers have started cranking out books and holding conferences on What It All Means.

Dr. Daniels, who has been tracking millennium mania since 1992, keeps tabs on 1,200 sources concerned with the date.

Let's just say it's a growth industry.

Last year, there were six web sites devoted to issues surrounding the turn of the century; now there are 6,000. Religious broadcaster Pat Robertson and others are writing Christian apocalyptic novels that are flying off the shelves. Hal Lindsey's "The Late Great Planet Earth," which was the No. 1 selling book of the 1970s, continues to sell millions. Academics at the University of Chicago and Indiana University are working on a three-volume "Encyclopedia of Apocalypticism."

A Worldwide Countdown

Although the new millennium actually will not begin until 2001, the year 2000 will begin a huge Christian celebration because it marks the 2,000th anniversary of the approximate date of Jesus' birth. Christians have been anticipating the event for 1,000 years.

Because the Christian calendar is in common use worldwide, everyone else feels its effects. For the first time in history, satellite television and digital clocks will enable people on every continent and in nearly every country to mark the same turn of the century.

"When you have an unknown impending global event, you have to invent a meaning for it," Dr. Daniels says.

He says die-hard millennium watchers break down into four groups: evangelical Christians, some of whom believe that Christ will return and that the Battle of Armageddon will be fought sometime around the year 2000; environmentalists, who believe that we are polluting and populating ourselves into imminent apocalypse; UFO watchers, who believe that aliens are visiting the earth to warn humans that the end is near; and New Agers, who believe that 2000 signals the dawn of an enlightened era.

Many of them will use the occasion to latch onto theories that they believe prove the apocalypse is near. That's because most religious leaders don't know how to handle discussions about the end, according to

James Moorhead, professor of American church history at Princeton Theological Seminary.

"Mainline religions haven't found a convincing way of talking about the end, so that has left an opening for all sorts of surrogates," he says. "Not that anybody ought to take the Book of Revelation literally. My point is perhaps mainline religion hasn't offered a convincing understanding of this point in history, and people have a hunger for some sense of the end."

Symbols and Fears

And so New Year's Eve 1999 has huge significance. On the threshold of the Big One, many people are frightened—of depleted resources, increased terrorism, sudden bankruptcies, outmoded industries and spiritual change.

Certain symbols have long been associated with their fears: "The Four Horsemen of the Apocalypse" woodcutting by Albrecht Durer; the Virgin Mary, whom many people believe is appearing around the world with messages that the end is near; and the two-headed god Janus, looking backward and forward in time.

People have harbored fearful feelings at the end of every century since at least 1300, according to Hillel Schwartz, author of "Century's End: An Orientation Manual Toward the Year 2000" and probably the most celebrated scholar of the millennium.

People invent utopias, believe that the world must be punished with apocalypse or purified with sobriety and feel that events are spinning out of control. As a result, according to Dr. Schwartz, they tend to participate in activities that are characteristic of such times.

For instance, they perform acts of retrospect. At the turn of the 19th century, preachers delivered sermons and newspapers printed articles chronicling the accomplishments of the previous century and counting up its exact number of hours and days. Prophetic novels were all the rage.

These days, Dr. Schwartz says, Americans are erecting memorials. Last year the Korean War memorial was unveiled in Washington. There's a new one going up to honor Franklin D. Roosevelt and one in the works to commemorate black Revolutionary War patriots.

We're also interested in our origins. Thus, experts say, the round of new translations of the Book of Genesis, the Bill Moyers series this fall on Genesis and renewed debates about creationism.

New Spiritual Frontiers

Another typical behavior at century's end is inventing new spiritual frontiers, Dr. Schwartz says. In the 1890s, people tried to contact the dead to learn about people's "past lives." In the 1790s, people were fascinated with static electricity, which they believed could be harnessed to read others' minds.

In the 1990s, people are interested in the near-death experience, in which they believe they go through a tunnel toward death and then are transformed into "new" people.

Another example of transformation experience, Dr. Schwartz says, is belief in alien abduction. Tens of thousands of UFO watchers believe that they are being abducted by aliens, operated on and then transformed into prophets of the end-times.

Lacy Shields, president of the UFOlogy Society, based in Dallas, says aliens are visiting Earth to warn us that the world may soon end. She believes that a UFO touched down in her Plano neighborhood in 1978. Like thousands of others, she believes that she may have been abducted by aliens.

She says abductees like her may be saved from coming tribulation: "Maybe we'll be taken off the planet during the worst times by flying saucers. When it's safe, they'll come back later to try [to build a civilization] again."

But most Americans are going about their business of 1996, unaware that others are wringing their hands over impending apocalypse or hatching grand plans for 2000. While such attention to the millennium may seem silly, Dr. Schwartz says, the millennium watchers perform a valuable service.

"We can make this an important time," he says. "If nothing happens, there's going to be a tremendous feeling of frustration and disappointment. If people go through the year 2000 and do absolutely nothing different, years down the road people are going to ask what they did at the turn of the century and they won't have anything to show for it."

Dr. Schwartz is writing a book called "What Are You Going to Do in the Year 2000, Seriously?" In it, he proposes that people set aside time for spiritual change. He's helping a small college focus its attention on the turn of the millennium, assisting the National Cathedral in Washington with its events and consulting with architects and composers nationwide.

One of the composers is Robert Xavier Rodriguez, a professor at the

University of Texas at Dallas and composer-in-residence with the San Antonio Symphony. Mr. Rodriguez is writing "Forbidden Fire: Cantata for the New Millennium," which is about the dangers, responsibilities and lure of knowledge. The score will combine modernist-sounding music by composers such as Stravinsky with the more traditional music of Beethoven.

"I believe the music of the future lies in reconciling the past and the present," he says. "This is an optimistic work that says I hope in the next millennium people will get it right."

Revelation and Armageddon

Some people, especially some evangelical Christians, believe that the end of the millennium roughly coincides with predictions in the Book of Revelation.

At Hillcrest Church, a 3,000-member interdenominational congregation in North Dallas, for instance, the Rev. Lenny Allen teaches his members to be ready for Jesus' Second Coming. He believes that the founding of the state of Israel in 1948 was a signal that the end is near because it fulfilled biblical prophecy.

Now, he says, Christians await the rapture, when they believe they will be spirited to heaven just before the Lord returns and fights the antichrist in the Battle of Armageddon. Once the battle is over, Jesus reigns on Earth for 1,000 years.

"Something is in the air," Mr. Allen says. "Things can't go on the way they're going. So naturally, believers are going to have their eyebrows up even more than the secularists. But the secular world also realizes something is taking place. Sure, believers are anxious. Some are anxiously glad and others are anxiously concerned, depending on where they feel they are in their walk with the Lord."

Some people carry their end-time forecasts to extremes that are hard for many Americans to fathom.

Richard Kieninger's plan for the apocalypse and the new civilization that he believes will follow is nearly always cited in books and articles as a particularly poignant example of millennium mania.

Mr. Kieninger moved to Garland in 1976, attracted a small following and began building a utopian community called Adelphi 50 miles east of Dallas. A few years ago, he predicted a cataclysmic earth shift on May 5, 2000, that will cause floods, tidal waves, earthquakes and volcanoes. But, he said, he would be ready.

The last time he talked publicly, he was working on technology to air-lift himself in a blimp 14 miles above the chaos.

A Time for Joy

For some people, the turn of the century will bring joy. A mellow guy who calls himself the Millennium Doctor is the top cheerleader for what he hopes will be a uniquely Christian celebration.

"I'm a physician of the soul," says Jay Gary, a Baptist whose focus is on Dec. 25 rather than Dec. 31.

He has written a book called "The Star of 2000" and created an Internet forum to promote the idea that the world should focus millennium mania on Jesus.

"My vision is to put magic back into Christmas for the new millennium" he says.

He also plans to re-enact the Journey of the Magi in the Middle East, starting from Iraq on Aug. 6, 1998, and traveling over land on camels to arrive in Bethlehem by Jan. 6, 1999.

"Rather than looking at what's wrong with life, I say, as the Millennium Doctor, we should look at what's right and how did it get that way, due to Christ," Mr. Gary says.

But it's not all that simple, even for Christians, says Gerald Barney, head of the Millennium Institute in Arlington, Va.

"My sense of what Christianity is all about is being out in the world doing what you understand God wants done," Dr. Barney says. "I don't think we're doing a good job right now with regard to each other or caring for the Earth. I'm not expecting a Second Coming, frankly."

Getting Back on Track

So while the millennium brings out people's apocalyptic nightmares, it also gives them an opportunity to step back and contemplate history, Dr. Barney says.

"The 21st century can't be a continuation of the past," he says. "It was our bloodiest century ever. The inter-religious hatred, the damage to the environment, the despair of our young people, the sick way in which magazines and television present the relationship between men and women—there's something sick going on and there've got to be some big changes."

Dr. Barney has a few ideas.

He's organizing a series of sacred celebrations around the world to mark the millennium. The first will be held in 1999 in South Africa, during the Parliament of World Religions. It will open a year of meditation and preparation for the new century. In 2000, Iceland will host an observance in a natural amphitheater that will include world religious leaders and world youth leaders pledging partnership in making changes. The following year, youth in Costa Rica plan to host a final celebration at sunrise.

Meanwhile, Dr. Barney's group is also writing what it calls "The Millennium Report to the World," which will outline ways to sustain ourselves ecologically. He says the world's major institutions—religions, corporations, universities and media—aren't providing any leadership.

Their task in the next century is to get the world back on track.

So many plans to make, so much to fix, so little time. Can we pull it all off?

"I've got two pictures in my mind," Dr. Barney says. "I think the 21st century could be a very, very enjoyable time. We could get to the point where, in effect, we've brought a measure of development and reasonable living conditions for the poorest countries of the world and we stop having a rat race in the industrial world and enjoy things and are careful about not wasting and the arts will flourish."

But there's a flip side.

"I can also see the possibility of a world in which the developing countries essentially are abandoned, and they get to feeling hostile and there's a lot of terrorism," he says. "I can see parts of the world where I think it's likely the situation will simply get to the point where the population can't be supported and there will be Rwanda-like situations."

Which scenario prevails? At this point, it's a draw, he says. So we'd better start working for change and saying our prayers.

"The first couple of decades of the 21st century," he says, "are a time when we decide which path we're going on."

Acknowledgments

The editors and publisher thank the following newspapers for their help and courtesy in allowing the works in this anthology to be printed. Copyright permissions are listed by order of appearance in the text.

CHAPTER 14

© 1923 Time Inc. for "Who Is Fundamental?" Reprinted by permission of Time Inc.

© 1923 Time Inc. for "Fosdick," "Baptists," and "Science Serves God." Reprinted by permission Time Inc.

© 1925 *Arkansas Gazette* for "Why the Anti-Evolution Law Was Introduced," by John W. Butler. Reprinted by permission of the *Arkansas Gazette*.

© 1925 *The Baltimore Sun* for "Evolution Case Serious Matter to Older Folk," by Frank R. Kent. Reprinted by permission of *The Baltimore Sun*.

CHAPTER 15

© 1940 by the New York Times Co. for "Bigotry Imperils All, Murphy Says." Reprinted by permission.

© 1941 by the New York Times Co. for "Use of Nation's Force in Spirit of the Policing Urged by Sockman, Who Decries Hatred." Reprinted by permission.

© 1942 by the New York Times Co. for "War Ban on Liquor Urged by Women." Reprinted by permission.

© 1944 *Associated Press* for "Clergymen, Writers Ask End to Bombings," as it appeared in both the March 6, 1944, *Denver Post* and *Rocky Mountain News*. Reprinted by permission of *The Associated Press*.

© 1941 by the New York Times Co. for "Sect Members Ask Draft Exemption." Reprinted by permission.

© 1943 *Associated Press* for "Compulsory Salute to Flag Barred by High Court Decision," as it appeared in *The Washington Post*. Reprinted by permission of *The Associated Press*.

CHAPTER 16

© 1949 Hearst Newspapers for "Great Religious Revival to Continue Sixth Week." Reprinted by permission of the *Los Angeles Examiner.*

© 1949 Hearst Newspapers for "Revival Stirs 'Colonel Zack.'" Reprinted by permission of the *Los Angeles Examiner.*

© 1951 *Associated Press* for "Trends in American Religous Life" series written by George Cornell. Reprinted by permission of *The Associated Press.*

CHAPTER 17

© 1957 *The New Republic* for "A Catholic For President?" by Helen Hill Miller. Reprinted by permission of *The New Republic.*

© 1962 *The Baltimore Sun* for "Ecumenical Meeting in Rome Opens," by Weldon Wallace. Reprinted by permission of *The Baltimore Sun.*

CHAPTER 18

© 1966 Time Inc. for "Toward a Hidden God." Reprinted by permission.

CHAPTER 19

© 1969 *Detroit Free Press* for "How to Read Manifesto," by Hiley Ward. Reprinted by permission of the *Detroit Free Press.*

© 1969 *Los Angeles Times* for "A Church for Homosexuals" by John Dart. Reprinted by permission.

© 1986 *St. Petersburg Times* for "Faith and the Revolution Are Intertwined for Padre Jaime," by Jeanne Pugh. Reprinted by permission of the *St. Petersburg Times.*

© 1983 *The Providence Journal-Bulletin* for "Bishops Call Arms Race 'A Curse On Mankind,' Vote 238–9 for Letter," by Richard C. Dujardin. Reprinted by permission of *The Providence Journal-Bulletin.*

CHAPTER 20

© 1978 *Religious Broadcasting Becomes Big Business, Spreading Across U.S.*, by Jim Montgomery. Reprinted by permission of the *The Wall Street Jounal.*

© 1982 *Richmond Times-Dispatch* for "Richmonders Watching Religious Shows at 2½ Times National Rate," by Thomas R. Morris and Ed Briggs. Reprinted by permission of the *Richmond Times-Dispatch.*